Sweet & Sensitive

Creator
Park Eun-Ah

ADV Manga™
www.adv-manga.com

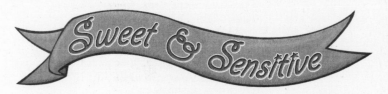

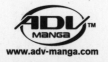

SWEET & SENSITIVE VOLUME TWO

© 2000 Park Eun-Ah, DAIWON C.I., Inc.
All Rights Reserved.
First published in Korea in 2000 by DAIWON C.I., Inc.
English translation righs in USA, Canada, UK, IRIE, NZ and Australia
arranged by DAIWON C.I., Inc.

Translator **JIYOON KIM**
Lead Translator/Translation Supervisor **JAVIER LOPEZ**
ADV Manga Translation Staff **JASON AN AND SIMON JUNG**

Print Production/ Art Studio Manager **LISA PUCKETT**
Pre-press Manager **KLYS REEDYK**
Art Production Manager **RYAN MASON**
Sr. Designer/Creative Manager **JORGE ALVARADO**
Graphic Designer/Group Leader **SCOTT SAVAGE**
Graphic Designer **NATALIA MORALES**
Graphic Artists **CHY LING, LISA RAPER, CHRIS LAPP AND NANAKO TSUKIHASHI**
Graphic Intern **MARK MEZA**

Publishing Editor **SUSAN ITIN**
Assistant Editor **MARGARET SCHAROLD**
Editorial Assistant **VARSHA BHUCHAR**
Proofreaders **SHERIDAN JACOBS AND STEVEN REED**
Editorial Intern **JENNIFER VACCA**

Research/ Traffic Coordinator **MARSHA ARNOLD**

Executive VP, CFO, COO **KEVIN CORCORAN**

President, CEO & Publisher **JOHN LEDFORD**

Email: editor@adv-manga.com
www.adv-manga.com
www.advfilms.com

For sales and distribution inquiries please call 1.800.282.7202

ADV MANGA™

is a division of A.D. Vision, Inc.
10114 W. Sam Houston Parkway, Suite 200, Houston, Texas 77099

English text © 2004 published by A.D. Vision, Inc. under exclusive license.
ADV MANGA is a trademark of A.D. Vision, Inc.

ISBN: 1-4139-0095-X
First printing, September 2004
10 9 8 7 6 5 4 3 2 1
Printed in Canada

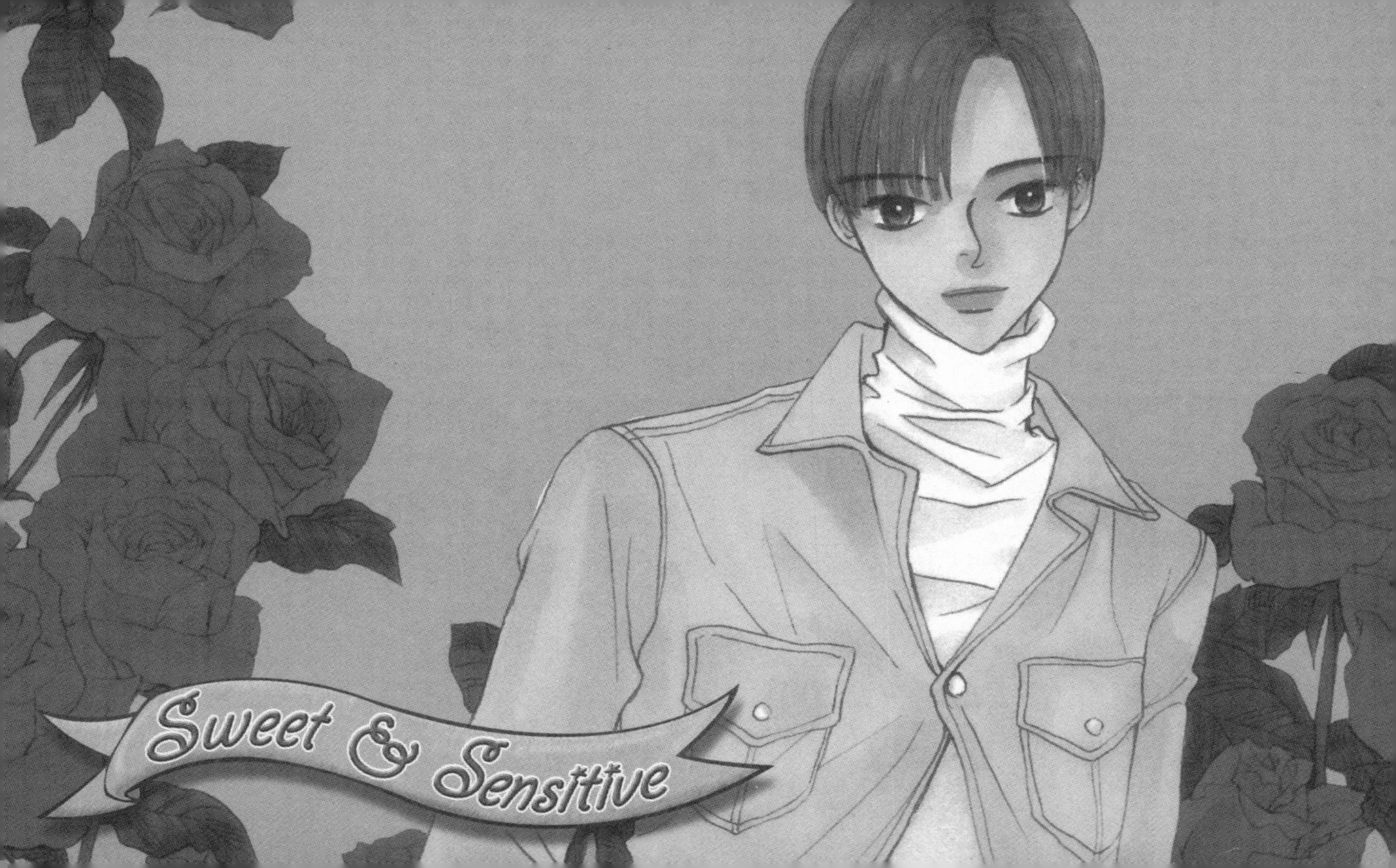
Sweet & Sensitive

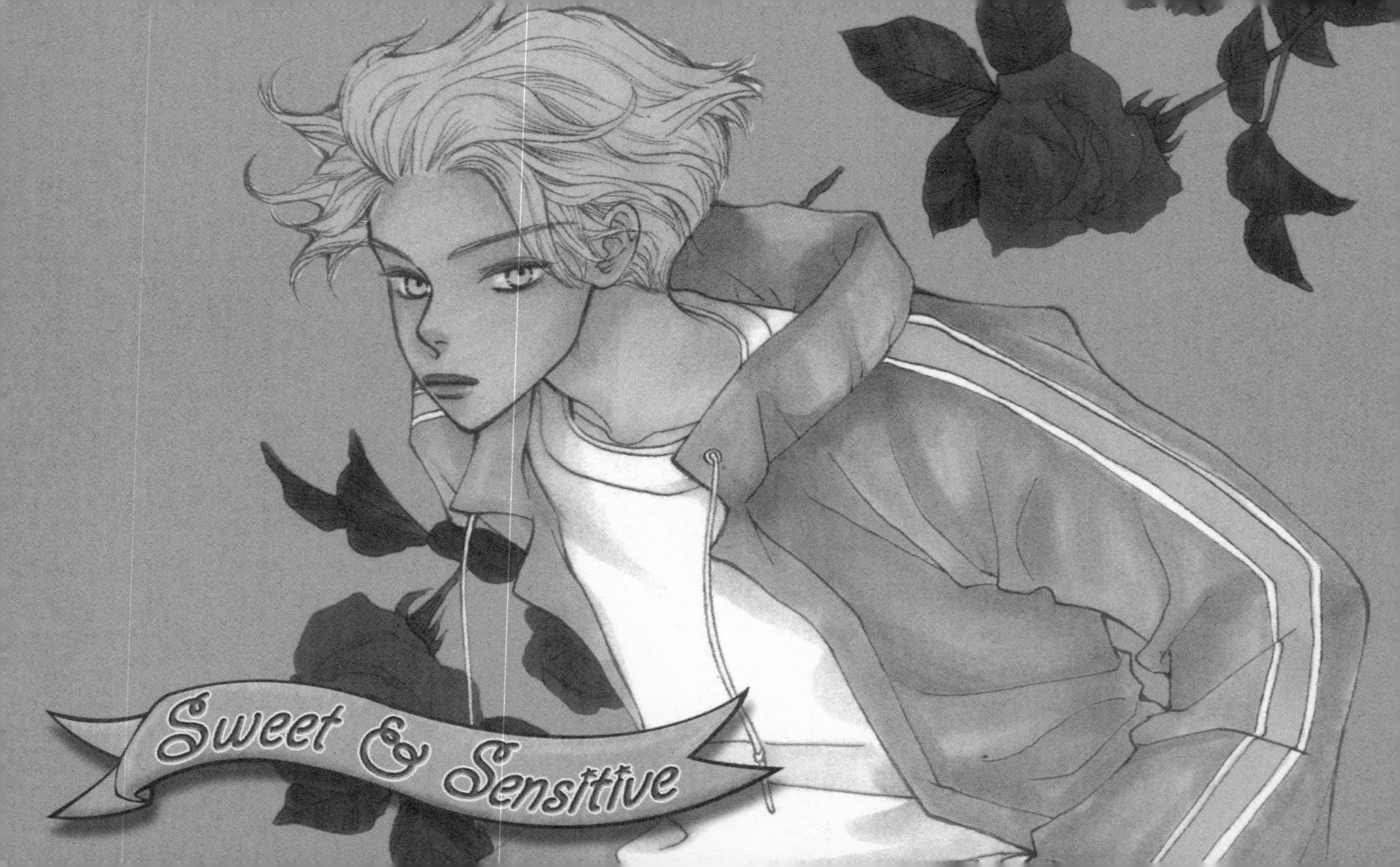
Sweet & Sensitive

Sweet & Sensitive

2

Park
Eun-Ah

CONTENTS

Chapter 7
Confession.................................. 7

Chapter 8
Ee-Ji Bae 29

Chapter 9
Parent-Teacher Conference.... 50

Chapter 10
Wind of Change...................... 95

ParKeuNuh Brand
     Shabby Atelier *Journal* ..191

Sweet & Sensitive
     Readers' Poll Results........195

Sweet & Sensitive

Chapter 7
Confession

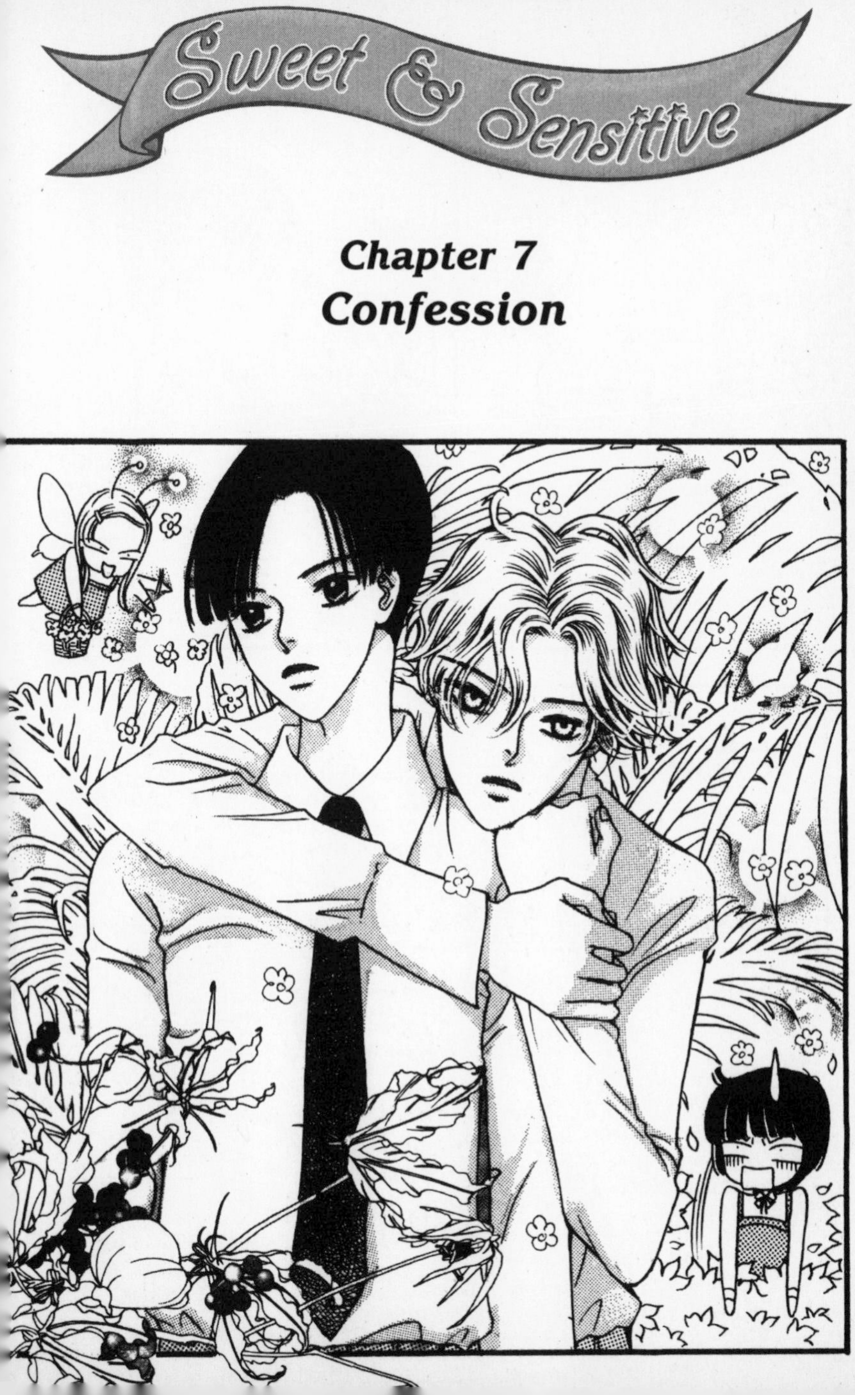

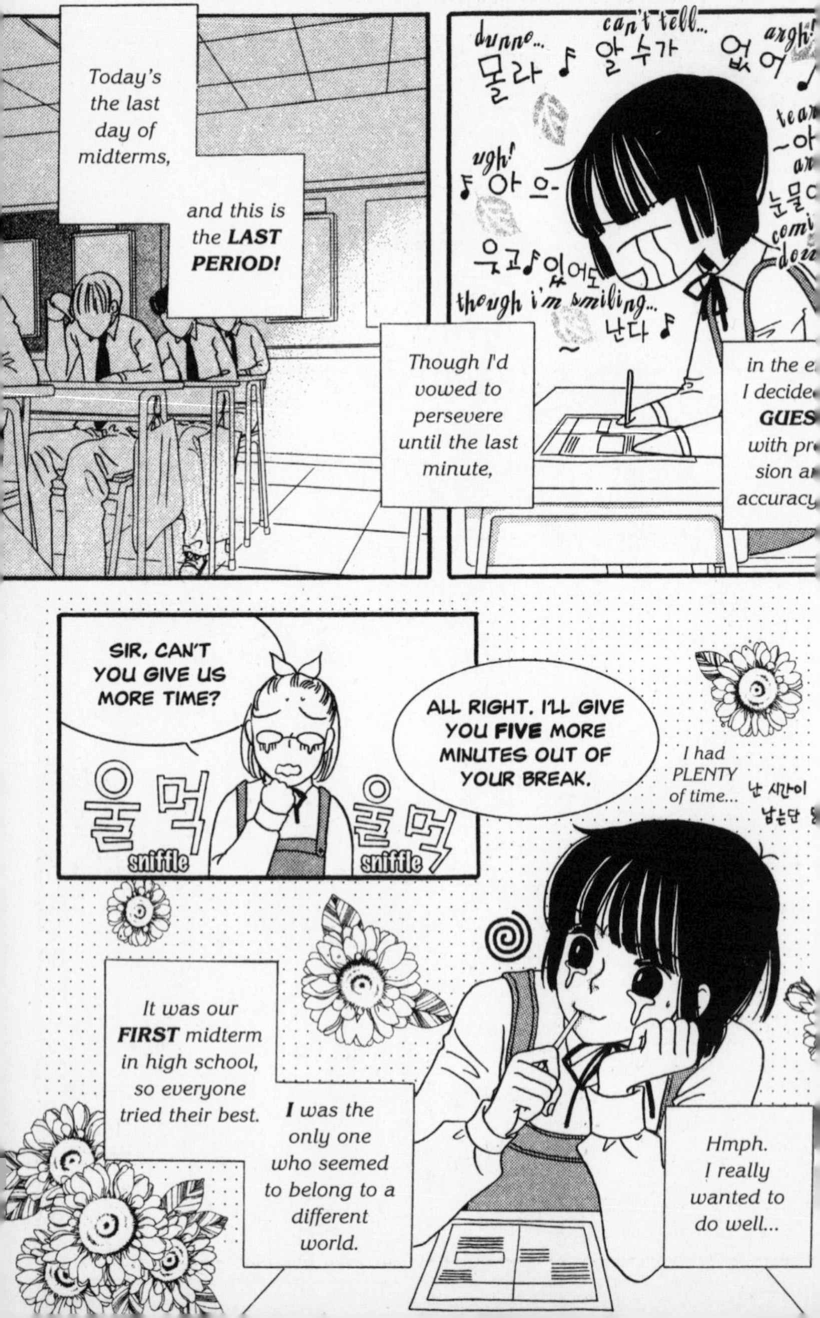
Today's the last day of midterms,
and this is the LAST PERIOD!
dunno...
몰라 ♪
can't tell...
알 수가
없어
ugh!
♪ 아으-
웃고♪있어도
though i'm smiling...
난다 ♪
Though I'd vowed to persevere until the last minute,
SIR, CAN'T YOU GIVE US MORE TIME?
울먹
sniffle
울먹
sniffle
ALL RIGHT. I'LL GIVE YOU FIVE MORE MINUTES OUT OF YOUR BREAK.
I had PLENTY of time...
It was our FIRST midterm in high school, so everyone tried their best.
I was the only one who seemed to belong to a different world.
Hmph. I really wanted to do well...

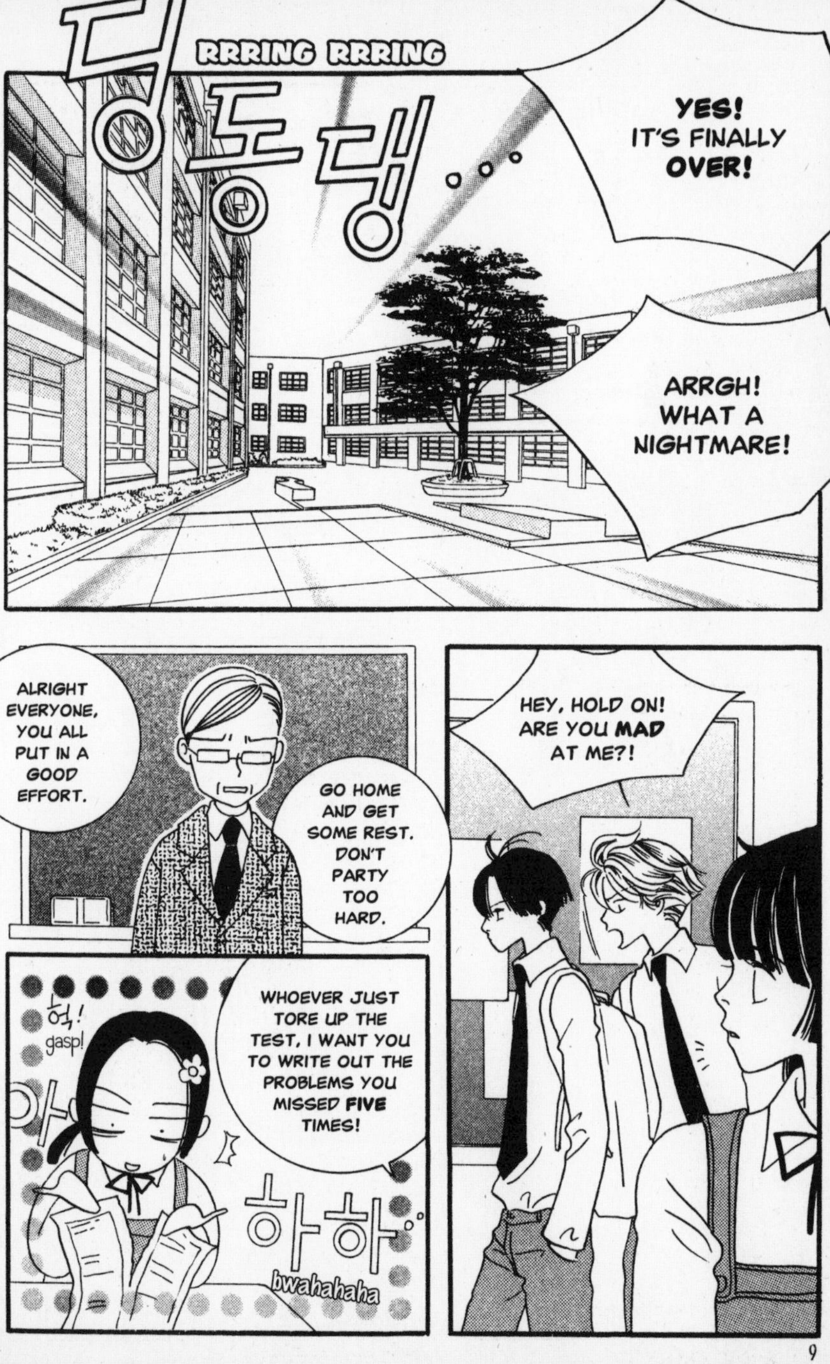

딩동댕...
RRRING RRRING
YES! IT'S FINALLY OVER!
ARRGH! WHAT A NIGHTMARE!
ALRIGHT EVERYONE, YOU ALL PUT IN A GOOD EFFORT.
GO HOME AND GET SOME REST. DON'T PARTY TOO HARD.
WHOEVER JUST TORE UP THE TEST, I WANT YOU TO WRITE OUT THE PROBLEMS YOU MISSED FIVE TIMES!
헉!
gasp!
아하하
bwahahaha
HEY, HOLD ON! ARE YOU MAD AT ME?!

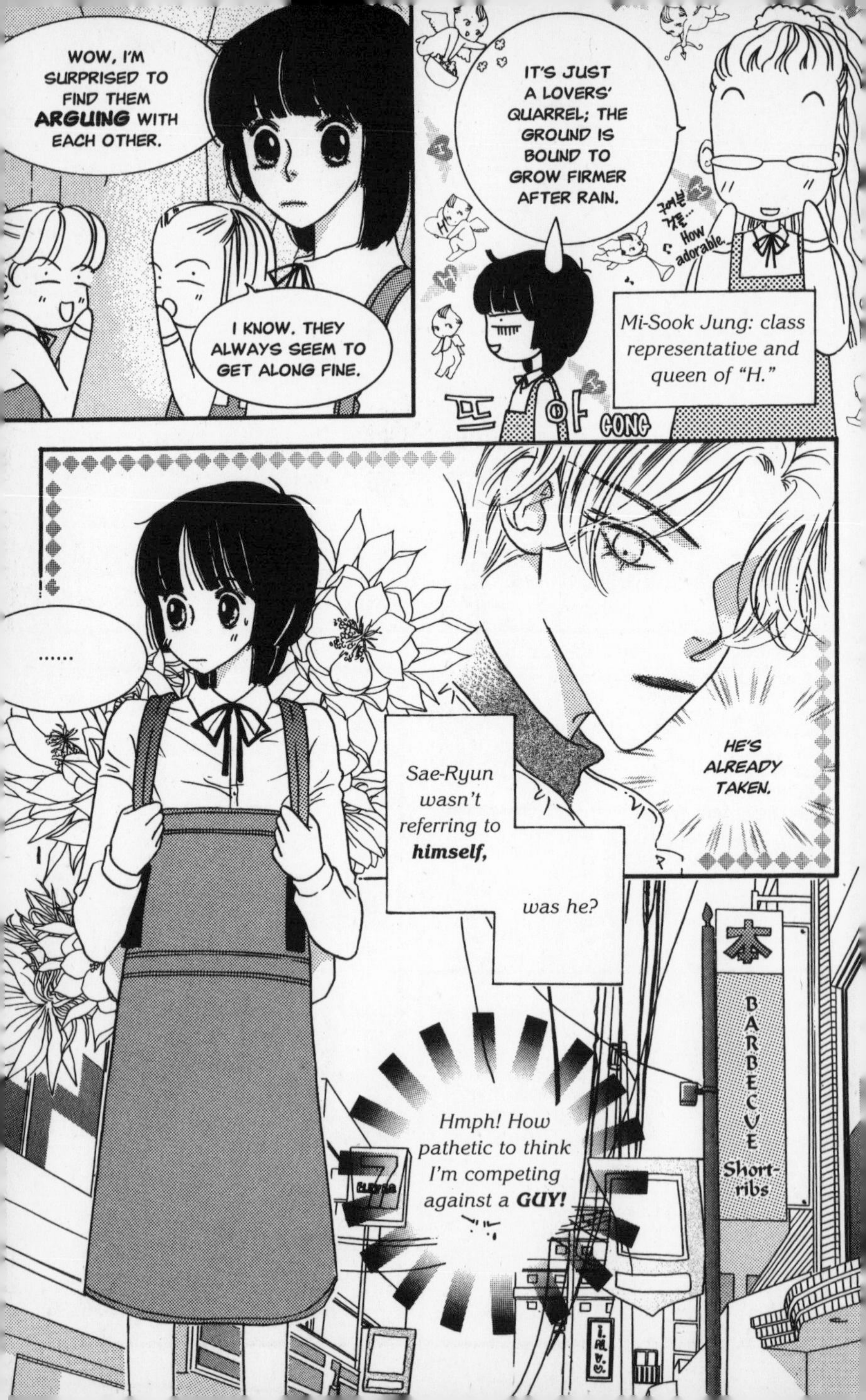
WOW, I'M SURPRISED TO FIND THEM ARGUING WITH EACH OTHER.
I KNOW. THEY ALWAYS SEEM TO GET ALONG FINE.
IT'S JUST A LOVERS' QUARREL; THE GROUND IS BOUND TO GROW FIRMER AFTER RAIN.
귀여운 것들… How adorable.
Mi-Sook Jung: class representative and queen of "H."
꽁 야 GONG
......
HE'S ALREADY TAKEN.
Sae-Ryun wasn't referring to himself,
was he?
Hmph! How pathetic to think I'm competing against a GUY!
BARBECUE Short-ribs

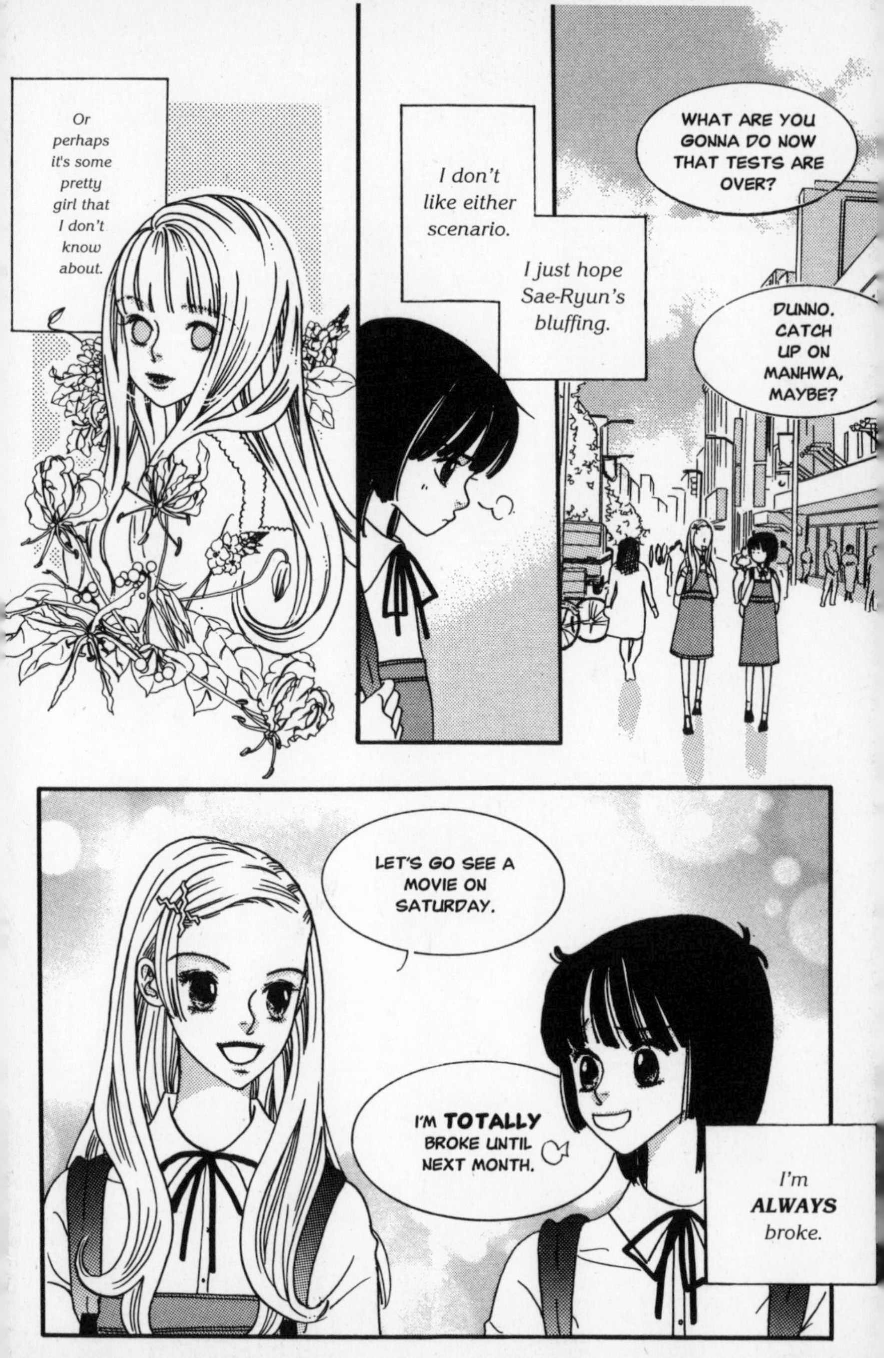
Or perhaps it's some pretty girl that I don't know about.
I don't like either scenario.
I just hope Sae-Ryun's bluffing.
WHAT ARE YOU GONNA DO NOW THAT TESTS ARE OVER?
DUNNO. CATCH UP ON MANHWA, MAYBE?
LET'S GO SEE A MOVIE ON SATURDAY.
I'M TOTALLY BROKE UNTIL NEXT MONTH.
I'm ALWAYS broke.

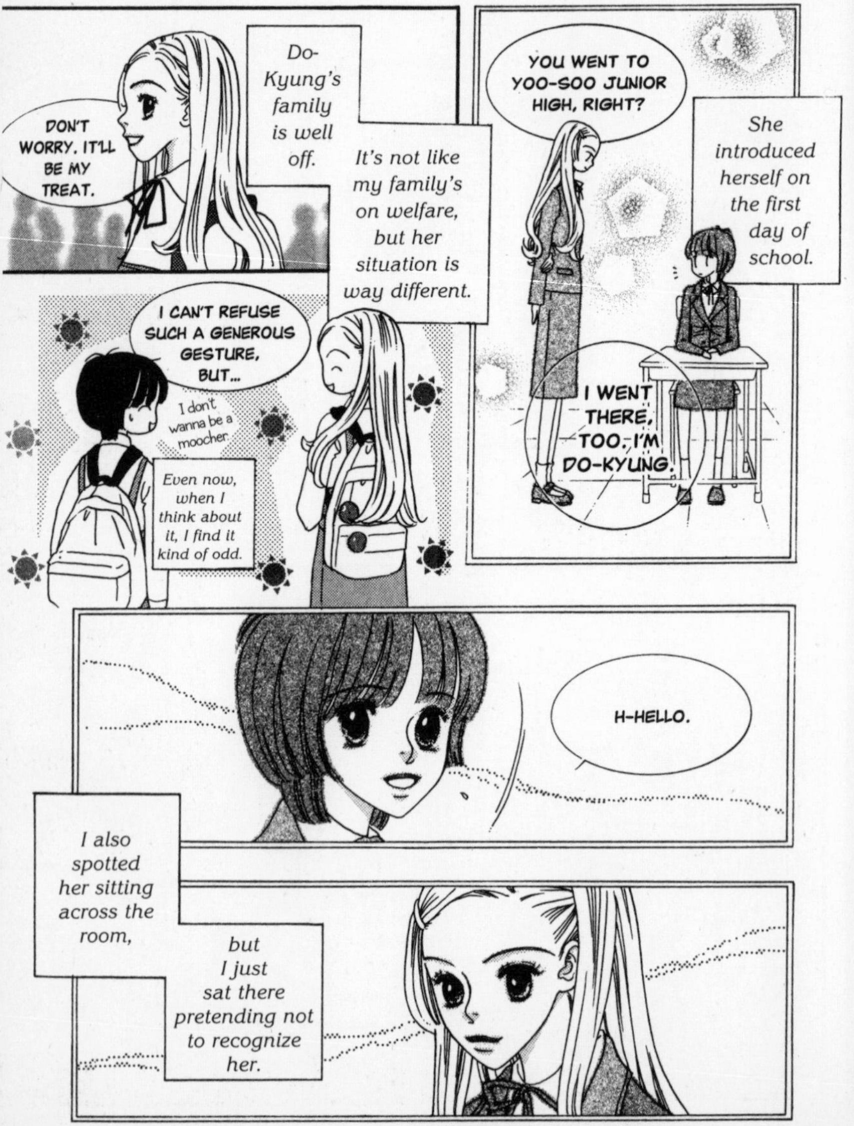
DON'T WORRY. IT'LL BE MY TREAT.
Do-Kyung's family is well off.
It's not like my family's on welfare, but her situation is way different.
I CAN'T REFUSE SUCH A GENEROUS GESTURE, BUT...
I don't wanna be a moocher.
Even now, when I think about it, I find it kind of odd.
YOU WENT TO YOO-SOO JUNIOR HIGH, RIGHT?
She introduced herself on the first day of school.
I WENT THERE, TOO. I'M DO-KYUNG.
H-HELLO.
I also spotted her sitting across the room,
but I just sat there pretending not to recognize her.

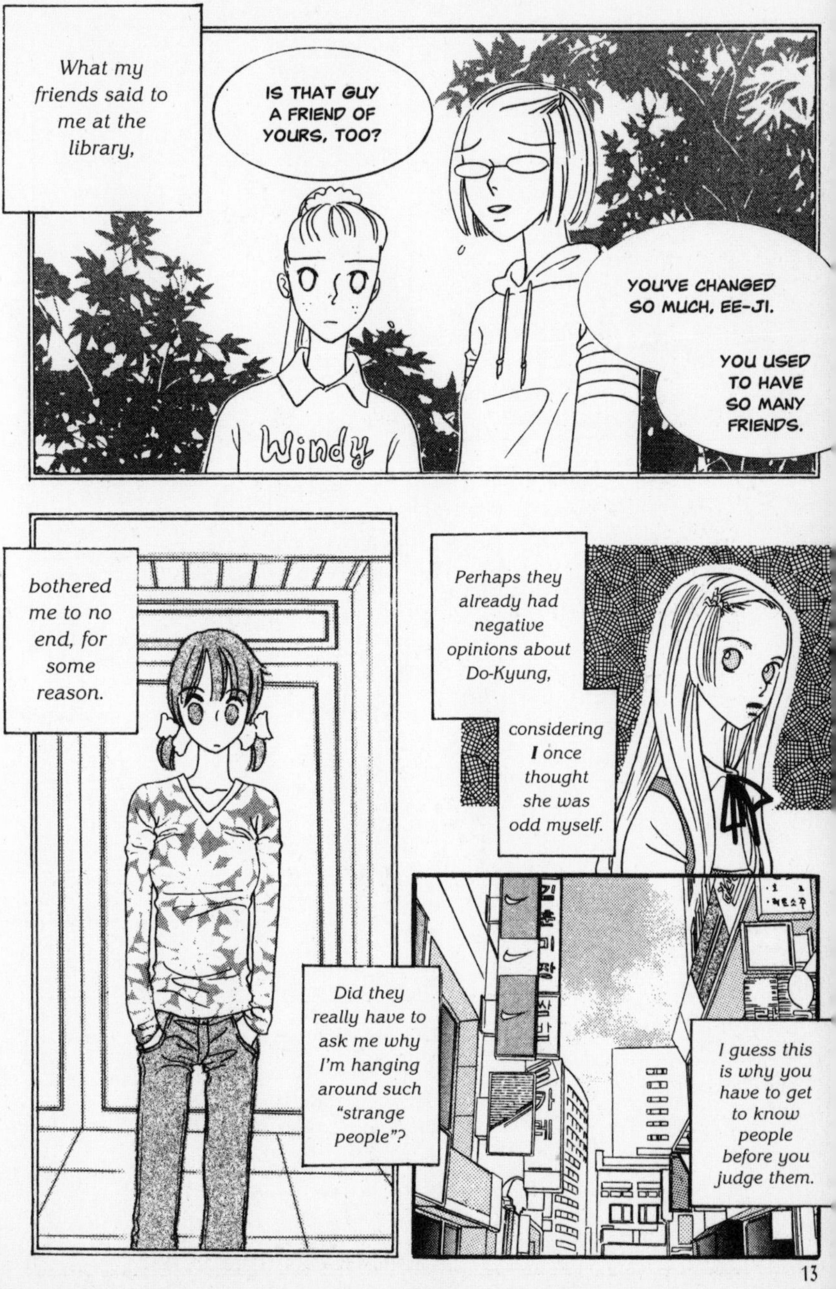
What my friends said to me at the library,
IS THAT GUY A FRIEND OF YOURS, TOO?
YOU'VE CHANGED SO MUCH, EE-JI.
YOU USED TO HAVE SO MANY FRIENDS.
Windy
bothered me to no end, for some reason.
Perhaps they already had negative opinions about Do-Kyung,
considering I once thought she was odd myself.
Did they really have to ask me why I'm hanging around such "strange people"?
I guess this is why you have to get to know people before you judge them.

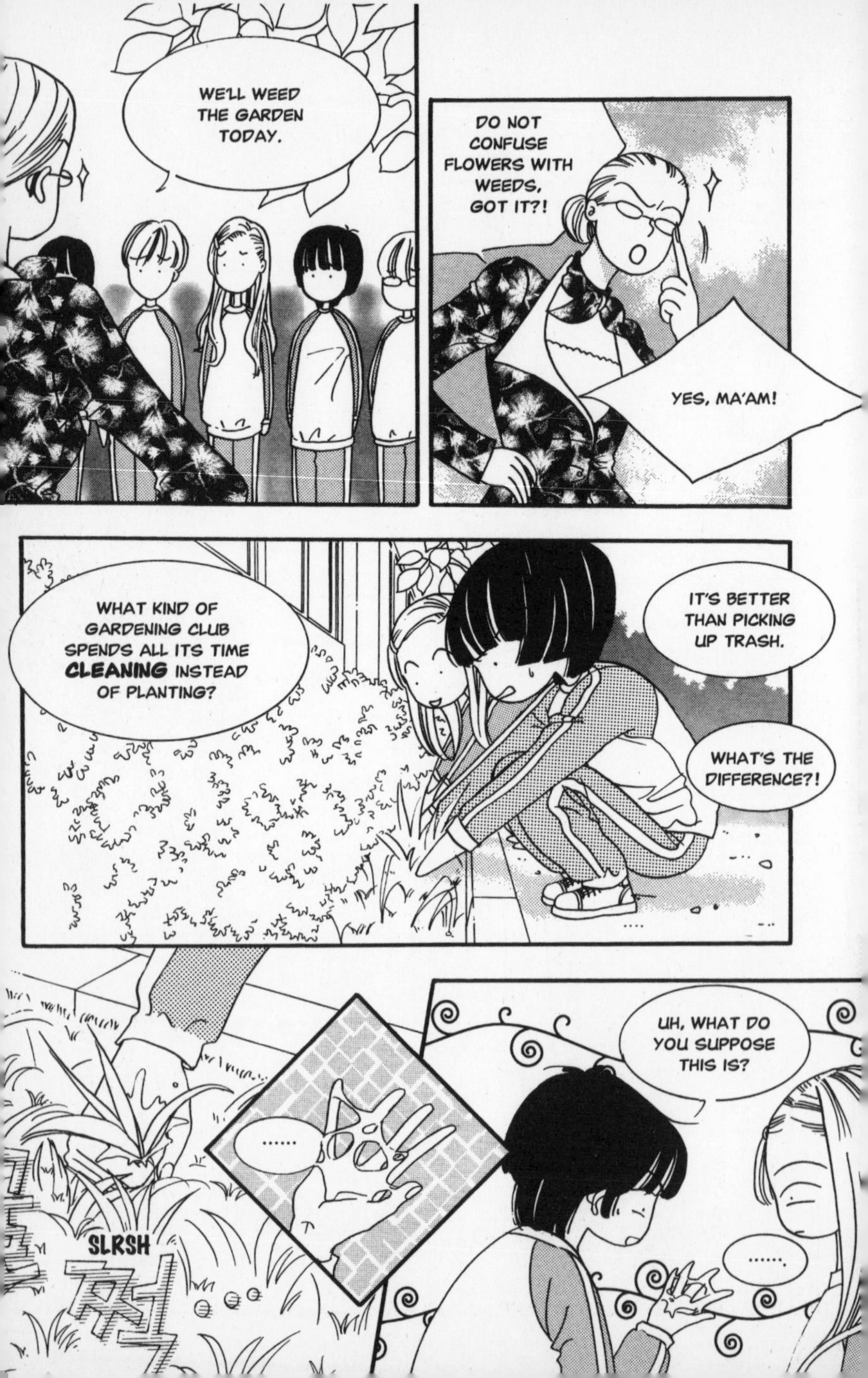
WE'LL WEED THE GARDEN TODAY.
DO NOT CONFUSE FLOWERS WITH WEEDS, GOT IT?!
YES, MA'AM!
WHAT KIND OF GARDENING CLUB SPENDS ALL ITS TIME **CLEANING** INSTEAD OF PLANTING?
IT'S BETTER THAN PICKING UP TRASH.
WHAT'S THE DIFFERENCE?!
....
UH, WHAT DO YOU SUPPOSE THIS IS?
......
......,
SLRSH

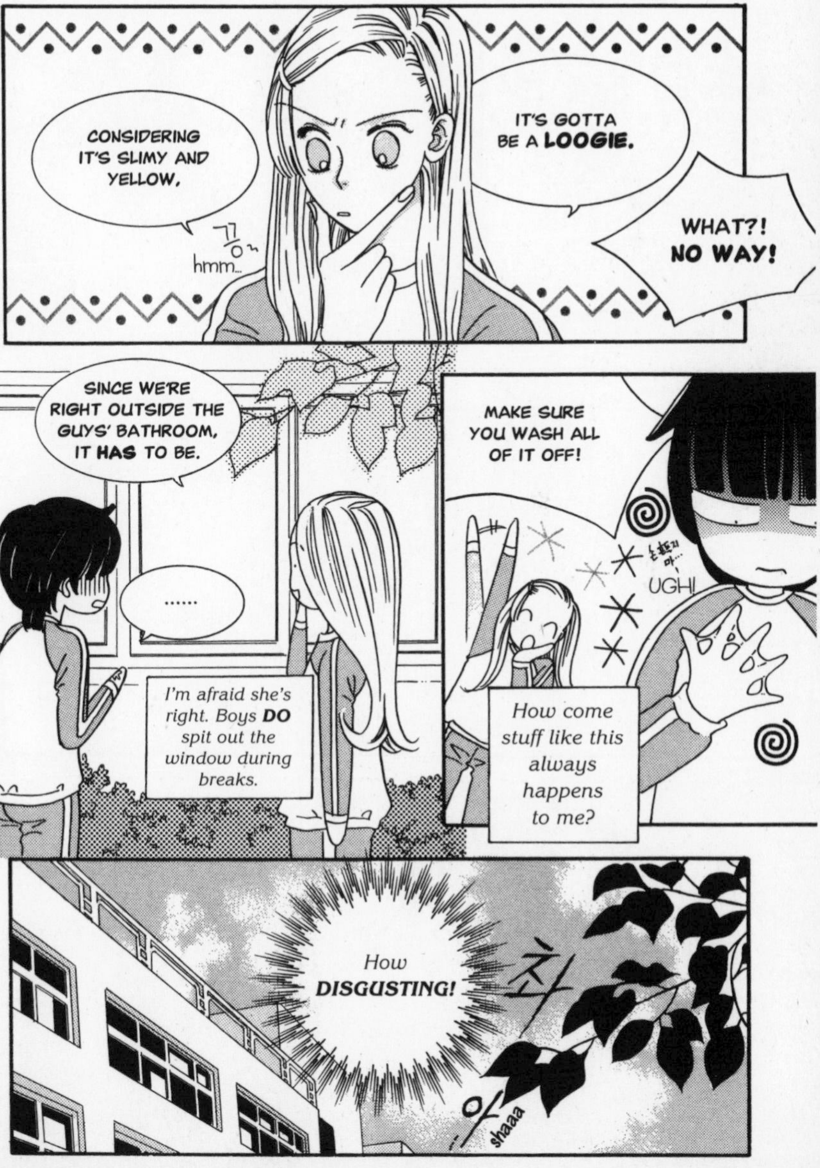
CONSIDERING IT'S SLIMY AND YELLOW,
hmm...
IT'S GOTTA BE A LOOGIE.
WHAT?! NO WAY!
SINCE WE'RE RIGHT OUTSIDE THE GUYS' BATHROOM, IT HAS TO BE.
......
I'm afraid she's right. Boys DO spit out the window during breaks.
MAKE SURE YOU WASH ALL OF IT OFF!
UGH!
How come stuff like this always happens to me?
How DISGUSTING!
shaaa

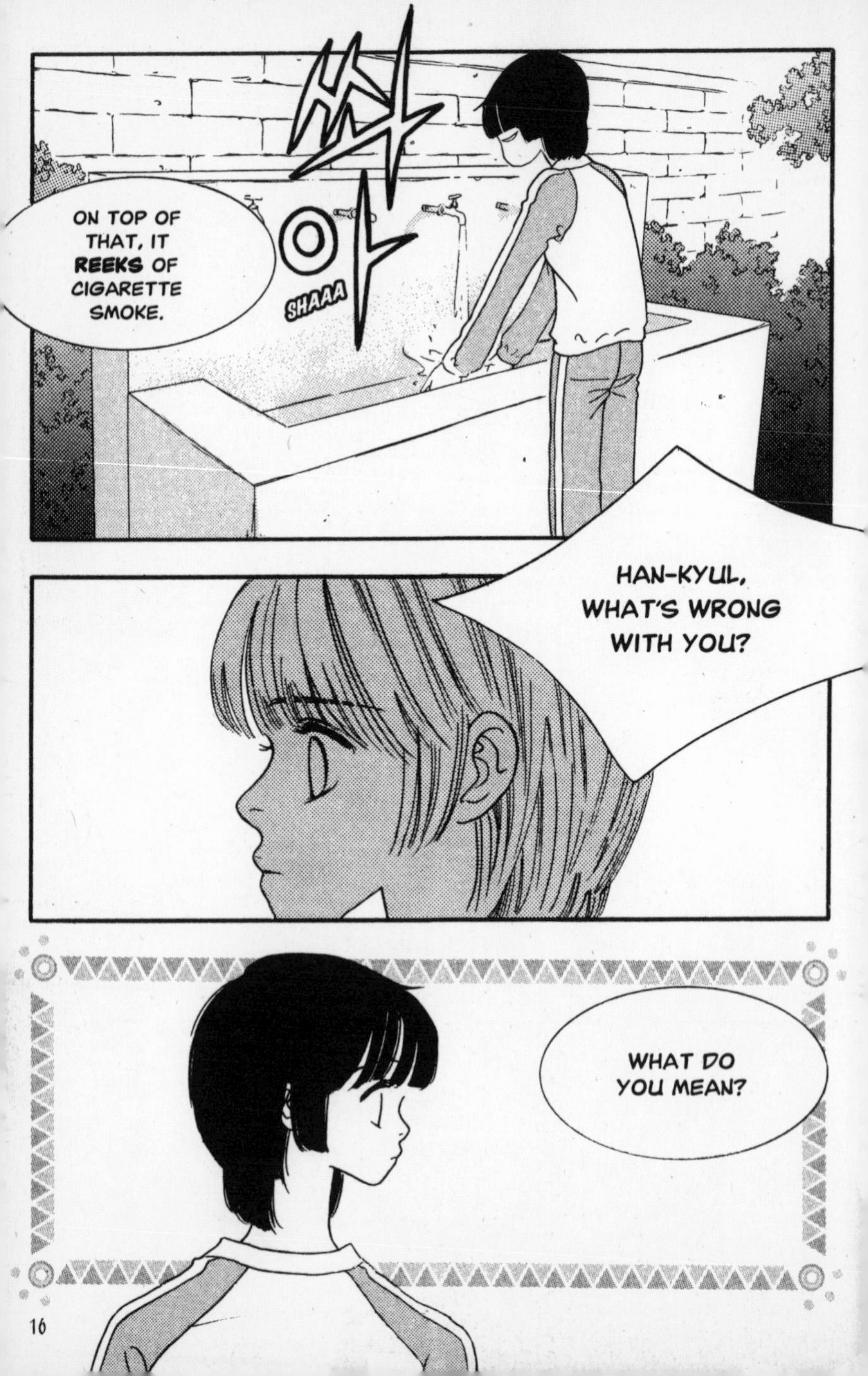
ON TOP OF THAT, IT REEKS OF CIGARETTE SMOKE.
SHAAA
HAN-KYUL, WHAT'S WRONG WITH YOU?
WHAT DO YOU MEAN?

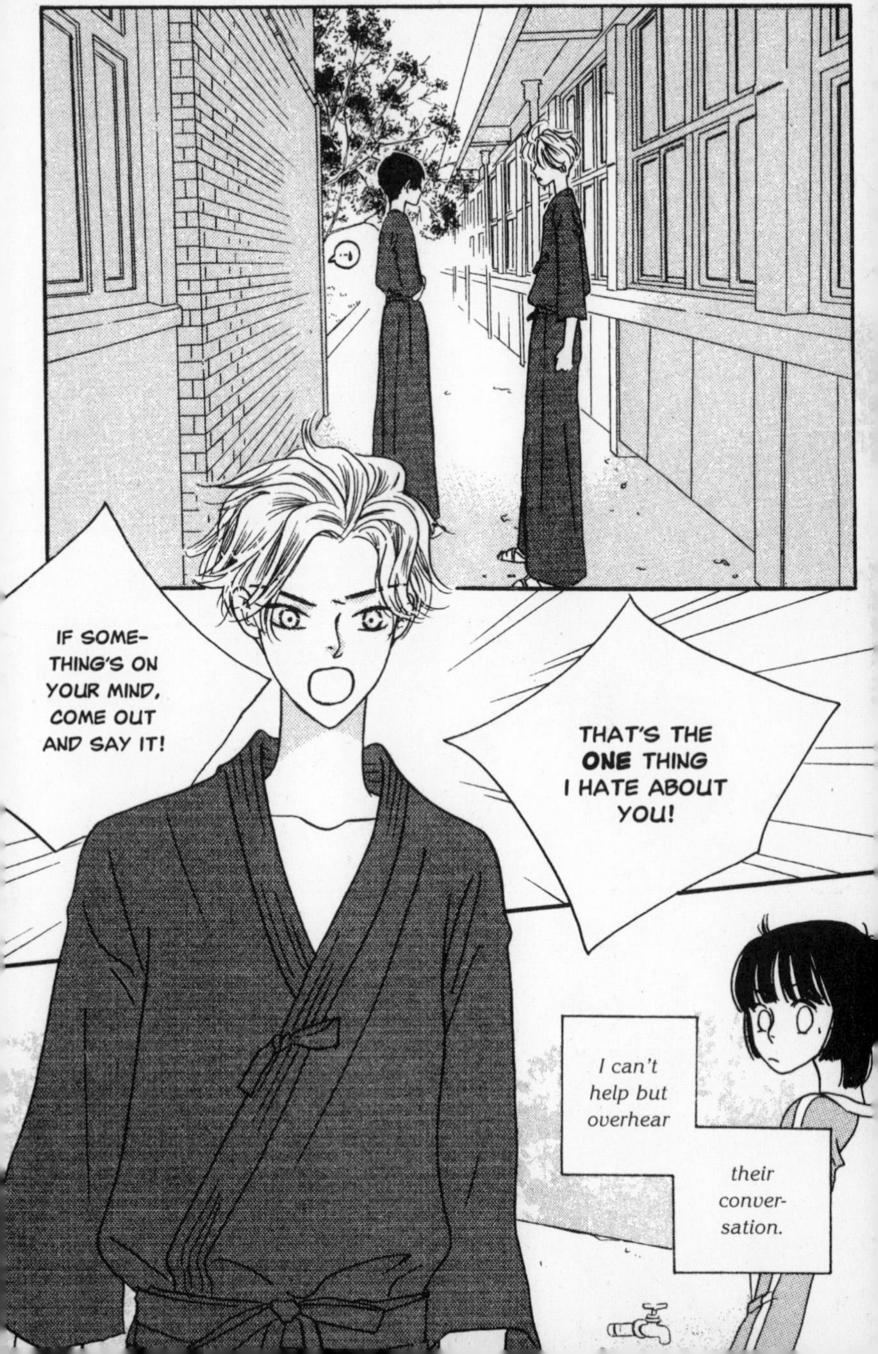
IF SOME-THING'S ON YOUR MIND, COME OUT AND SAY IT!
THAT'S THE ONE THING I HATE ABOUT YOU!
I can't help but overhear
their conver-sation.

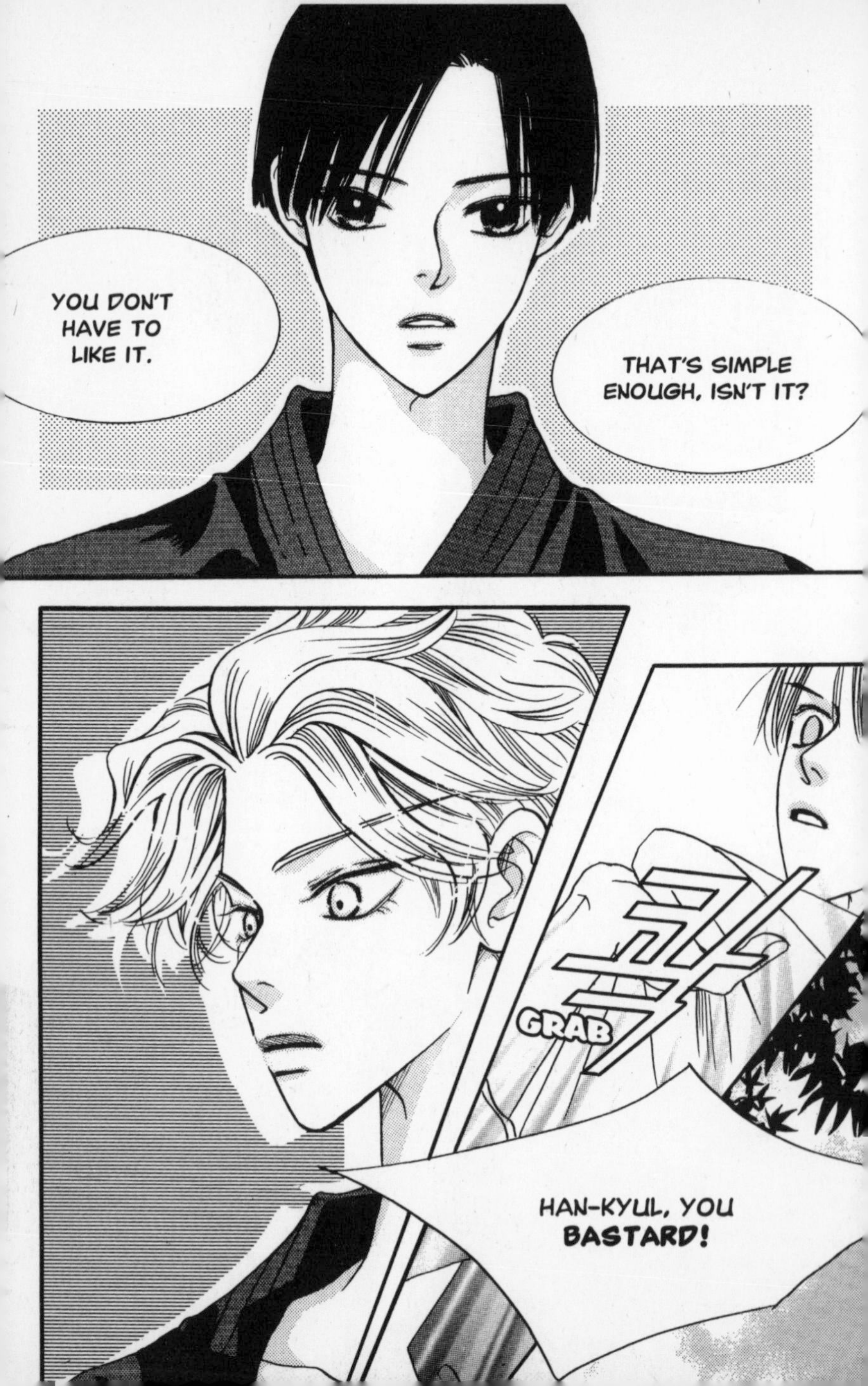
YOU DON'T HAVE TO LIKE IT.
THAT'S SIMPLE ENOUGH, ISN'T IT?
GRAB
HAN-KYUL, YOU BASTARD!

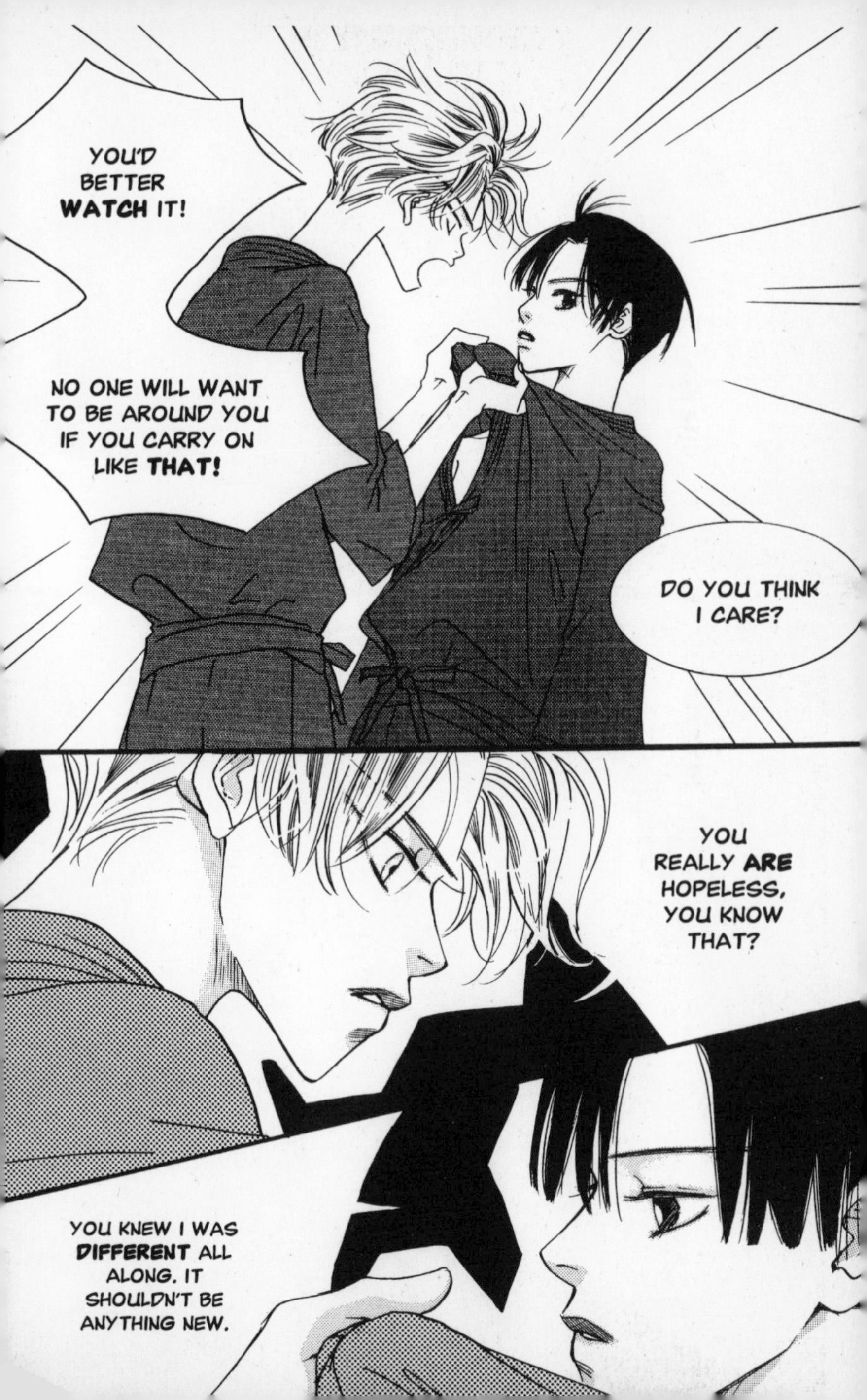
YOU'D BETTER **WATCH** IT!
NO ONE WILL WANT TO BE AROUND YOU IF YOU CARRY ON LIKE **THAT!**
DO YOU THINK I CARE?
YOU REALLY **ARE** HOPELESS, YOU KNOW THAT?
YOU KNEW I WAS **DIFFERENT** ALL ALONG. IT SHOULDN'T BE ANYTHING NEW.

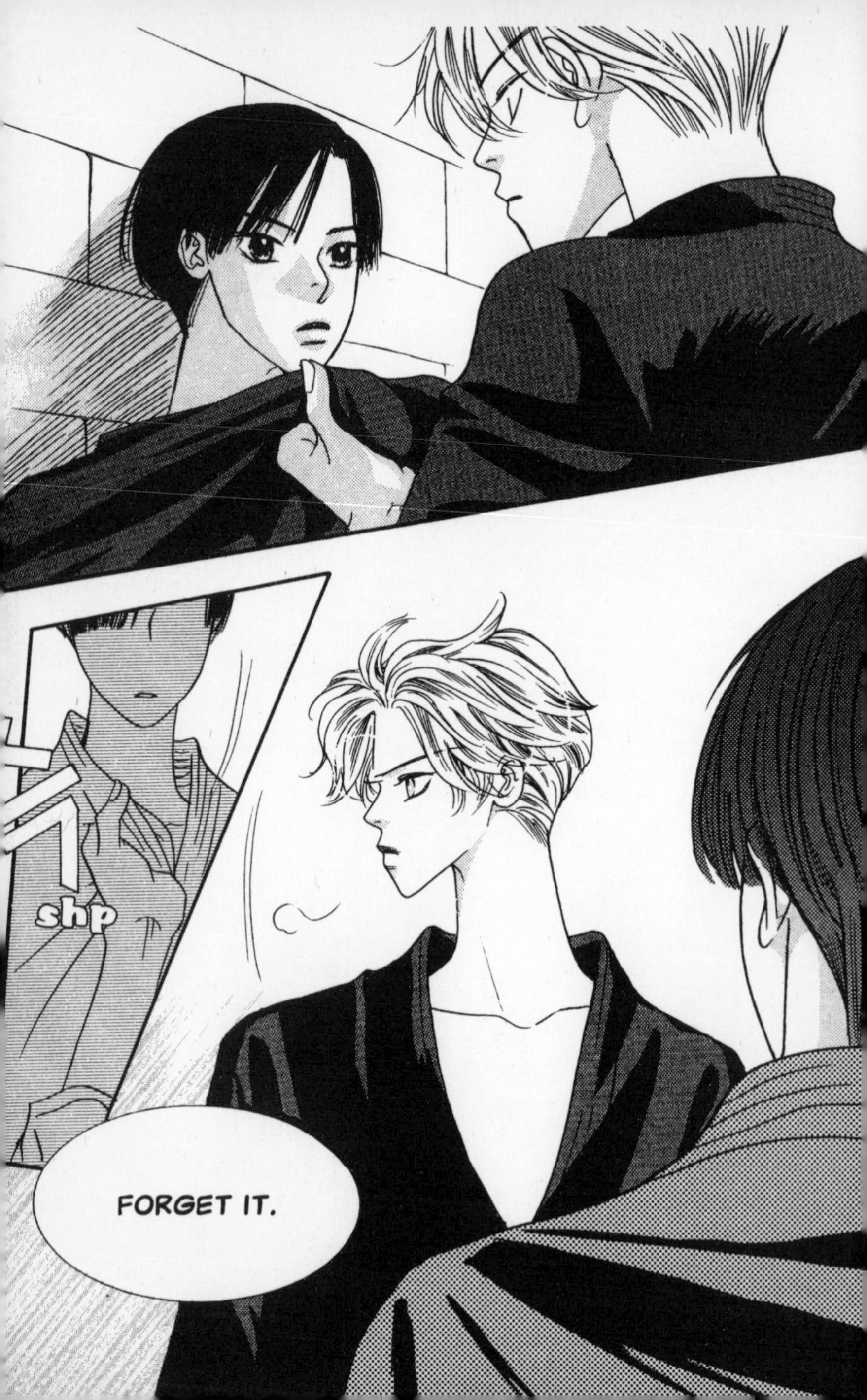
shp
FORGET IT.

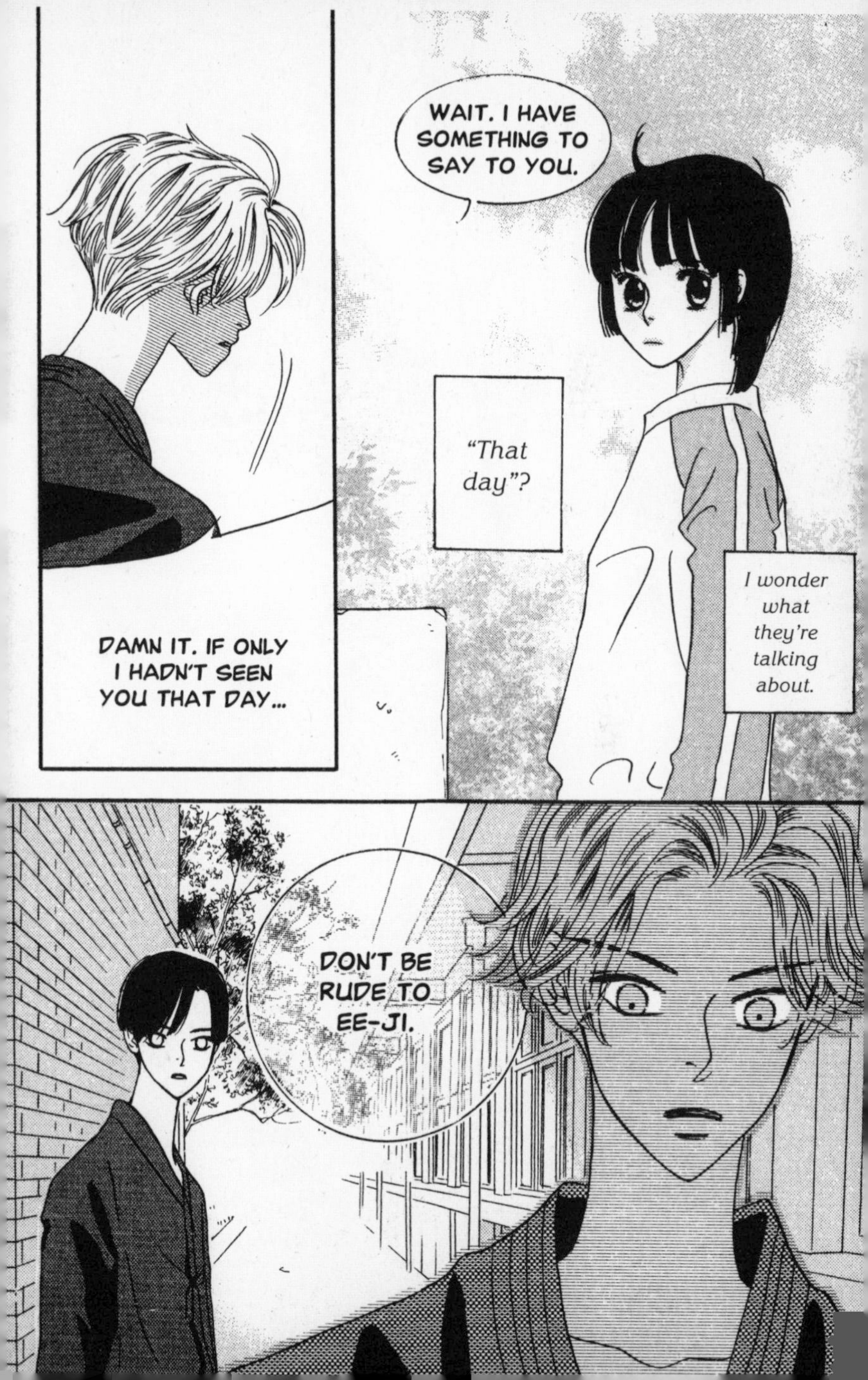

DAMN IT. IF ONLY I HADN'T SEEN YOU THAT DAY...
WAIT. I HAVE SOMETHING TO SAY TO YOU.
"That day"?
I wonder what they're talking about.
DON'T BE RUDE TO EE-JI.

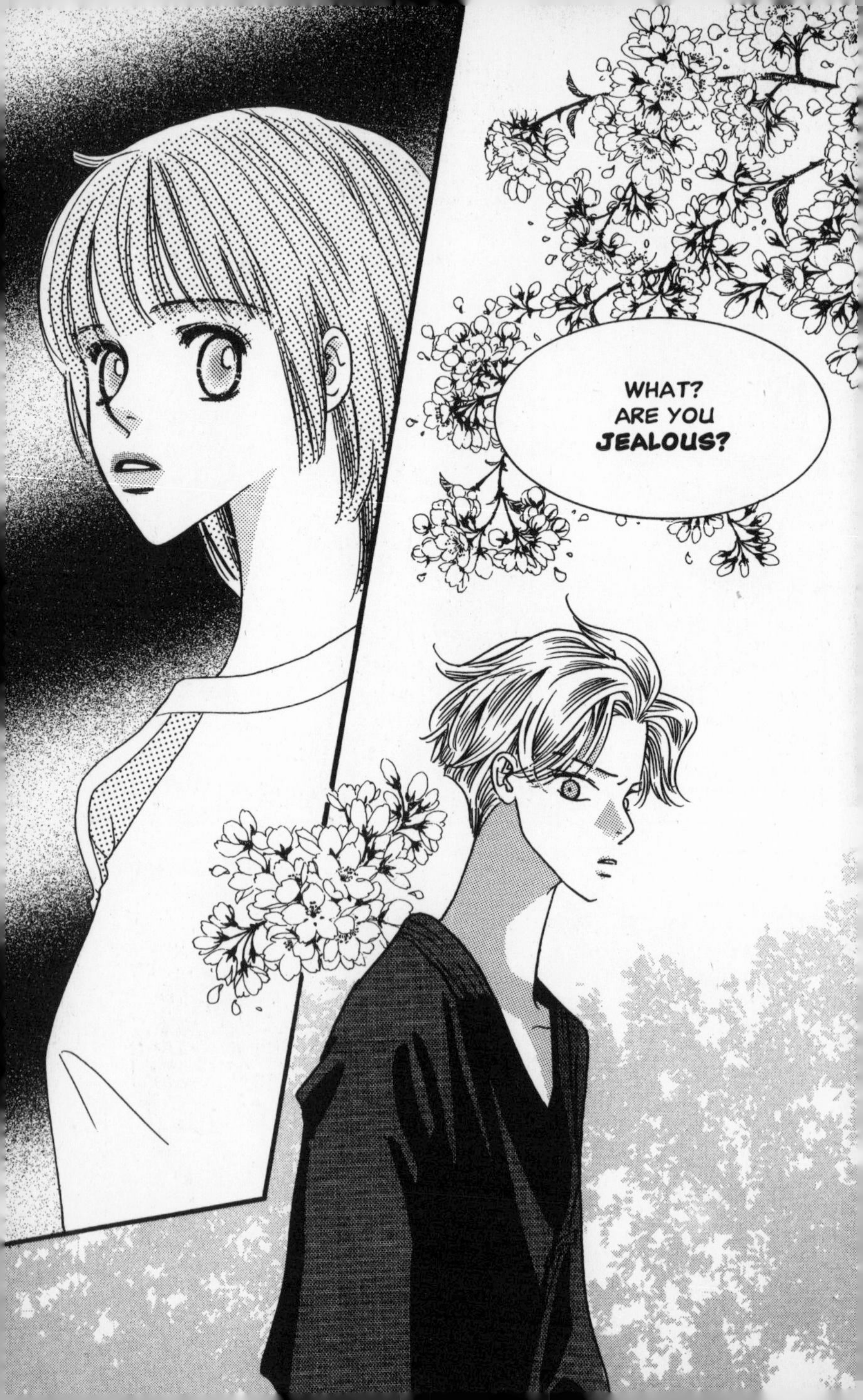
WHAT? ARE YOU JEALOUS?

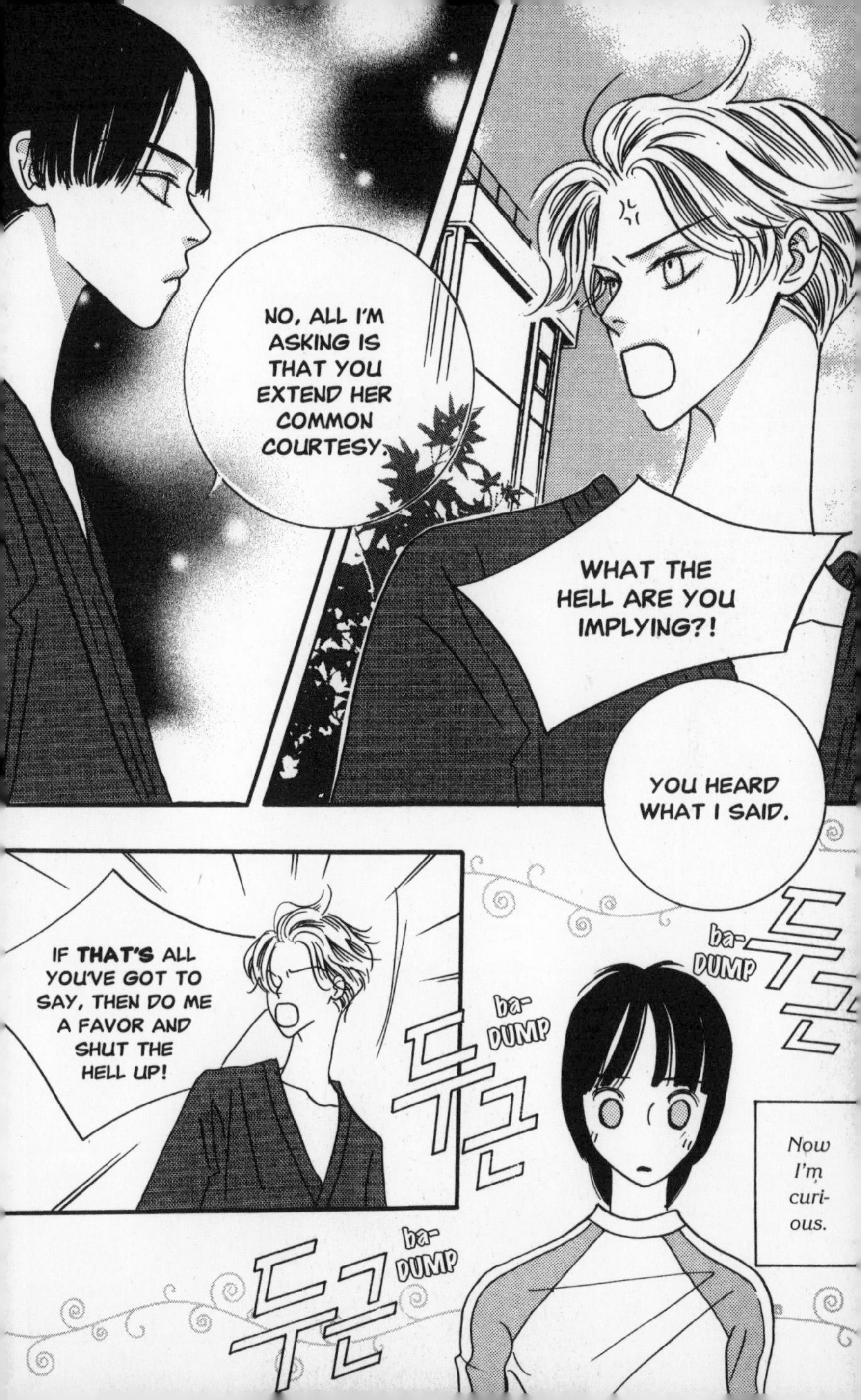
NO, ALL I'M ASKING IS THAT YOU EXTEND HER COMMON COURTESY.
WHAT THE HELL ARE YOU IMPLYING?!
YOU HEARD WHAT I SAID.
IF THAT'S ALL YOU'VE GOT TO SAY, THEN DO ME A FAVOR AND SHUT THE HELL UP!
ba-DUMP
ba-DUMP
ba-DUMP
Now I'm curious.

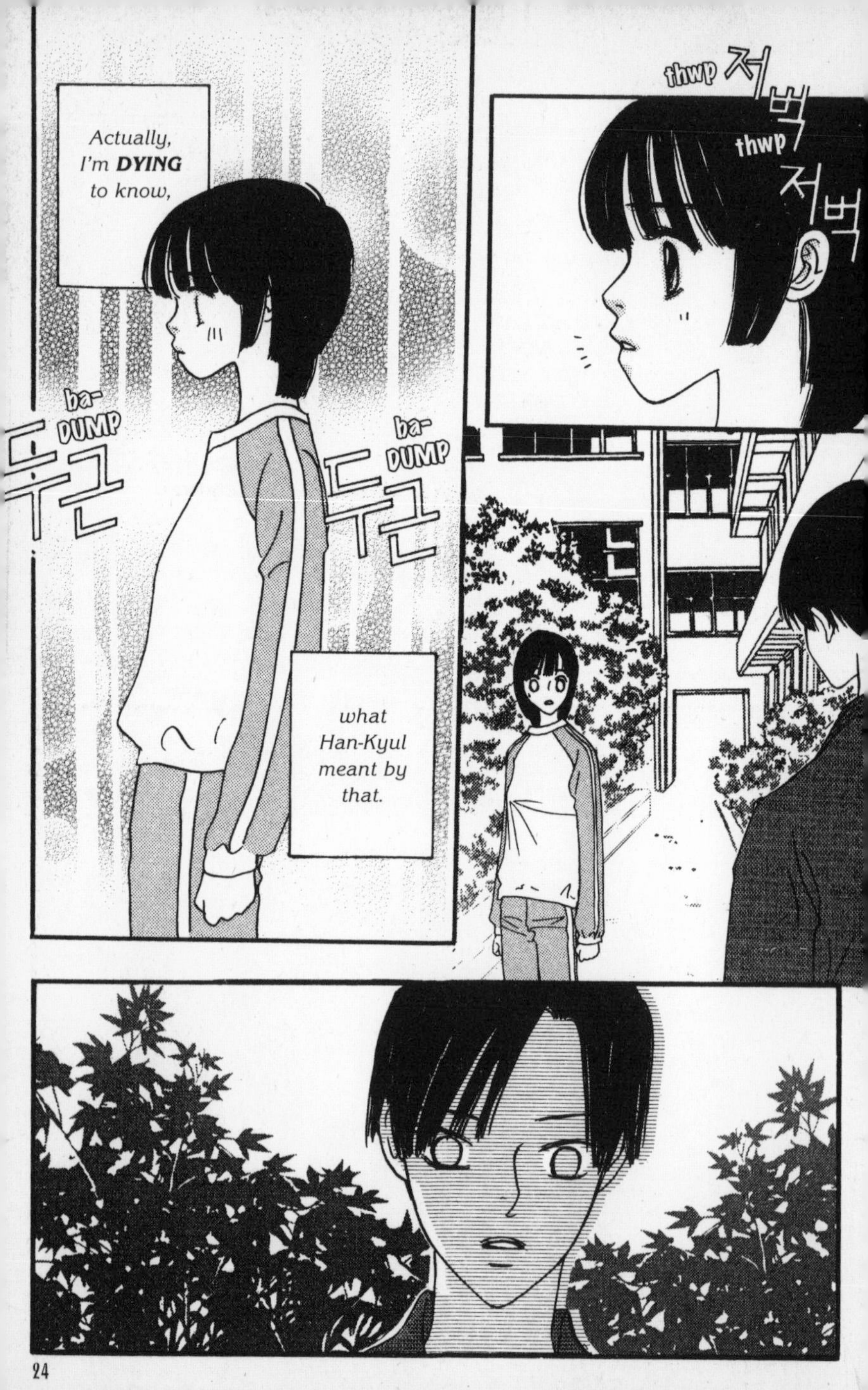
Actually, I'm **DYING** to know,
ba-DUMP
두근
ba-DUMP
두근
what Han-Kyul meant by that.
thwp
저벅
thwp
저벅

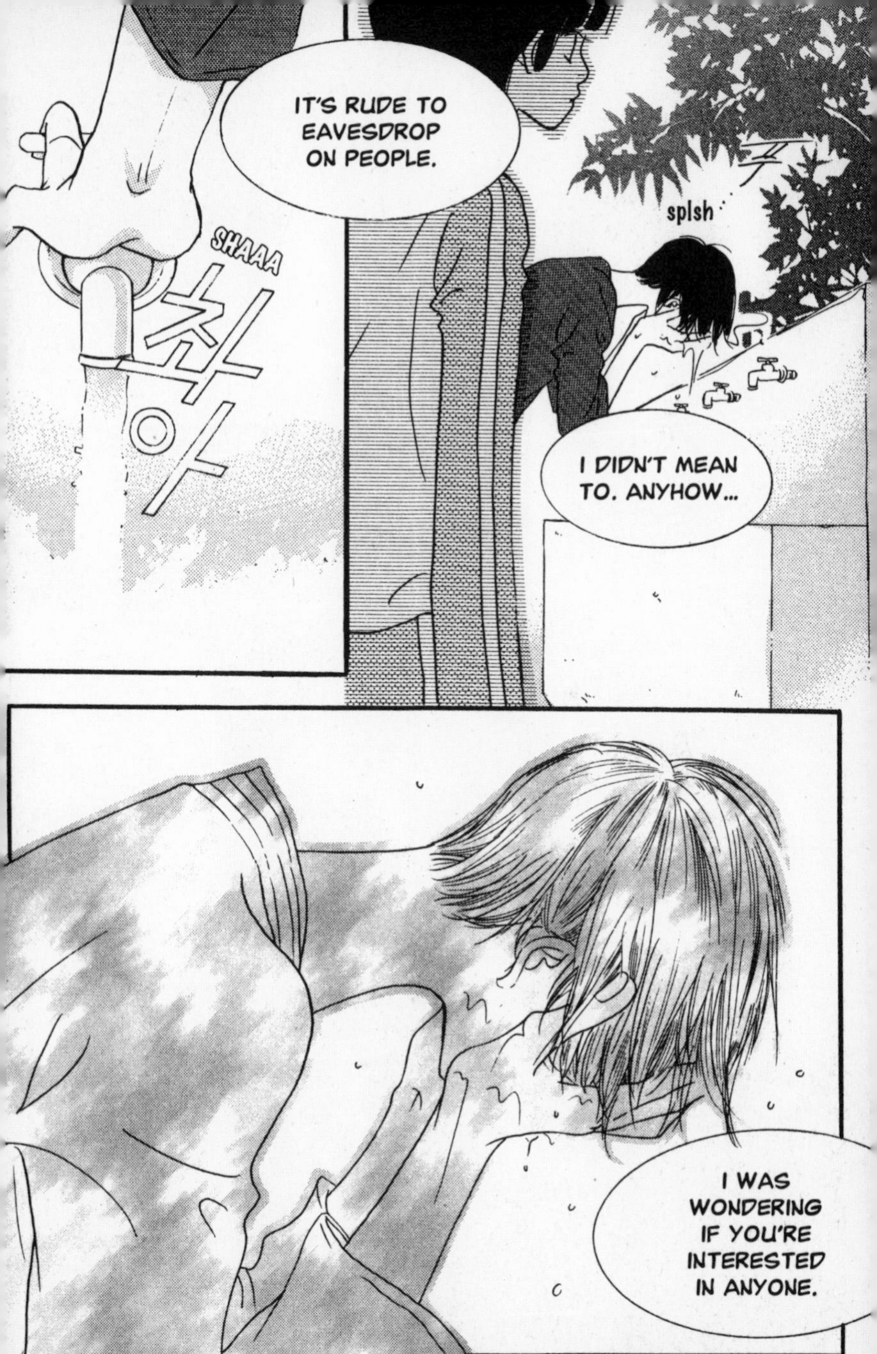
IT'S RUDE TO EAVESDROP ON PEOPLE.
SHAAA
촤아
splsh
I DIDN'T MEAN TO. ANYHOW...
I WAS WONDERING IF YOU'RE INTERESTED IN ANYONE.

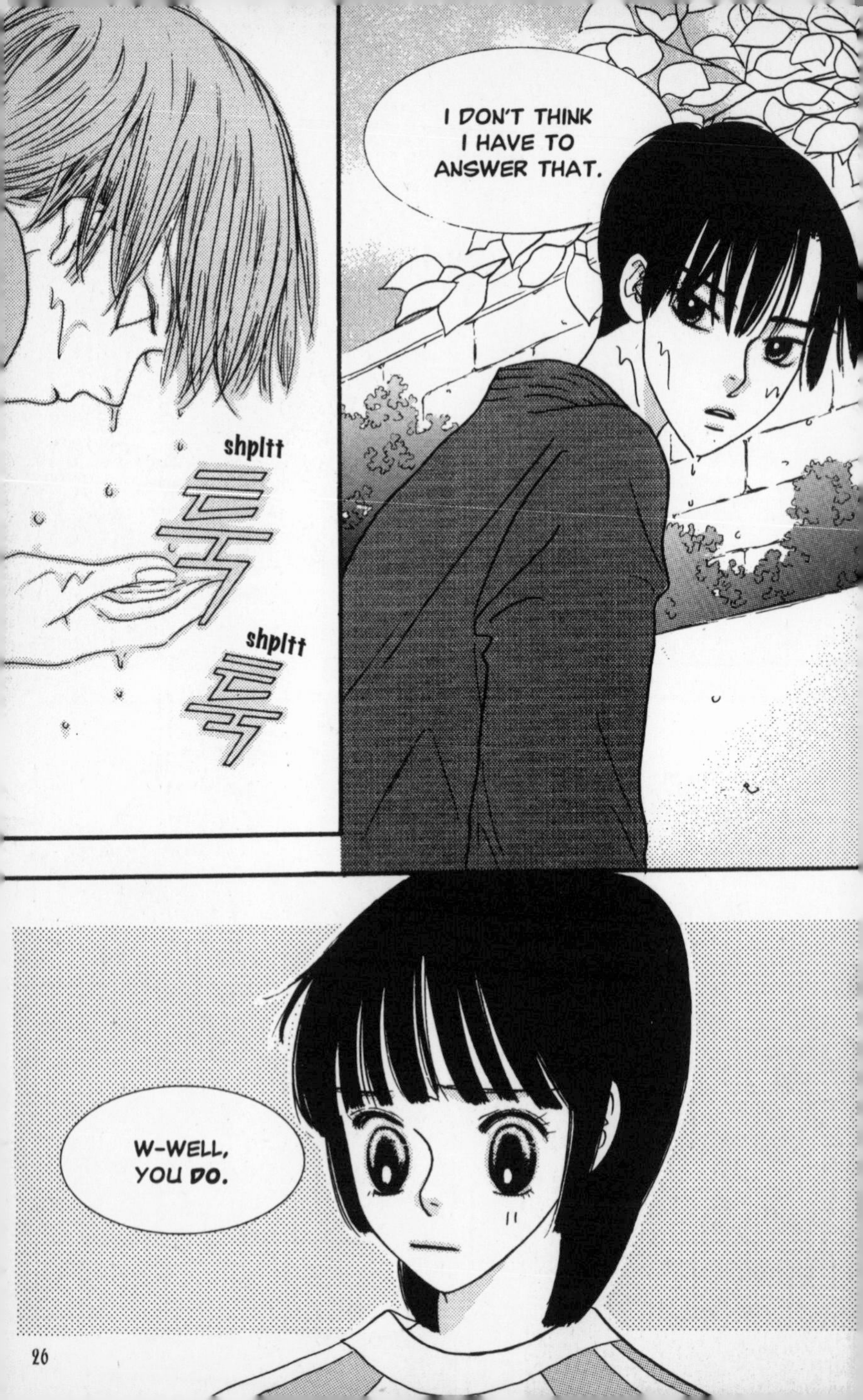
I DON'T THINK I HAVE TO ANSWER THAT.
shpltt
shpltt
W-WELL, YOU DO.

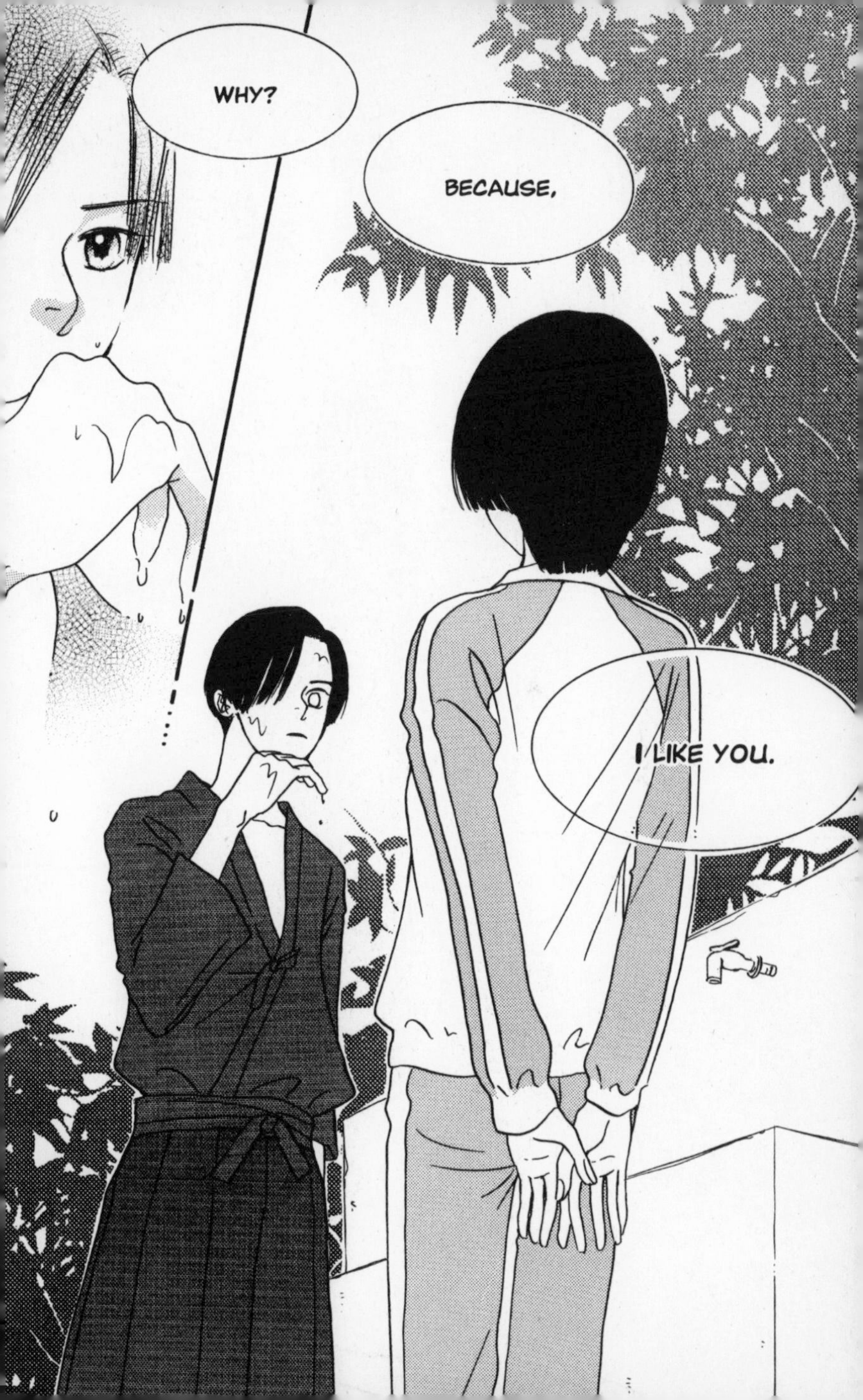
WHY?
BECAUSE,
I LIKE YOU.

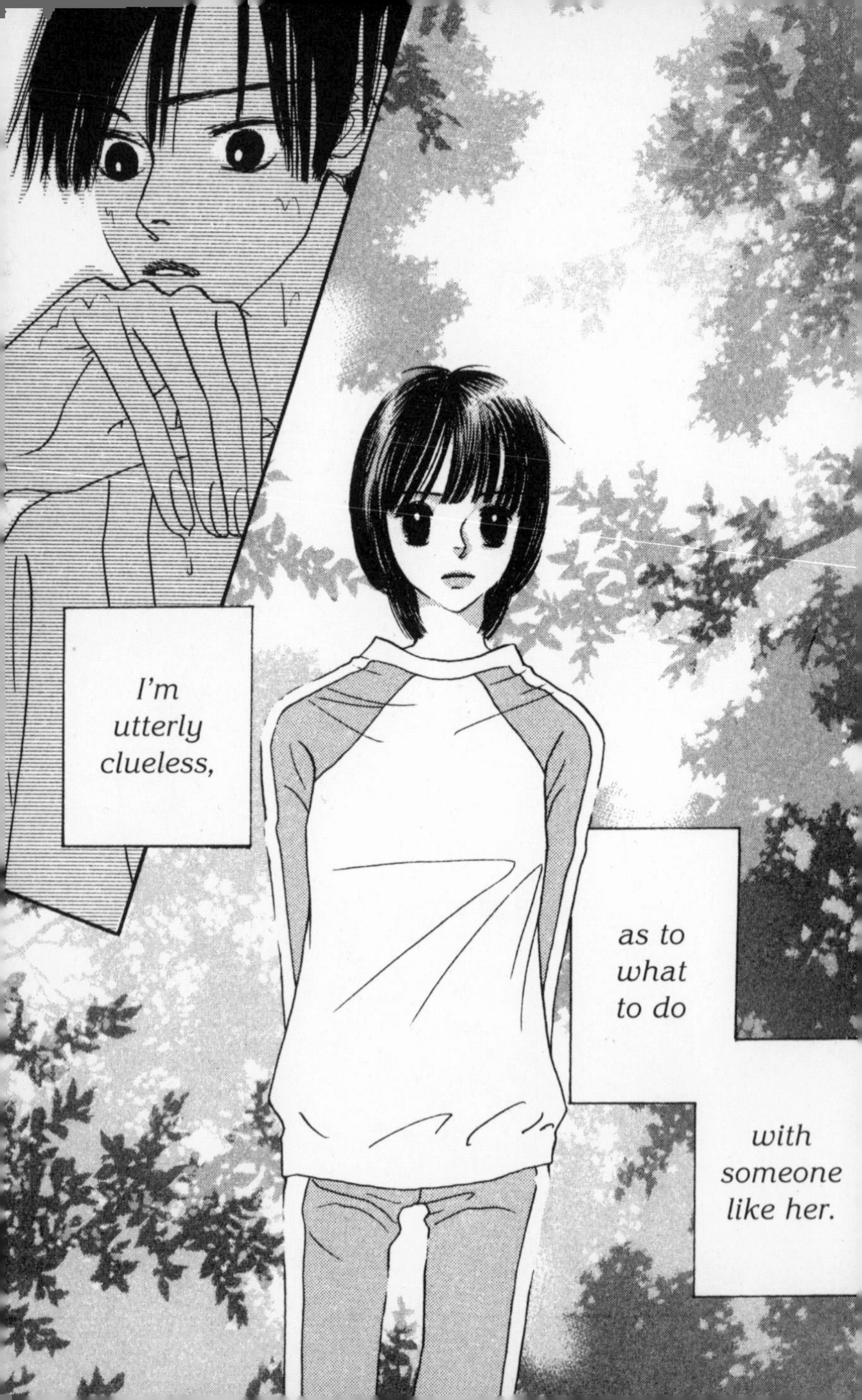
I'm utterly clueless,
as to what to do
with someone like her.

Chapter 8
Ee-Ji Bae

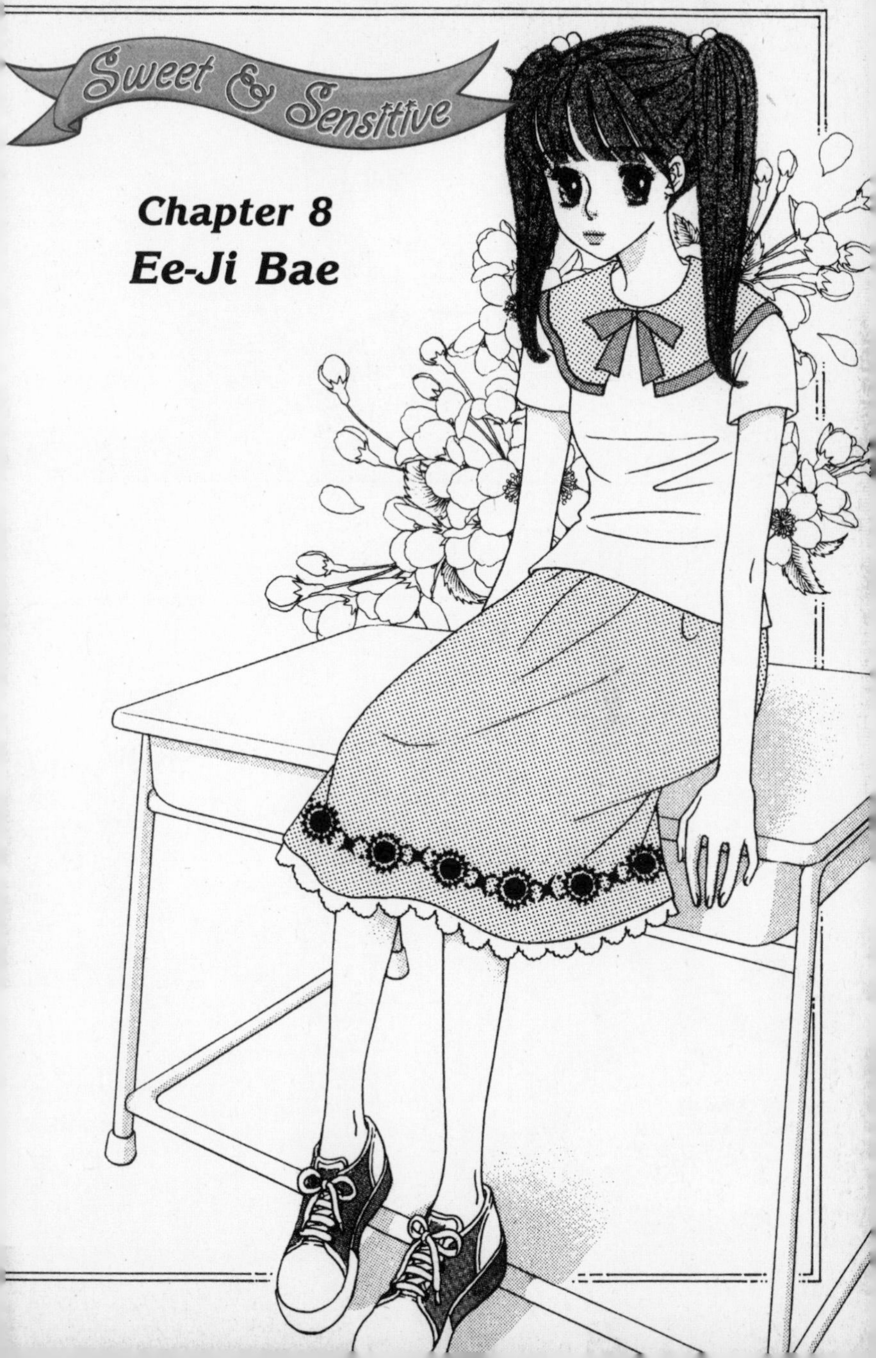
Sweet & Sensitive

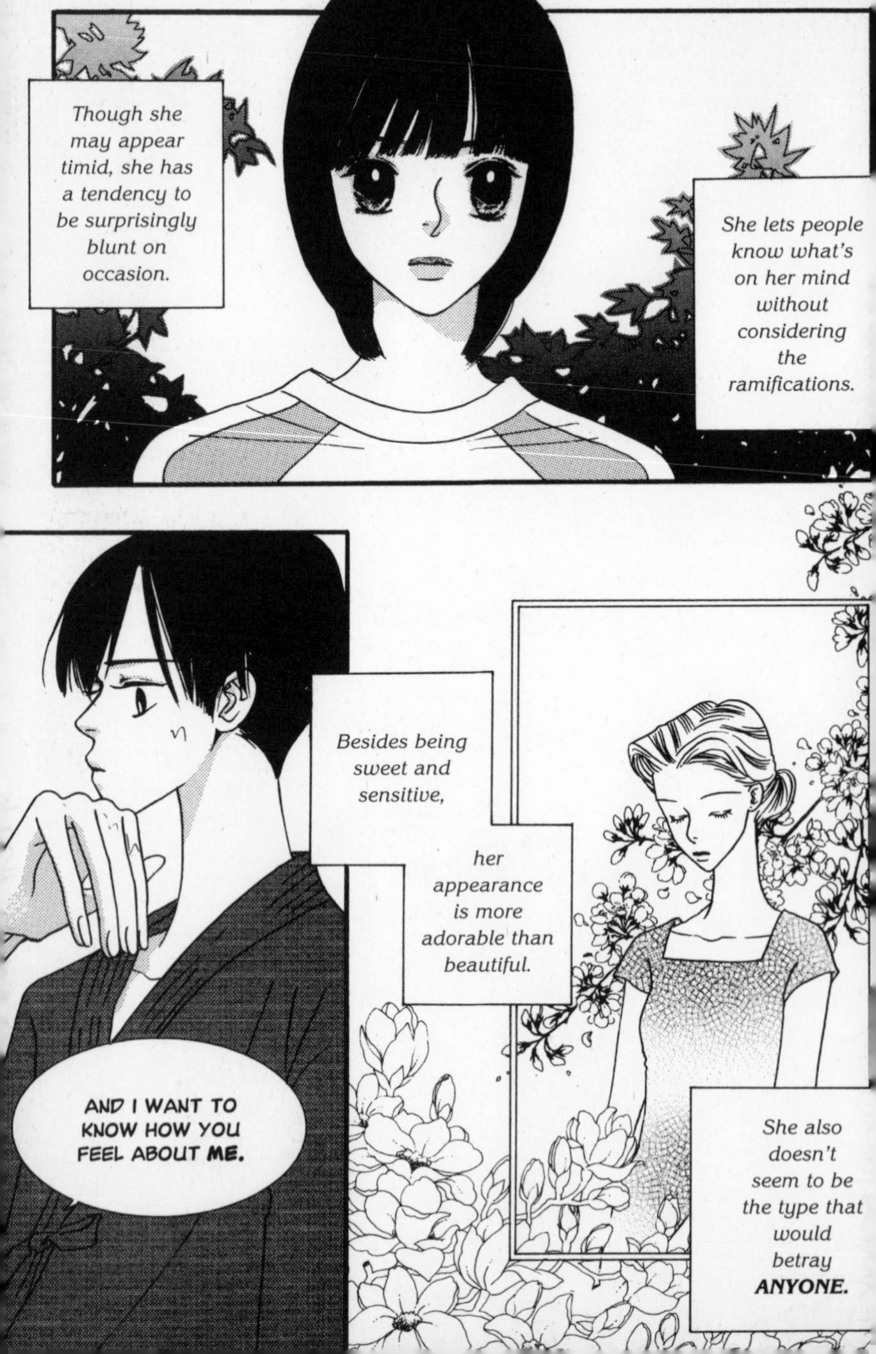

Though she may appear timid, she has a tendency to be surprisingly blunt on occasion.
She lets people know what's on her mind without considering the ramifications.
Besides being sweet and sensitive,
her appearance is more adorable than beautiful.
AND I WANT TO KNOW HOW YOU FEEL ABOUT ME.
She also doesn't seem to be the type that would betray ANYONE.

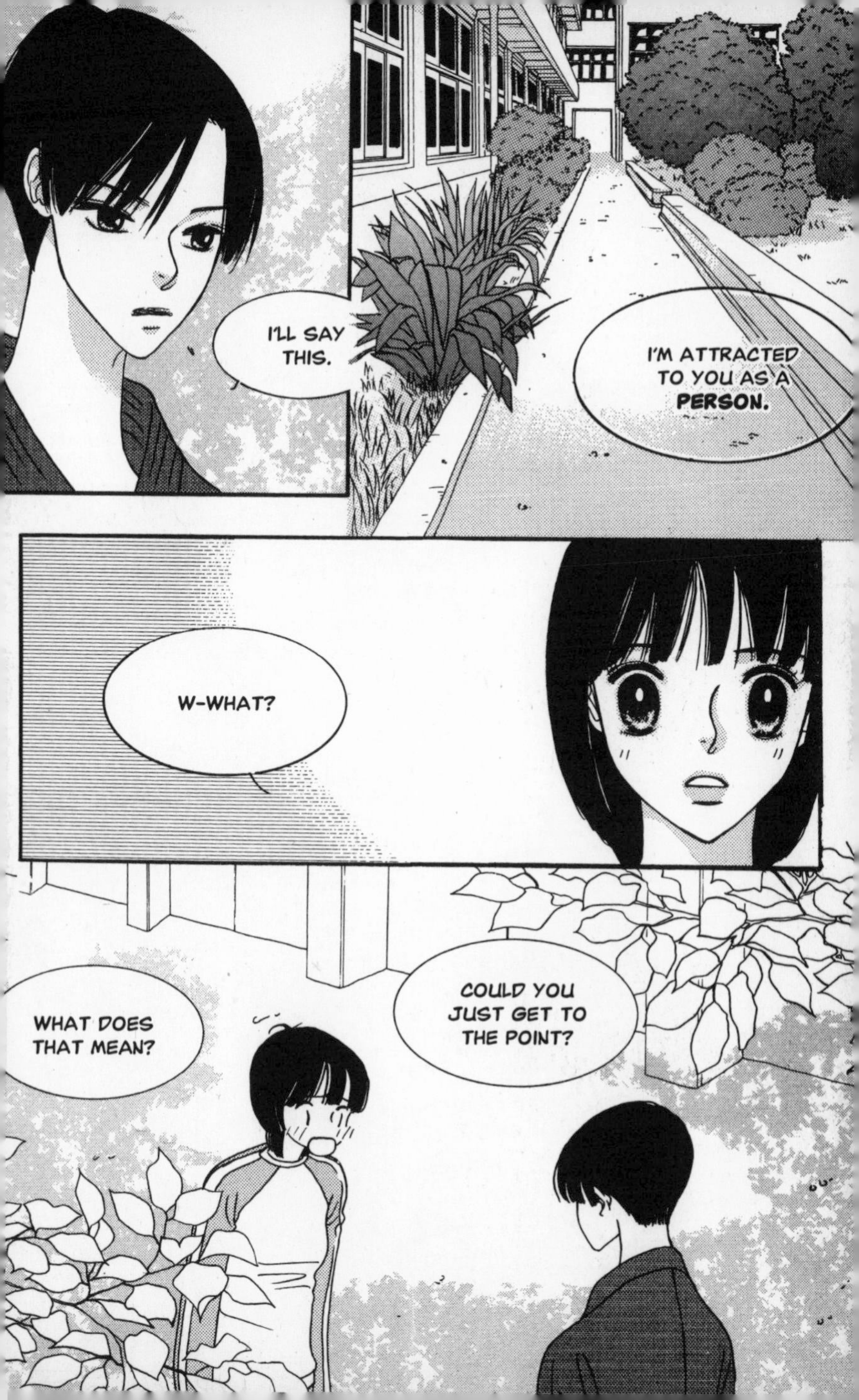
I'LL SAY THIS.
I'M ATTRACTED TO YOU AS A PERSON.
W-WHAT?
COULD YOU JUST GET TO THE POINT?
WHAT DOES THAT MEAN?

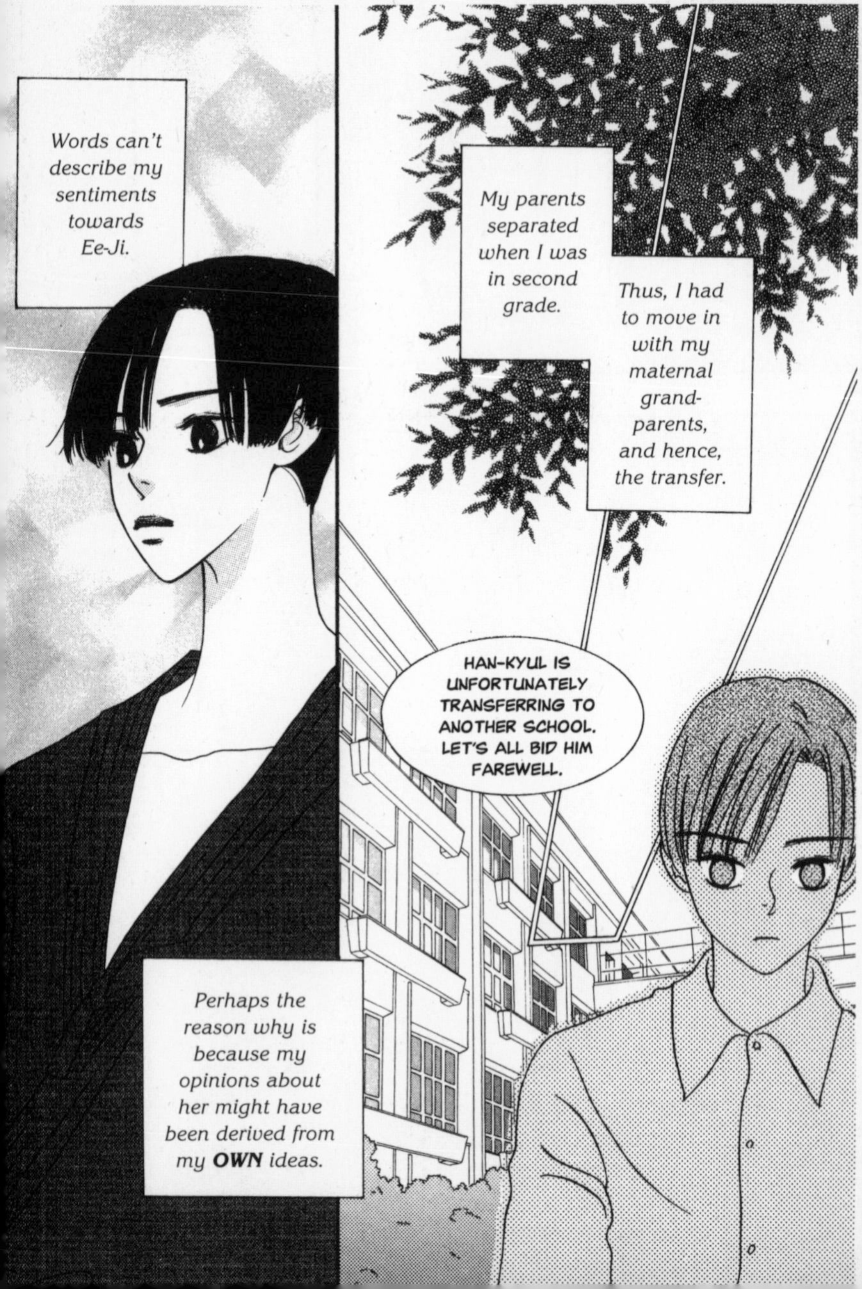
Words can't describe my sentiments towards Ee-Ji.
My parents separated when I was in second grade.
Thus, I had to move in with my maternal grand-parents, and hence, the transfer.
HAN-KYUL IS UNFORTUNATELY TRANSFERRING TO ANOTHER SCHOOL. LET'S ALL BID HIM FAREWELL.
Perhaps the reason why is because my opinions about her might have been derived from my OWN ideas.

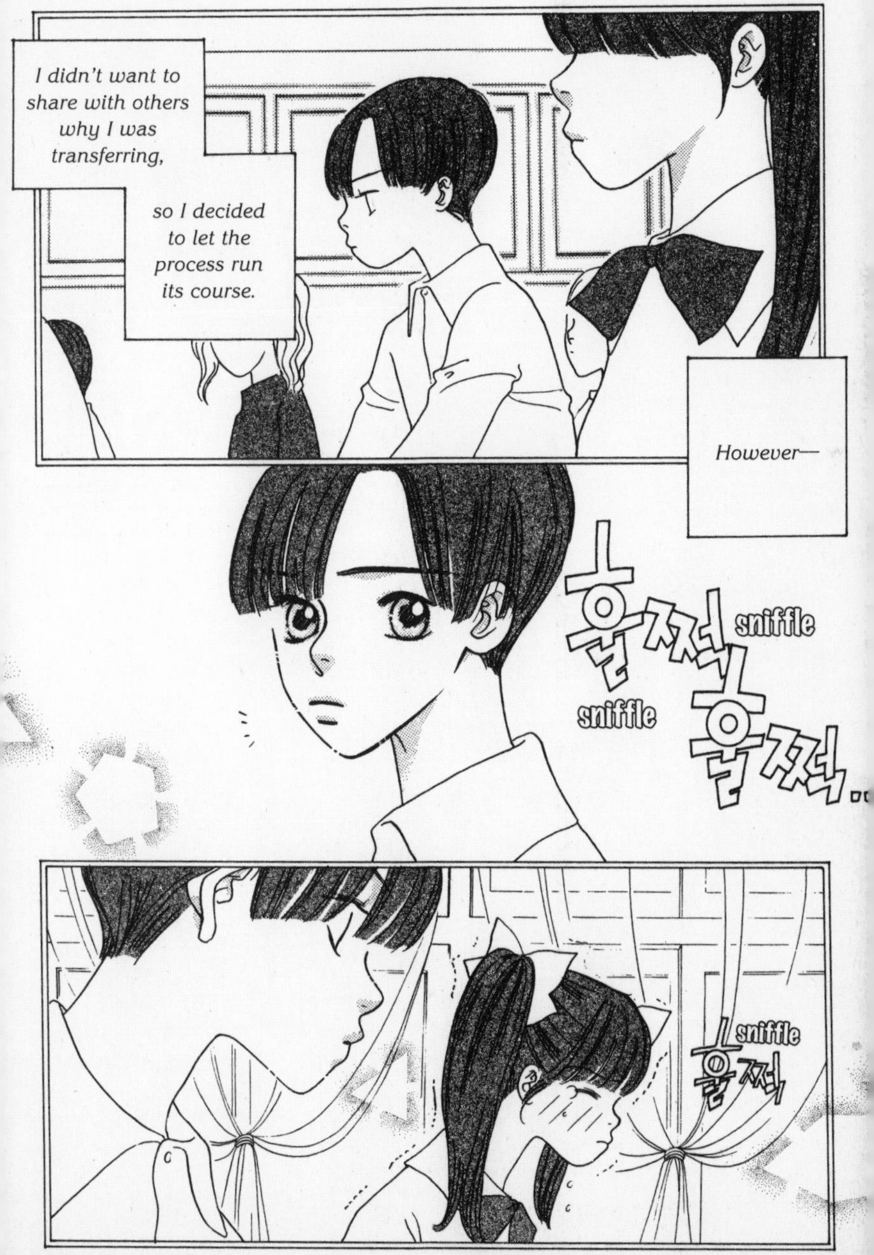
I didn't want to share with others why I was transferring,
so I decided to let the process run its course.
However—
훌쩍
sniffle
훌쩍..
sniffle
훌쩍
sniffle

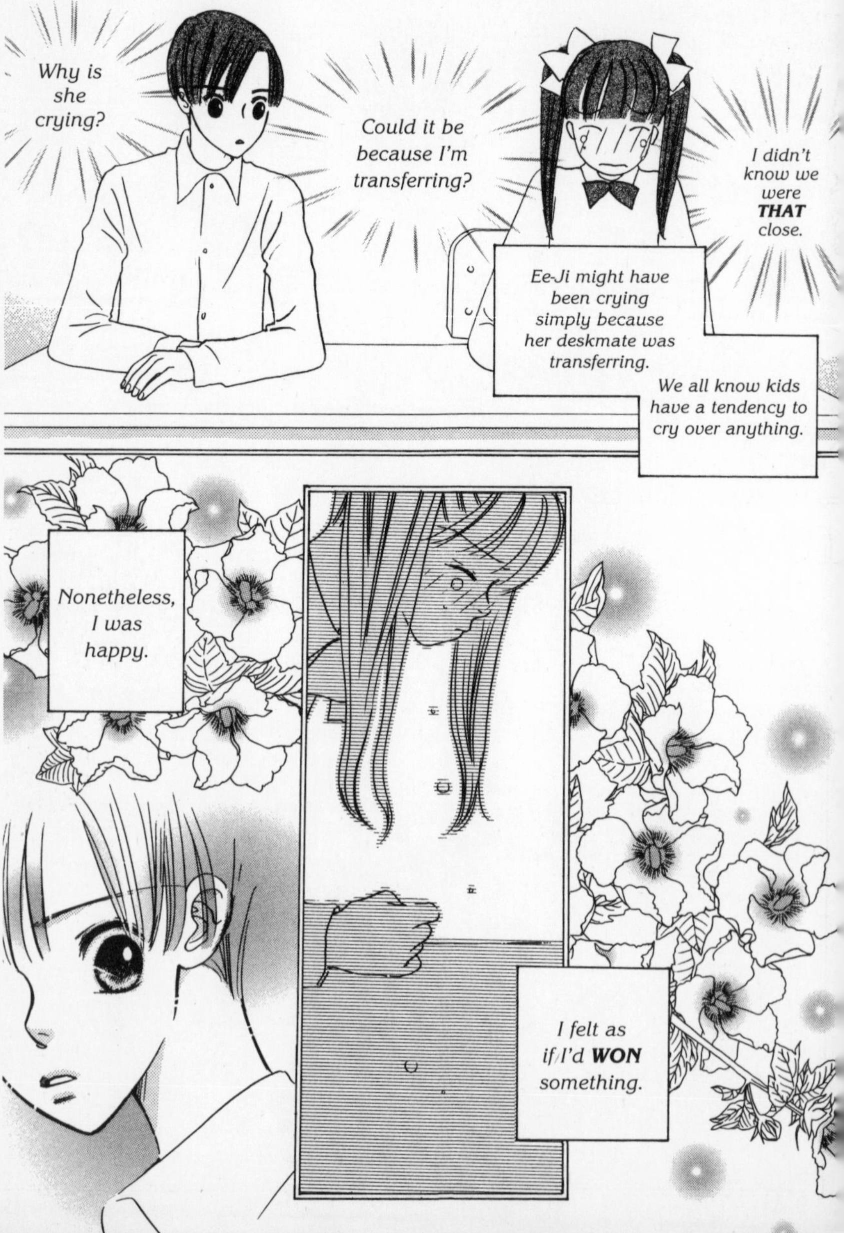
Why is she crying?
Could it be because I'm transferring?
I didn't know we were **THAT** close.
Ee-Ji might have been crying simply because her deskmate was transferring.
We all know kids have a tendency to cry over anything.
Nonetheless, I was happy.
I felt as if I'd **WON** something.

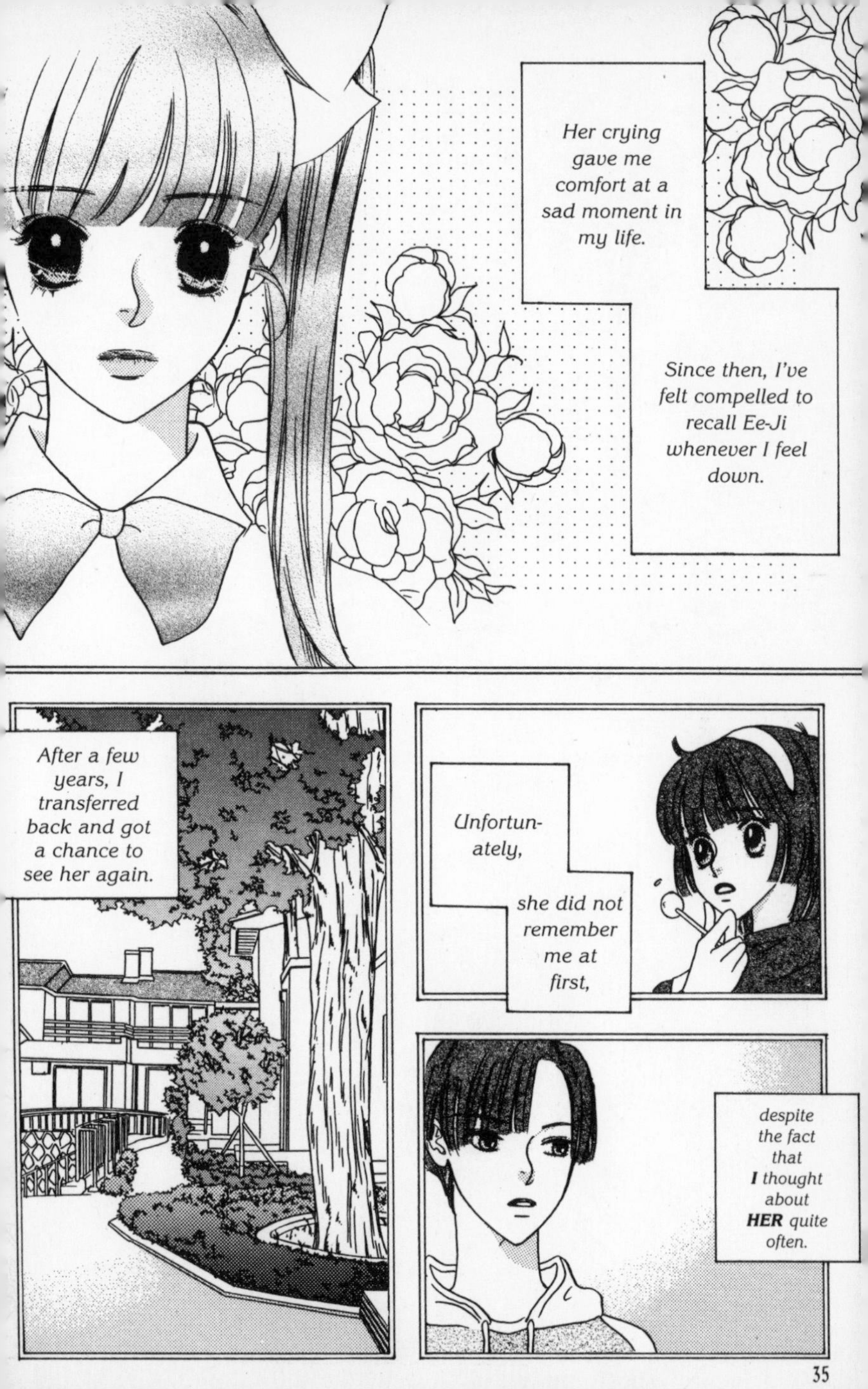
Her crying gave me comfort at a sad moment in my life.
Since then, I've felt compelled to recall Ee-Ji whenever I feel down.
After a few years, I transferred back and got a chance to see her again.
Unfortun-ately,
she did not remember me at first,
despite the fact that I thought about HER quite often.

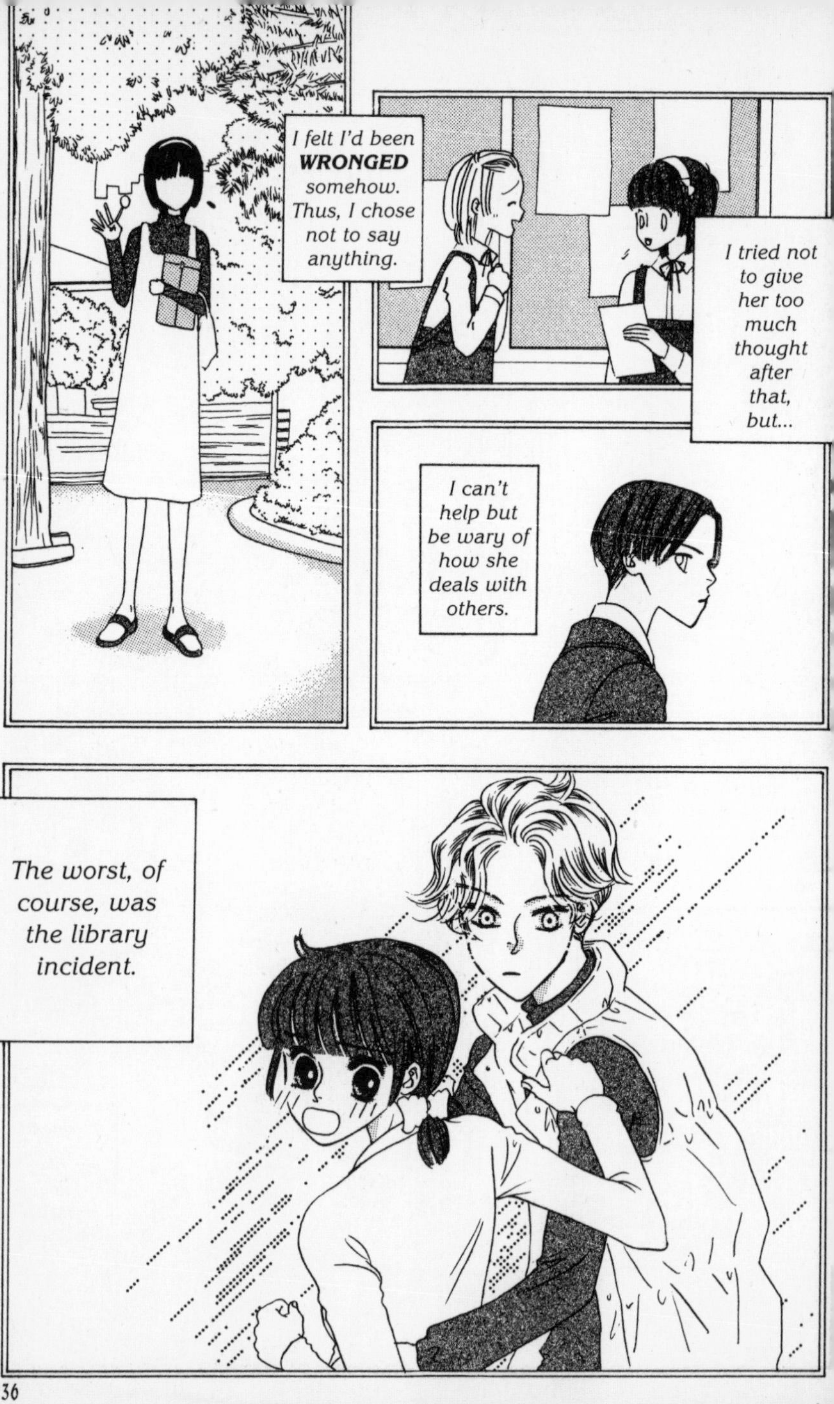
I felt I'd been **WRONGED** somehow. Thus, I chose not to say anything.
I tried not to give her too much thought after that, but...
I can't help but be wary of how she deals with others.
The worst, of course, was the library incident.

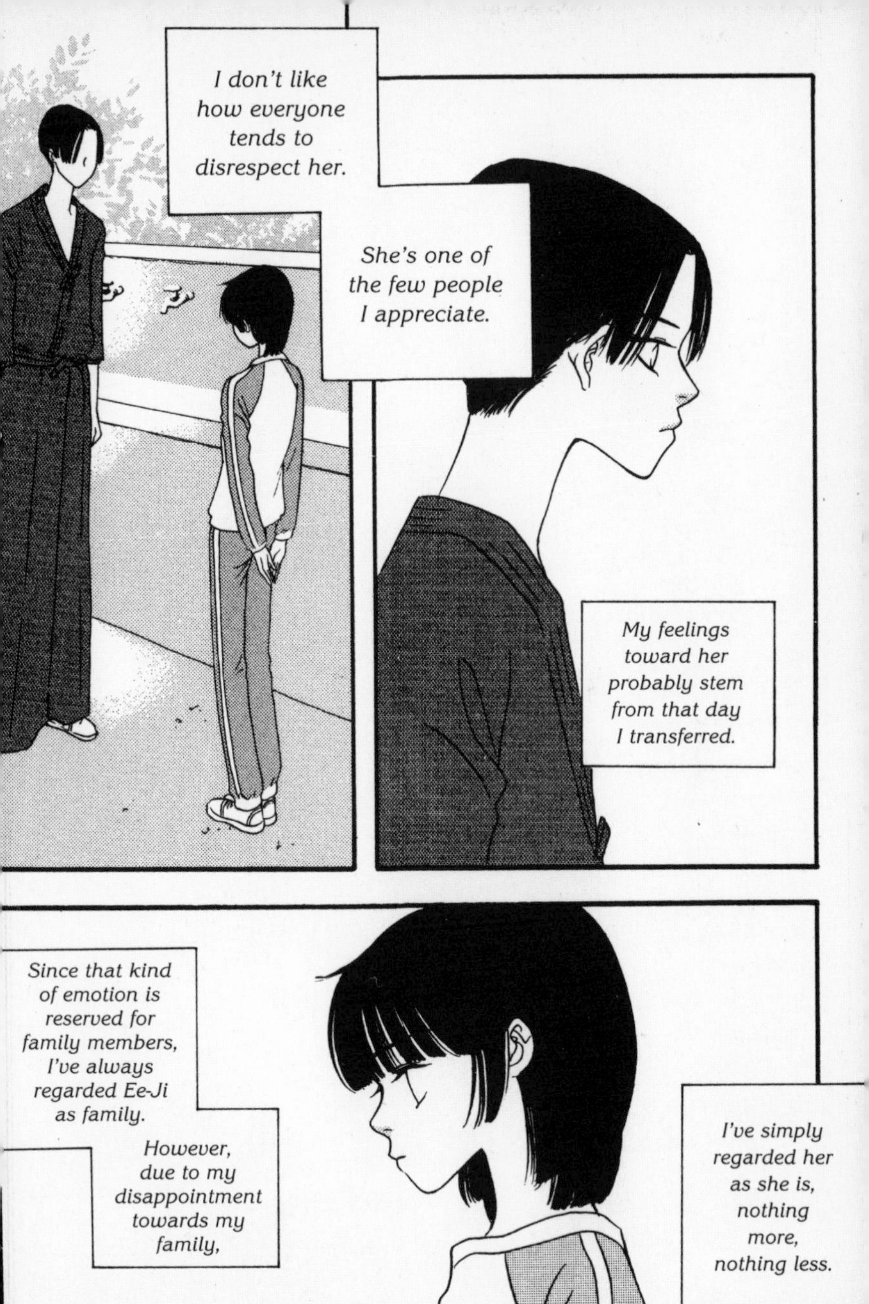
I don't like how everyone tends to disrespect her.
She's one of the few people I appreciate.
My feelings toward her probably stem from that day I transferred.
Since that kind of emotion is reserved for family members, I've always regarded Ee-Ji as family.
However, due to my disappointment towards my family,
I've simply regarded her as she is, nothing more, nothing less.

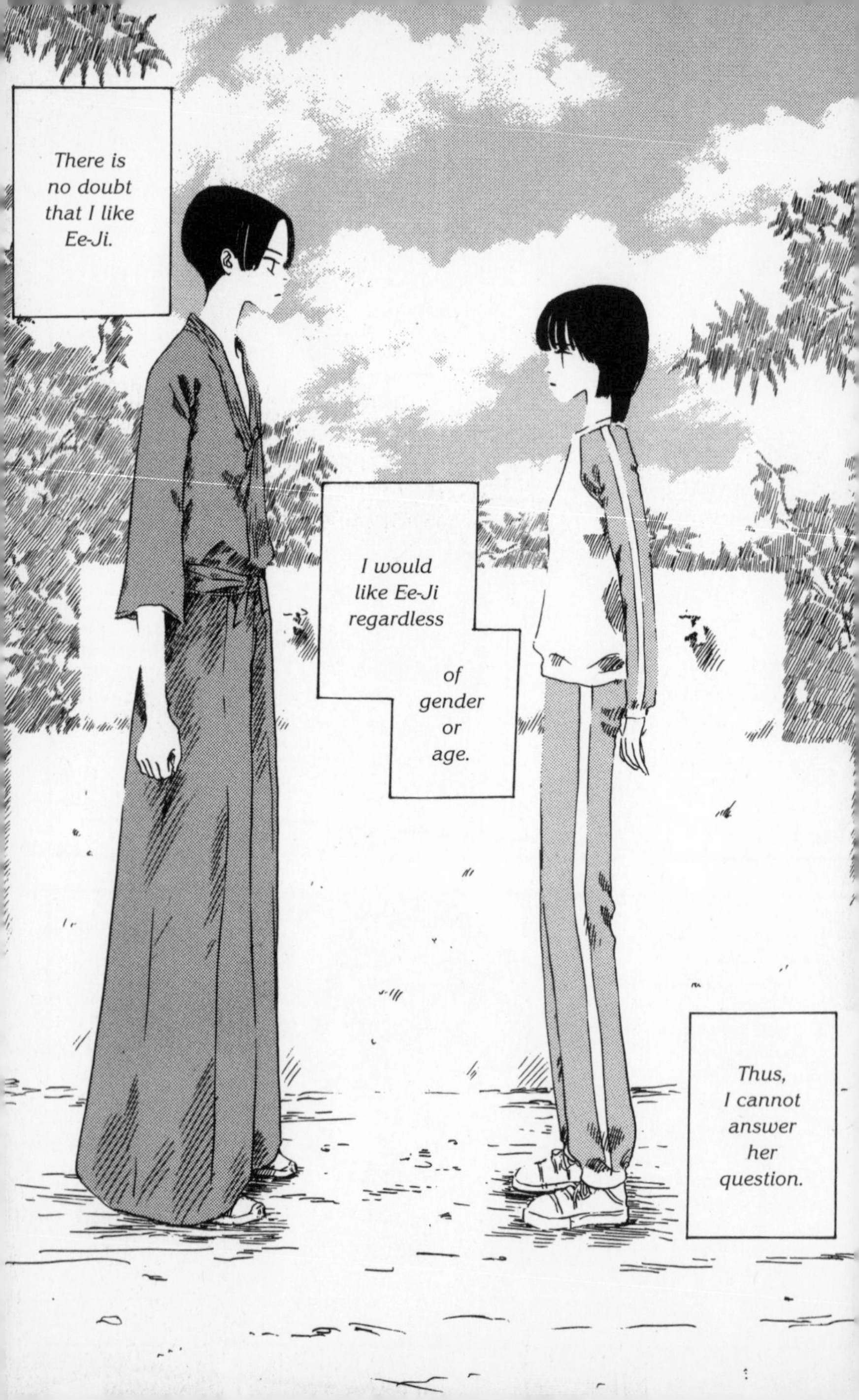

There is no doubt that I like Ee-Ji.
I would like Ee-Ji regardless of gender or age.
Thus, I cannot answer her question.

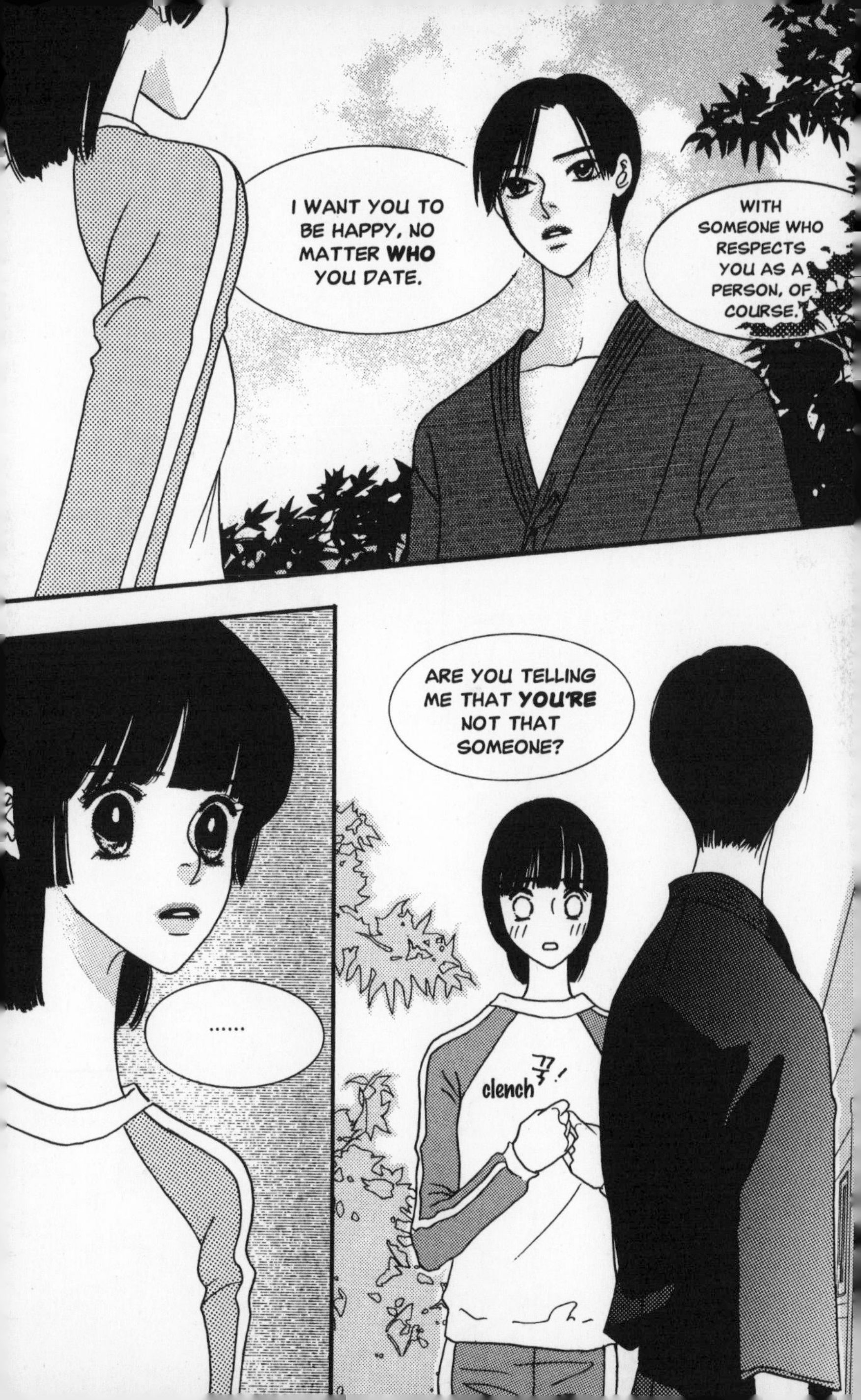
I WANT YOU TO BE HAPPY, NO MATTER WHO YOU DATE.
WITH SOMEONE WHO RESPECTS YOU AS A PERSON, OF COURSE.
ARE YOU TELLING ME THAT YOU'RE NOT THAT SOMEONE?
......
clench

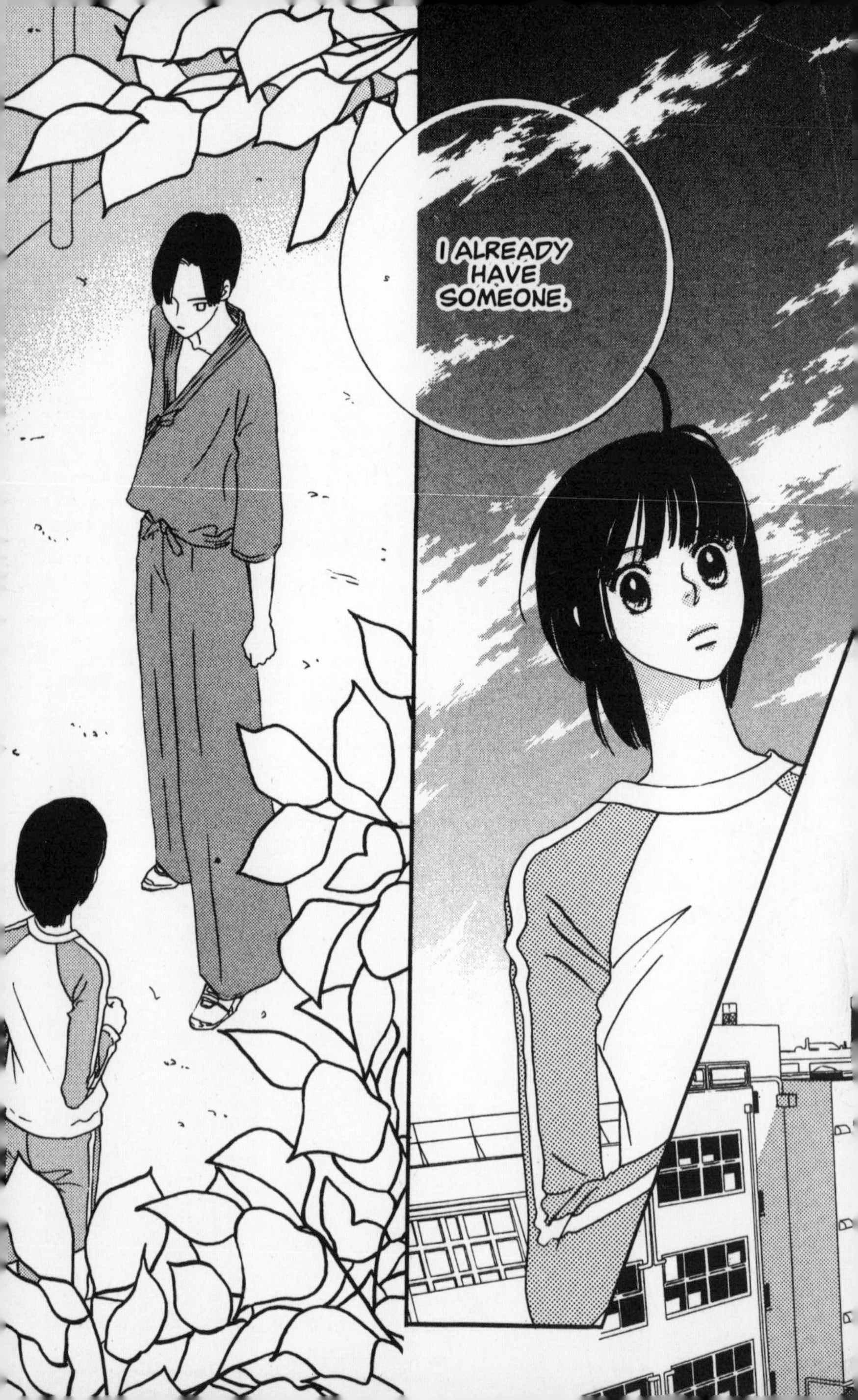
I ALREADY HAVE SOMEONE.

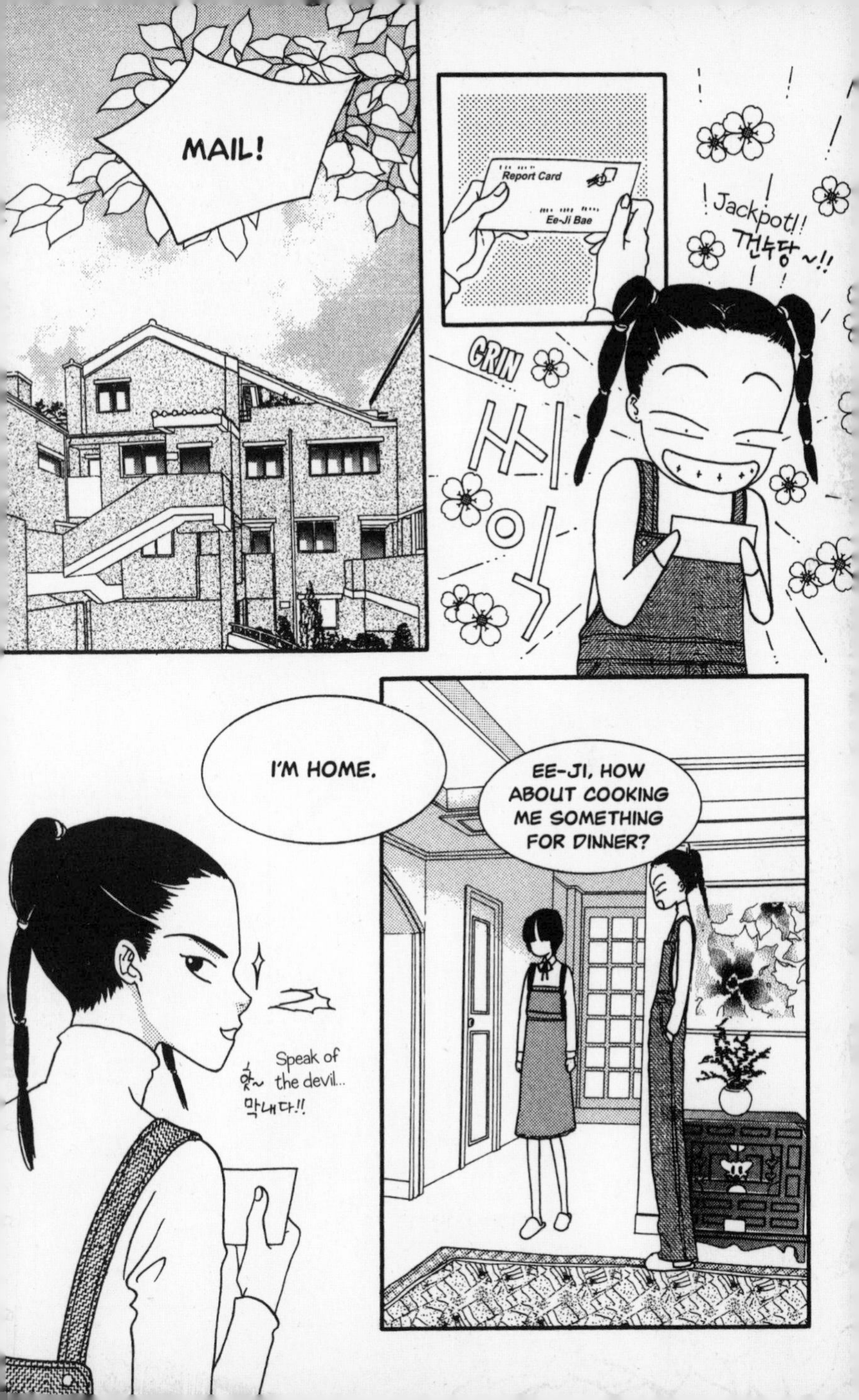
MAIL!
Report Card
Ee-Ji Bae
Jackpot!!
껀수당~!!
GRIN
씨익
I'M HOME.
EE-JI, HOW ABOUT COOKING ME SOMETHING FOR DINNER?
Speak of the devil...
앗~ 막내다!!

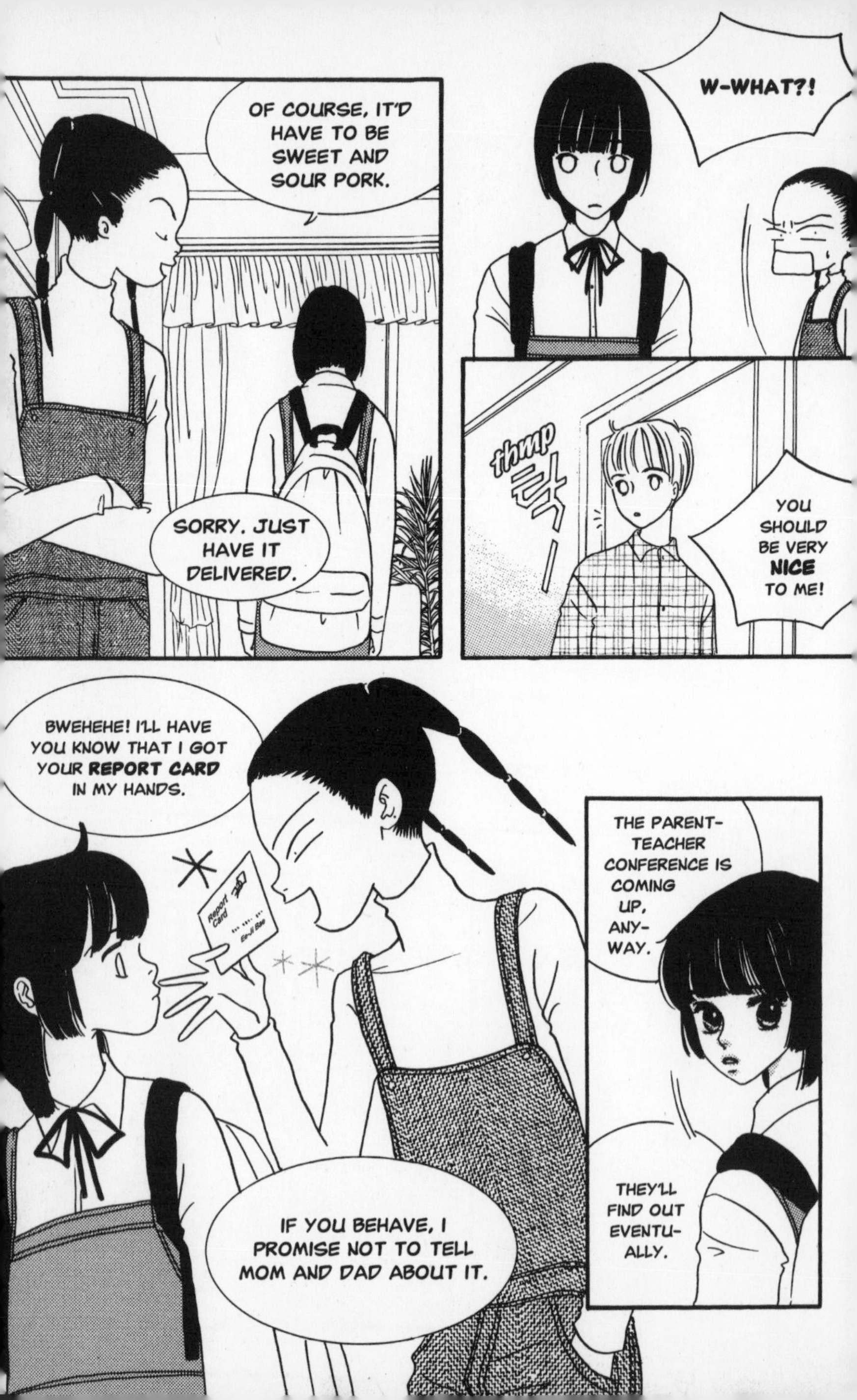
OF COURSE, IT'D HAVE TO BE SWEET AND SOUR PORK.
SORRY. JUST HAVE IT DELIVERED.
W-WHAT?!
thmp
YOU SHOULD BE VERY NICE TO ME!
BWEHEHE! I'LL HAVE YOU KNOW THAT I GOT YOUR REPORT CARD IN MY HANDS.
Report Card
Ee-Ji Bae
IF YOU BEHAVE, I PROMISE NOT TO TELL MOM AND DAD ABOUT IT.
THE PARENT-TEACHER CONFERENCE IS COMING UP, ANYWAY.
THEY'LL FIND OUT EVENTUALLY.

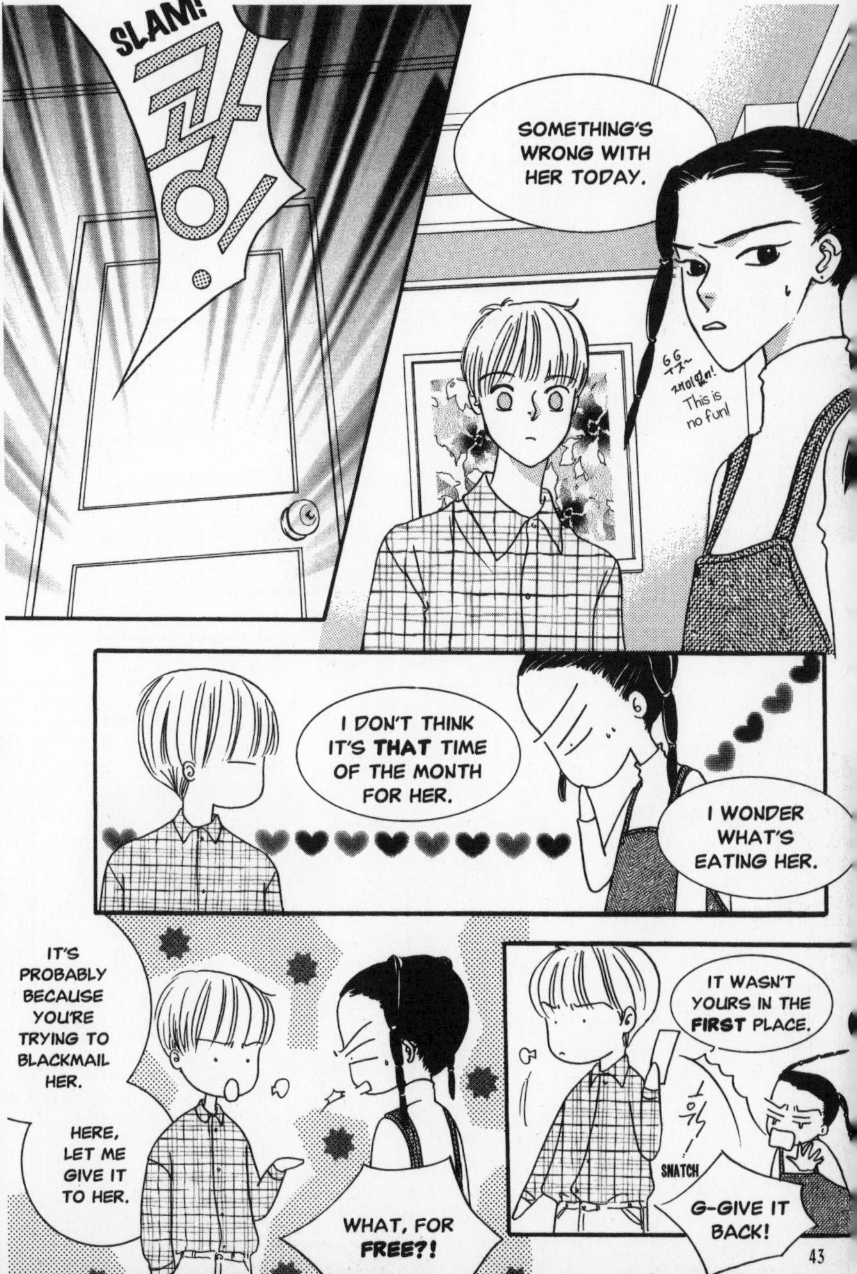
SLAM!
SOMETHING'S WRONG WITH HER TODAY.
This is no fun!
I DON'T THINK IT'S THAT TIME OF THE MONTH FOR HER.
I WONDER WHAT'S EATING HER.
IT'S PROBABLY BECAUSE YOU'RE TRYING TO BLACKMAIL HER.
HERE, LET ME GIVE IT TO HER.
WHAT, FOR FREE?!
IT WASN'T YOURS IN THE FIRST PLACE.
SNATCH
G-GIVE IT BACK!

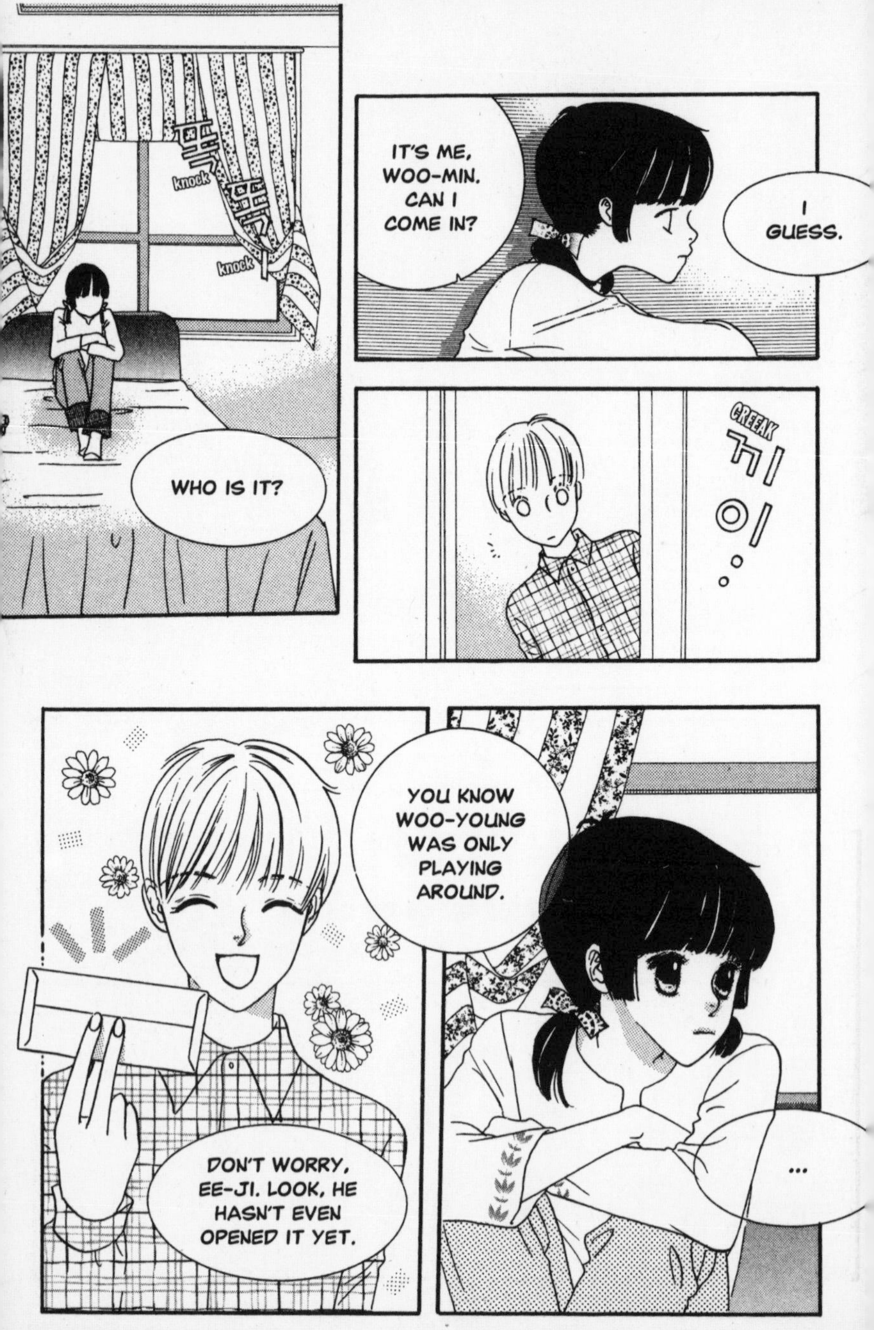
knock
knock
WHO IS IT?
IT'S ME, WOO-MIN. CAN I COME IN?
I GUESS.
CREEAK
YOU KNOW WOO-YOUNG WAS ONLY PLAYING AROUND.
DON'T WORRY, EE-JI. LOOK, HE HASN'T EVEN OPENED IT YET.
...

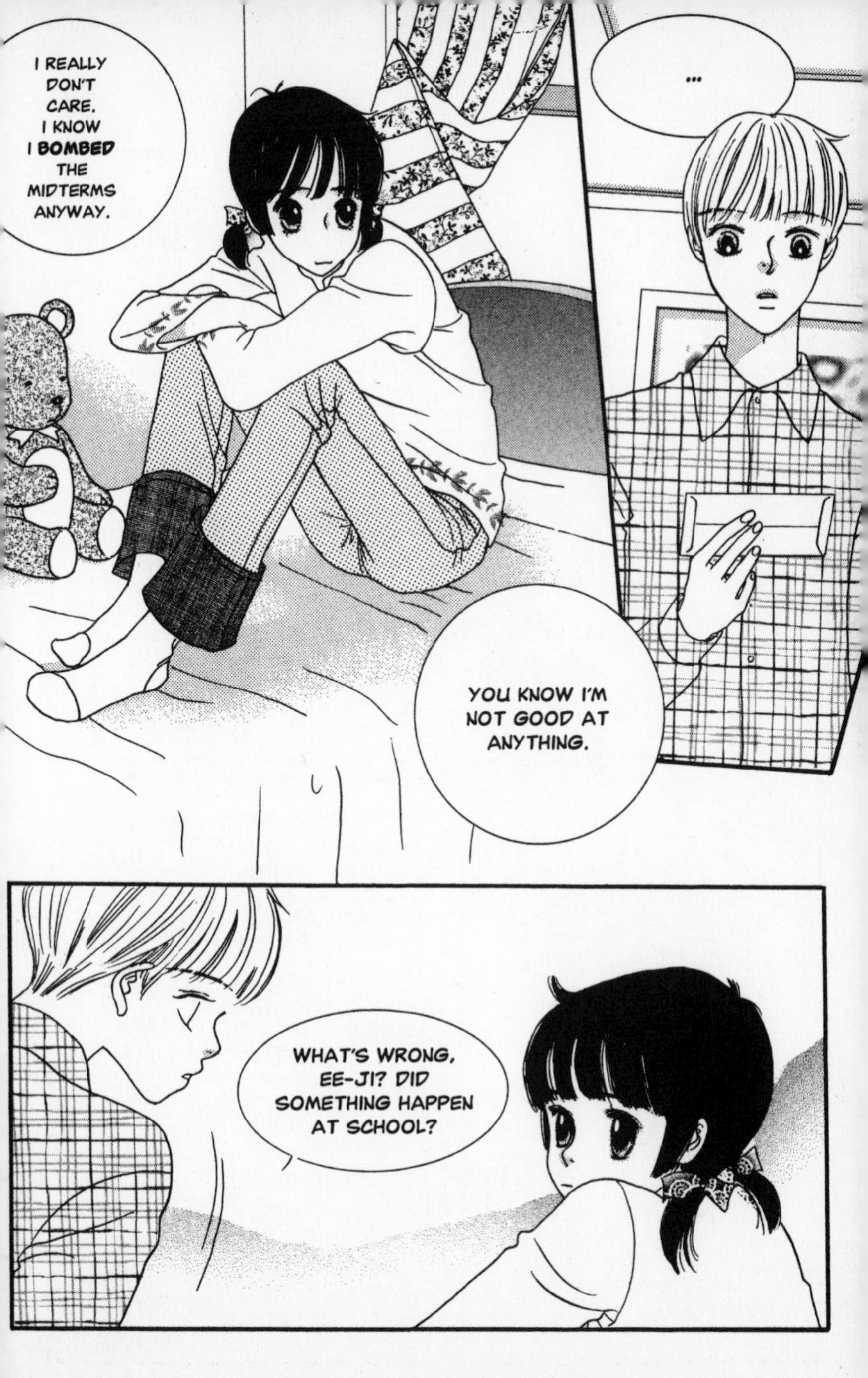
I REALLY DON'T CARE. I KNOW I **BOMBED** THE MIDTERMS ANYWAY.
...
YOU KNOW I'M NOT GOOD AT ANYTHING.
WHAT'S WRONG, EE-JI? DID SOMETHING HAPPEN AT SCHOOL?

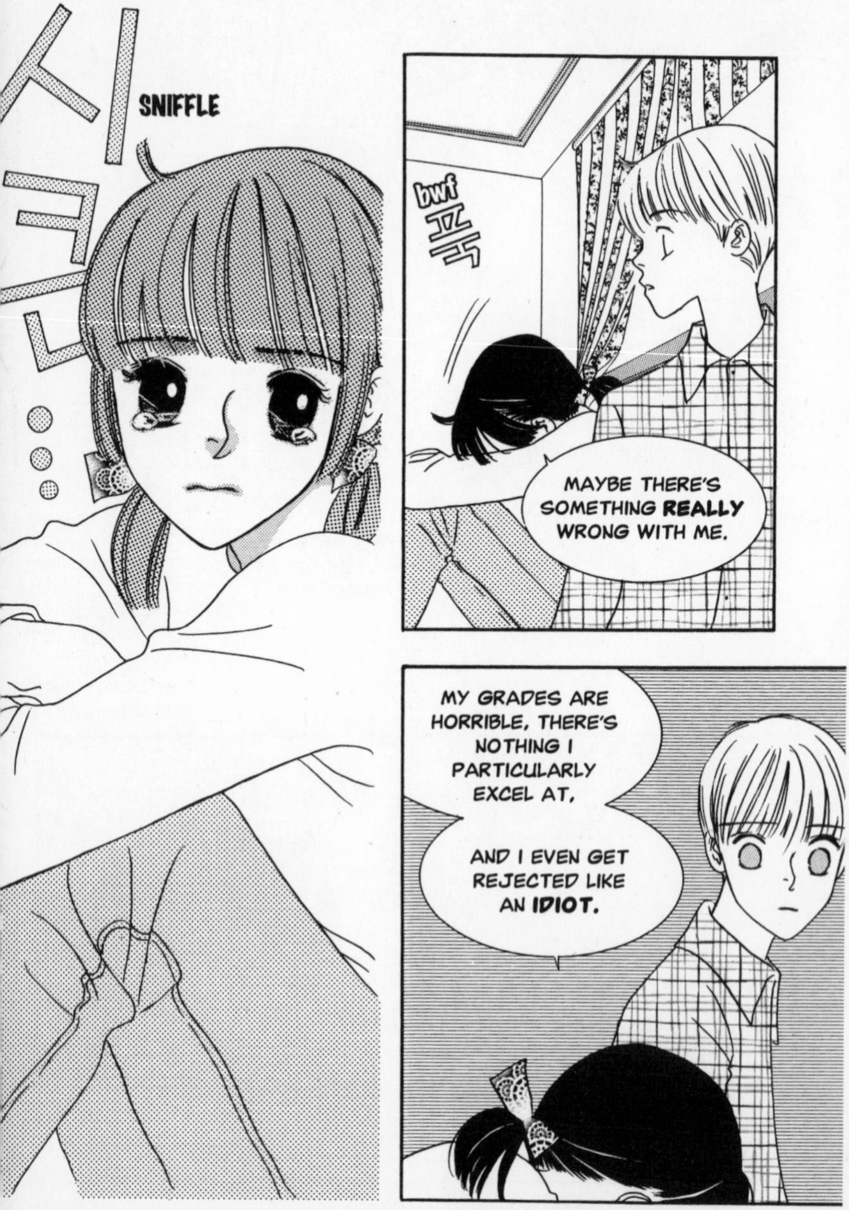
SNIFFLE
bwf
MAYBE THERE'S SOMETHING **REALLY** WRONG WITH ME.
MY GRADES ARE HORRIBLE, THERE'S NOTHING I PARTICULARLY EXCEL AT,
AND I EVEN GET REJECTED LIKE AN **IDIOT.**

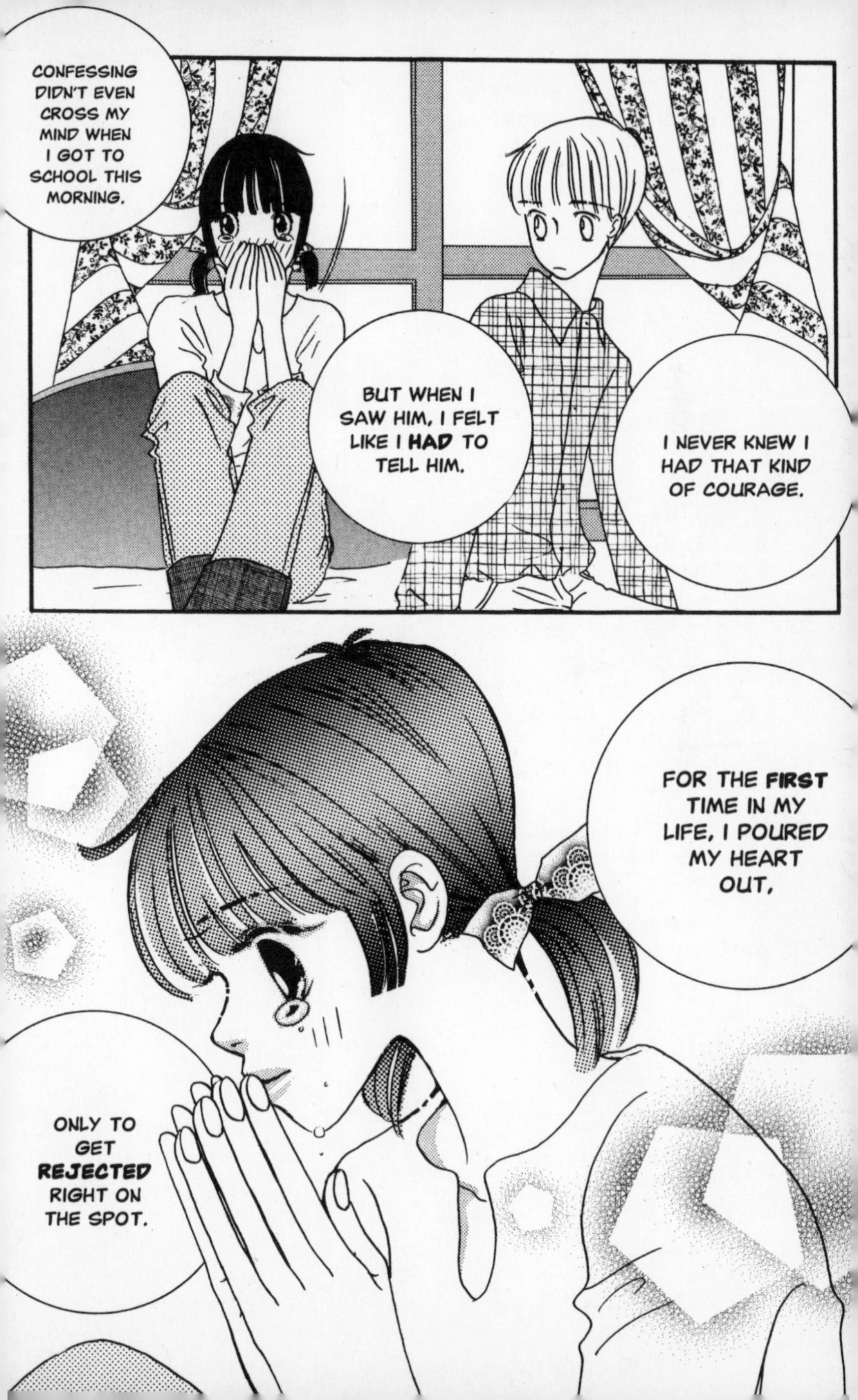
CONFESSING DIDN'T EVEN CROSS MY MIND WHEN I GOT TO SCHOOL THIS MORNING.
BUT WHEN I SAW HIM, I FELT LIKE I **HAD** TO TELL HIM.
I NEVER KNEW I HAD THAT KIND OF COURAGE.
FOR THE **FIRST** TIME IN MY LIFE, I POURED MY HEART OUT,
ONLY TO GET **REJECTED** RIGHT ON THE SPOT.

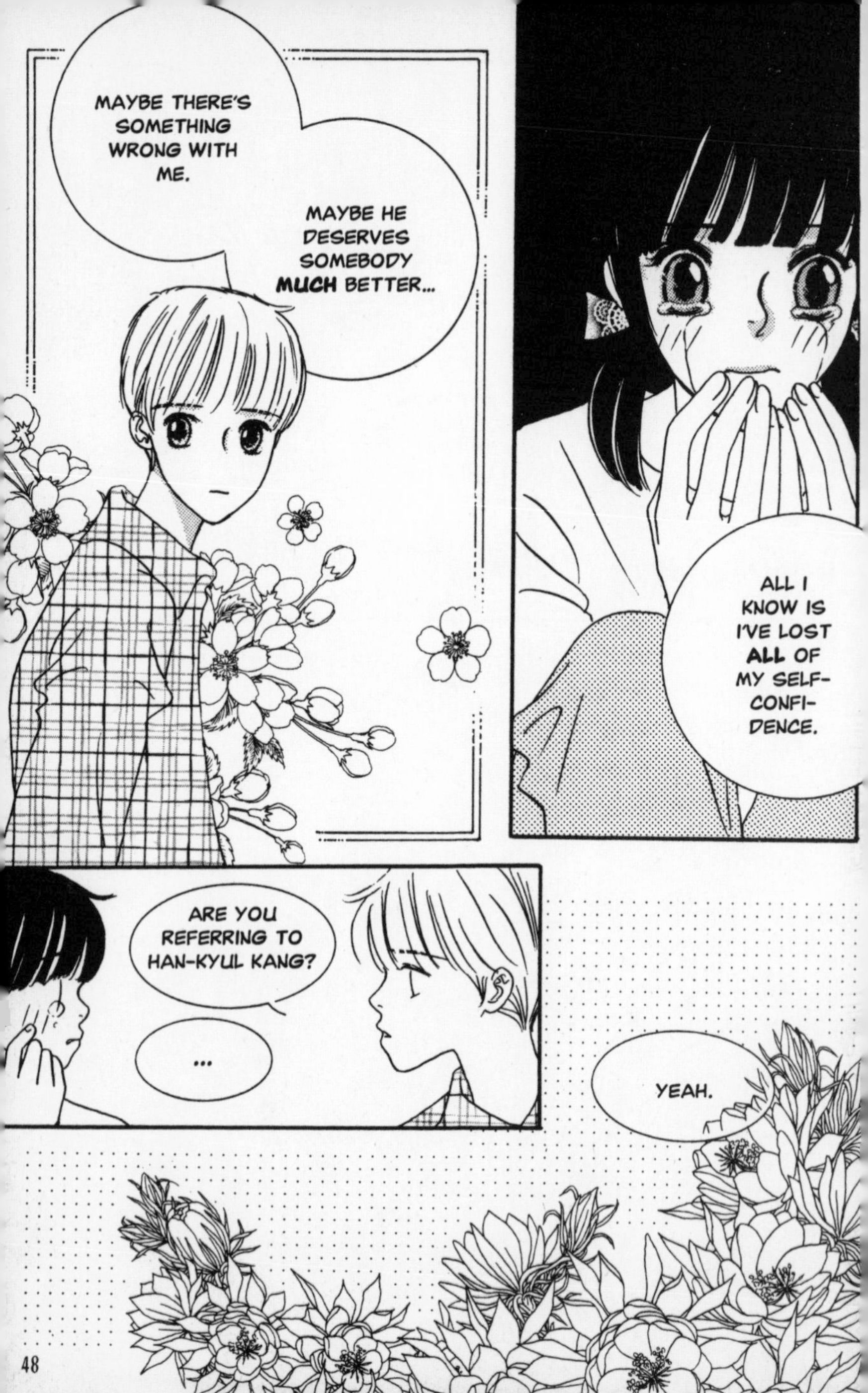

MAYBE THERE'S SOMETHING WRONG WITH ME.
MAYBE HE DESERVES SOMEBODY MUCH BETTER...
ALL I KNOW IS I'VE LOST ALL OF MY SELF-CONFIDENCE.
ARE YOU REFERRING TO HAN-KYUL KANG?
...
YEAH.

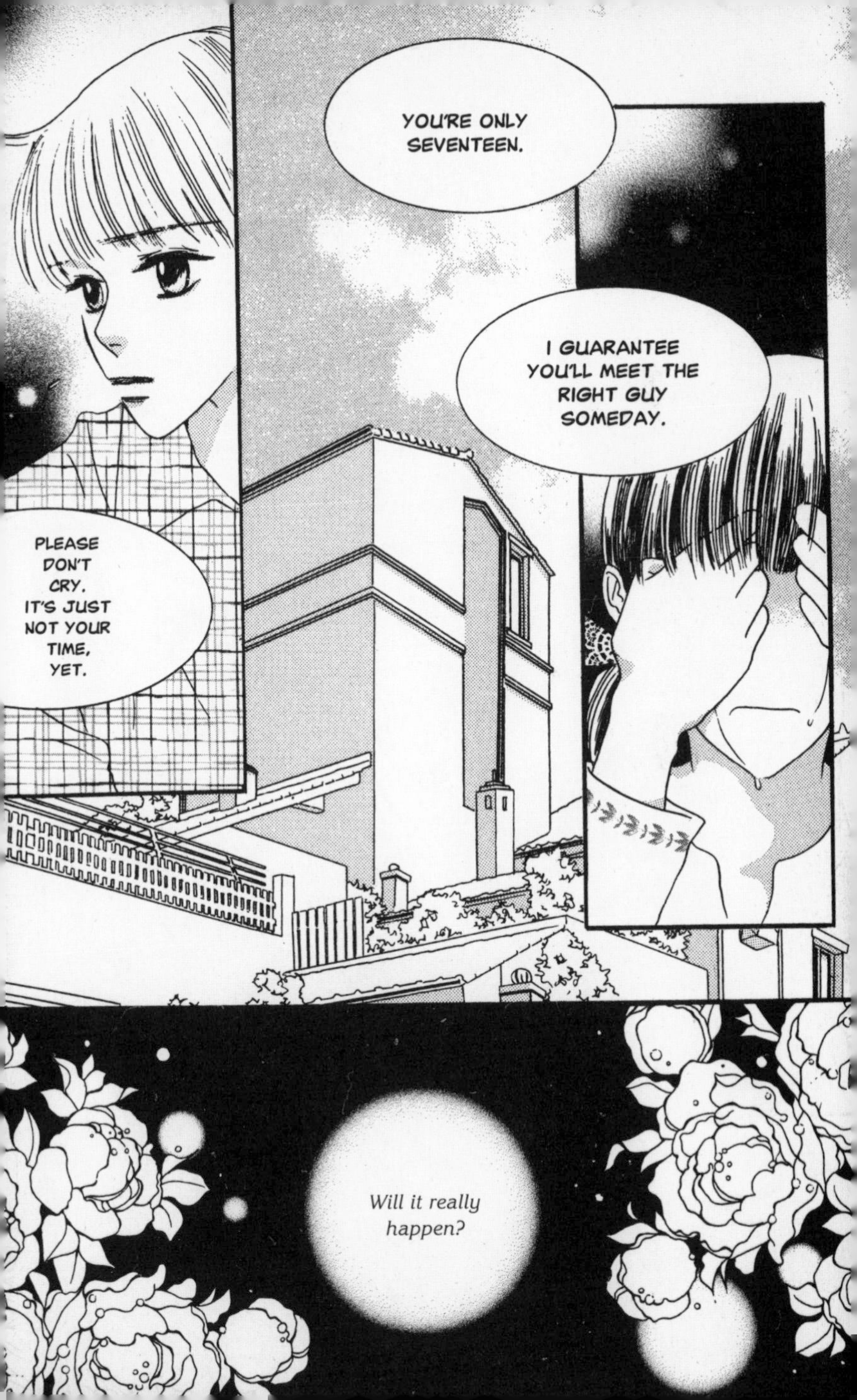
YOU'RE ONLY SEVENTEEN.
I GUARANTEE YOU'LL MEET THE RIGHT GUY SOMEDAY.
PLEASE DON'T CRY. IT'S JUST NOT YOUR TIME, YET.
Will it really happen?

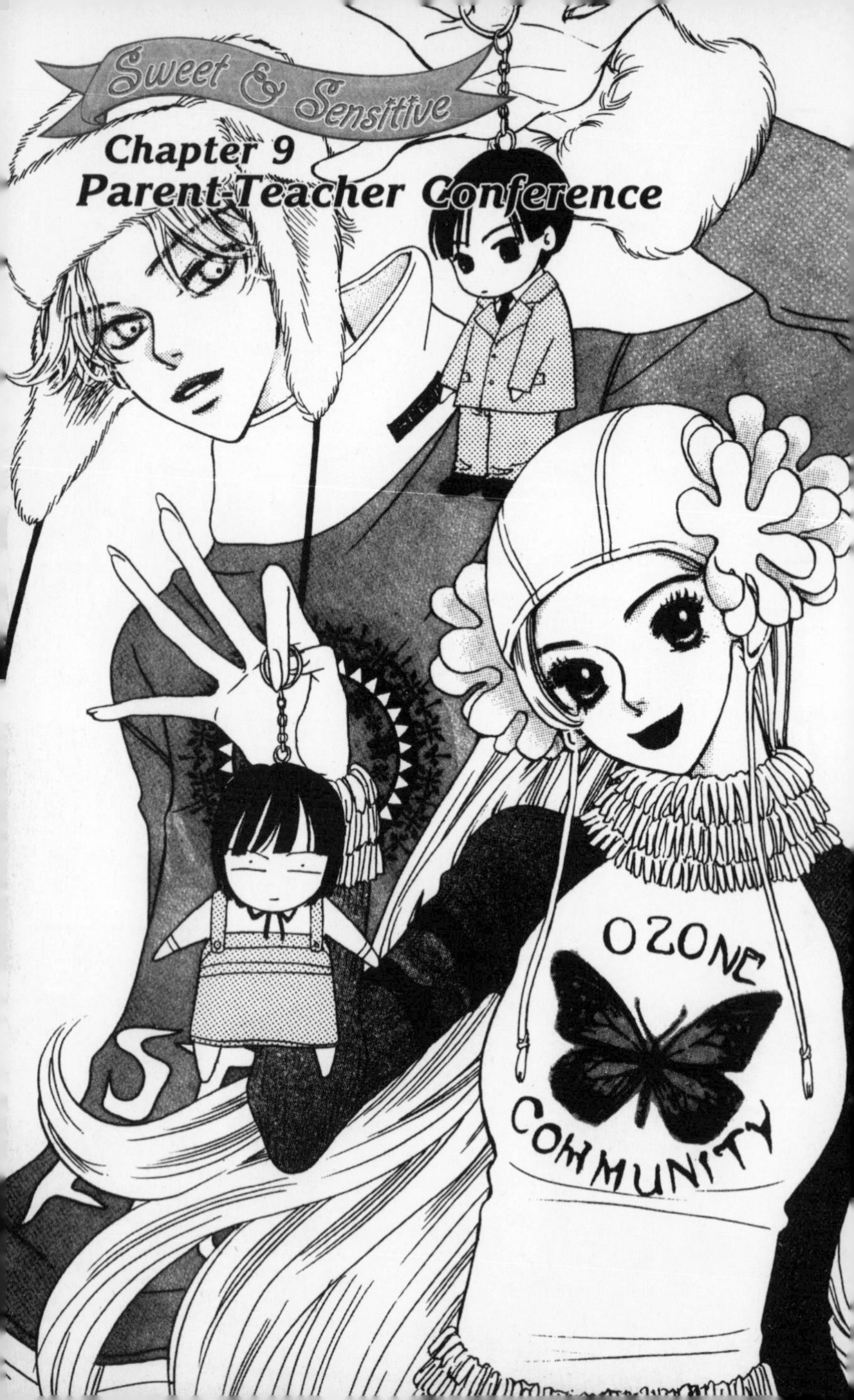

Sweet & Sensitive
Chapter 9
Parent-Teacher Conference
OZONE
COMMUNITY

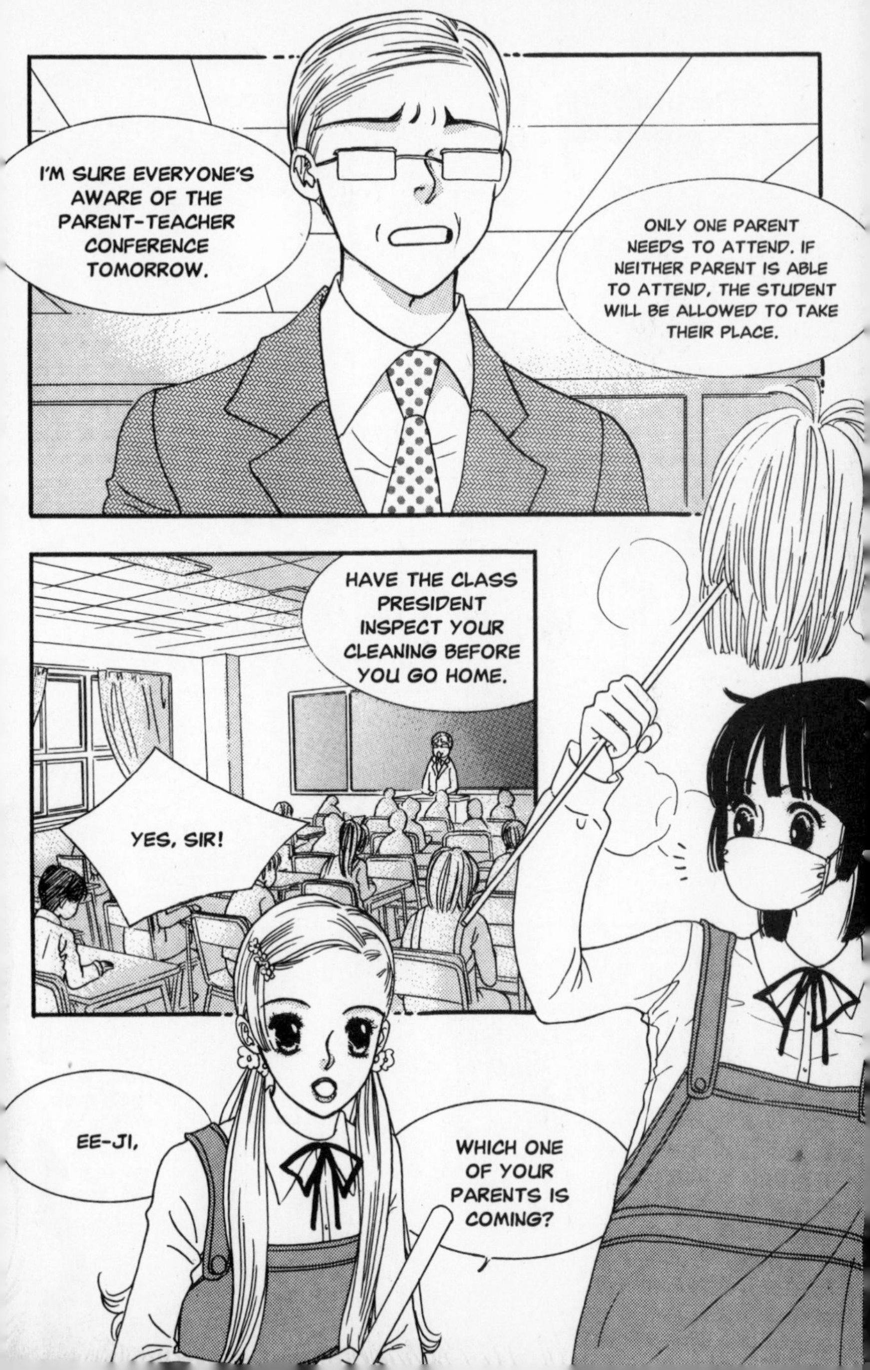
I'M SURE EVERYONE'S AWARE OF THE PARENT-TEACHER CONFERENCE TOMORROW.
ONLY ONE PARENT NEEDS TO ATTEND. IF NEITHER PARENT IS ABLE TO ATTEND, THE STUDENT WILL BE ALLOWED TO TAKE THEIR PLACE.
HAVE THE CLASS PRESIDENT INSPECT YOUR CLEANING BEFORE YOU GO HOME.
YES, SIR!
EE-JI,
WHICH ONE OF YOUR PARENTS IS COMING?

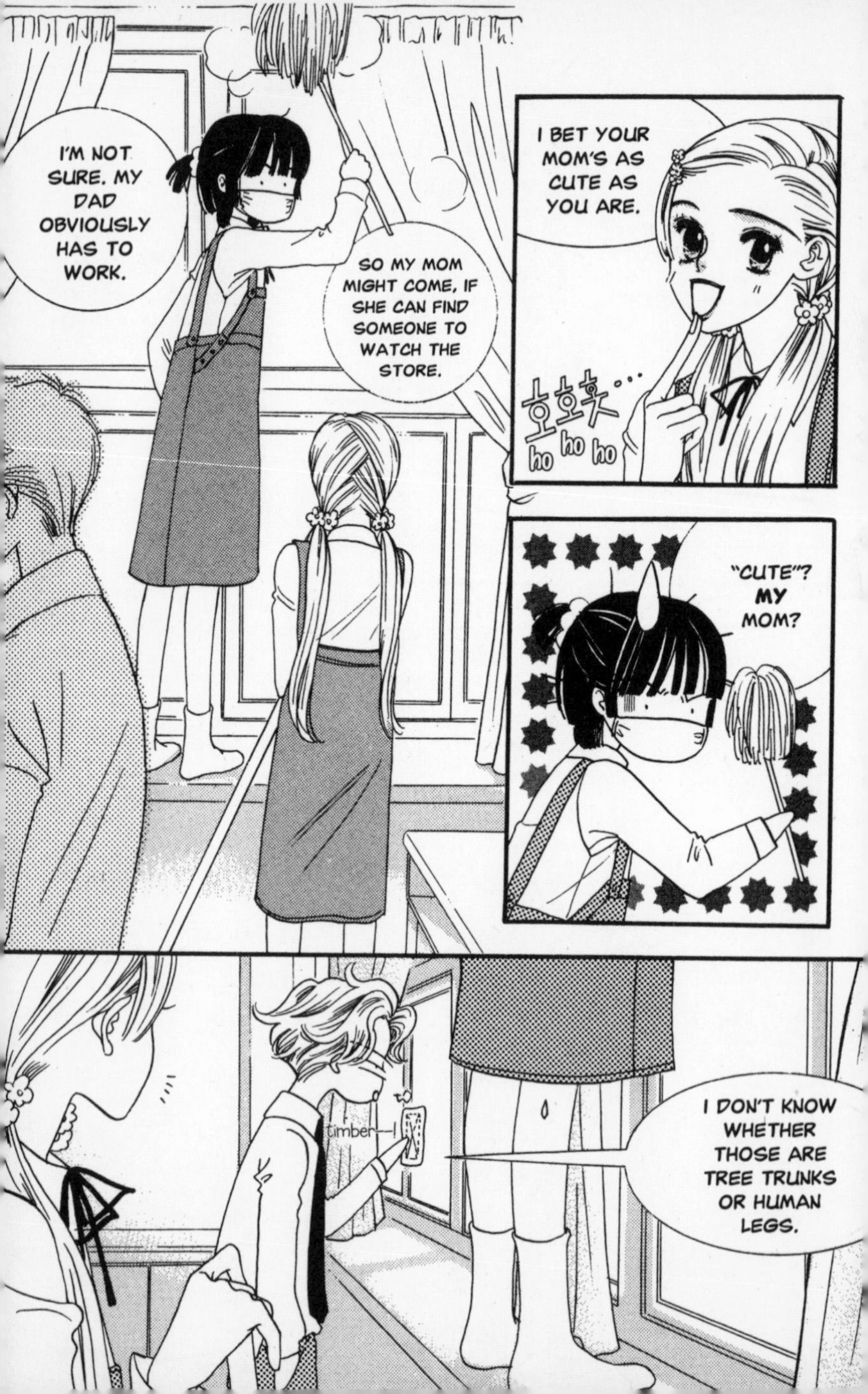

I'M NOT SURE. MY DAD OBVIOUSLY HAS TO WORK.
SO MY MOM MIGHT COME, IF SHE CAN FIND SOMEONE TO WATCH THE STORE.
I BET YOUR MOM'S AS CUTE AS YOU ARE.
호호홋...
ho ho ho
"CUTE"? MY MOM?
timber—!
I DON'T KNOW WHETHER THOSE ARE TREE TRUNKS OR HUMAN LEGS.

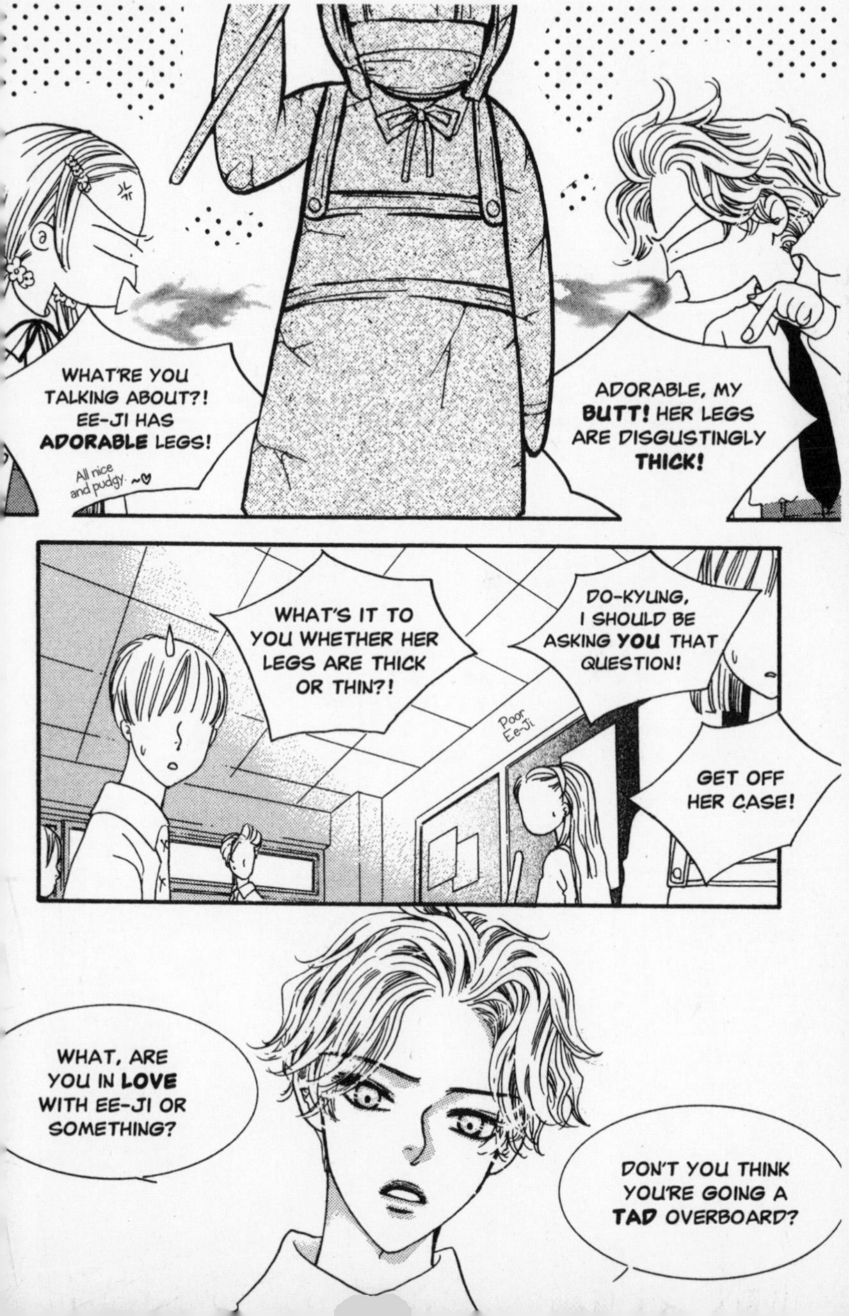
WHAT'RE YOU TALKING ABOUT?! EE-JI HAS ADORABLE LEGS!
All nice and pudgy. ~♡
ADORABLE, MY BUTT! HER LEGS ARE DISGUSTINGLY THICK!
WHAT'S IT TO YOU WHETHER HER LEGS ARE THICK OR THIN?!
DO-KYUNG, I SHOULD BE ASKING YOU THAT QUESTION!
Poor Ee-Ji
GET OFF HER CASE!
WHAT, ARE YOU IN LOVE WITH EE-JI OR SOMETHING?
DON'T YOU THINK YOU'RE GOING A TAD OVERBOARD?

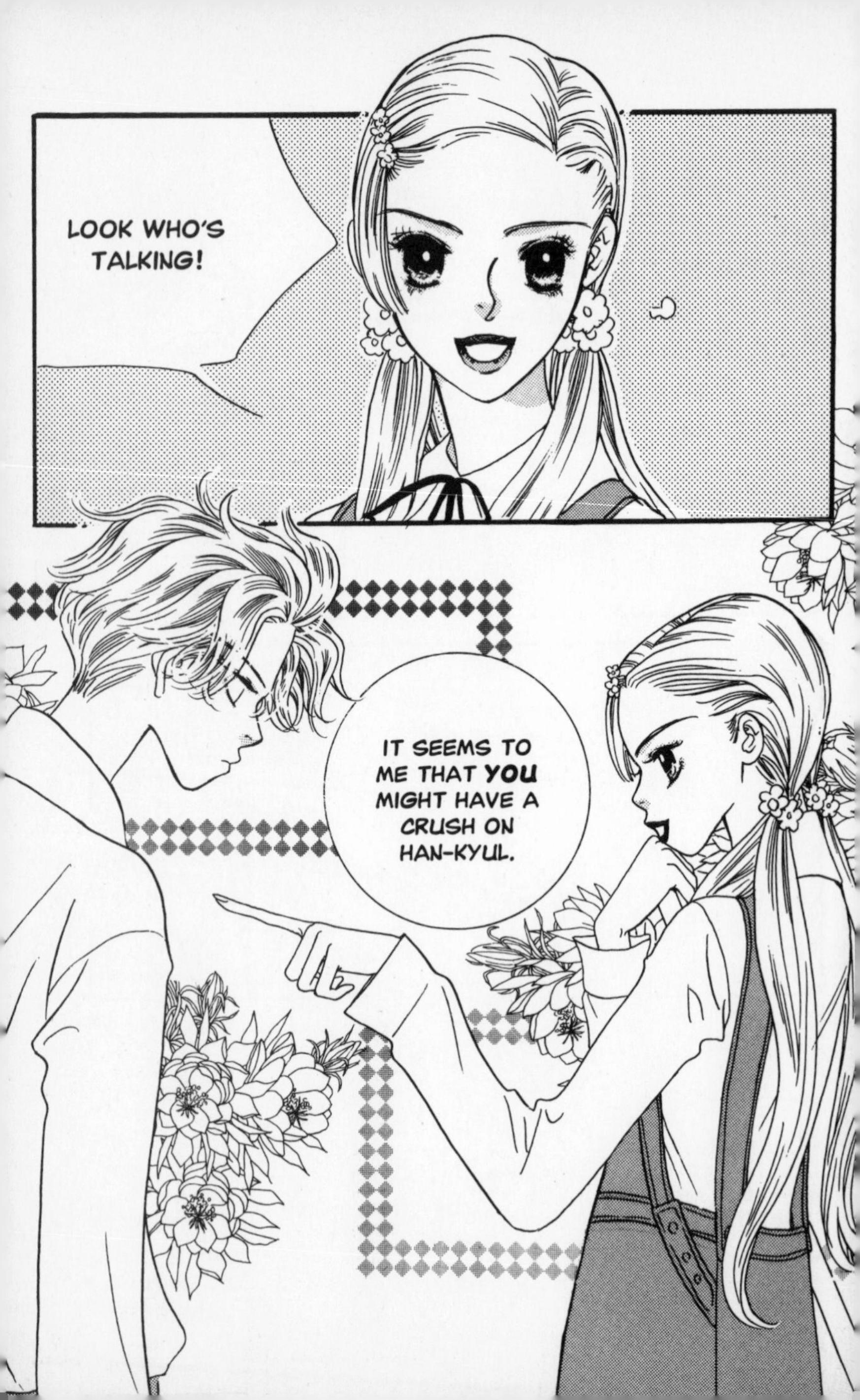
LOOK WHO'S TALKING!
IT SEEMS TO ME THAT **YOU** MIGHT HAVE A CRUSH ON HAN-KYUL.

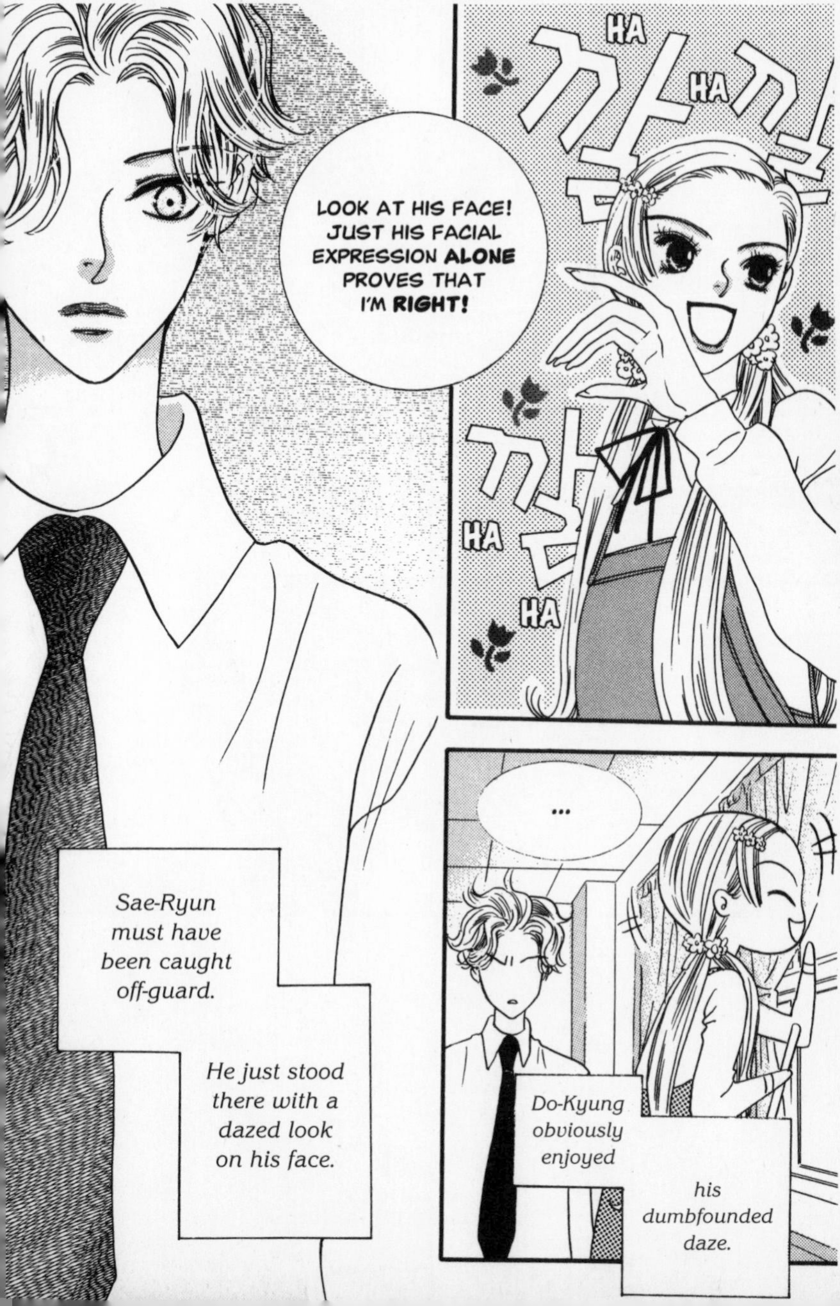
LOOK AT HIS FACE! JUST HIS FACIAL EXPRESSION ALONE PROVES THAT I'M RIGHT!
HA HA HA HA
Sae-Ryun must have been caught off-guard.
He just stood there with a dazed look on his face.
...
Do-Kyung obviously enjoyed
his dumbfounded daze.

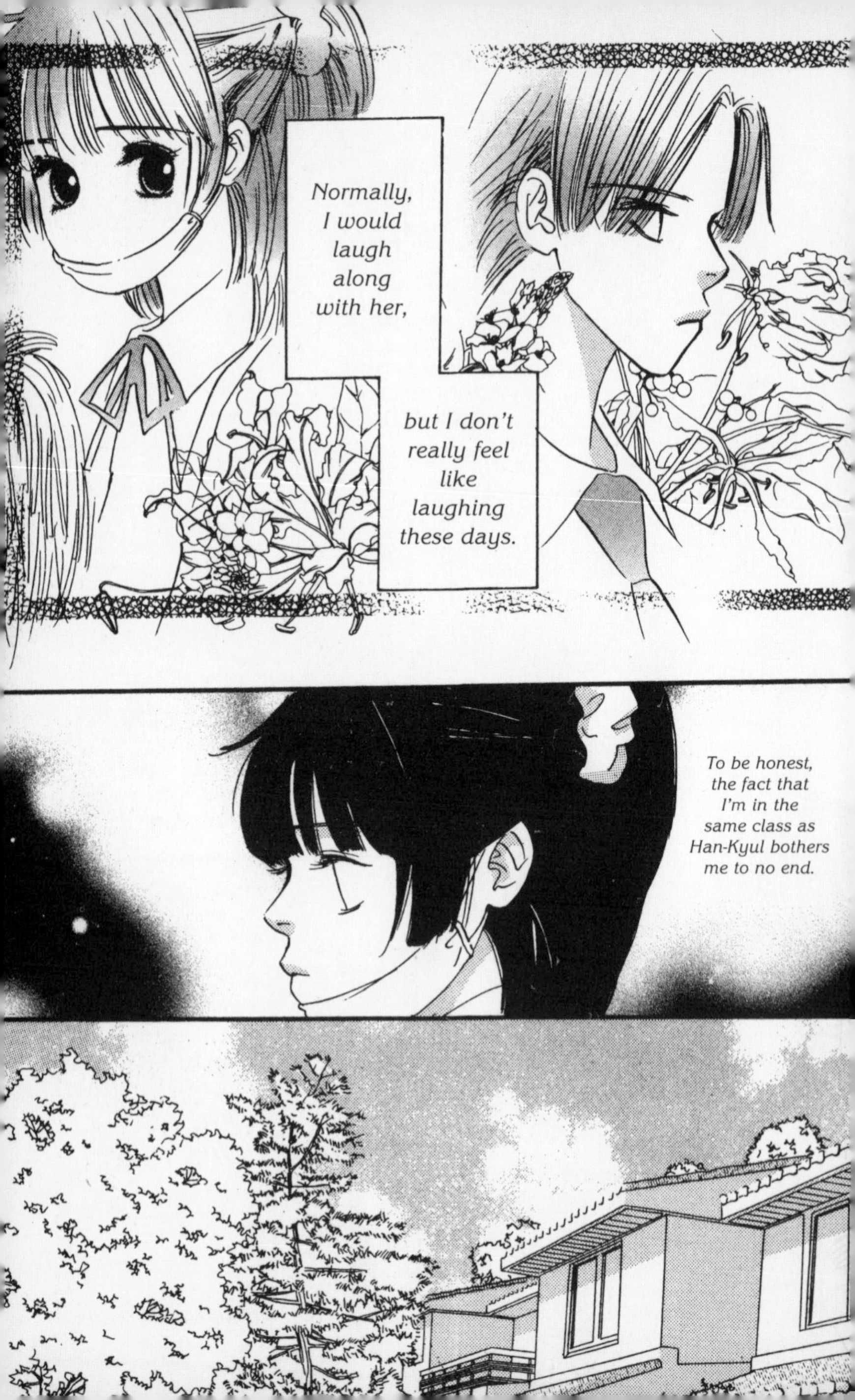
Normally, I would laugh along with her,
but I don't really feel like laughing these days.
To be honest, the fact that I'm in the same class as Han-Kyul bothers me to no end.

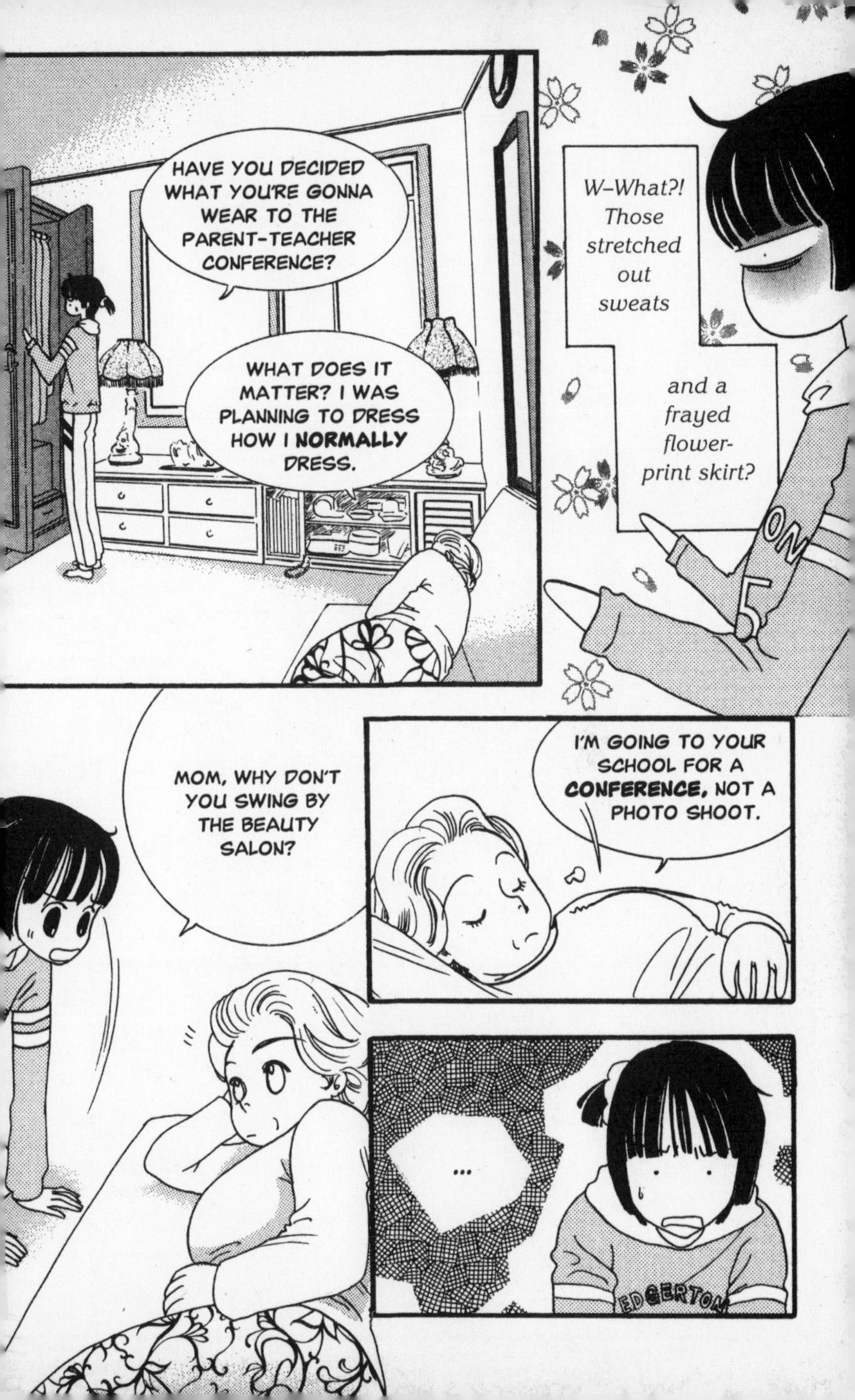
HAVE YOU DECIDED WHAT YOU'RE GONNA WEAR TO THE PARENT-TEACHER CONFERENCE?
WHAT DOES IT MATTER? I WAS PLANNING TO DRESS HOW I NORMALLY DRESS.
W-What?! Those stretched out sweats
and a frayed flower-print skirt?
ON
5
MOM, WHY DON'T YOU SWING BY THE BEAUTY SALON?
I'M GOING TO YOUR SCHOOL FOR A CONFERENCE, NOT A PHOTO SHOOT.
...
EDGERTON

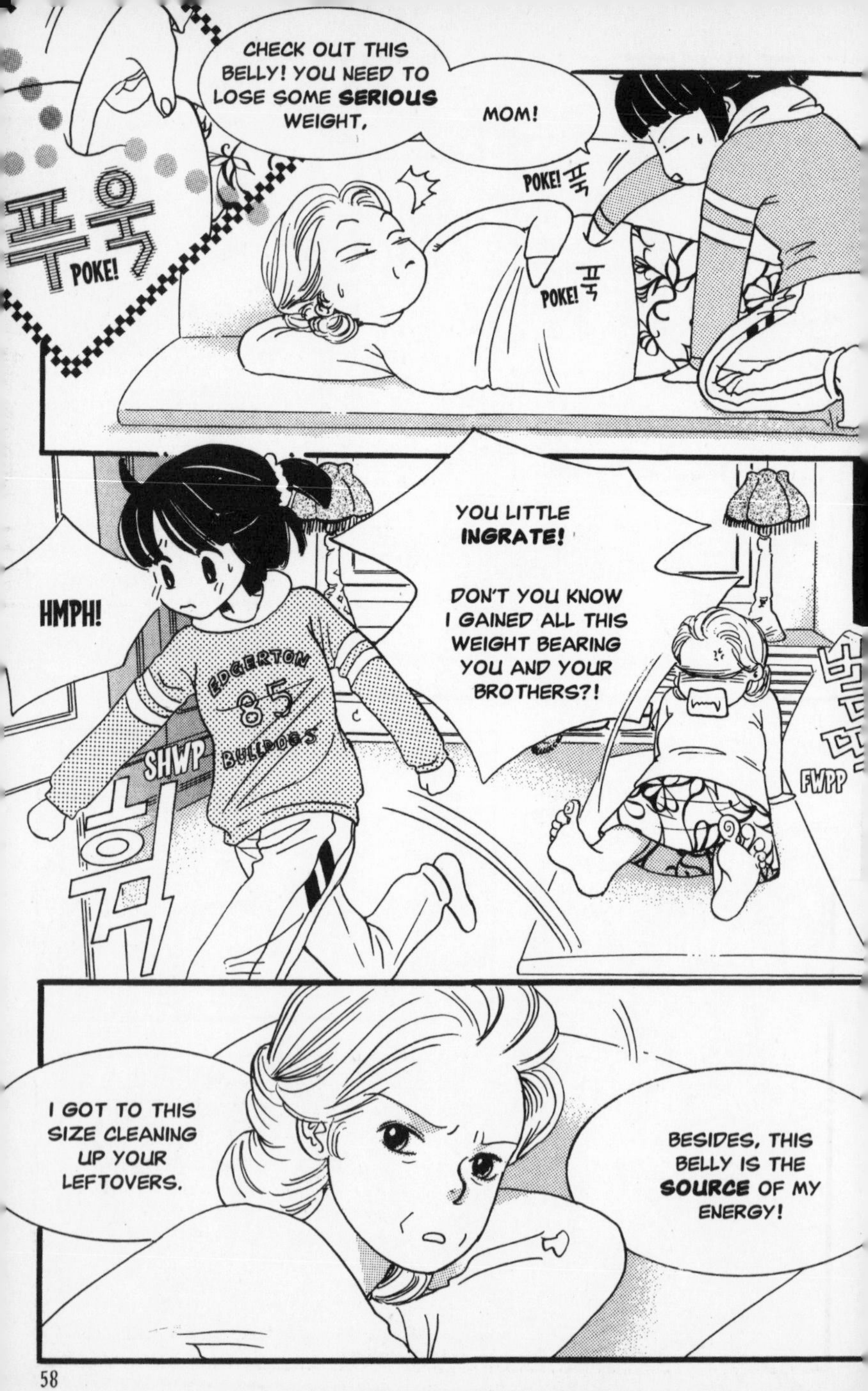
CHECK OUT THIS BELLY! YOU NEED TO LOSE SOME **SERIOUS** WEIGHT,
MOM!
푸욱
POKE!
POKE! 푹
POKE! 푹
HMPH!
SHWP
YOU LITTLE **INGRATE!**
DON'T YOU KNOW I GAINED ALL THIS WEIGHT BEARING YOU AND YOUR BROTHERS?!
FWPP
I GOT TO THIS SIZE CLEANING UP YOUR LEFTOVERS.
BESIDES, THIS BELLY IS THE **SOURCE** OF MY ENERGY!

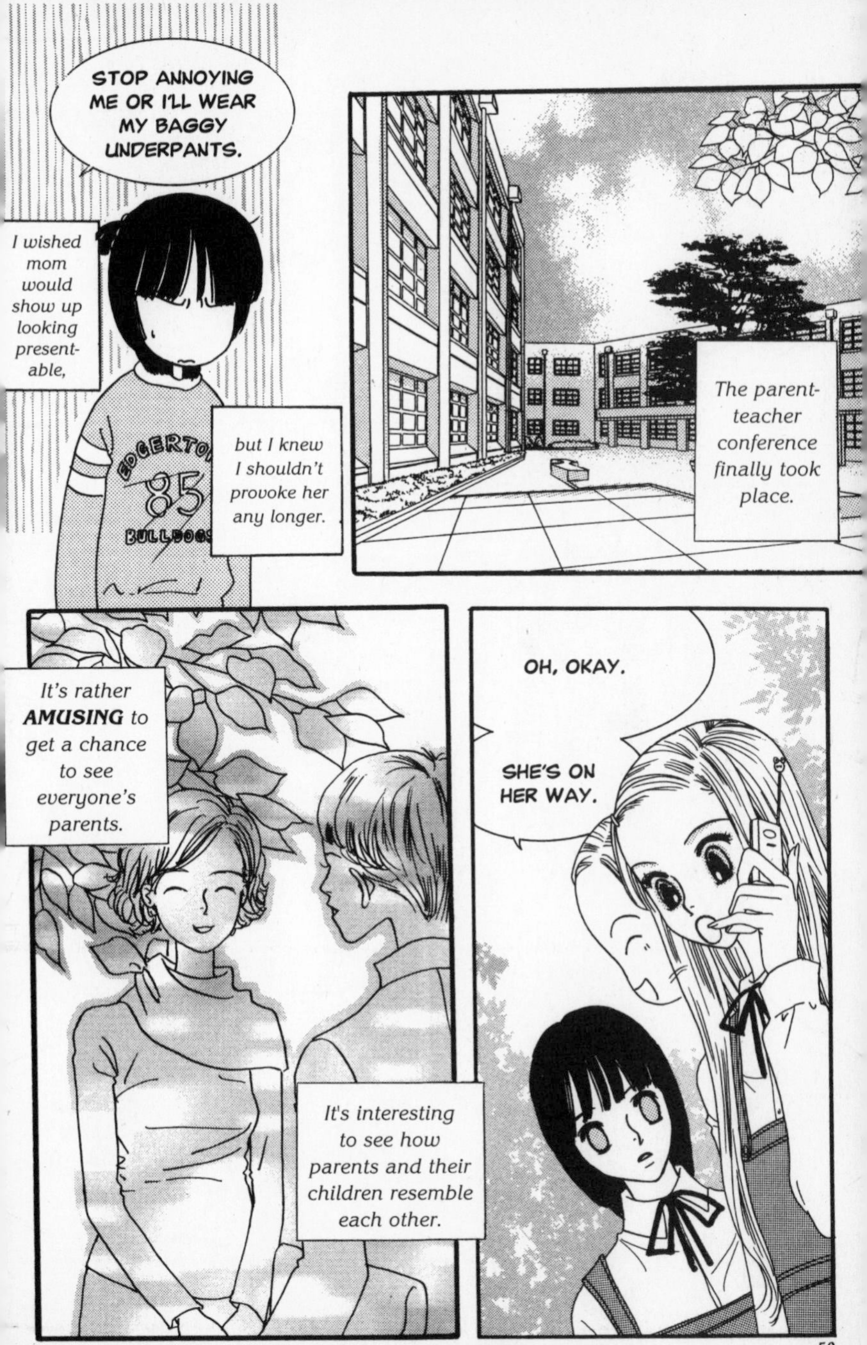
STOP ANNOYING ME OR I'LL WEAR MY BAGGY UNDERPANTS.
I wished mom would show up looking present-able,
but I knew I shouldn't provoke her any longer.
EDGERTON 85 BULLDOGS
The parent-teacher conference finally took place.
It's rather **AMUSING** to get a chance to see everyone's parents.
It's interesting to see how parents and their children resemble each other.
OH, OKAY.
SHE'S ON HER WAY.

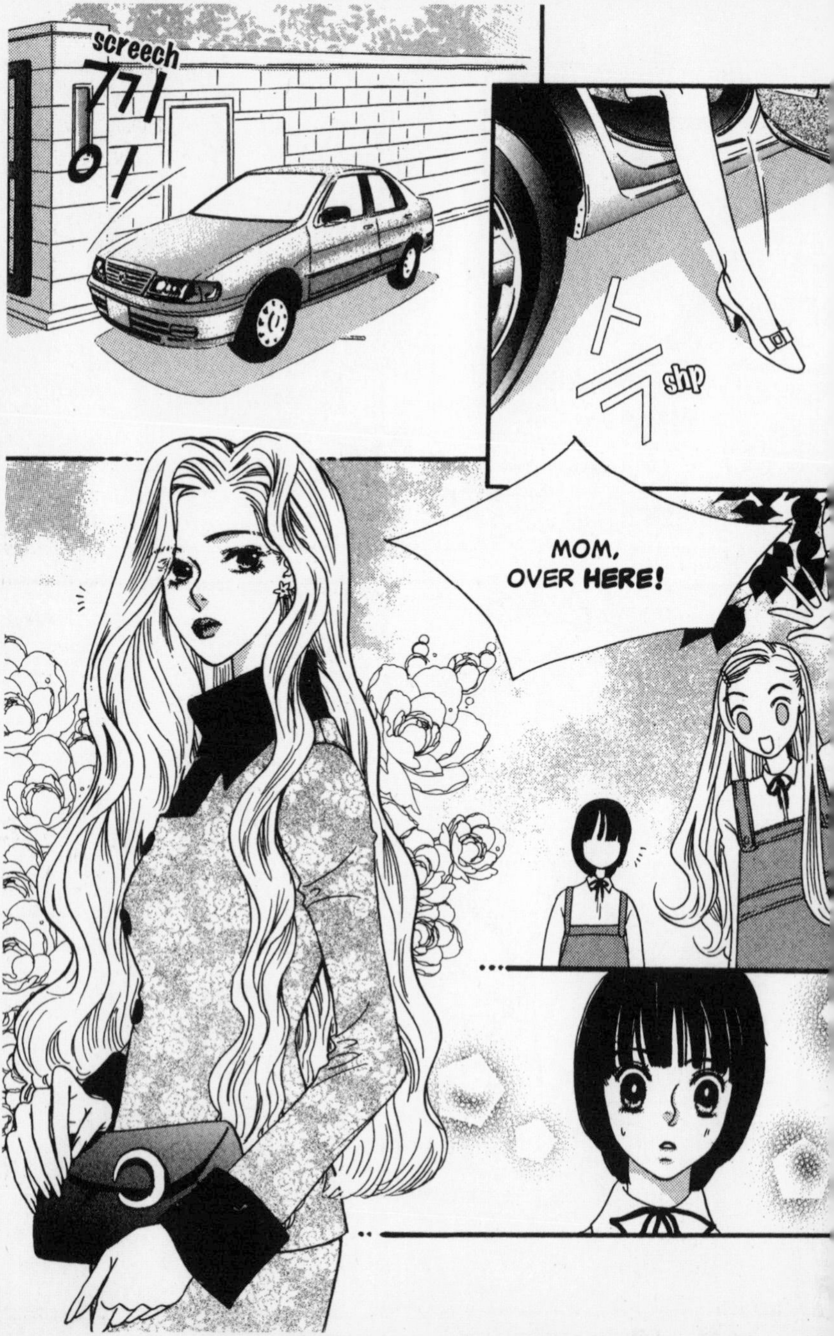
screech
shp
MOM, OVER HERE!

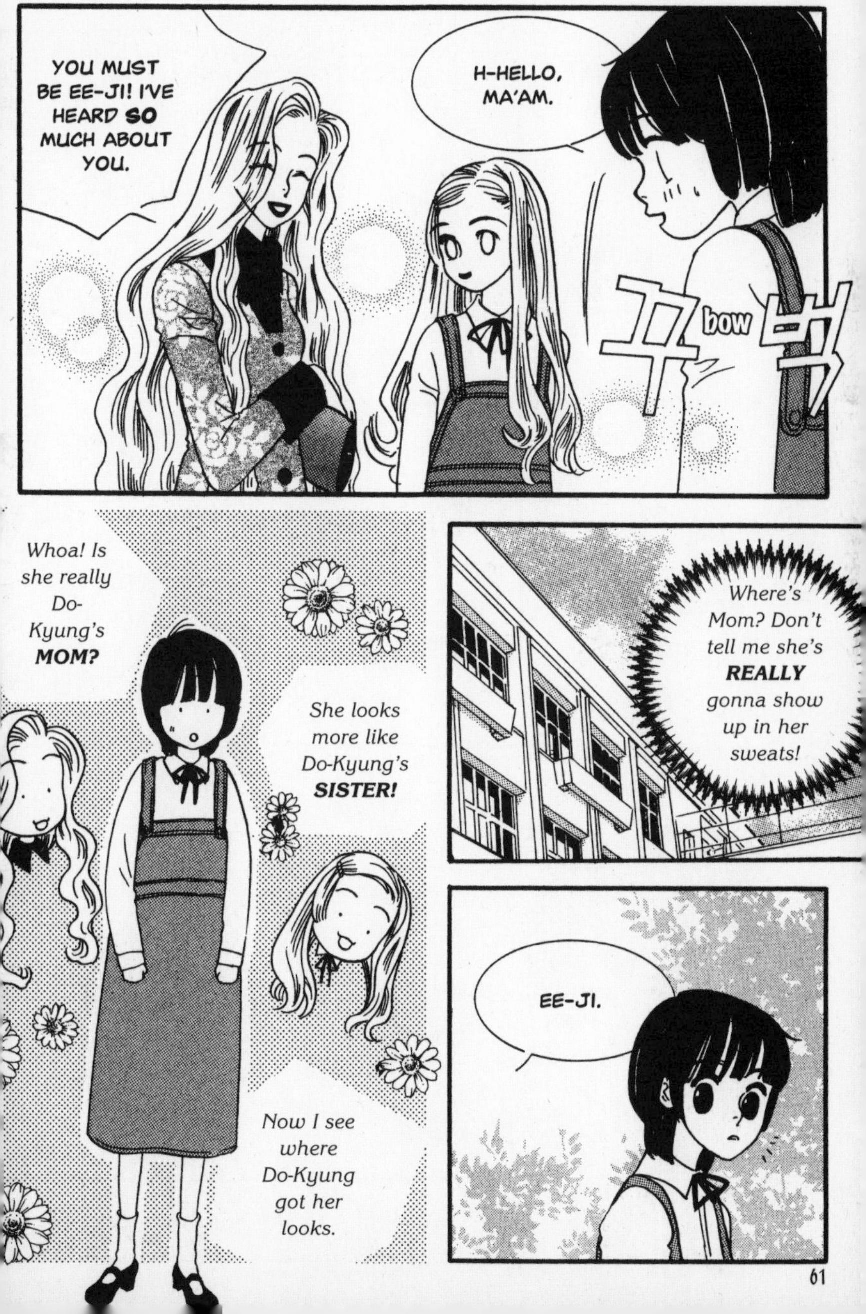
YOU MUST BE EE-JI! I'VE HEARD SO MUCH ABOUT YOU.
H-HELLO, MA'AM.
bow
Whoa! Is she really Do-Kyung's MOM?
She looks more like Do-Kyung's SISTER!
Now I see where Do-Kyung got her looks.
Where's Mom? Don't tell me she's REALLY gonna show up in her sweats!
EE-JI.

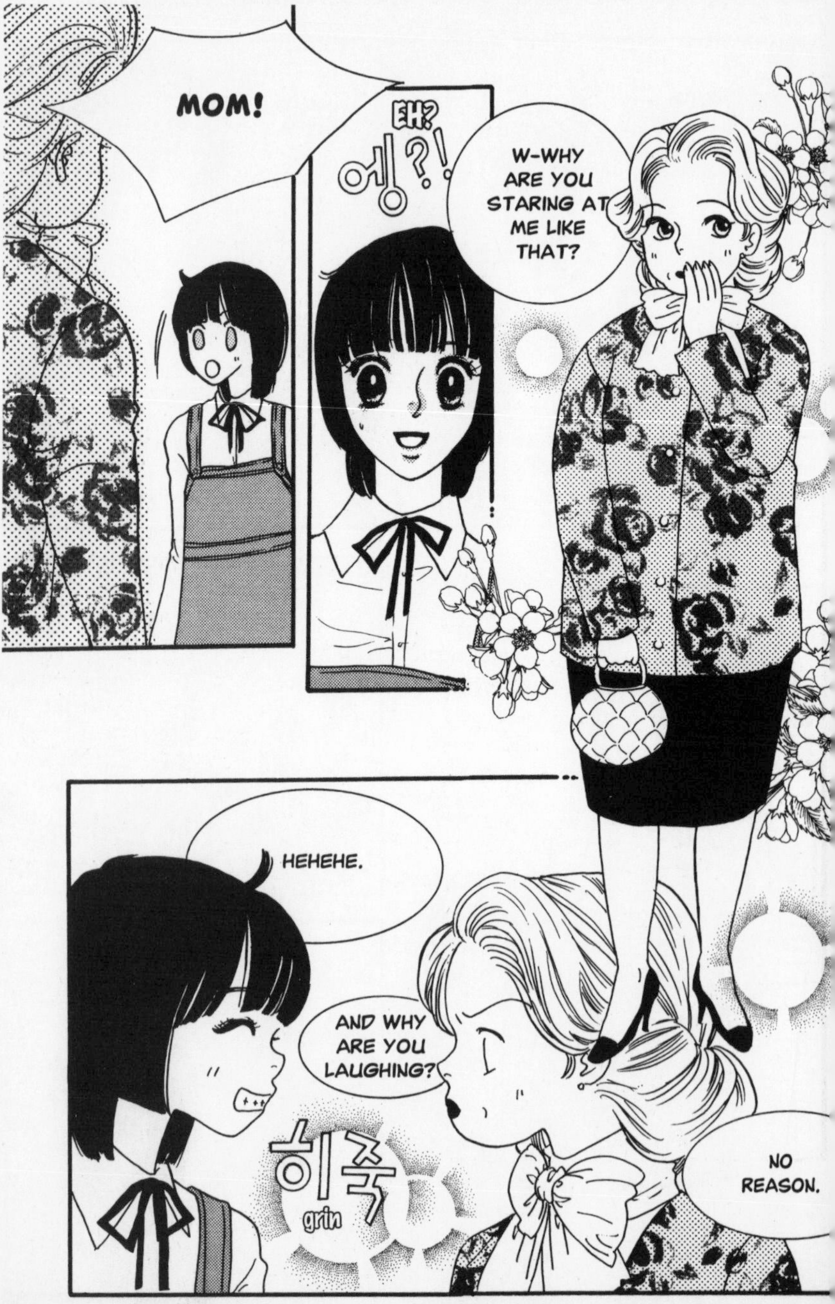
MOM!
EH?
엥?!
W-WHY ARE YOU STARING AT ME LIKE THAT?
HEHEHE.
AND WHY ARE YOU LAUGHING?
히죽
grin
NO REASON.

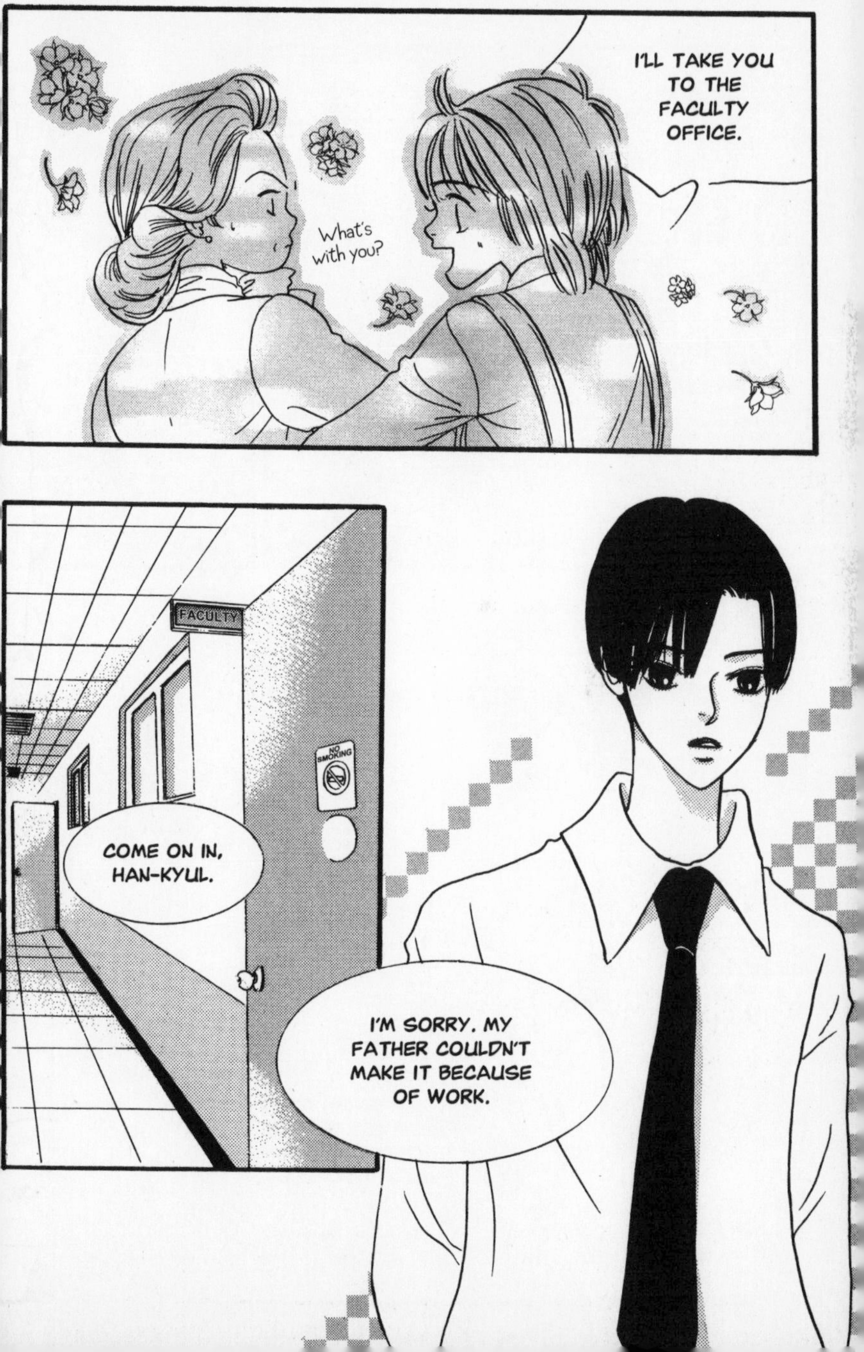
I'LL TAKE YOU TO THE FACULTY OFFICE.
What's with you?
FACULTY
NO SMOKING
COME ON IN, HAN-KYUL.
I'M SORRY. MY FATHER COULDN'T MAKE IT BECAUSE OF WORK.

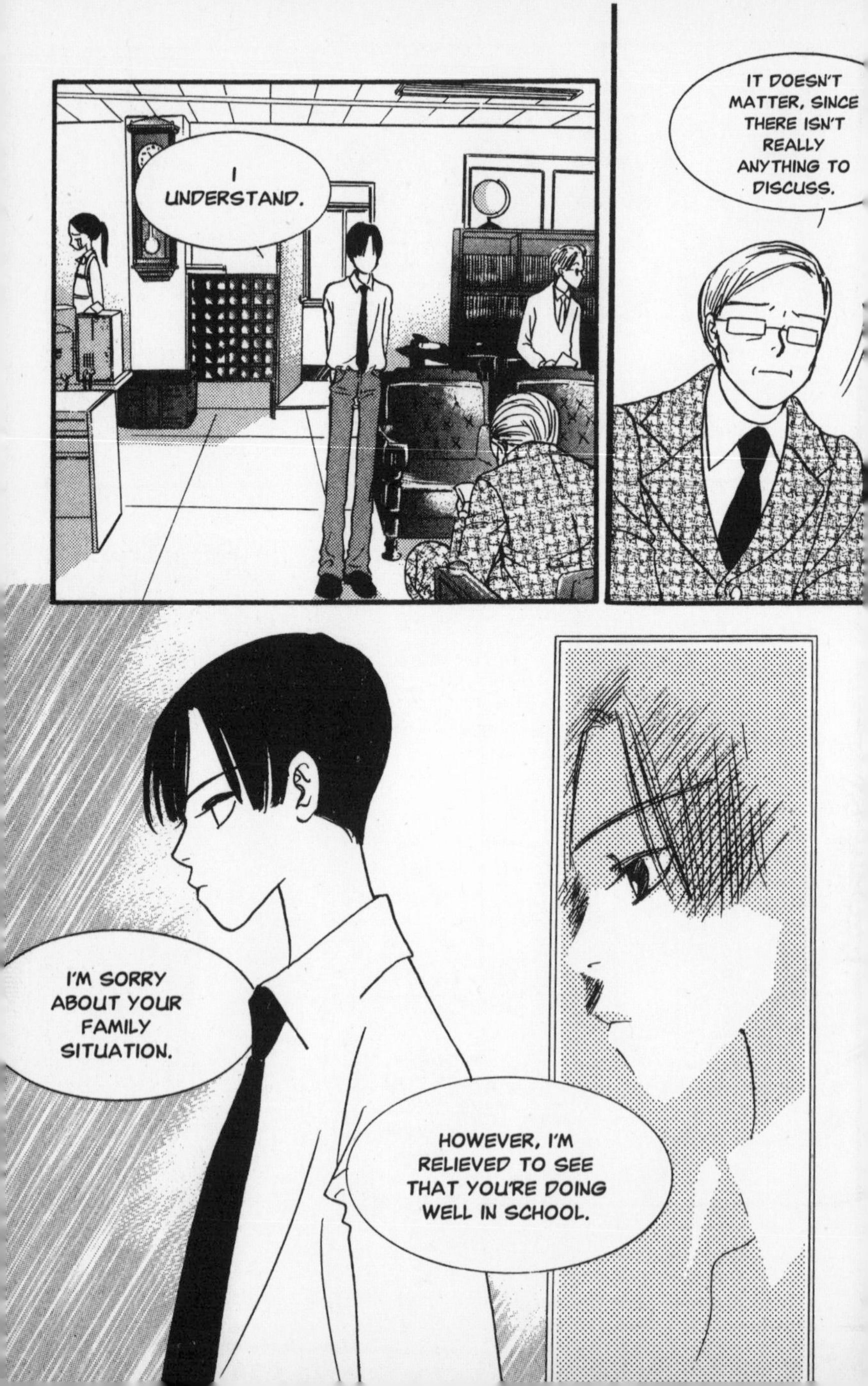
I UNDERSTAND.
IT DOESN'T MATTER, SINCE THERE ISN'T REALLY ANYTHING TO DISCUSS.
I'M SORRY ABOUT YOUR FAMILY SITUATION.
HOWEVER, I'M RELIEVED TO SEE THAT YOU'RE DOING WELL IN SCHOOL.

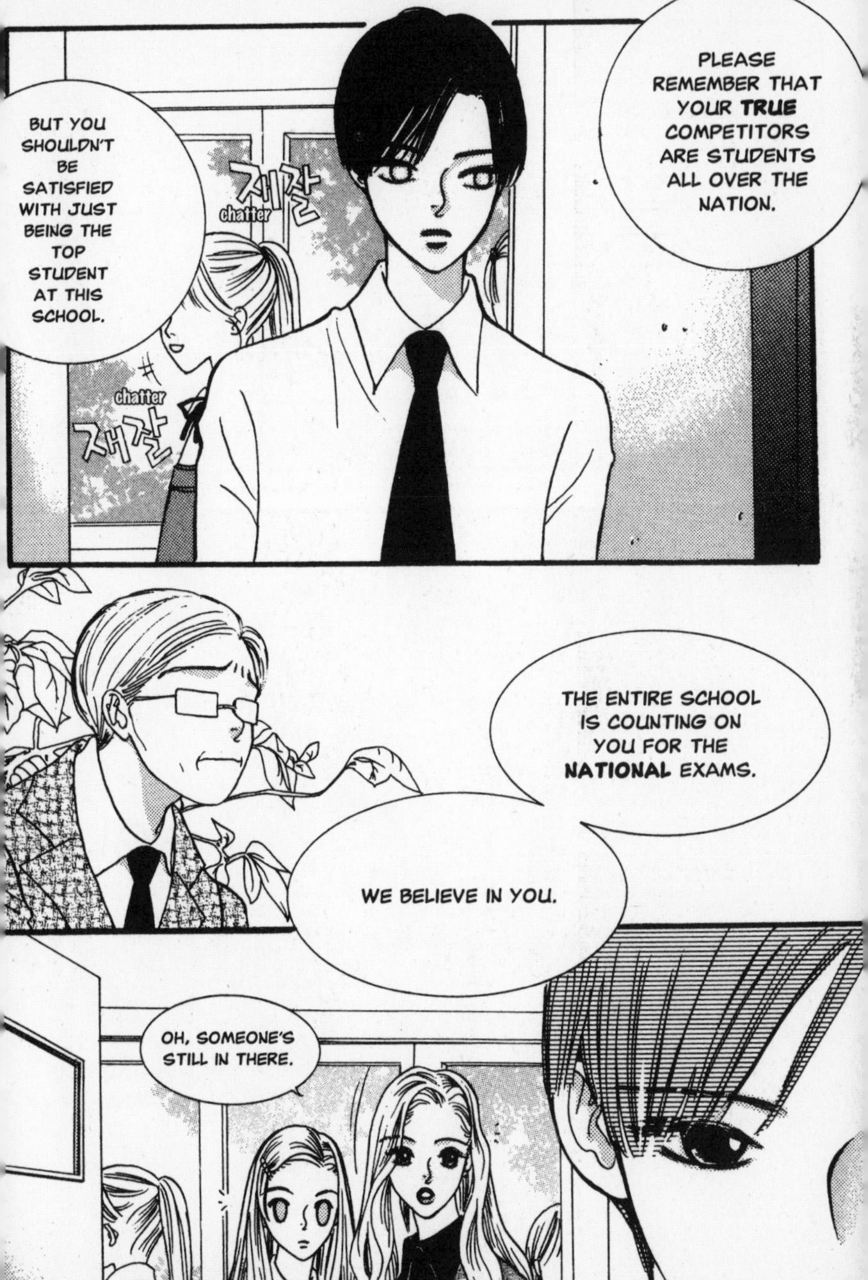
BUT YOU SHOULDN'T BE SATISFIED WITH JUST BEING THE TOP STUDENT AT THIS SCHOOL.
재잘
chatter
재잘
chatter
PLEASE REMEMBER THAT YOUR TRUE COMPETITORS ARE STUDENTS ALL OVER THE NATION.
THE ENTIRE SCHOOL IS COUNTING ON YOU FOR THE NATIONAL EXAMS.
WE BELIEVE IN YOU.
OH, SOMEONE'S STILL IN THERE.

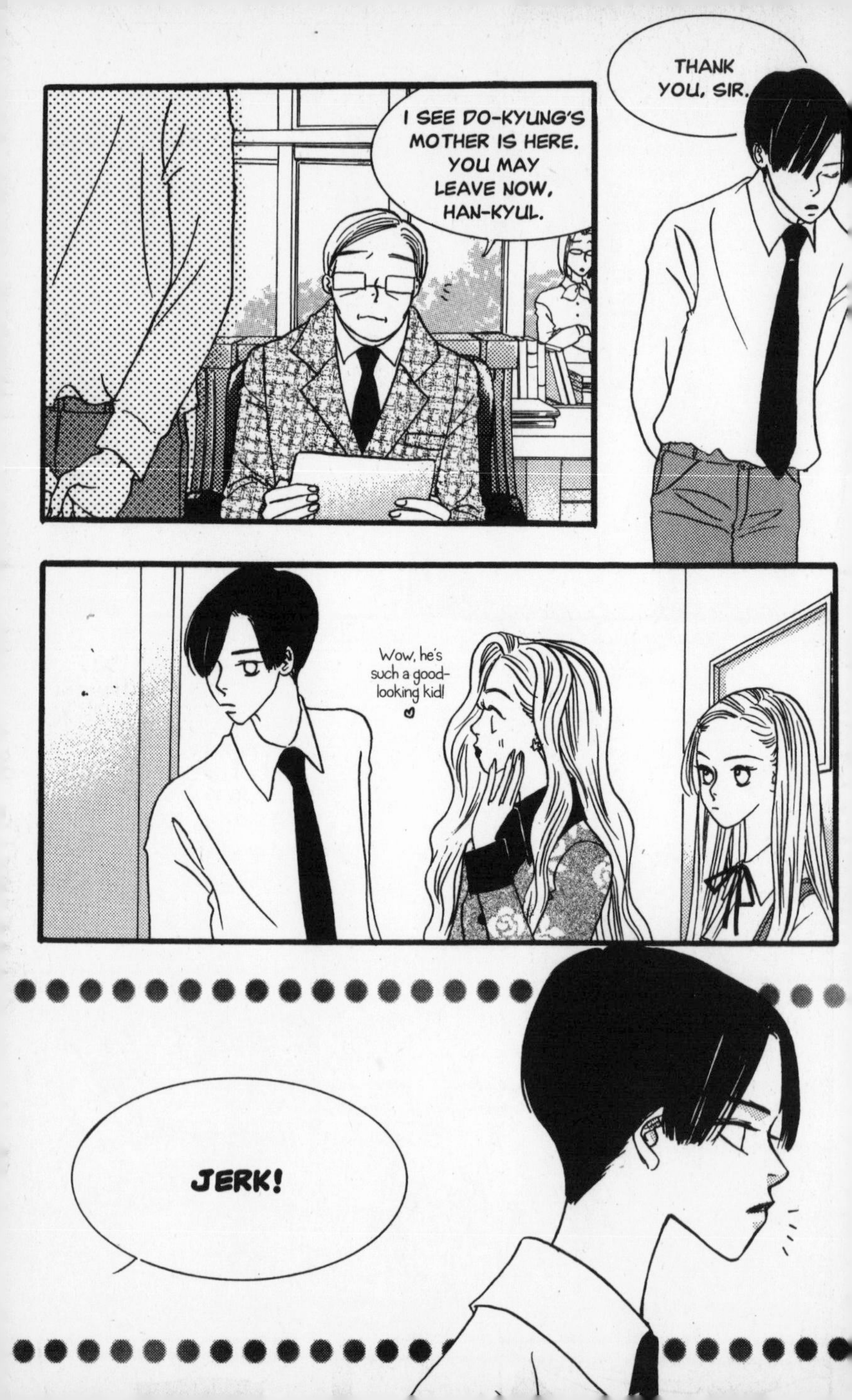
I SEE DO-KYUNG'S MOTHER IS HERE. YOU MAY LEAVE NOW, HAN-KYUL.
THANK YOU, SIR.
Wow, he's such a good-looking kid!
JERK!

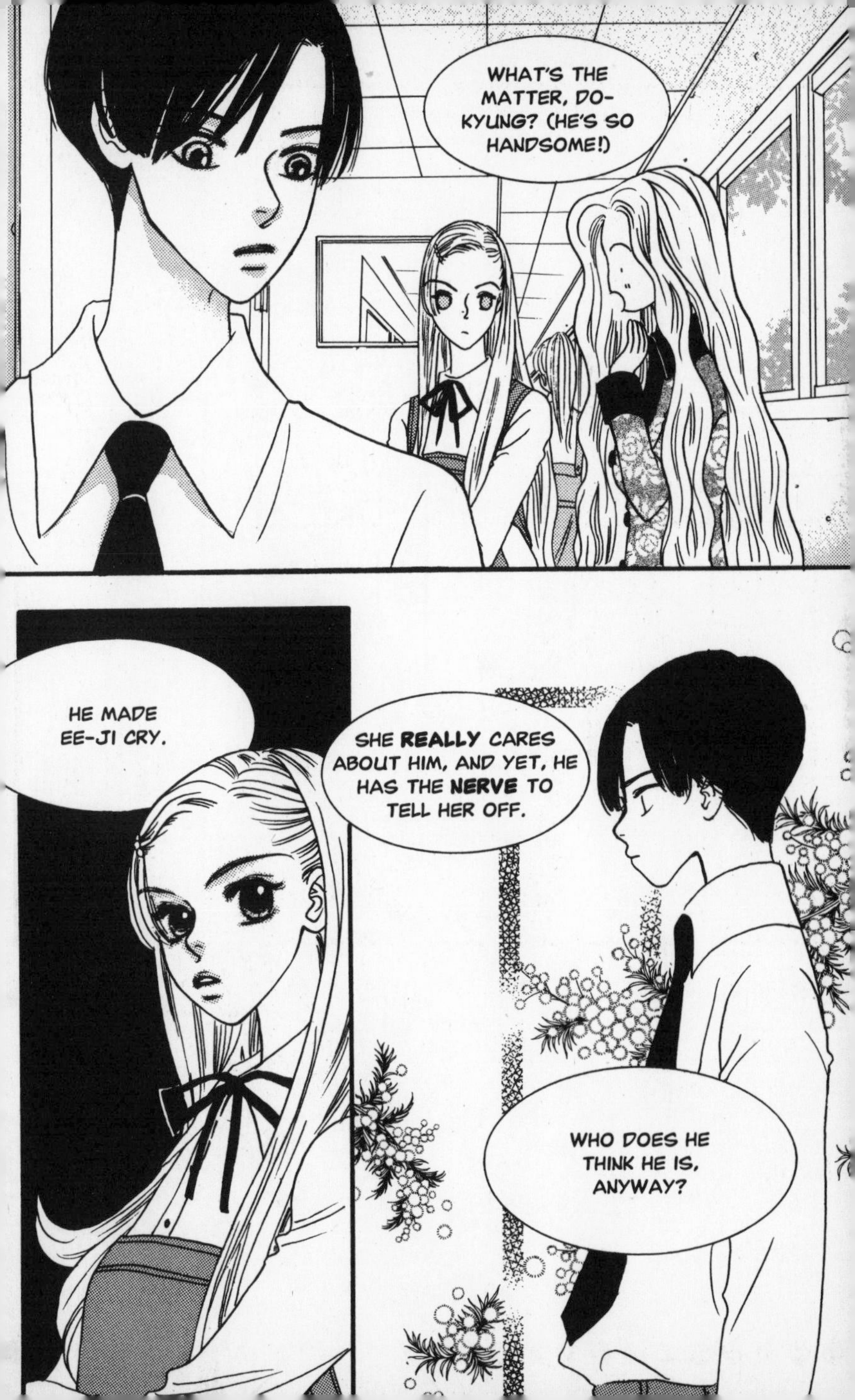
WHAT'S THE MATTER, DO-KYUNG? (HE'S SO HANDSOME!)
HE MADE EE-JI CRY.
SHE **REALLY** CARES ABOUT HIM, AND YET, HE HAS THE **NERVE** TO TELL HER OFF.
WHO DOES HE THINK HE IS, ANYWAY?

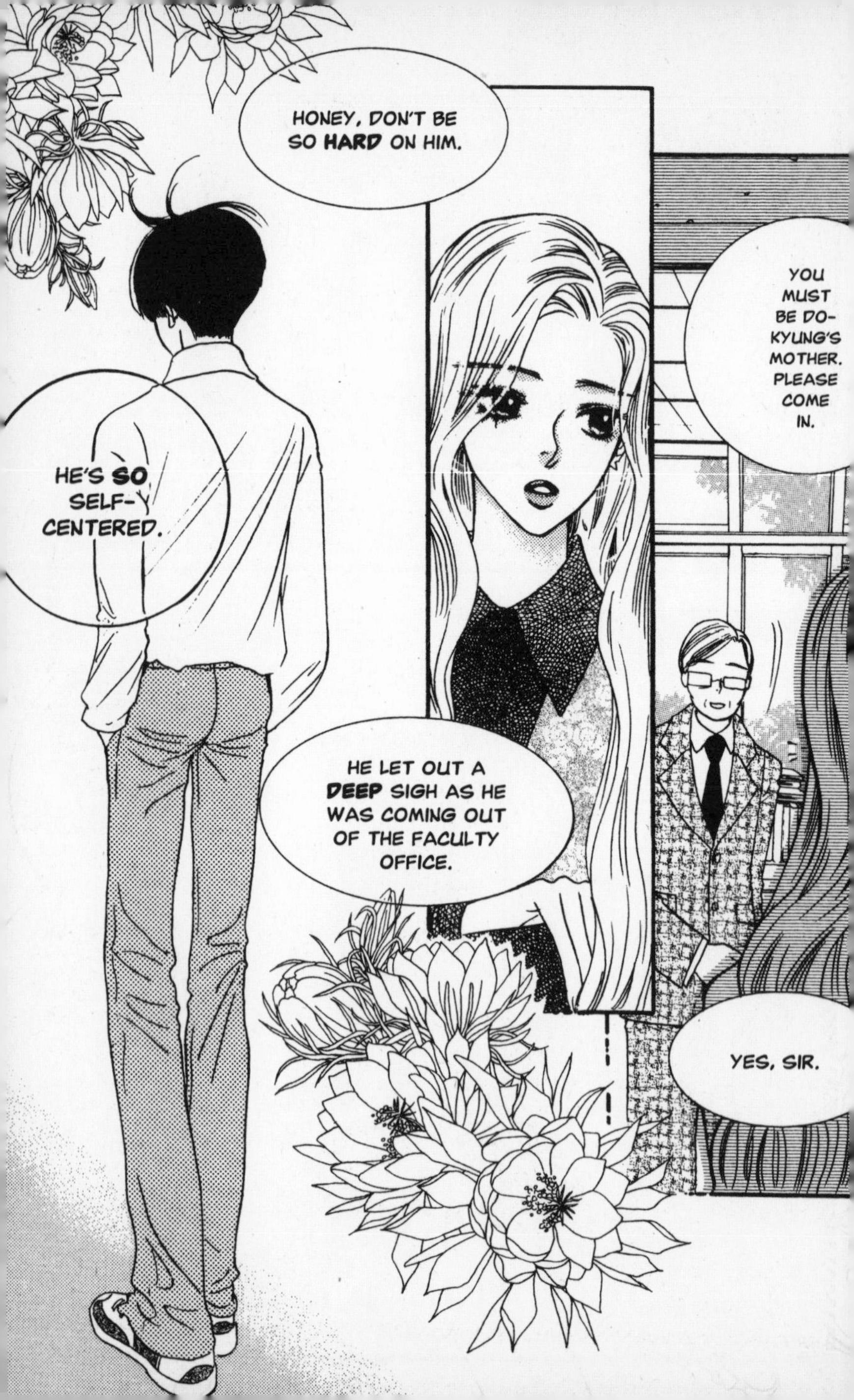
HONEY, DON'T BE SO HARD ON HIM.
HE'S SO SELF-CENTERED.
HE LET OUT A DEEP SIGH AS HE WAS COMING OUT OF THE FACULTY OFFICE.
YOU MUST BE DO-KYUNG'S MOTHER. PLEASE COME IN.
YES, SIR.

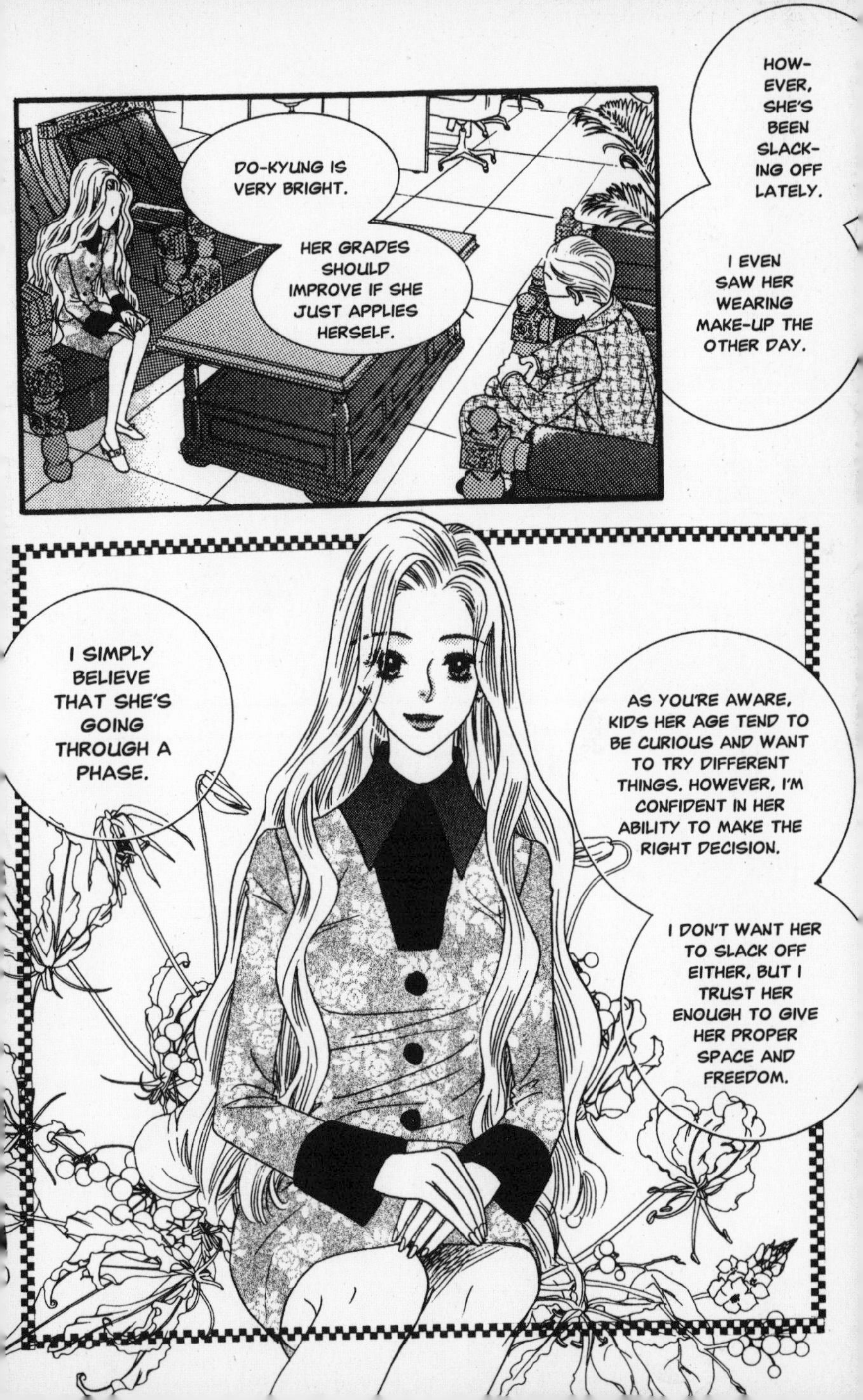
HOW-EVER, SHE'S BEEN SLACK-ING OFF LATELY.
I EVEN SAW HER WEARING MAKE-UP THE OTHER DAY.
DO-KYUNG IS VERY BRIGHT.
HER GRADES SHOULD IMPROVE IF SHE JUST APPLIES HERSELF.
AS YOU'RE AWARE, KIDS HER AGE TEND TO BE CURIOUS AND WANT TO TRY DIFFERENT THINGS. HOWEVER, I'M CONFIDENT IN HER ABILITY TO MAKE THE RIGHT DECISION.
I DON'T WANT HER TO SLACK OFF EITHER, BUT I TRUST HER ENOUGH TO GIVE HER PROPER SPACE AND FREEDOM.
I SIMPLY BELIEVE THAT SHE'S GOING THROUGH A PHASE.

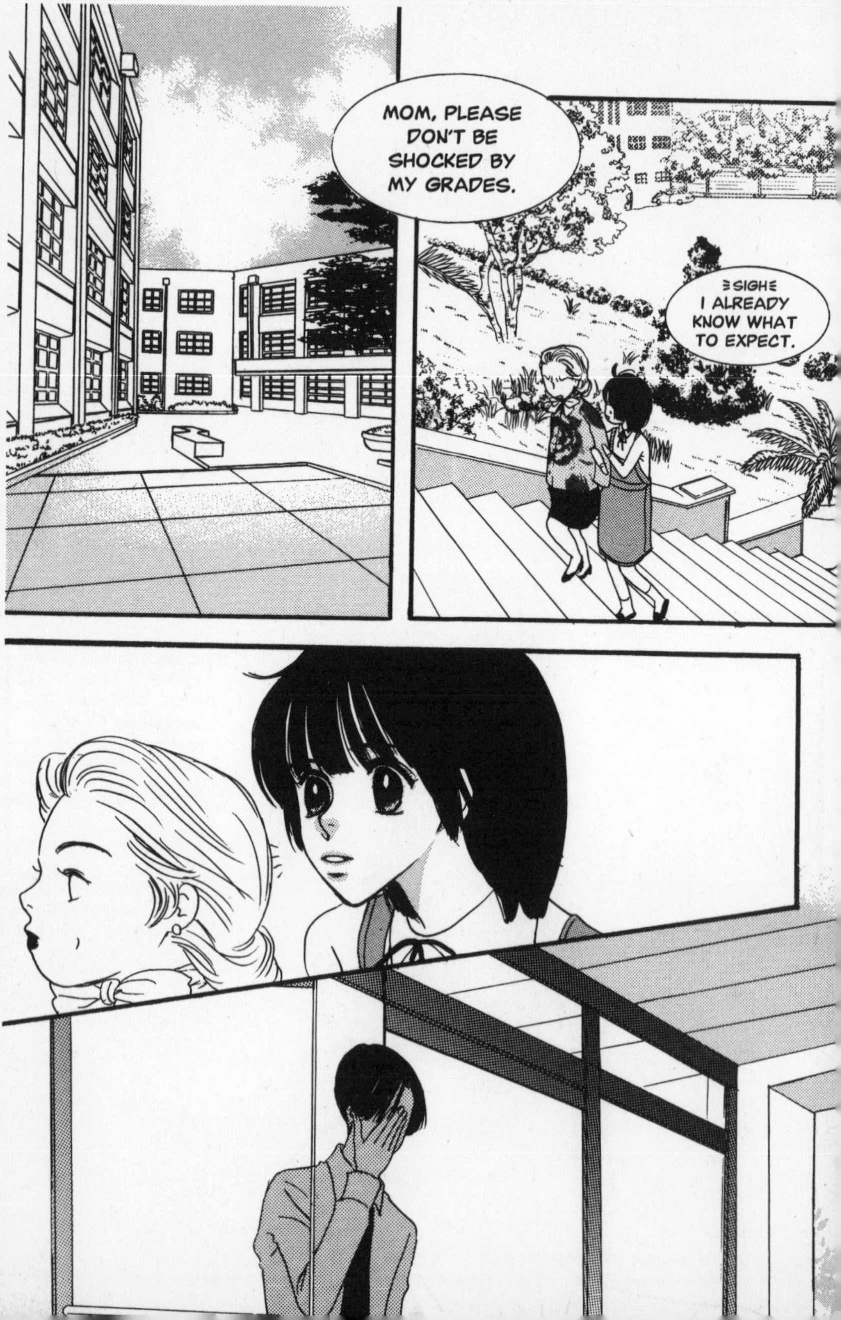
MOM, PLEASE DON'T BE SHOCKED BY MY GRADES.
≡SIGH≡
I ALREADY KNOW WHAT TO EXPECT.

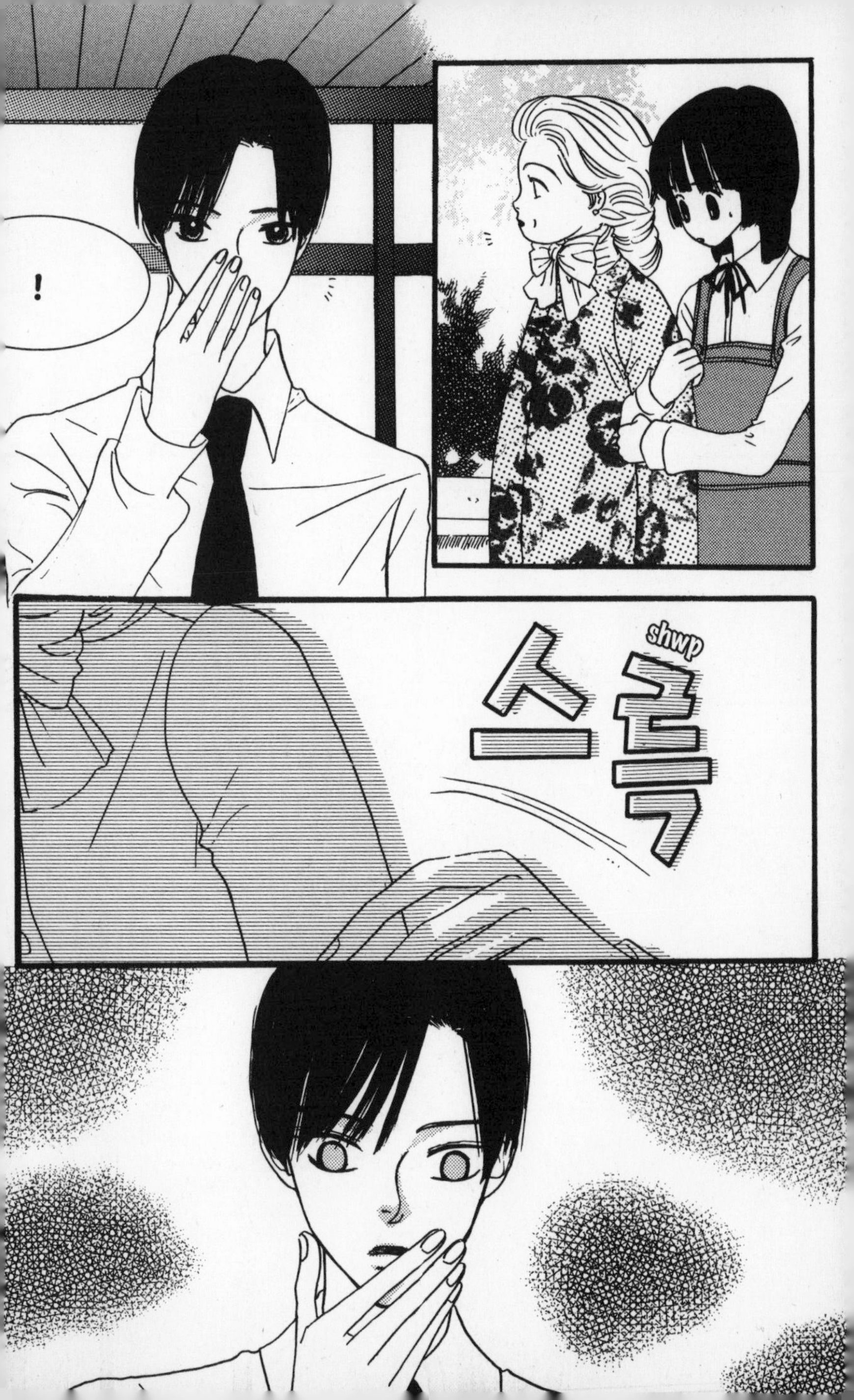
!
スー
shwp

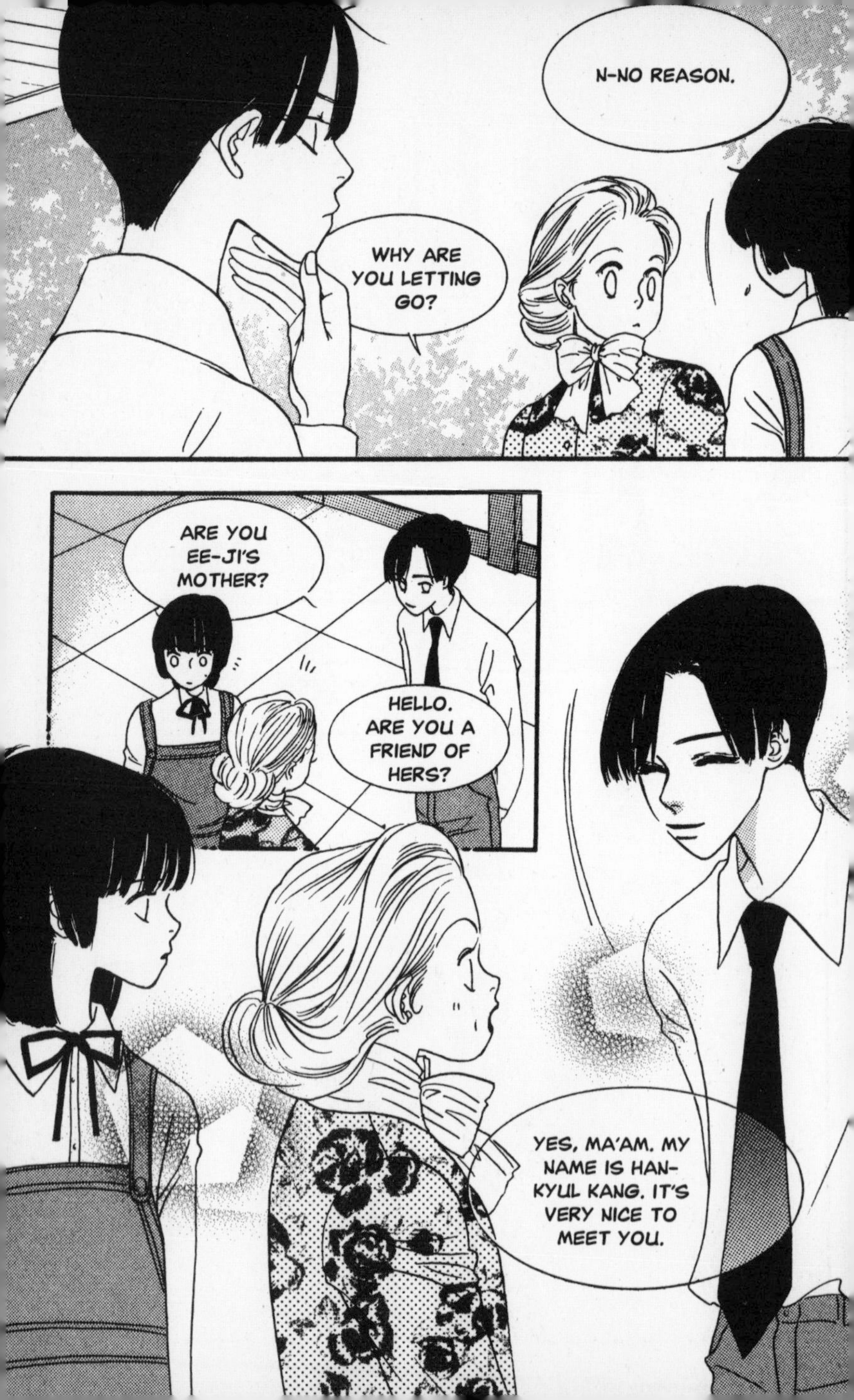
N-NO REASON.
WHY ARE YOU LETTING GO?
ARE YOU EE-JI'S MOTHER?
HELLO. ARE YOU A FRIEND OF HERS?
YES, MA'AM. MY NAME IS HAN-KYUL KANG. IT'S VERY NICE TO MEET YOU.

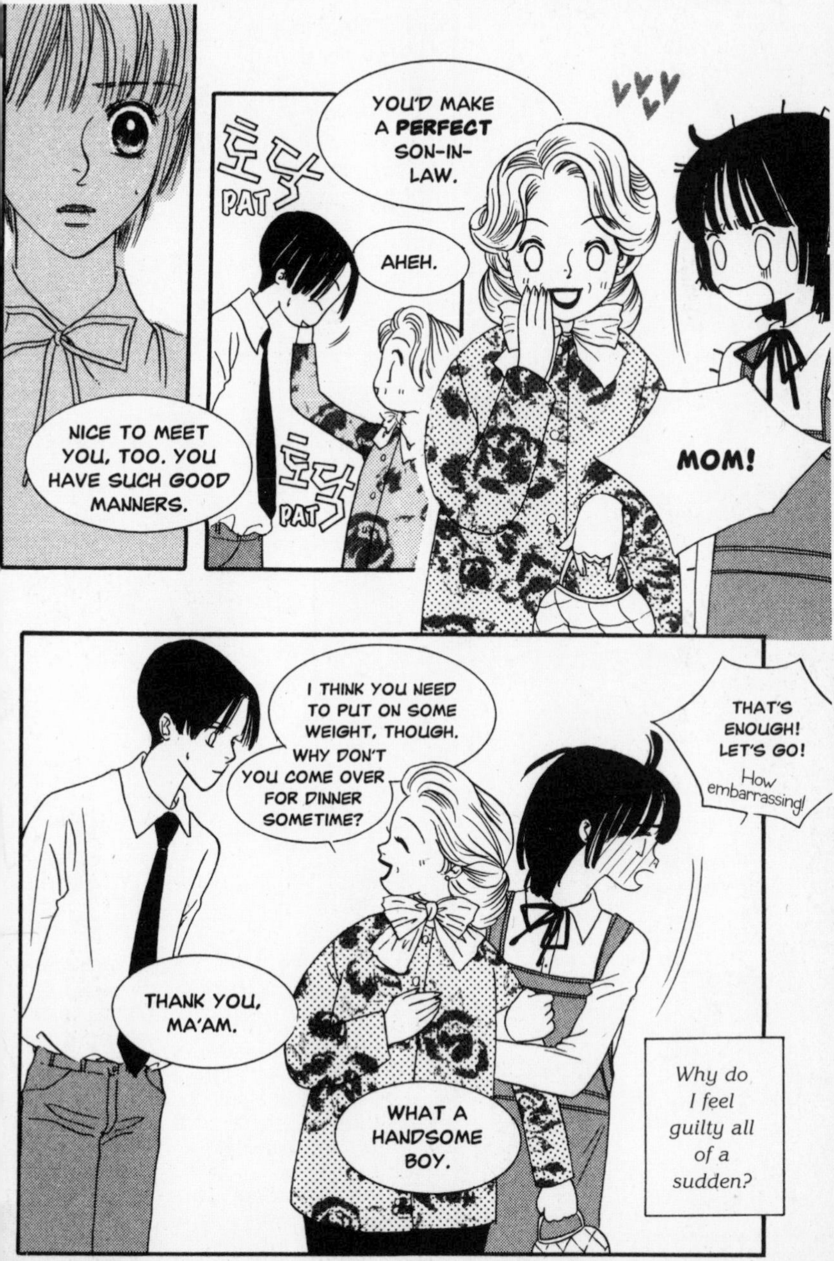
NICE TO MEET YOU, TOO. YOU HAVE SUCH GOOD MANNERS.
토닥 PAT
YOU'D MAKE A **PERFECT** SON-IN-LAW.
AHEH.
토닥 PAT
MOM!
I THINK YOU NEED TO PUT ON SOME WEIGHT, THOUGH.
WHY DON'T YOU COME OVER FOR DINNER SOMETIME?
THAT'S ENOUGH! LET'S GO!
How embarrassing!
THANK YOU, MA'AM.
WHAT A HANDSOME BOY.
Why do I feel guilty all of a sudden?

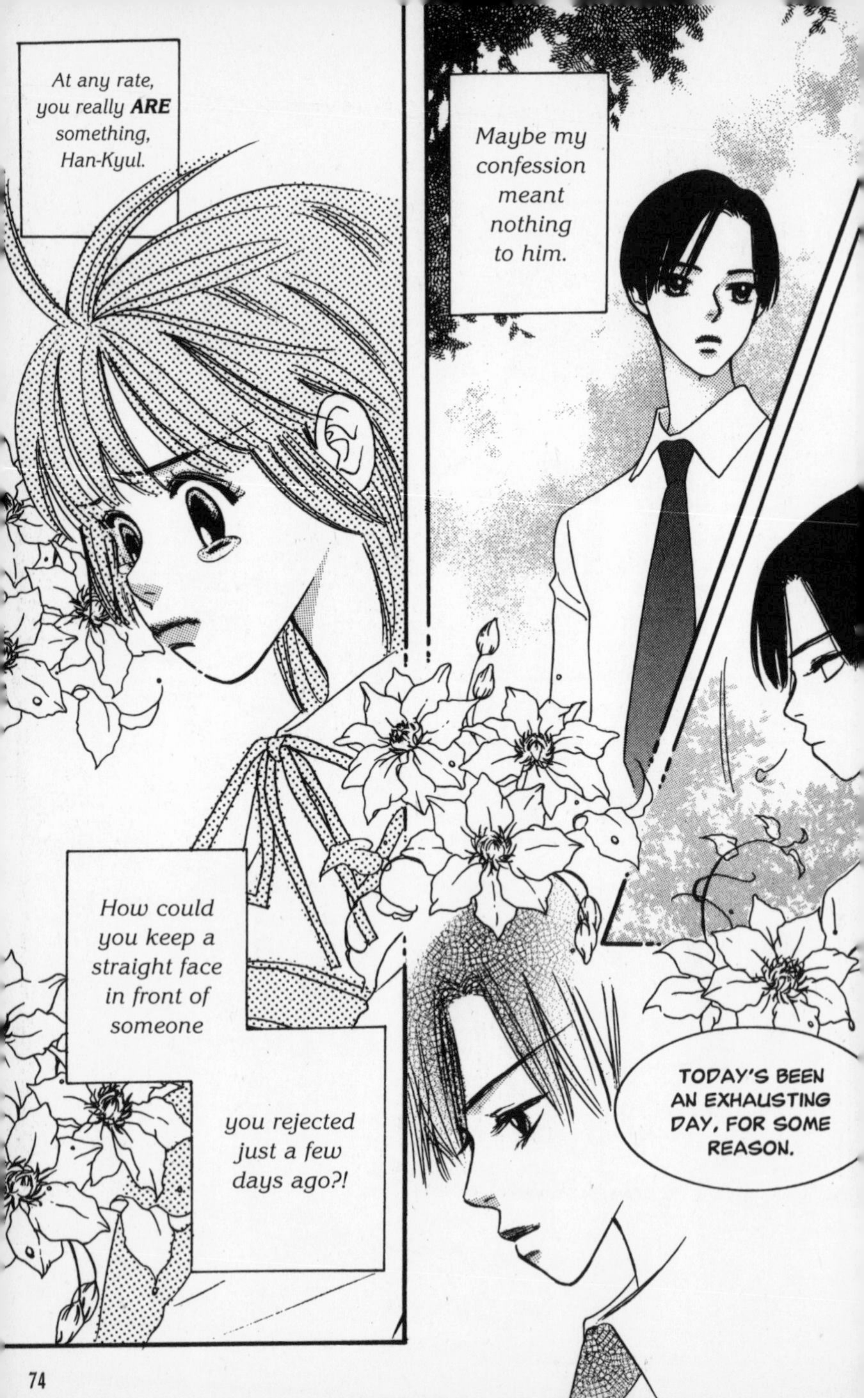

At any rate, you really ARE something, Han-Kyul.
Maybe my confession meant nothing to him.
How could you keep a straight face in front of someone
you rejected just a few days ago?!
TODAY'S BEEN AN EXHAUSTING DAY, FOR SOME REASON.

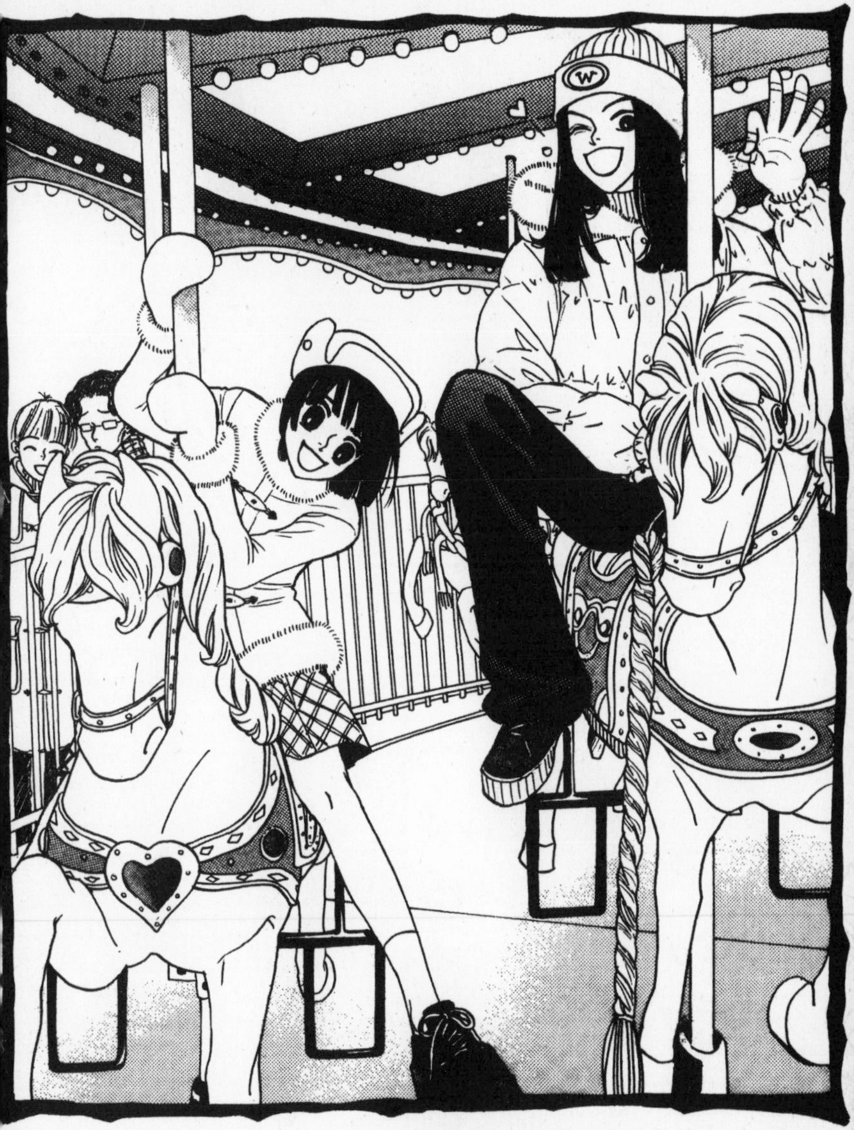

Sweet & Sensitive

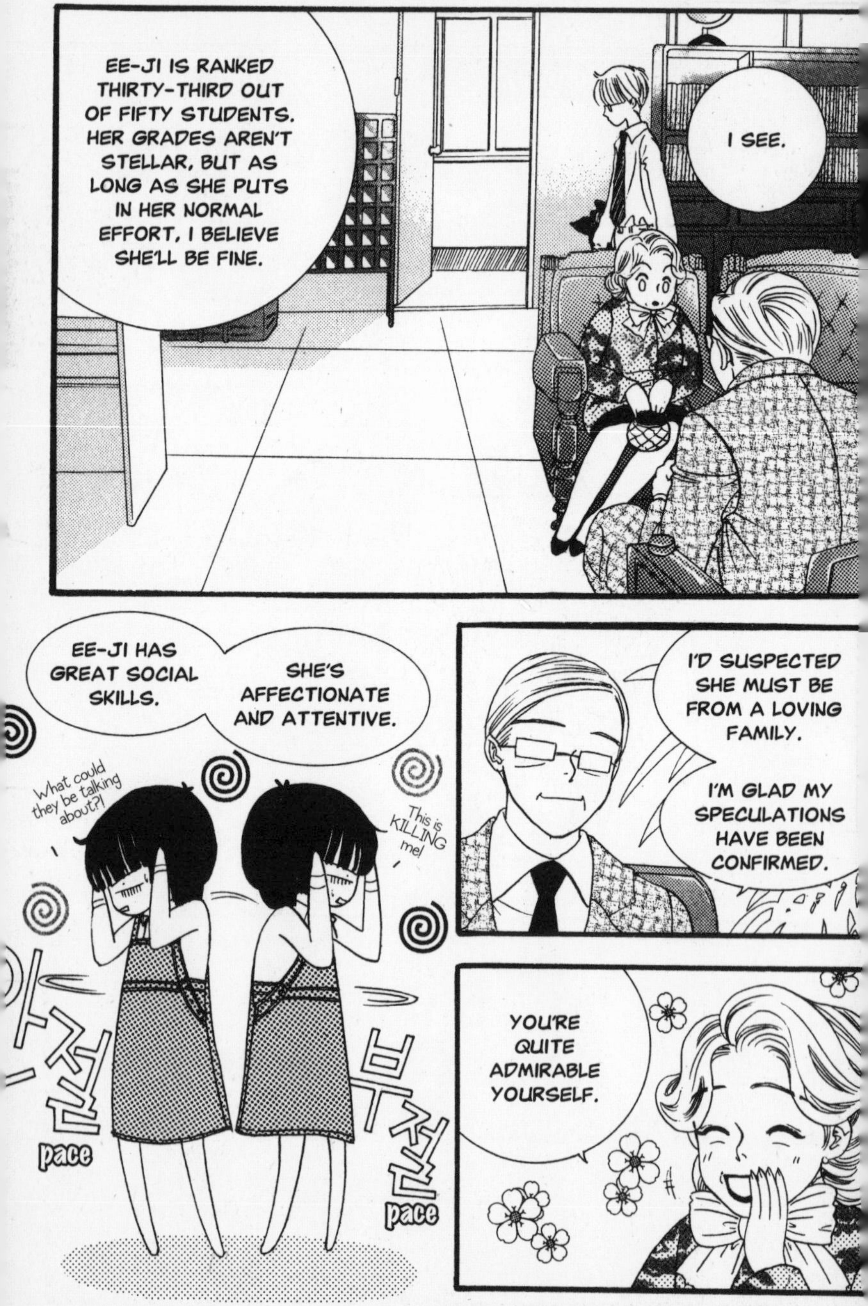

EE-JI IS RANKED THIRTY-THIRD OUT OF FIFTY STUDENTS. HER GRADES AREN'T STELLAR, BUT AS LONG AS SHE PUTS IN HER NORMAL EFFORT, I BELIEVE SHE'LL BE FINE.
I SEE.
EE-JI HAS GREAT SOCIAL SKILLS.
SHE'S AFFECTIONATE AND ATTENTIVE.
What could they be talking about?!
This is KILLING me!
pace
pace
I'D SUSPECTED SHE MUST BE FROM A LOVING FAMILY.
I'M GLAD MY SPECULATIONS HAVE BEEN CONFIRMED.
YOU'RE QUITE ADMIRABLE YOURSELF.

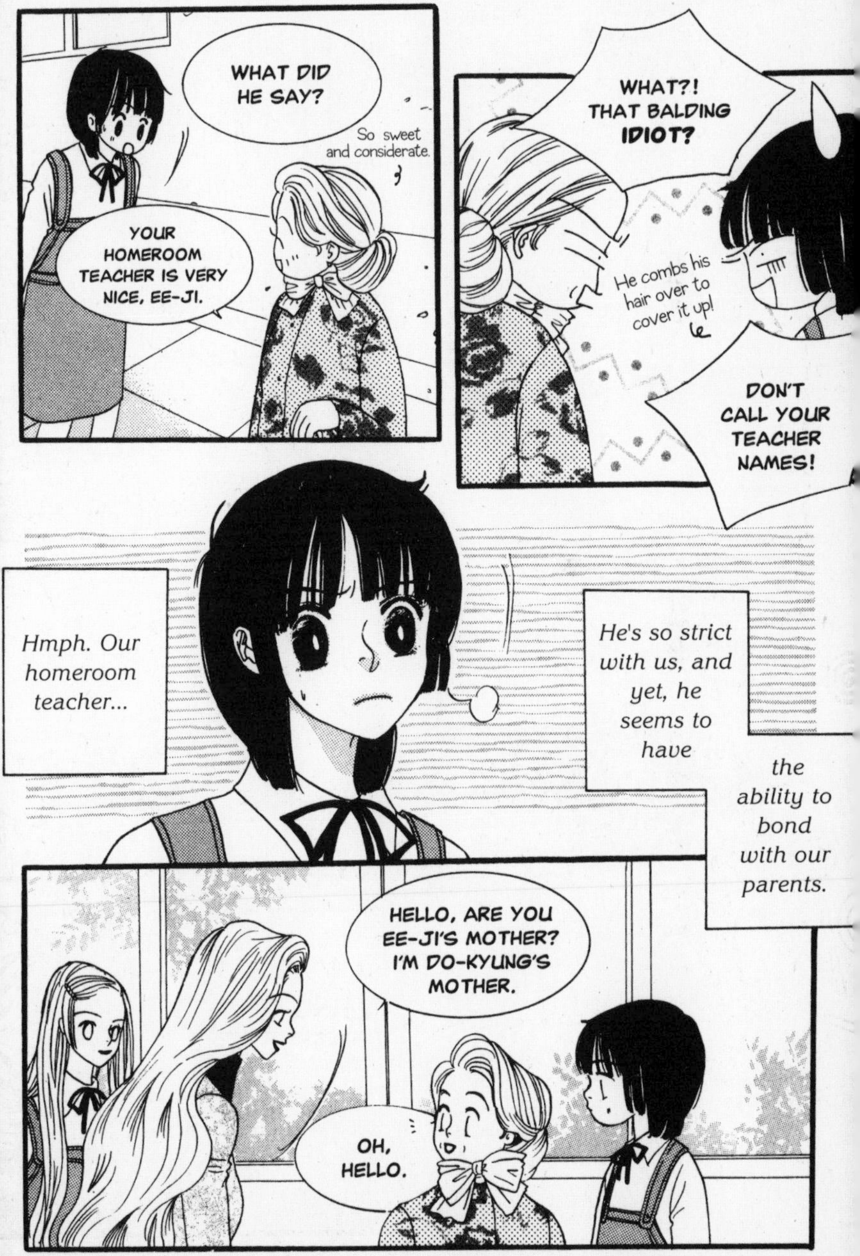
WHAT DID HE SAY?
YOUR HOMEROOM TEACHER IS VERY NICE, EE-JI.
So sweet and considerate.
WHAT?! THAT BALDING IDIOT?
He combs his hair over to cover it up!
DON'T CALL YOUR TEACHER NAMES!
Hmph. Our homeroom teacher...
He's so strict with us, and yet, he seems to have
the ability to bond with our parents.
HELLO, ARE YOU EE-JI'S MOTHER? I'M DO-KYUNG'S MOTHER.
OH, HELLO.

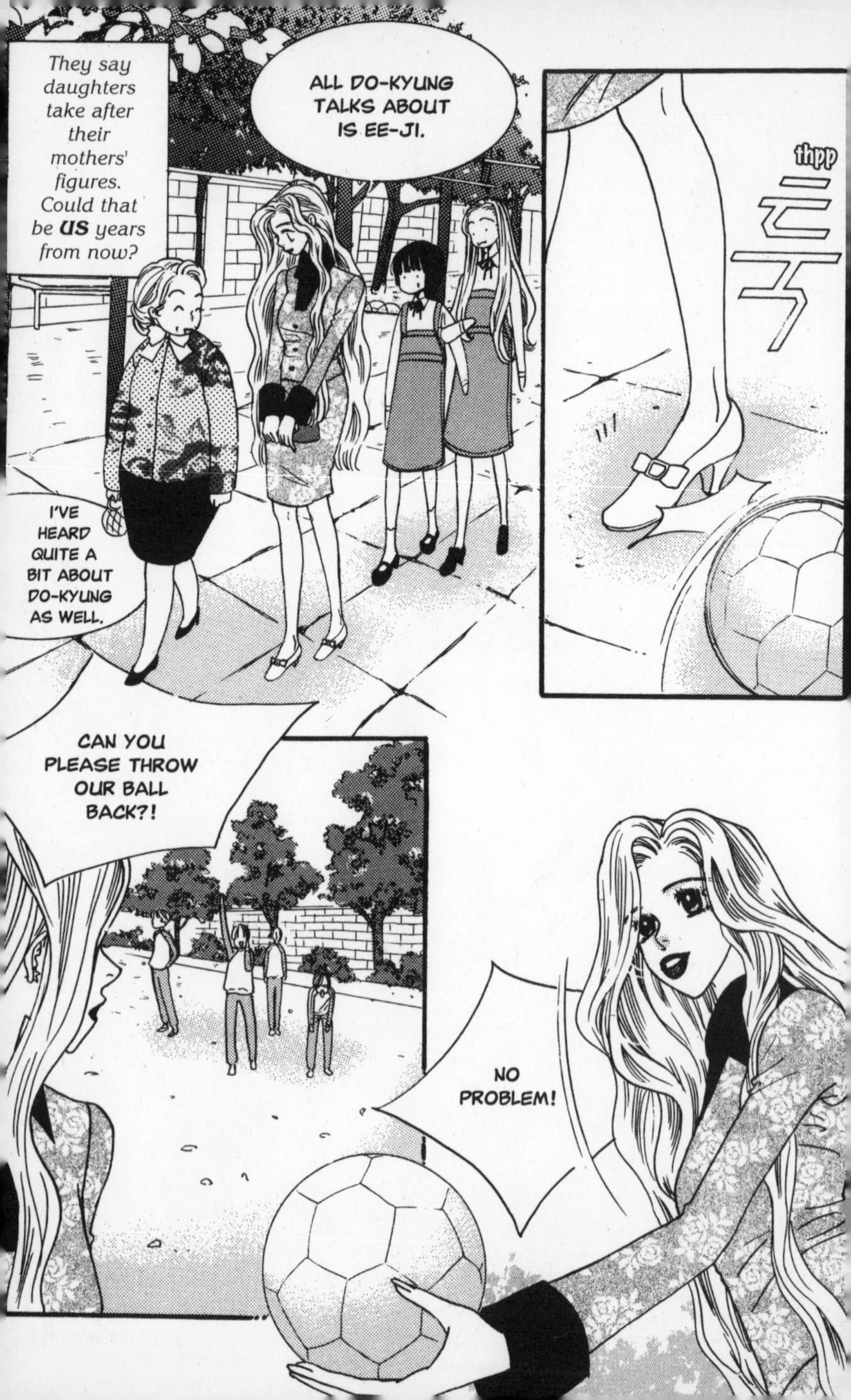
They say daughters take after their mothers' figures. Could that be **US** years from now?
ALL DO-KYUNG TALKS ABOUT IS EE-JI.
I'VE HEARD QUITE A BIT ABOUT DO-KYUNG AS WELL.
thpp
CAN YOU PLEASE THROW OUR BALL BACK?!
NO PROBLEM!

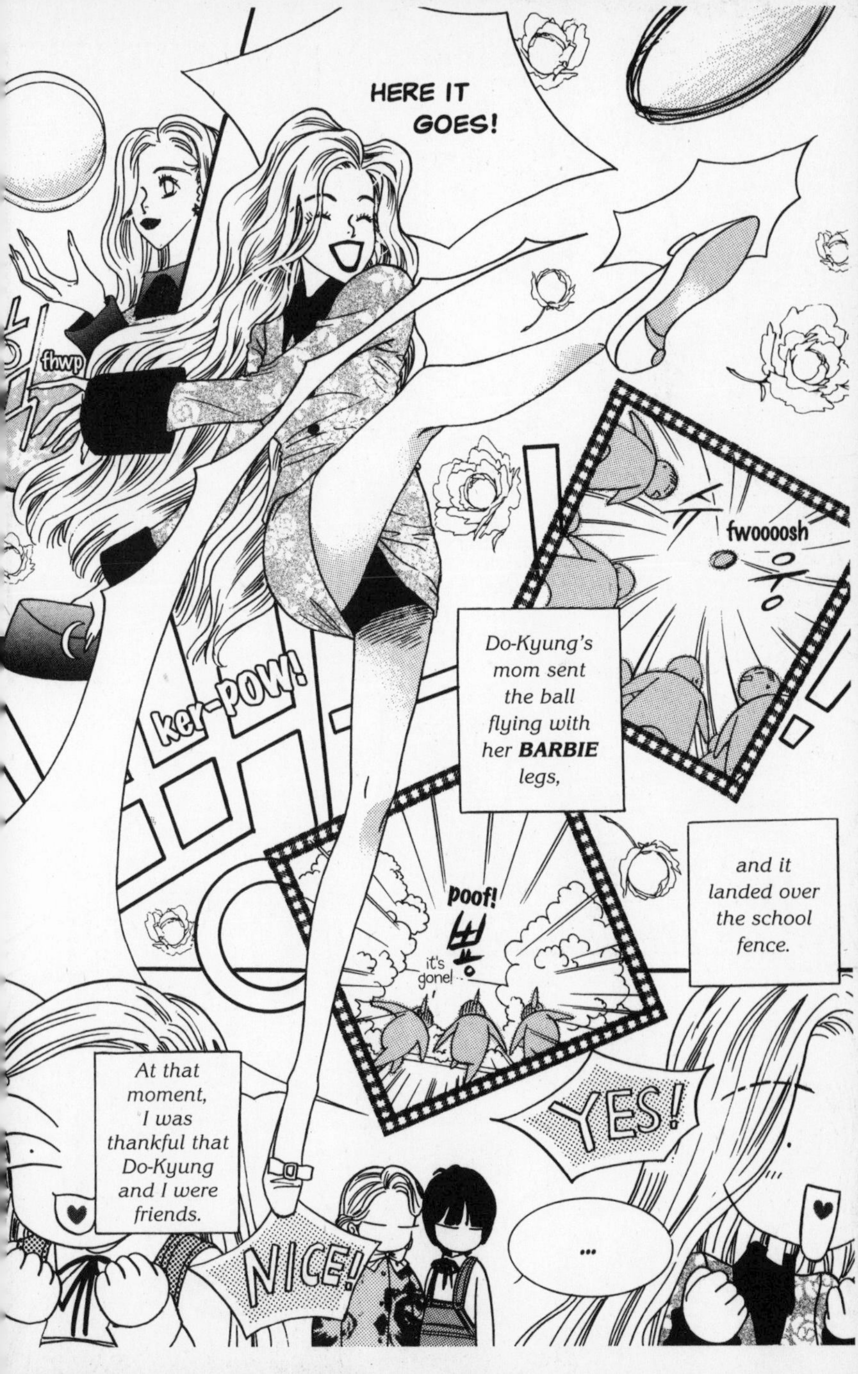
HERE IT GOES!
fhwp
ker-POW!
fwoooosh
Do-Kyung's mom sent the ball flying with her **BARBIE** legs,
poof!
it's gone!
and it landed over the school fence.
At that moment, I was thankful that Do-Kyung and I were friends.
YES!
NICE!
...

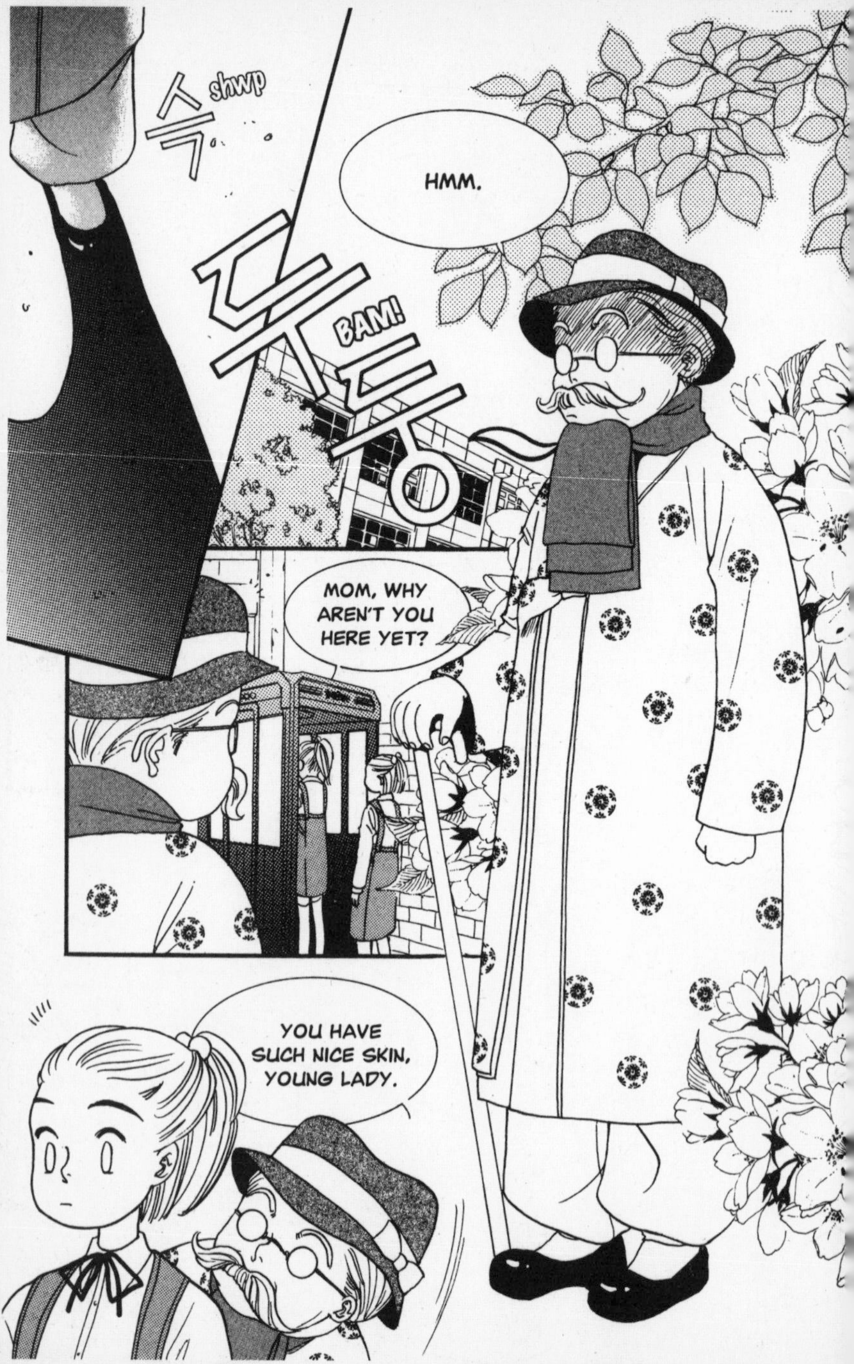
shwp
BAM!
HMM.
MOM, WHY AREN'T YOU HERE YET?
YOU HAVE SUCH NICE SKIN, YOUNG LADY.

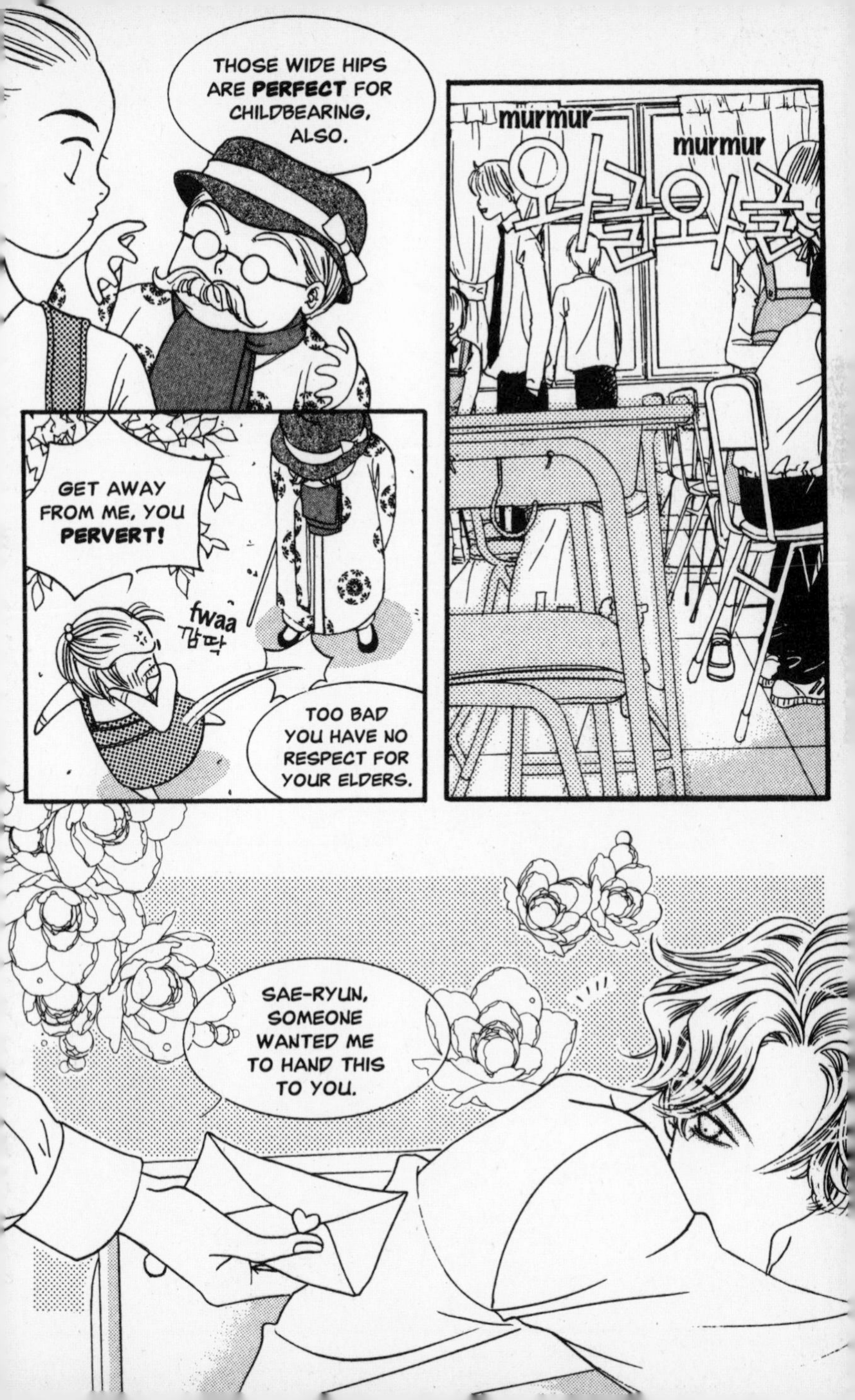
THOSE WIDE HIPS ARE **PERFECT** FOR CHILDBEARING, ALSO.
murmur
murmur
와글와글
GET AWAY FROM ME, YOU **PERVERT!**
fwaa
깜딱
TOO BAD YOU HAVE NO RESPECT FOR YOUR ELDERS.
SAE-RYUN, SOMEONE WANTED ME TO HAND THIS TO YOU.

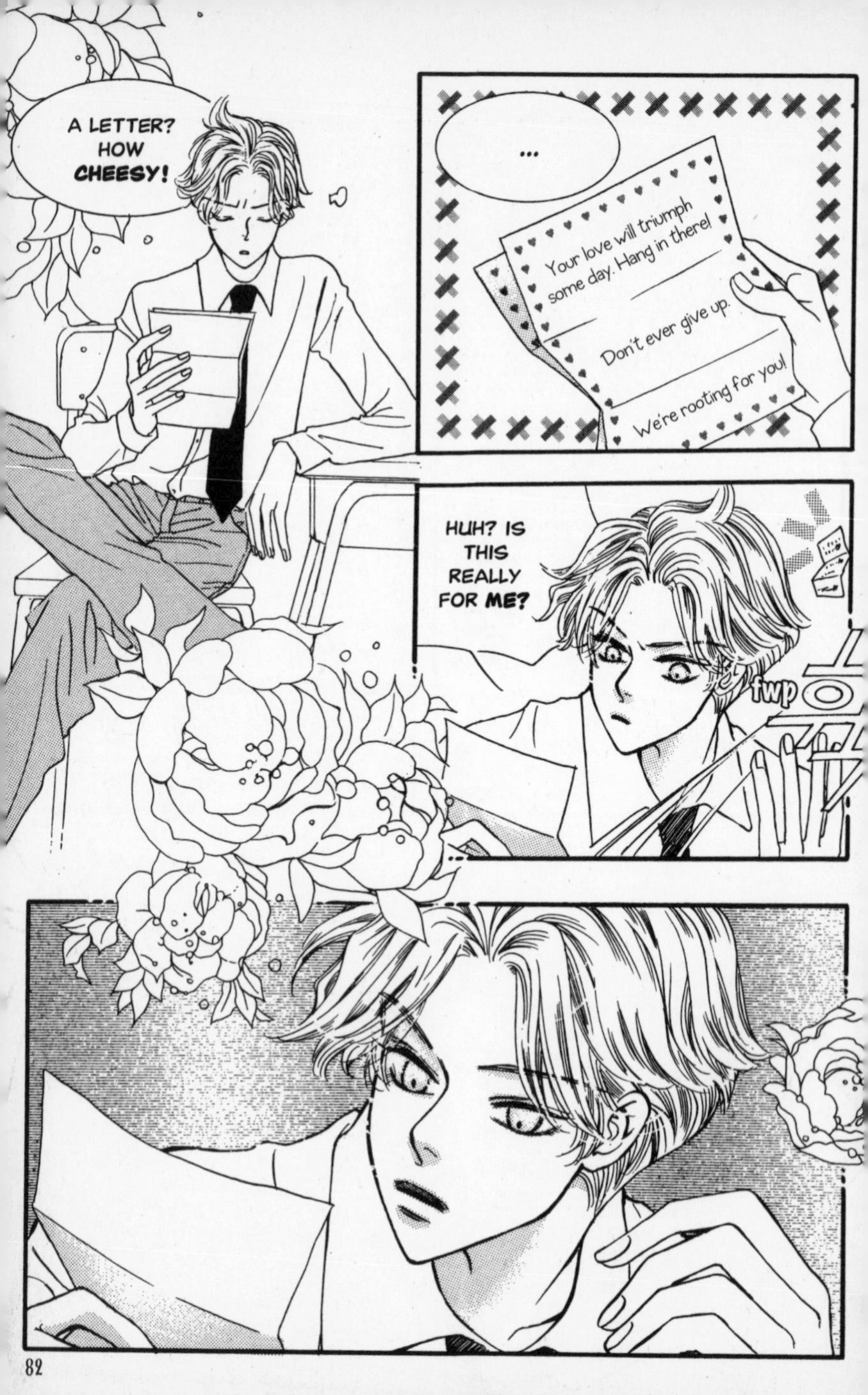
A LETTER? HOW CHEESY!
...
Your love will triumph some day. Hang in there!
Don't ever give up.
We're rooting for you!
HUH? IS THIS REALLY FOR ME?
fwp

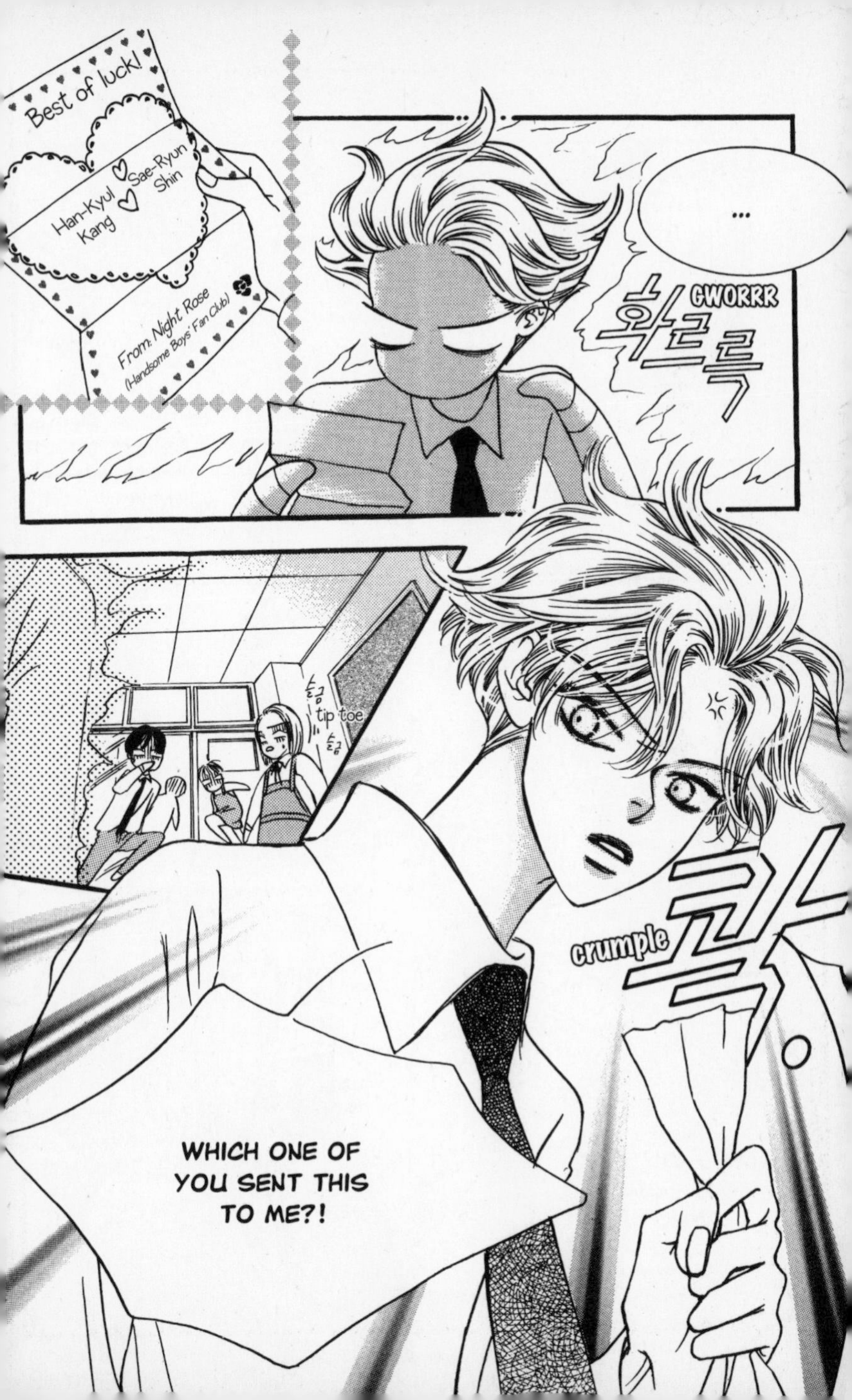

Best of luck!
Han-Kyul Kang ♡ Sae-Ryun Shin
From: Night Rose (Handsome Boys' Fan Club)
...
화르륵
GWORRR
살금 tip toe 살금
구깃
crumple
WHICH ONE OF YOU SENT THIS TO ME?!

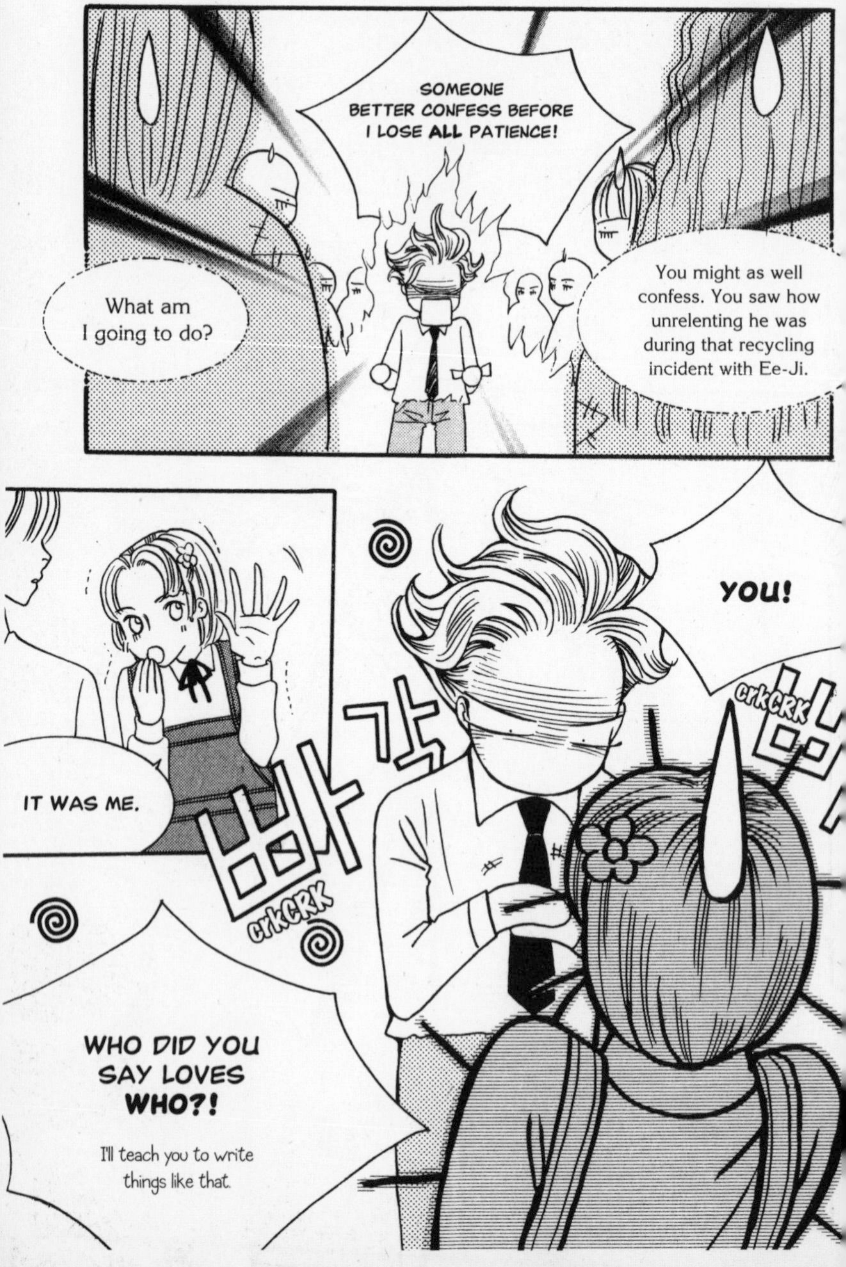

SOMEONE BETTER CONFESS BEFORE I LOSE **ALL** PATIENCE!
What am I going to do?
You might as well confess. You saw how unrelenting he was during that recycling incident with Ee-Ji.
IT WAS ME.
YOU!
crkCRK
crkCRK
WHO DID YOU SAY LOVES **WHO?!**
I'll teach you to write things like that.

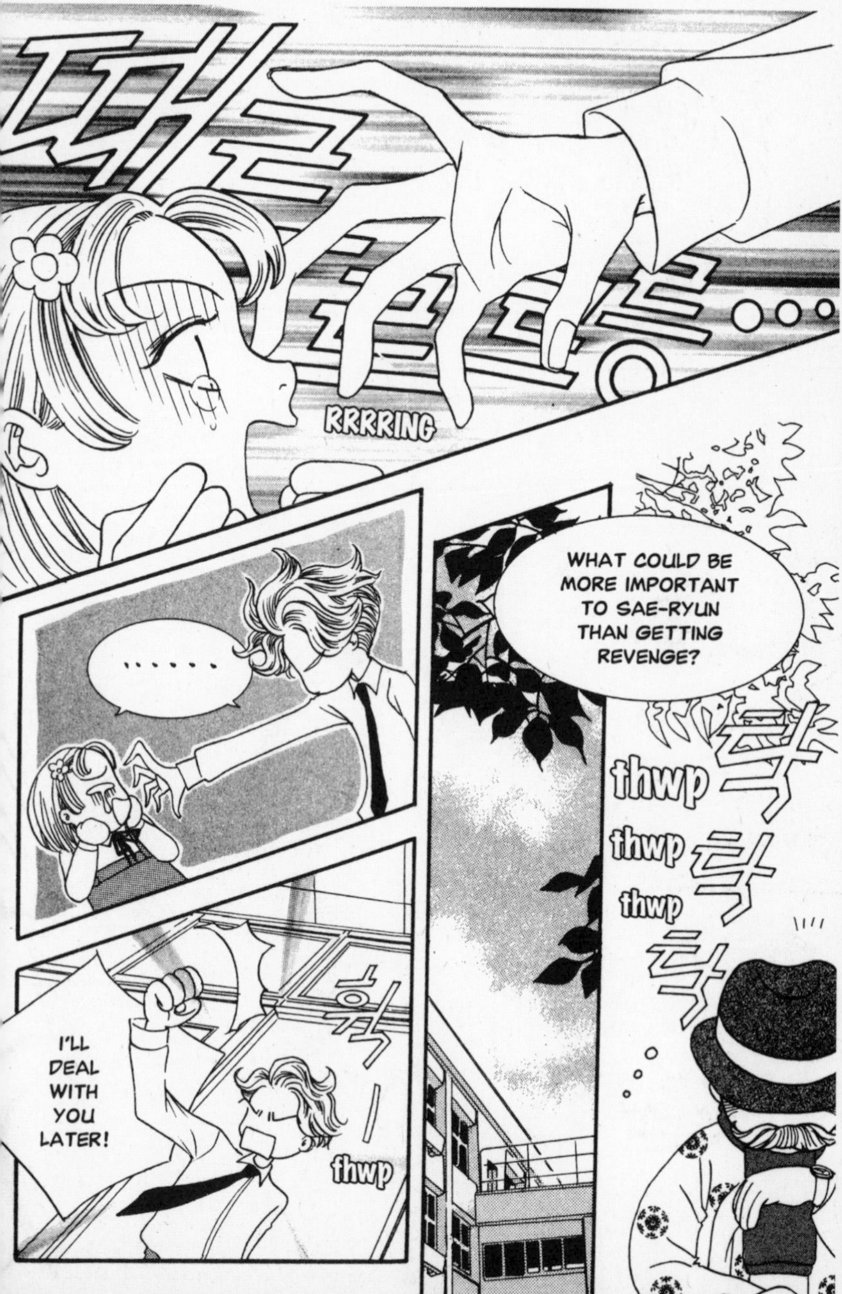

RRRRING
......
WHAT COULD BE MORE IMPORTANT TO SAE-RYUN THAN GETTING REVENGE?
thwp
thwp
thwp
I'LL DEAL WITH YOU LATER!
fhwp

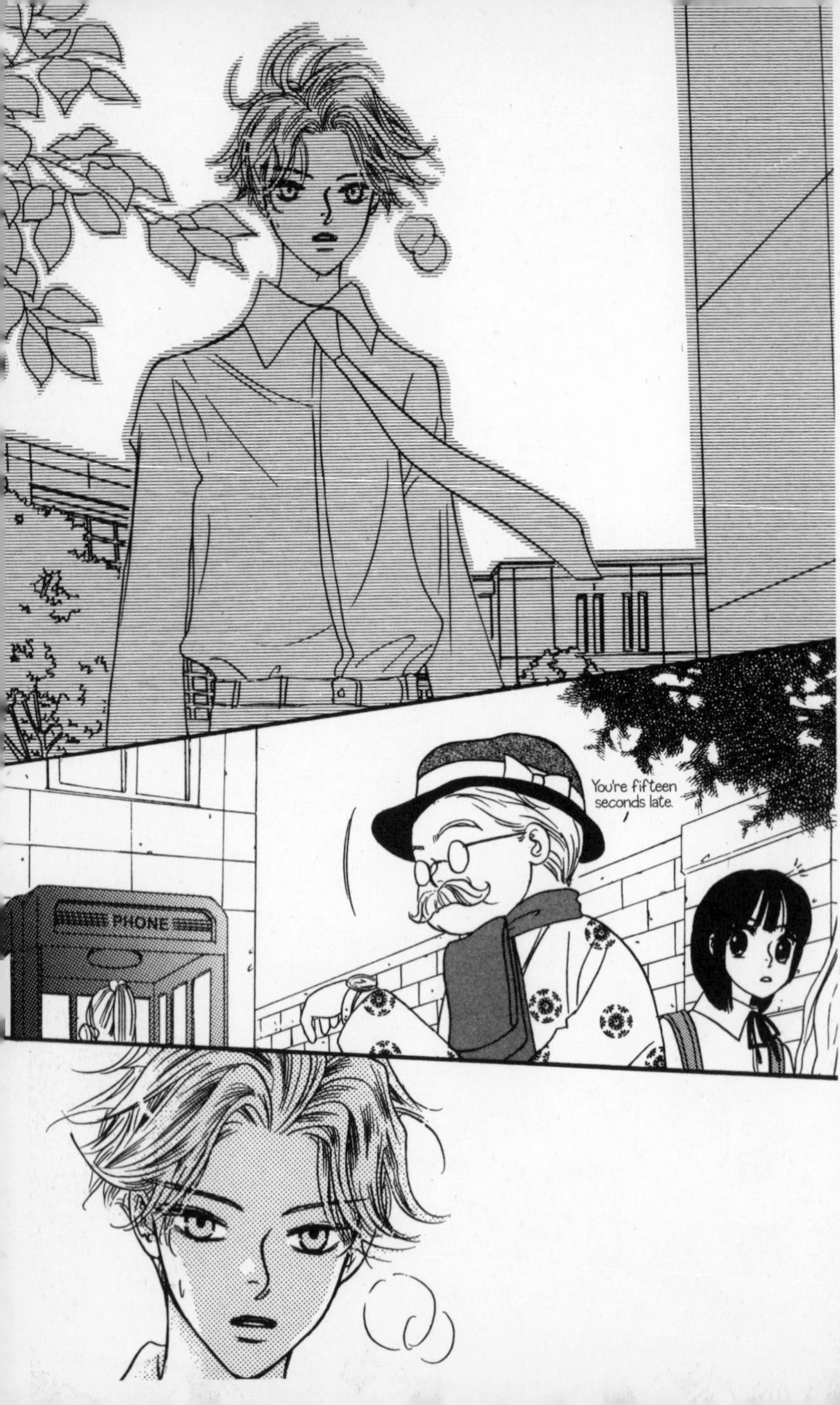
You're fifteen seconds late.
PHONE

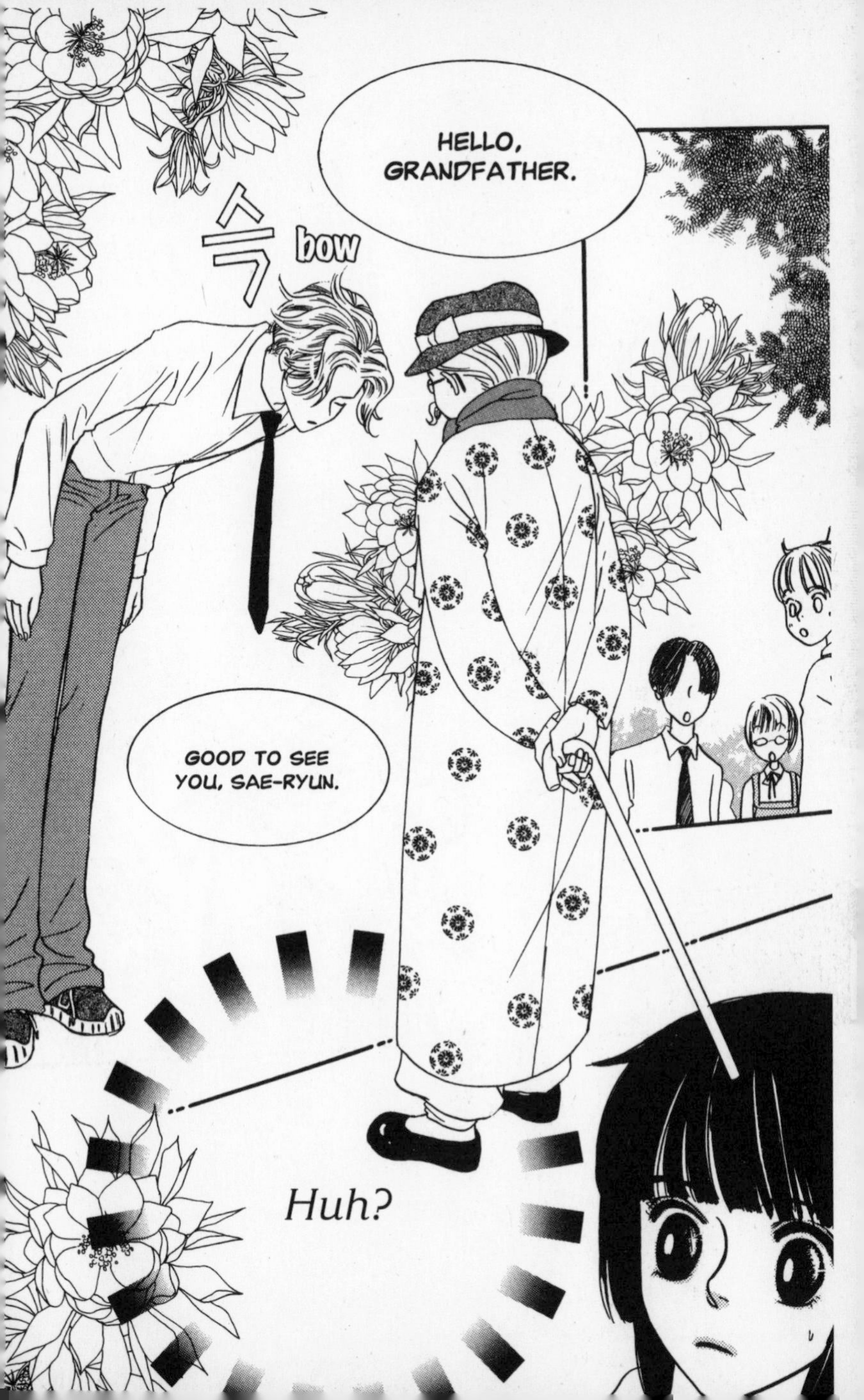
HELLO, GRANDFATHER.
bow
GOOD TO SEE YOU, SAE-RYUN.
Huh?

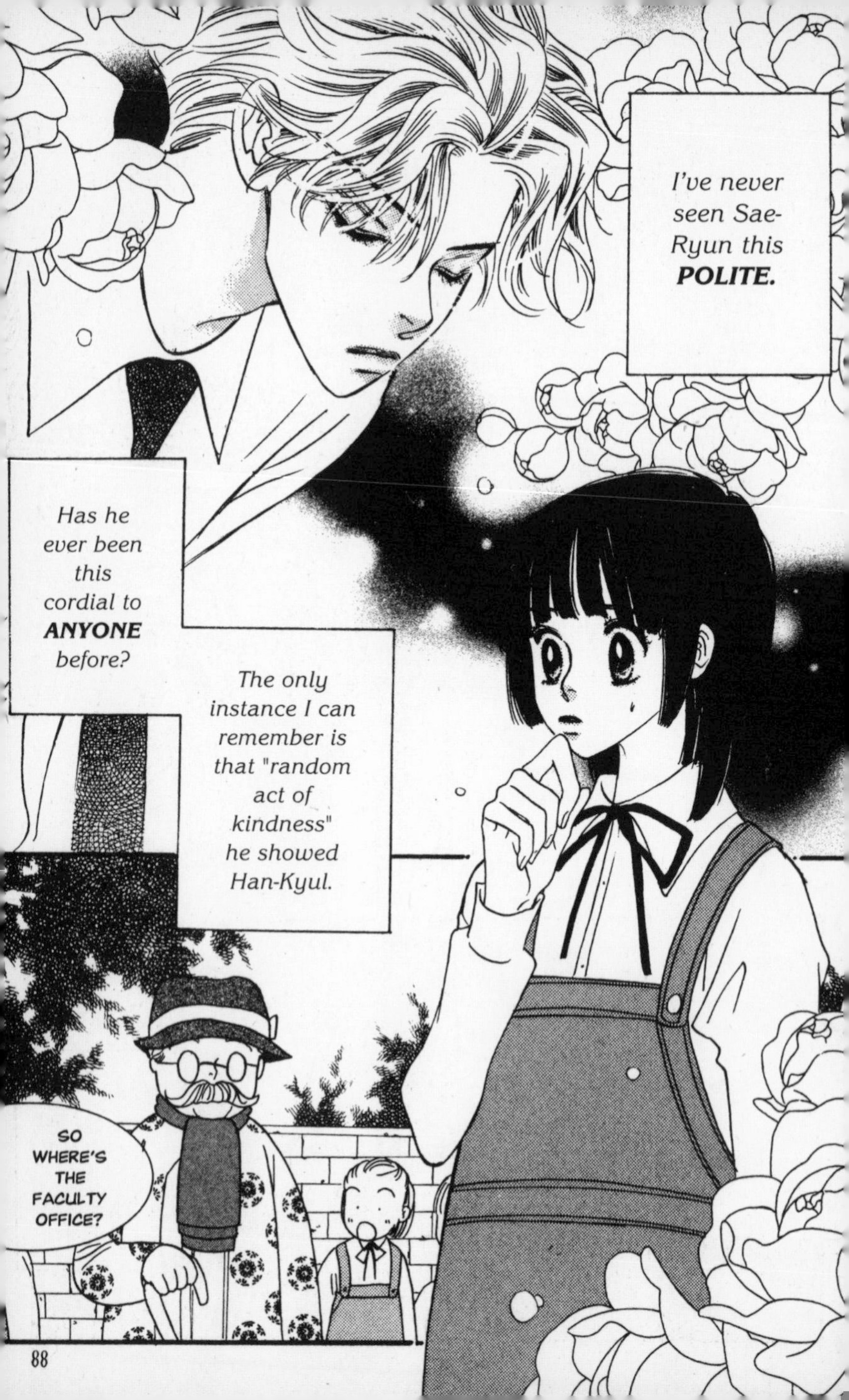
I've never seen Sae-Ryun this POLITE.
Has he ever been this cordial to ANYONE before?
The only instance I can remember is that "random act of kindness" he showed Han-Kyul.
SO WHERE'S THE FACULTY OFFICE?

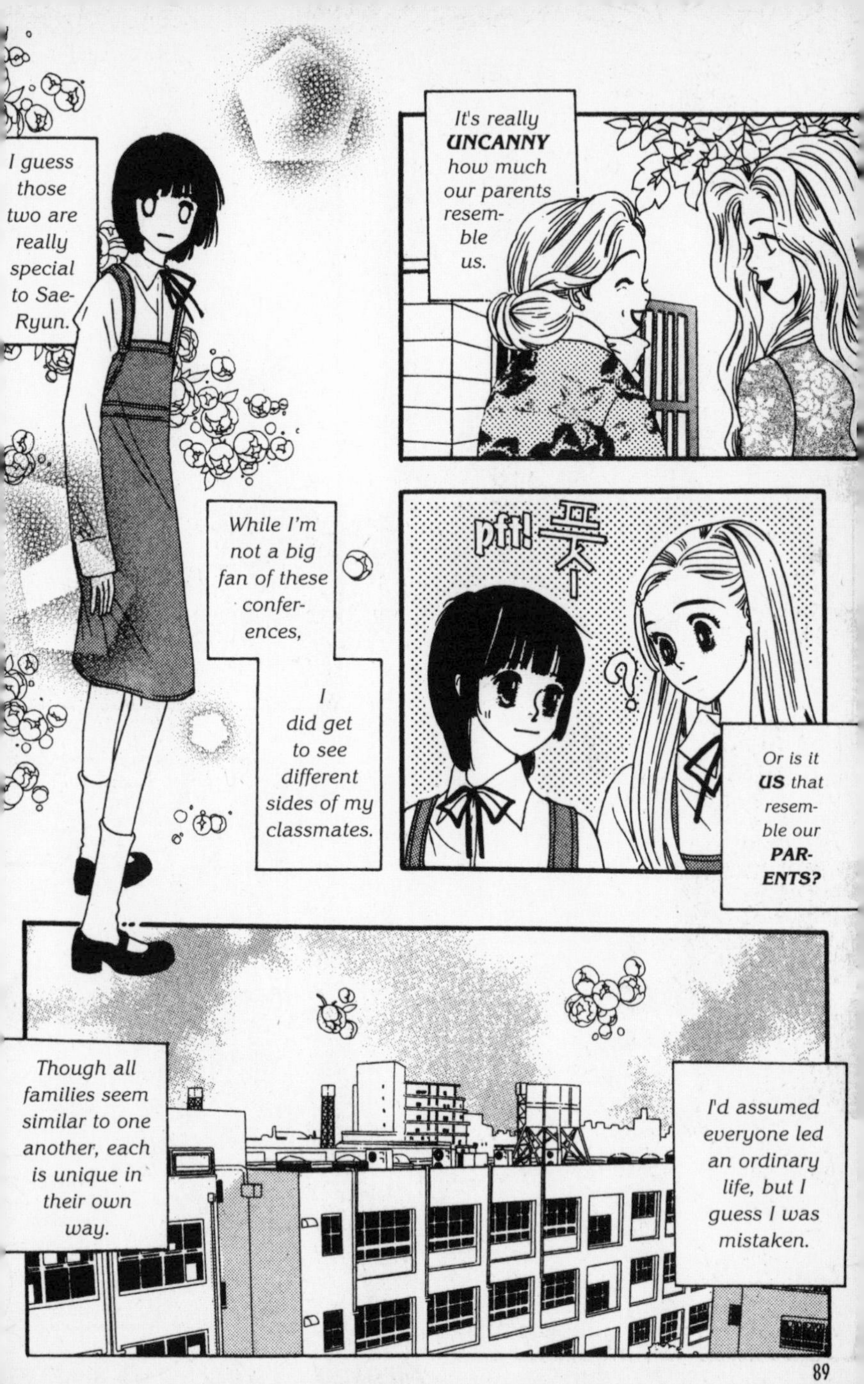
I guess those two are really special to Sae-Ryun.
It's really UNCANNY how much our parents resemble us.
pft!
While I'm not a big fan of these conferences,
I did get to see different sides of my classmates.
Or is it US that resemble our PARENTS?
Though all families seem similar to one another, each is unique in their own way.
I'd assumed everyone led an ordinary life, but I guess I was mistaken.

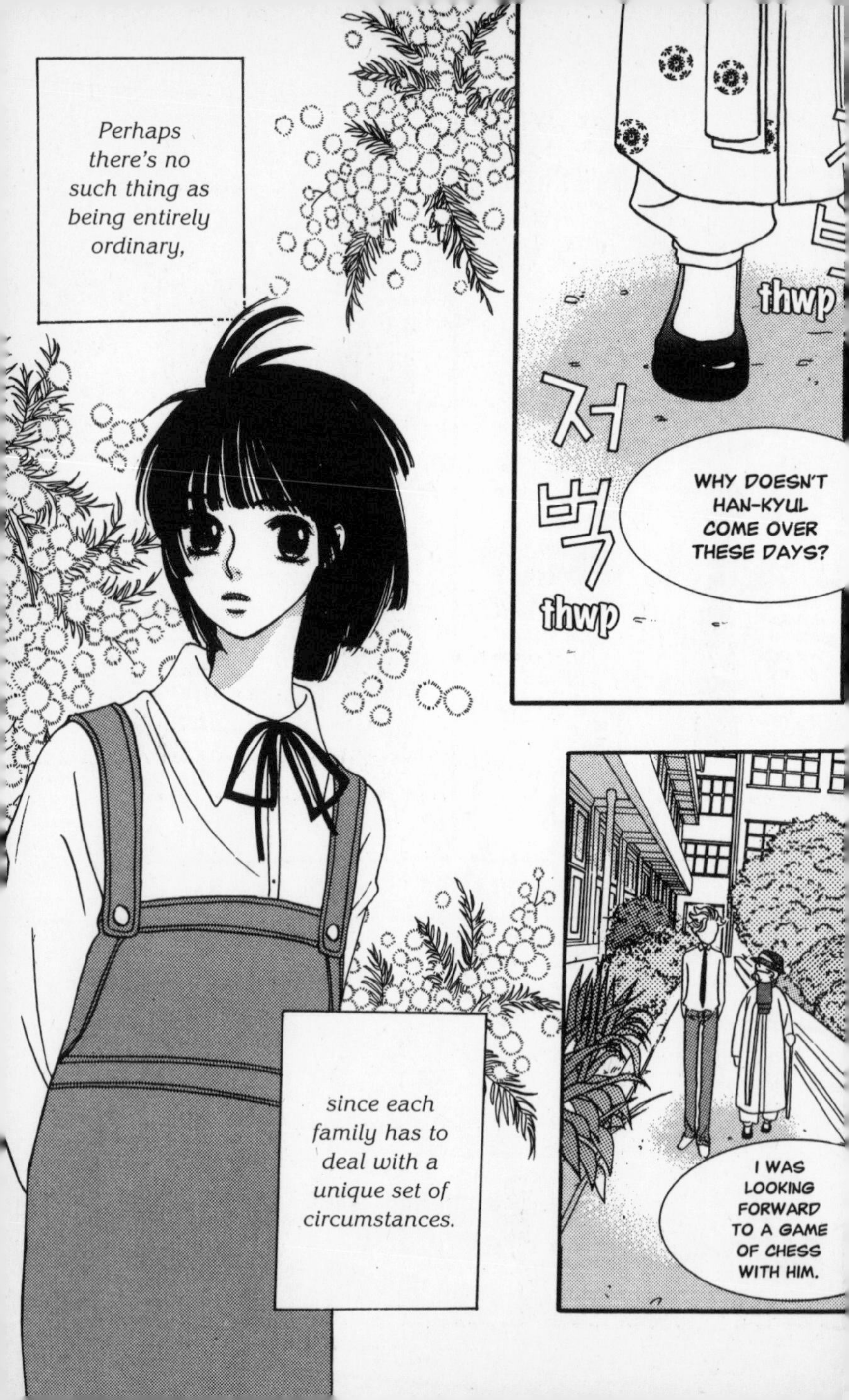
Perhaps there's no such thing as being entirely ordinary,
since each family has to deal with a unique set of circumstances.
thwp
저벅
thwp
WHY DOESN'T HAN-KYUL COME OVER THESE DAYS?
I WAS LOOKING FORWARD TO A GAME OF CHESS WITH HIM.

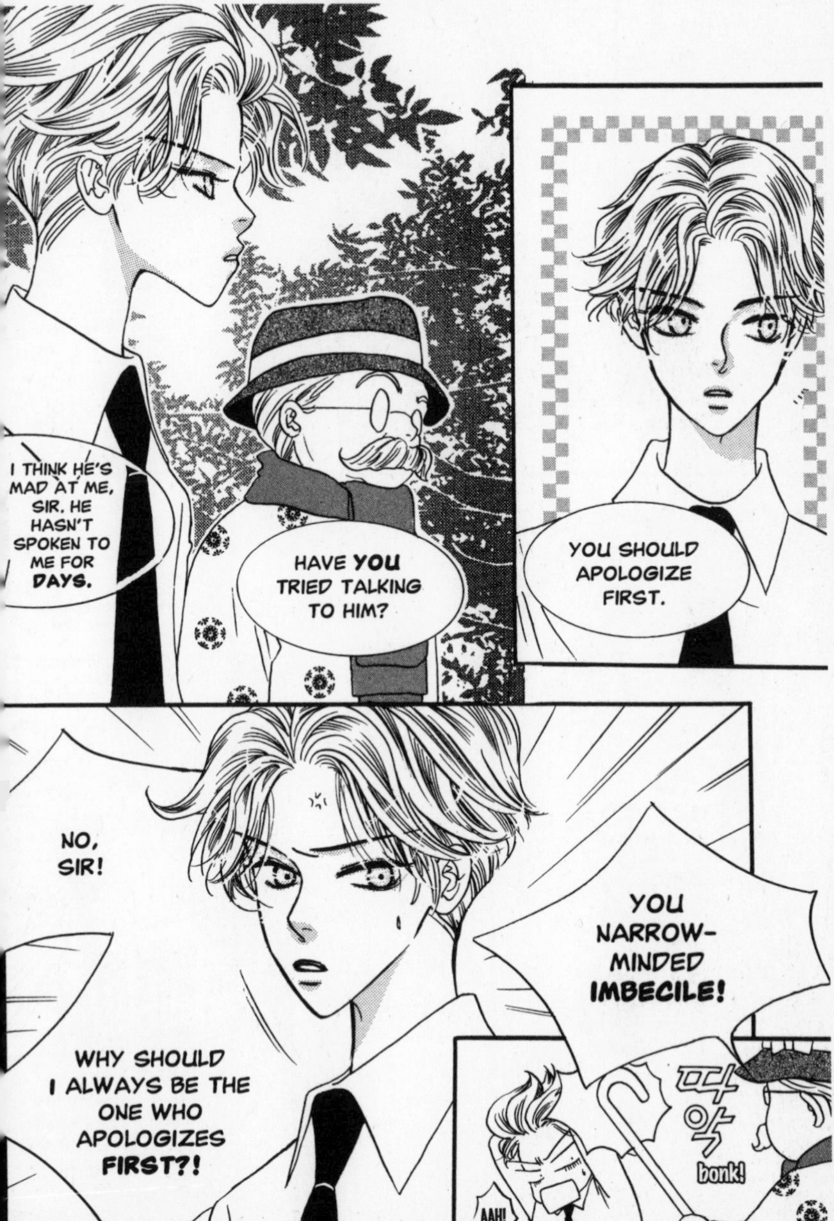
I THINK HE'S MAD AT ME, SIR. HE HASN'T SPOKEN TO ME FOR DAYS.
HAVE YOU TRIED TALKING TO HIM?
YOU SHOULD APOLOGIZE FIRST.
NO, SIR!
WHY SHOULD I ALWAYS BE THE ONE WHO APOLOGIZES FIRST?!
YOU NARROW-MINDED IMBECILE!
따악
bonk!
AAH!

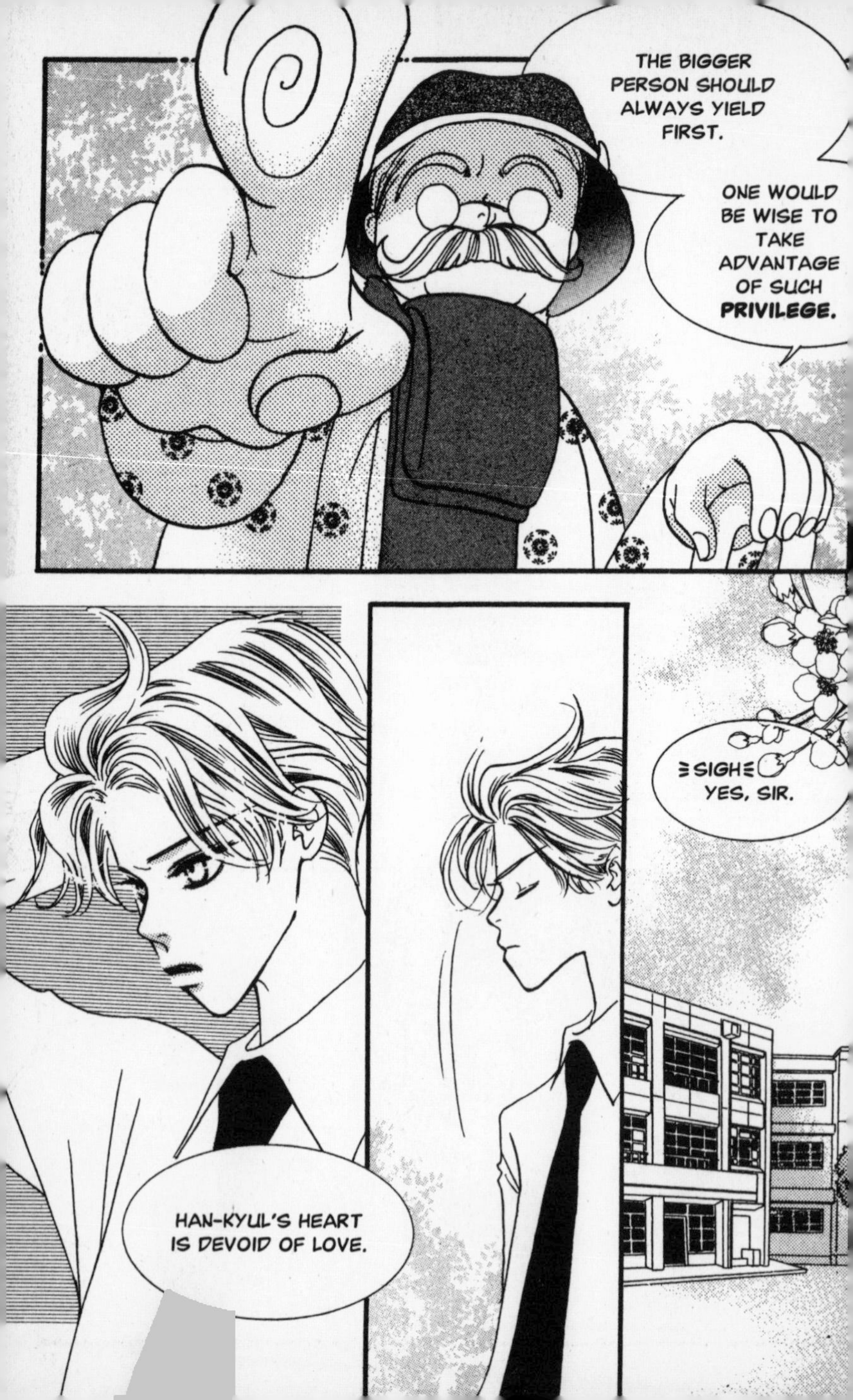
THE BIGGER PERSON SHOULD ALWAYS YIELD FIRST.
ONE WOULD BE WISE TO TAKE ADVANTAGE OF SUCH **PRIVILEGE.**
≡SIGH≡ YES, SIR.
HAN-KYUL'S HEART IS DEVOID OF LOVE.

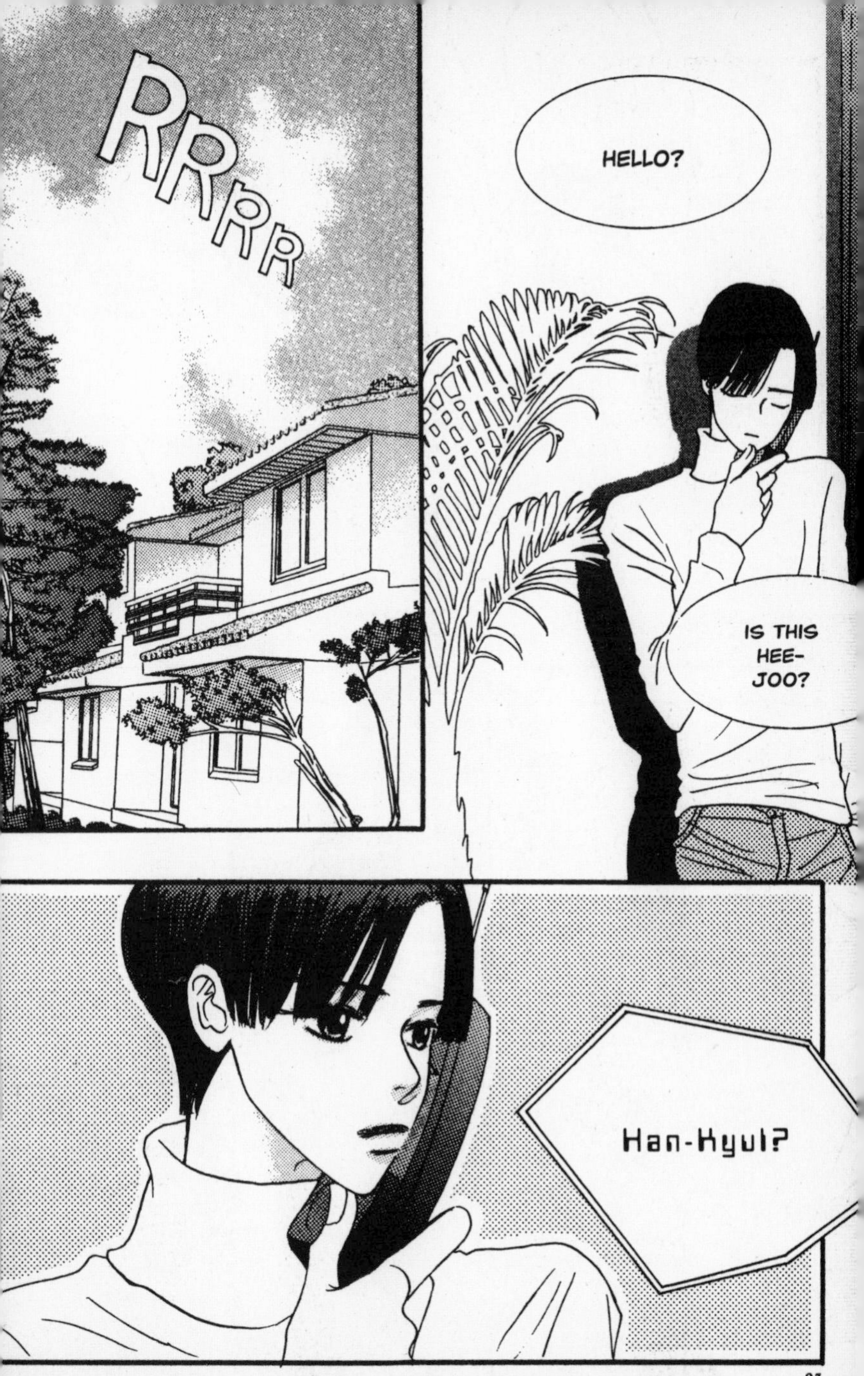
RRRRR
HELLO?
IS THIS HEE-JOO?
Han-Kyul?

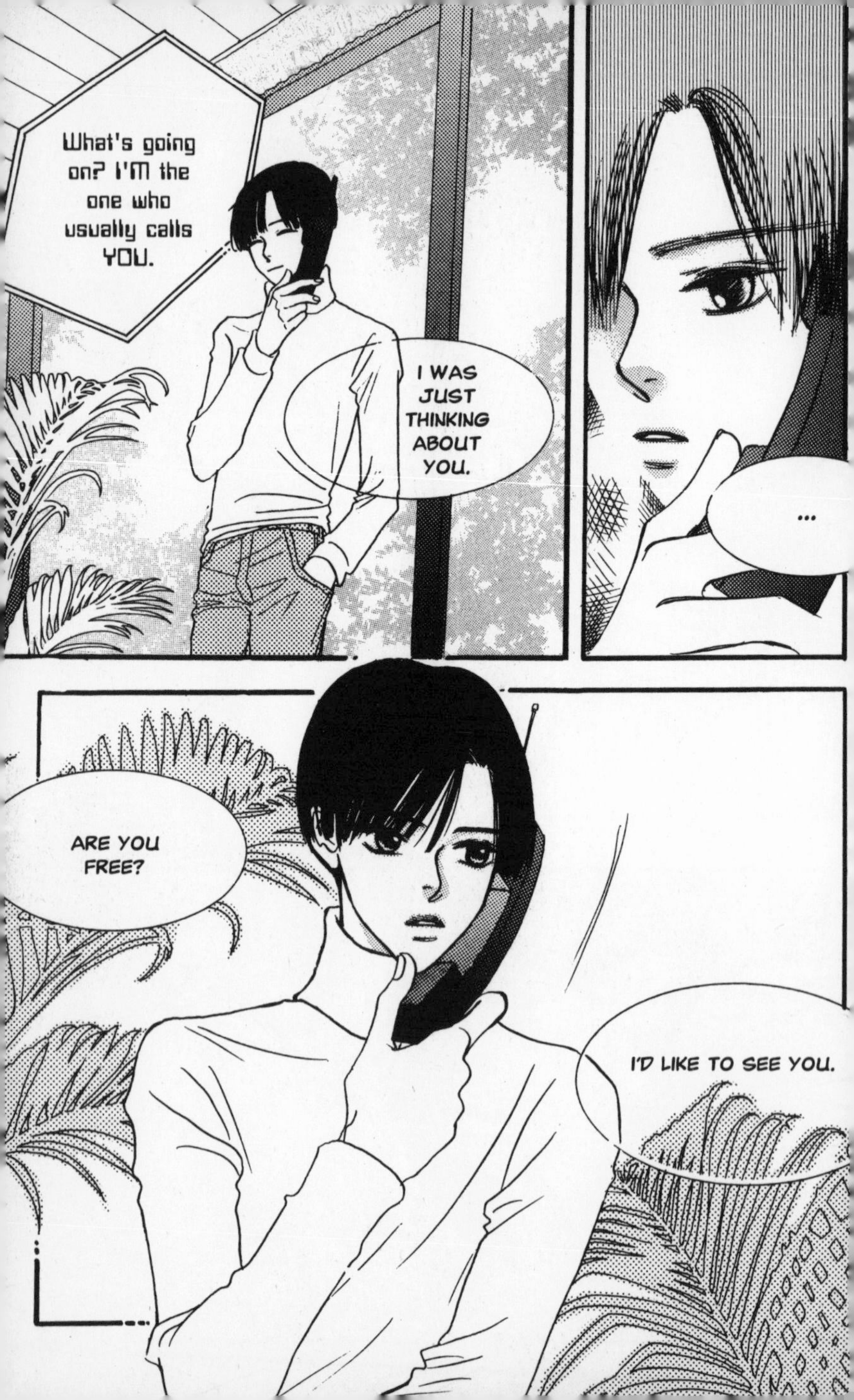
What's going on? I'M the one who usually calls YOU.
I WAS JUST THINKING ABOUT YOU.
...
ARE YOU FREE?
I'D LIKE TO SEE YOU.

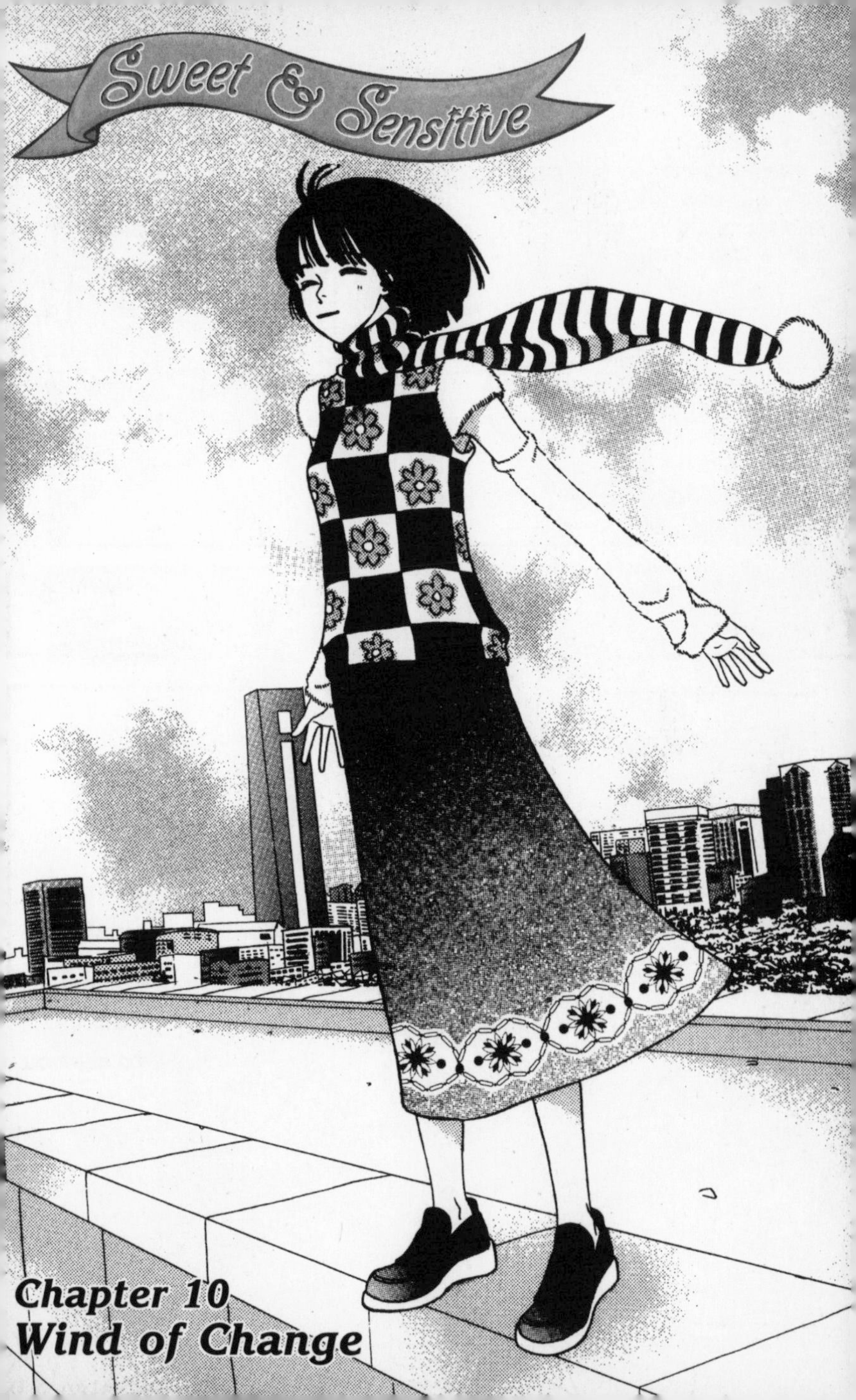
Sweet & Sensitive
Chapter 10
Wind of Change

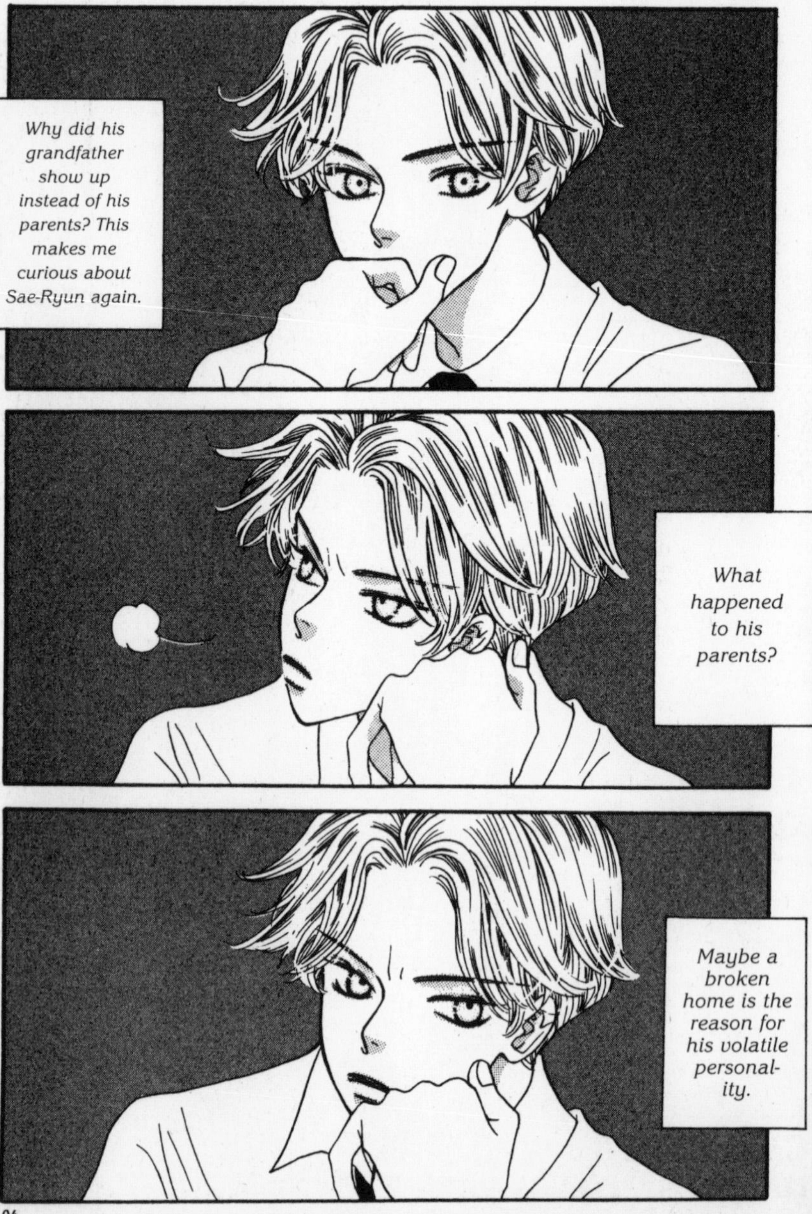
Why did his grandfather show up instead of his parents? This makes me curious about Sae-Ryun again.
What happened to his parents?
Maybe a broken home is the reason for his volatile personal-ity.

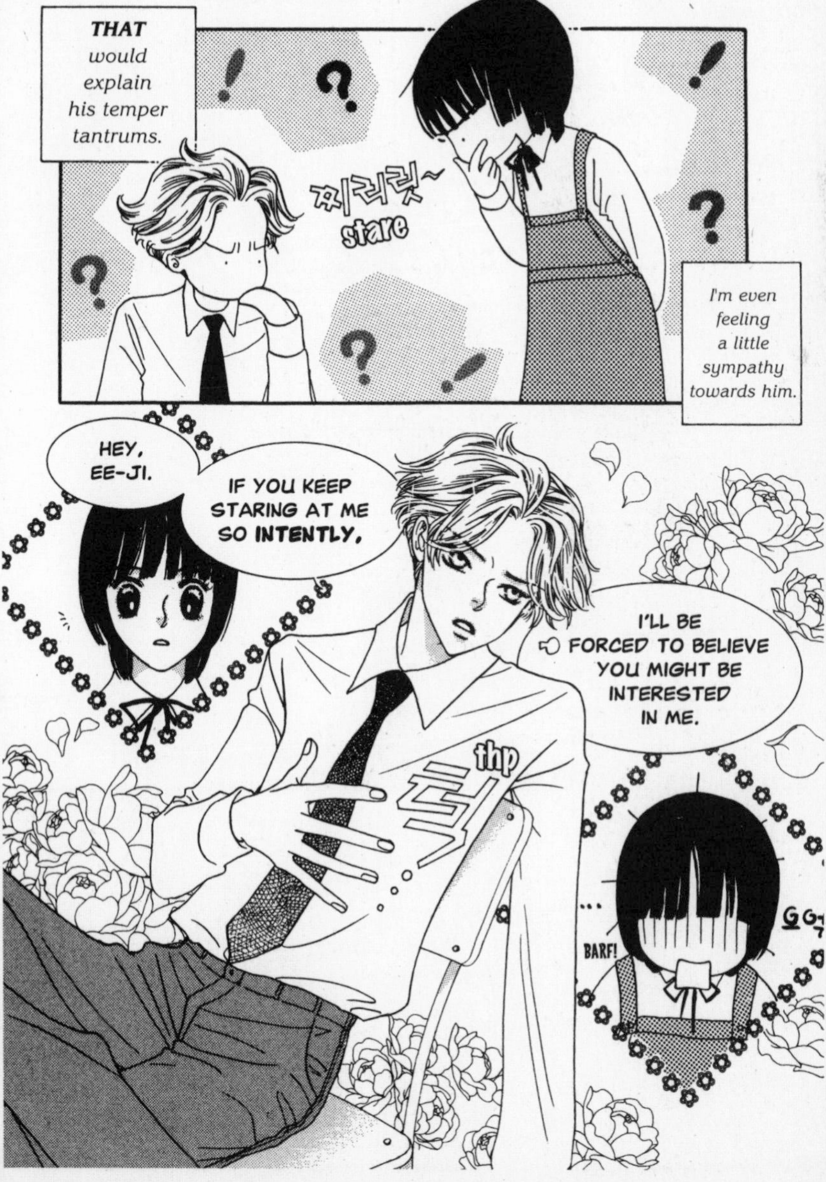
THAT would explain his temper tantrums.
찌리릿~
stare
I'm even feeling a little sympathy towards him.
HEY, EE-JI.
IF YOU KEEP STARING AT ME SO INTENTLY,
I'LL BE FORCED TO BELIEVE YOU MIGHT BE INTERESTED IN ME.
thp
...
BARF!

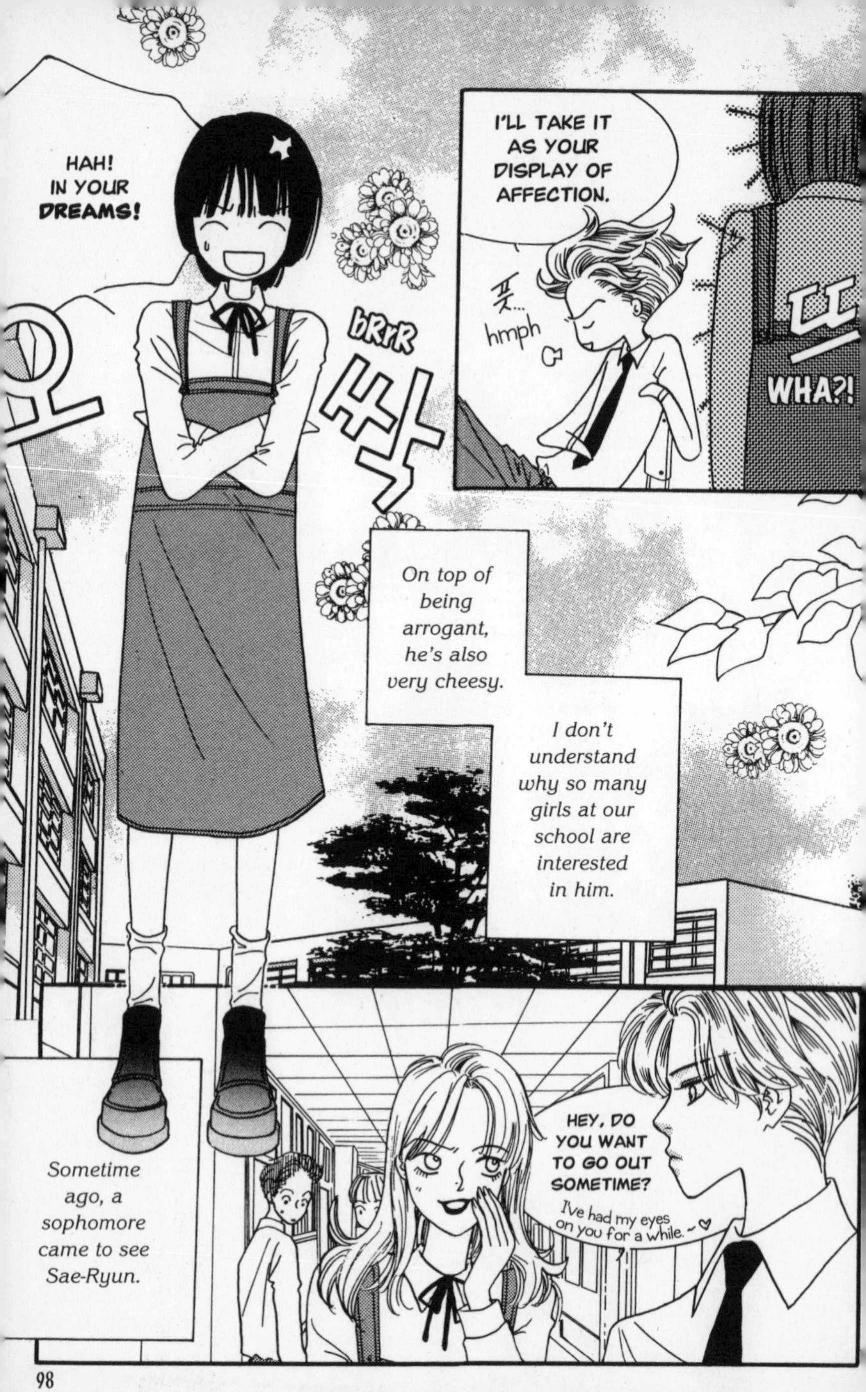
I'LL TAKE IT AS YOUR DISPLAY OF AFFECTION.
훗... hmph
뜨
WHA?!
HAH! IN YOUR DREAMS!
bRrR
싹
On top of being arrogant, he's also very cheesy.
I don't understand why so many girls at our school are interested in him.
Sometime ago, a sophomore came to see Sae-Ryun.
HEY, DO YOU WANT TO GO OUT SOMETIME?
I've had my eyes on you for a while. ~♡

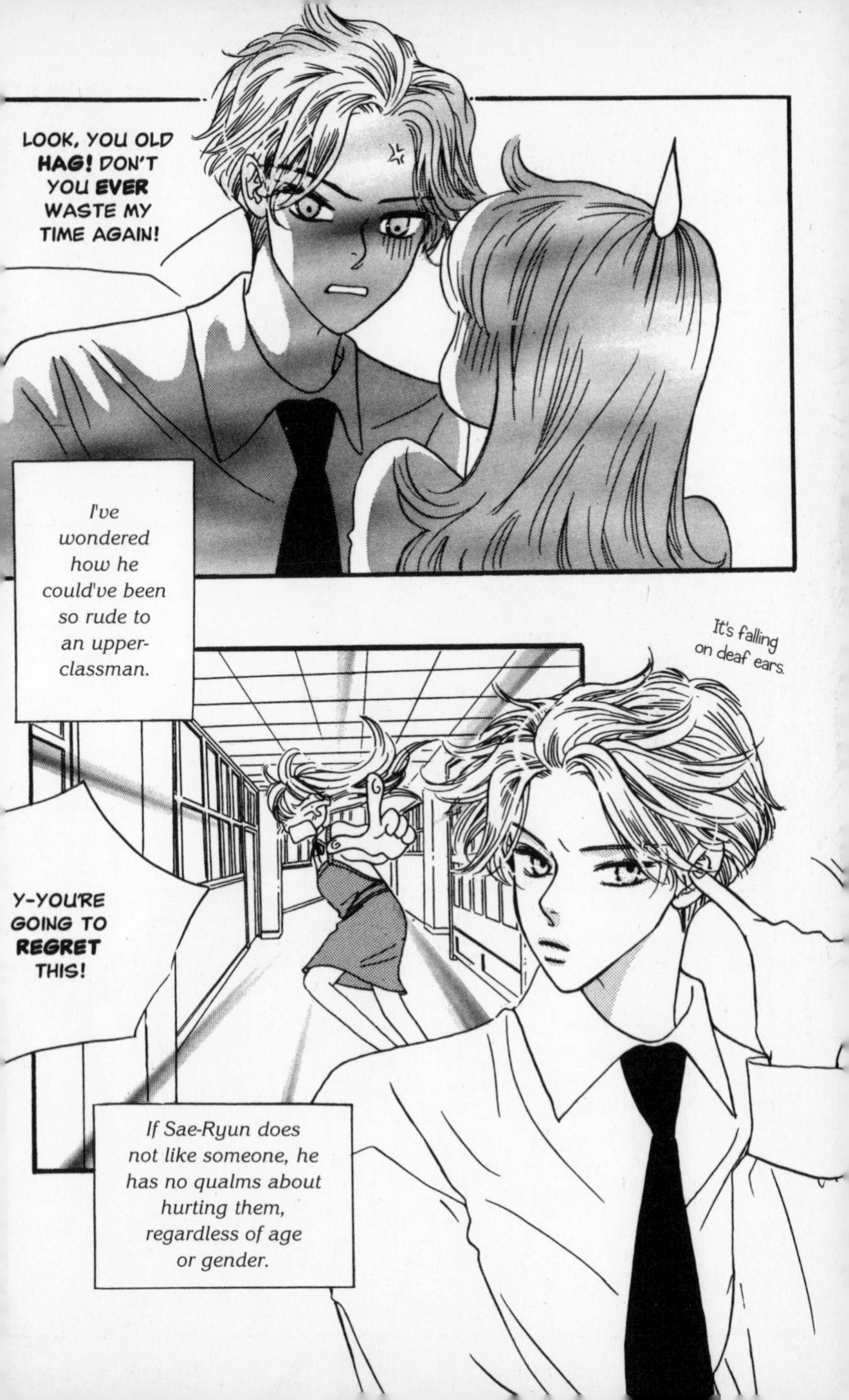
LOOK, YOU OLD HAG! DON'T YOU EVER WASTE MY TIME AGAIN!
I've wondered how he could've been so rude to an upper-classman.
It's falling on deaf ears.
Y-YOU'RE GOING TO REGRET THIS!
If Sae-Ryun does not like someone, he has no qualms about hurting them, regardless of age or gender.

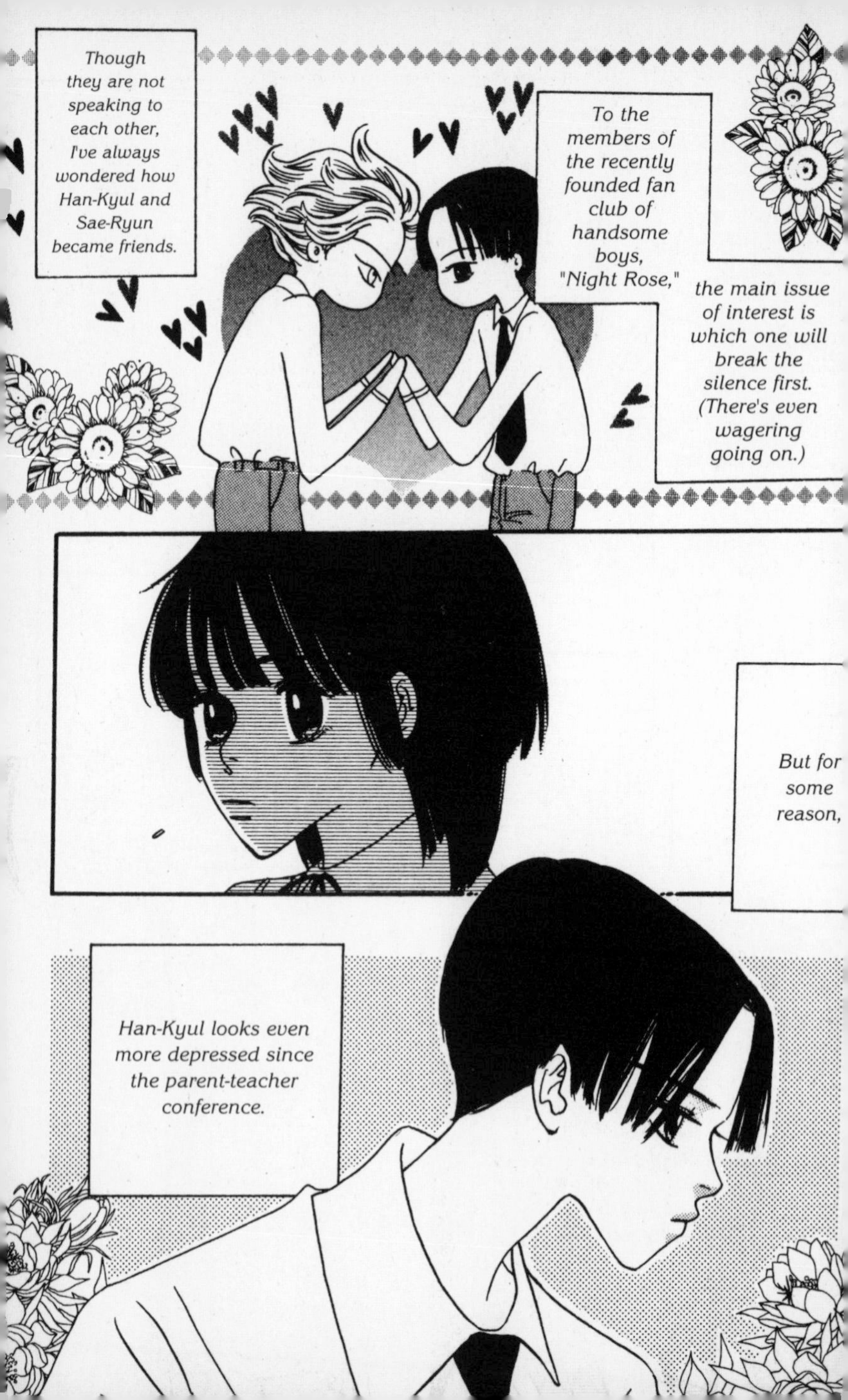

Though they are not speaking to each other, I've always wondered how Han-Kyul and Sae-Ryun became friends.
To the members of the recently founded fan club of handsome boys, "Night Rose,"
the main issue of interest is which one will break the silence first. (There's even wagering going on.)
But for some reason,
Han-Kyul looks even more depressed since the parent-teacher conference.

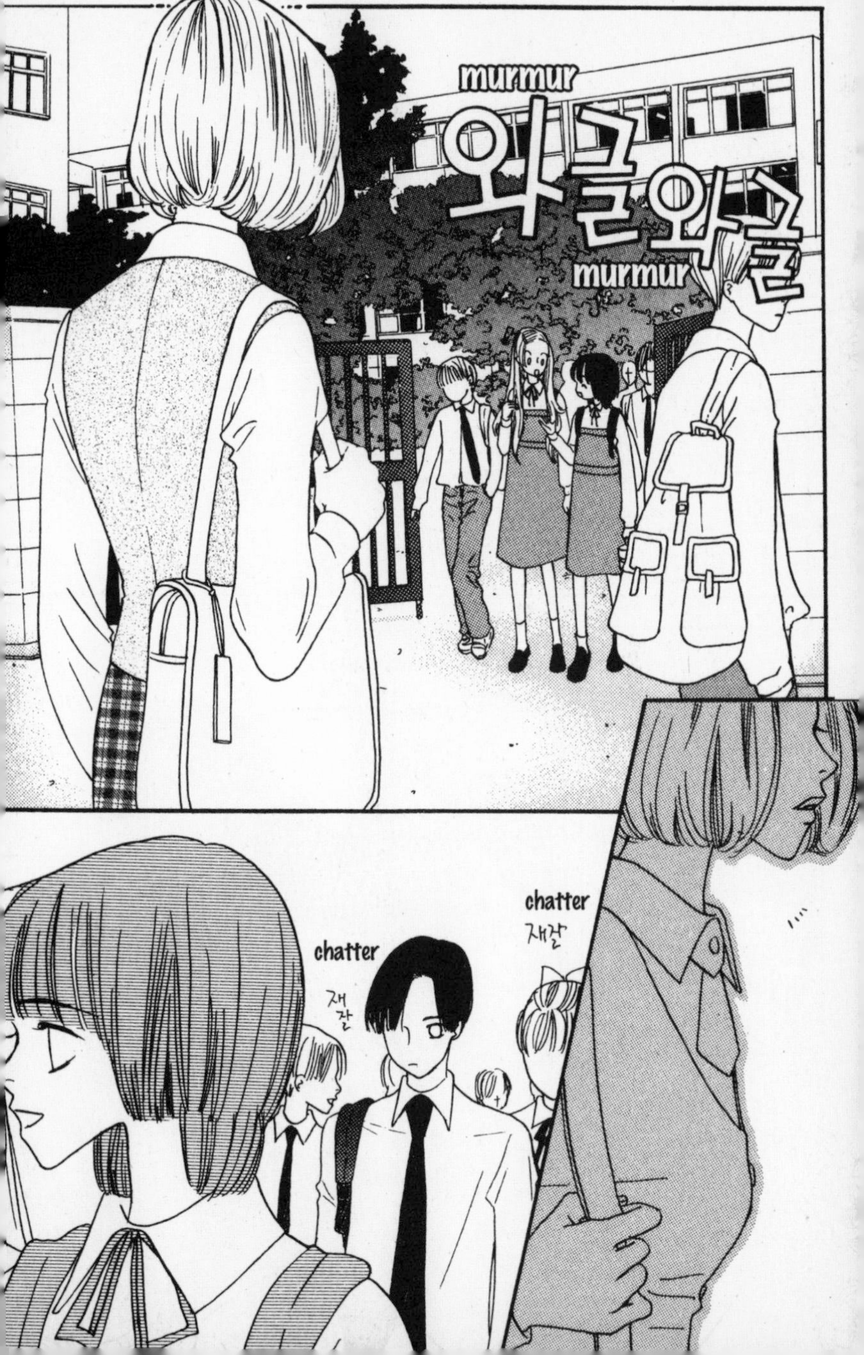

murmur
와글와글
murmur
chatter
재잘
chatter
재잘

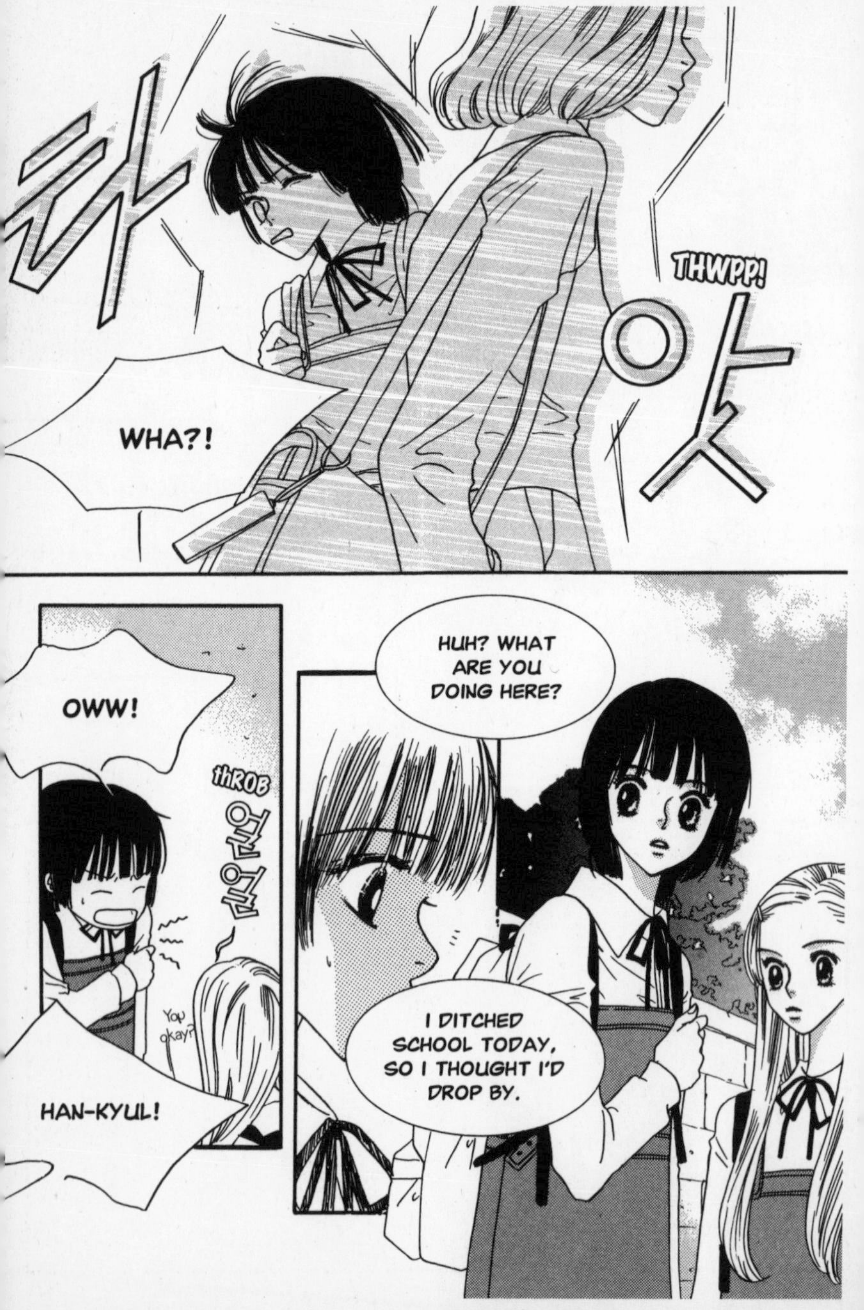
WHA?!
THWPP!
OWW!
thROB
You okay?
HAN-KYUL!
HUH? WHAT ARE YOU DOING HERE?
I DITCHED SCHOOL TODAY, SO I THOUGHT I'D DROP BY.

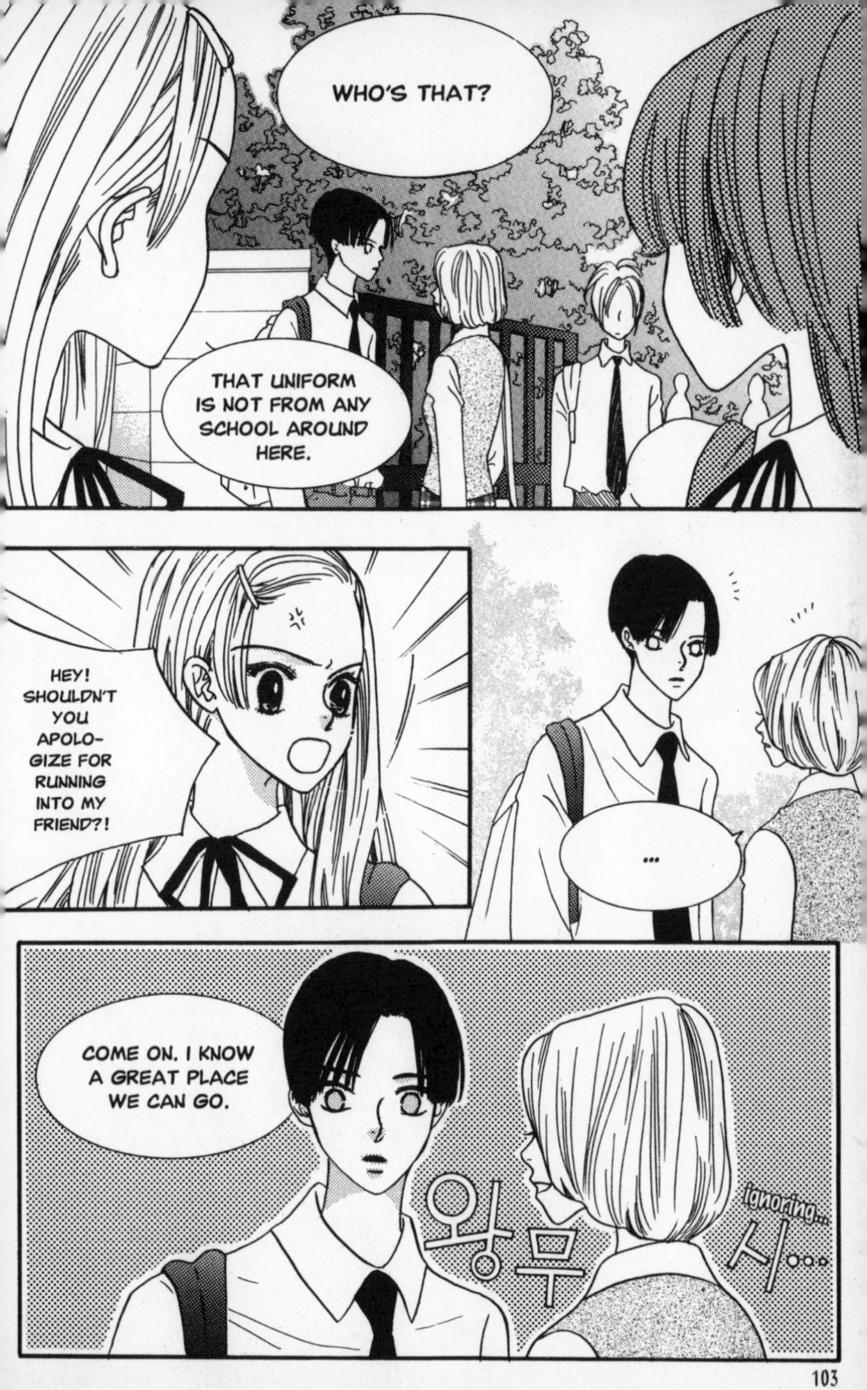
WHO'S THAT?
THAT UNIFORM IS NOT FROM ANY SCHOOL AROUND HERE.
HEY! SHOULDN'T YOU APOLO-GIZE FOR RUNNING INTO MY FRIEND?!
...
COME ON. I KNOW A GREAT PLACE WE CAN GO.
왕무시...
ignoring...

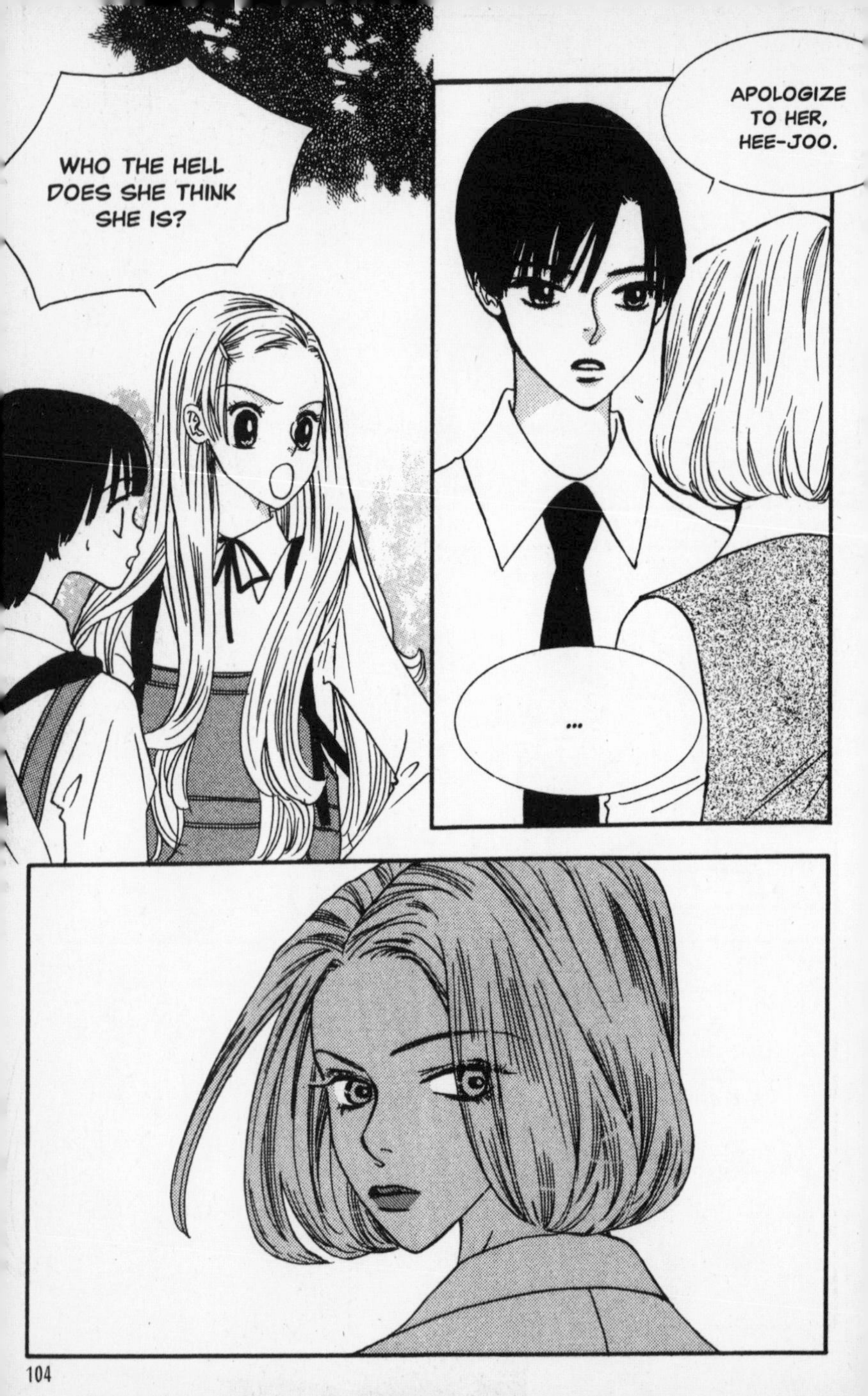
WHO THE HELL DOES SHE THINK SHE IS?
APOLOGIZE TO HER, HEE-JOO.
...

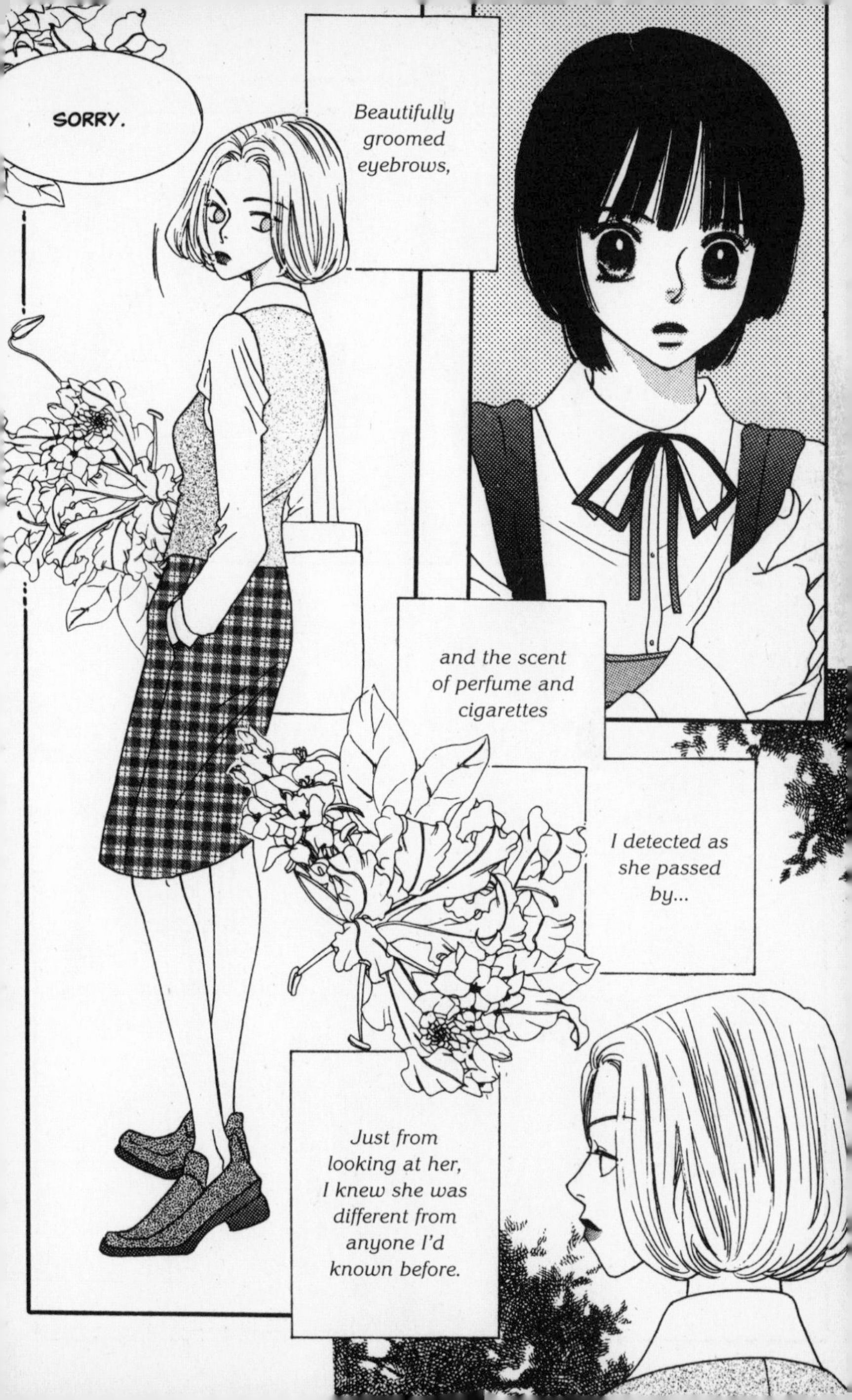

SORRY.
Beautifully groomed eyebrows,
and the scent of perfume and cigarettes
I detected as she passed by...
Just from looking at her, I knew she was different from anyone I'd known before.

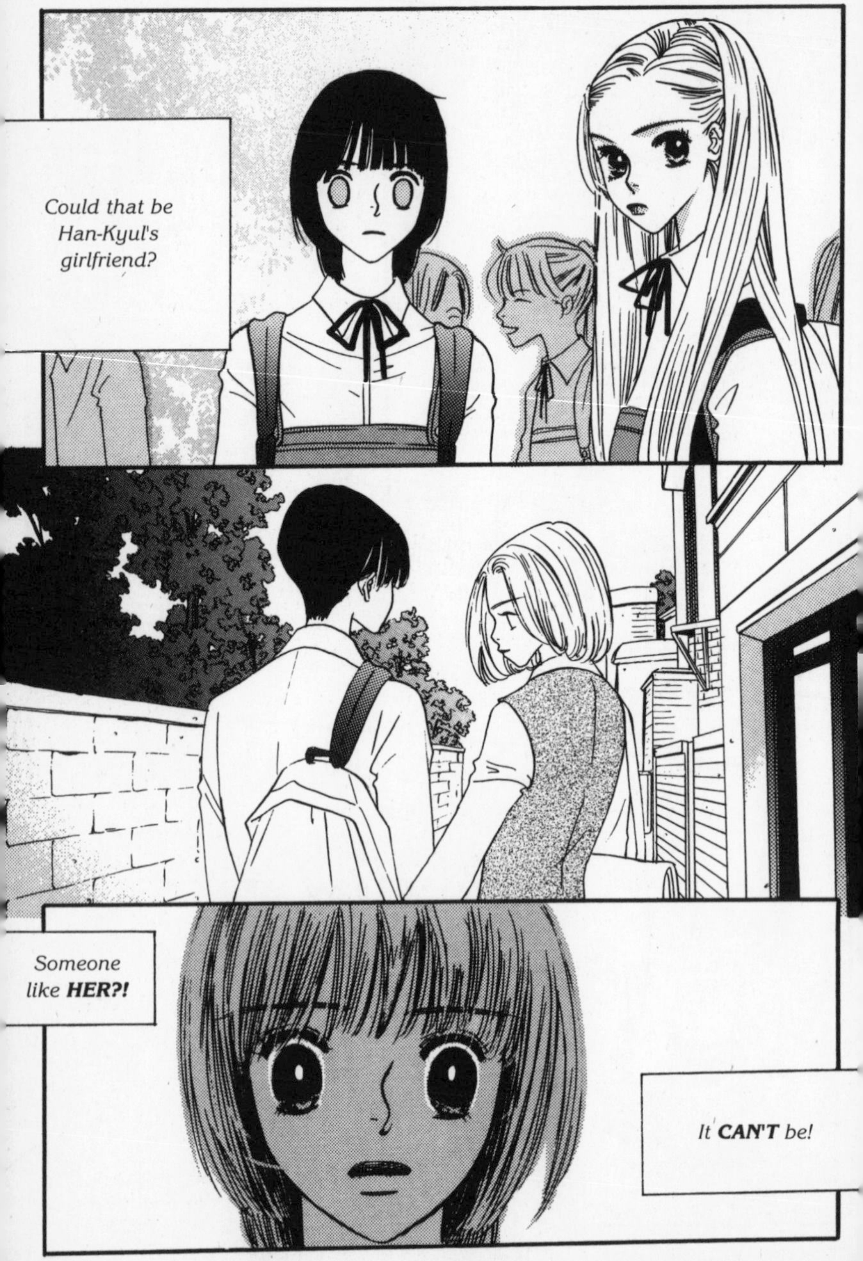
Could that be Han-Kyul's girlfriend?
Someone like **HER?!**
It **CAN'T** be!

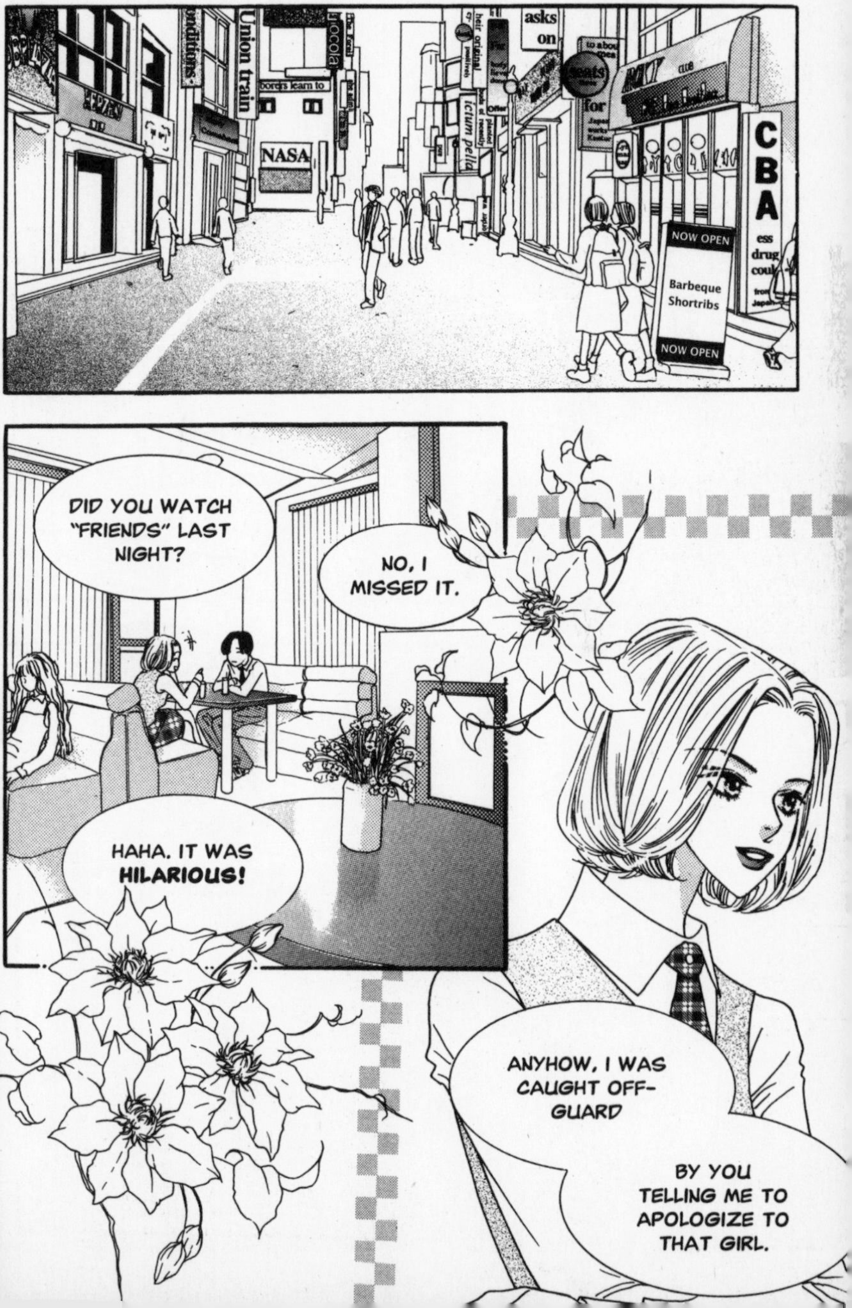
Union train
NASA
CBA
NOW OPEN
Barbeque Shortribs
NOW OPEN
DID YOU WATCH "FRIENDS" LAST NIGHT?
NO, I MISSED IT.
HAHA. IT WAS **HILARIOUS!**
ANYHOW, I WAS CAUGHT OFF-GUARD
BY YOU TELLING ME TO APOLOGIZE TO THAT GIRL.

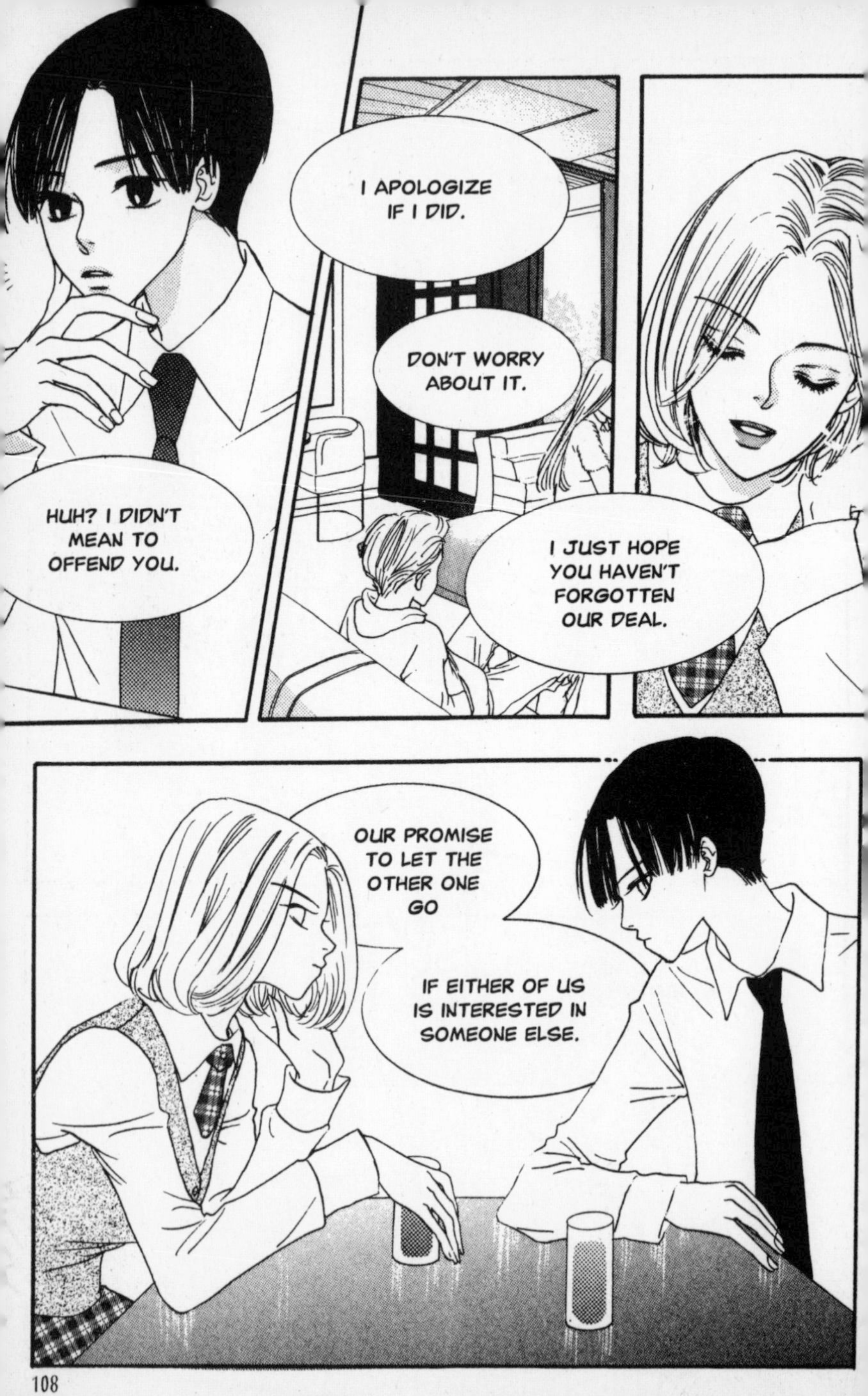
HUH? I DIDN'T MEAN TO OFFEND YOU.
I APOLOGIZE IF I DID.
DON'T WORRY ABOUT IT.
I JUST HOPE YOU HAVEN'T FORGOTTEN OUR DEAL.
OUR PROMISE TO LET THE OTHER ONE GO
IF EITHER OF US IS INTERESTED IN SOMEONE ELSE.

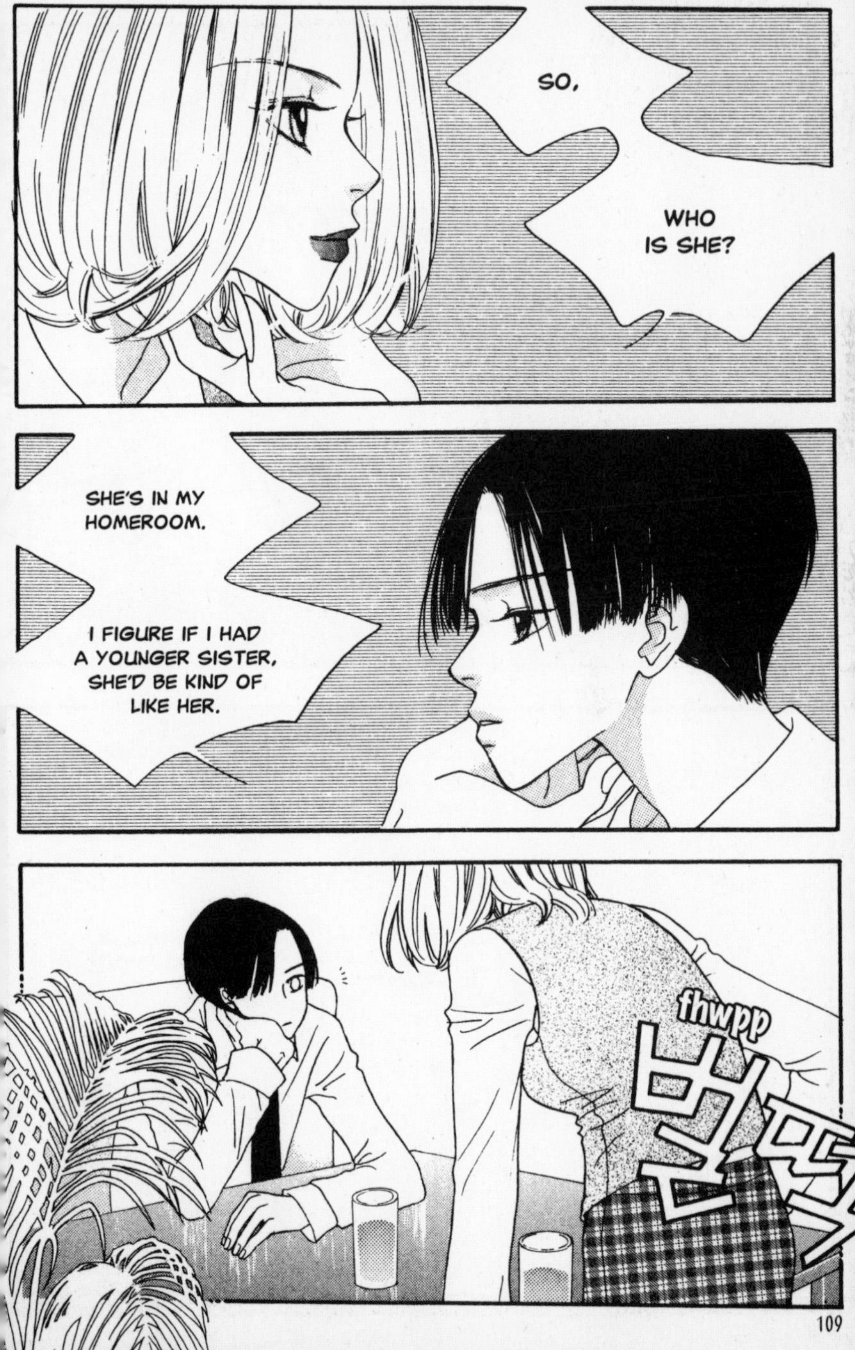
SO,
WHO IS SHE?
SHE'S IN MY HOMEROOM.
I FIGURE IF I HAD A YOUNGER SISTER, SHE'D BE KIND OF LIKE HER.
fhwpp

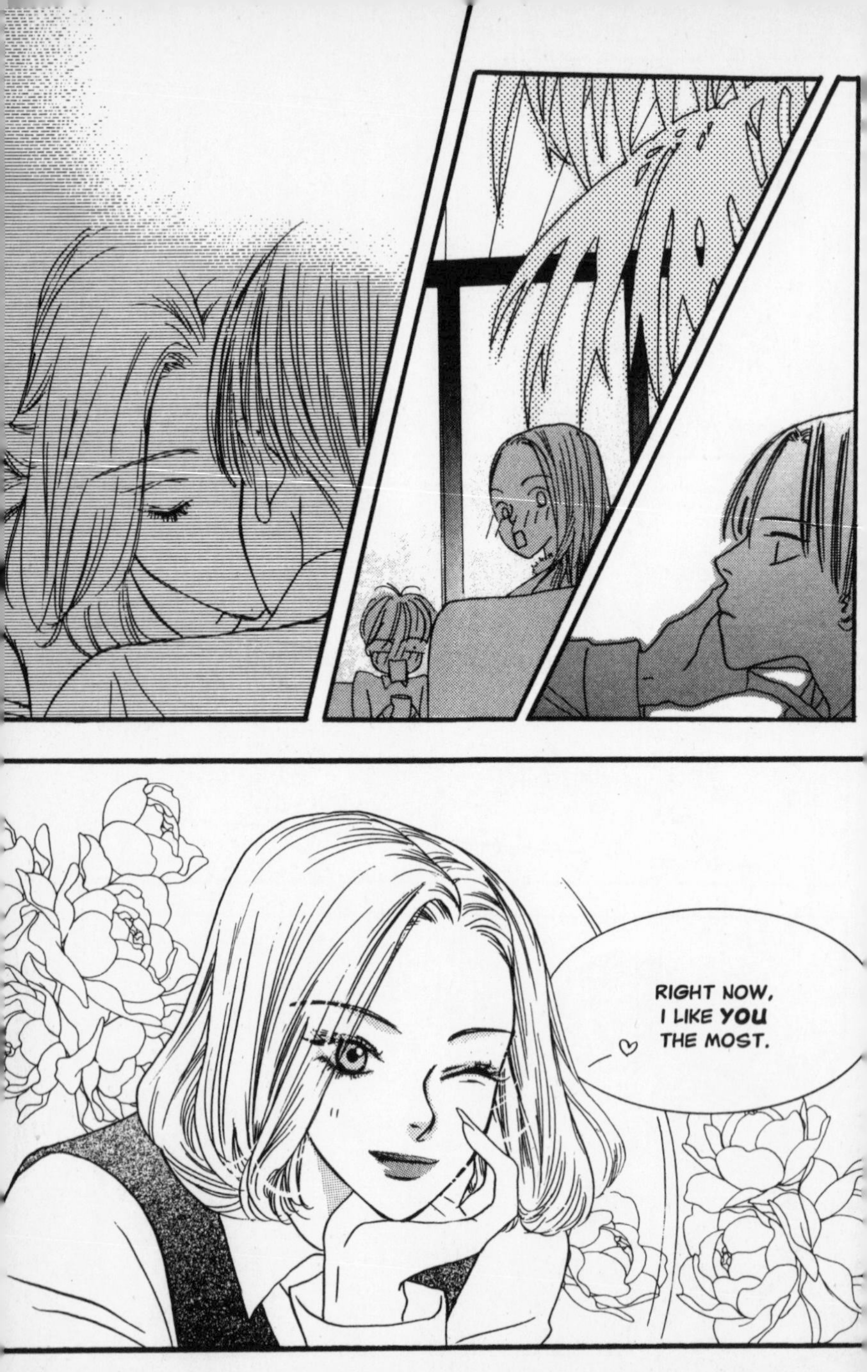
RIGHT NOW, I LIKE YOU THE MOST.

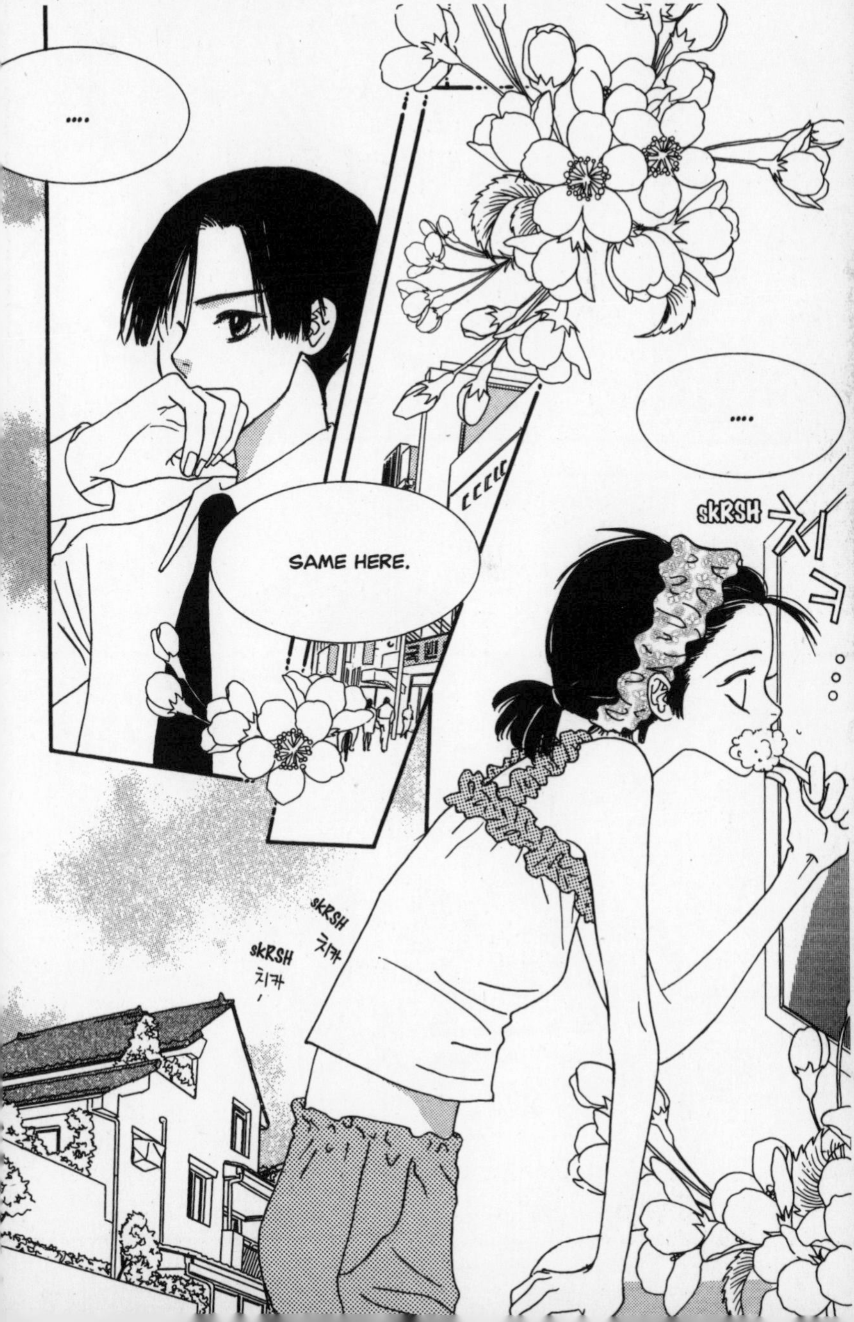
....
SAME HERE.
....
skRSH
skRSH
치카
skRSH
치카

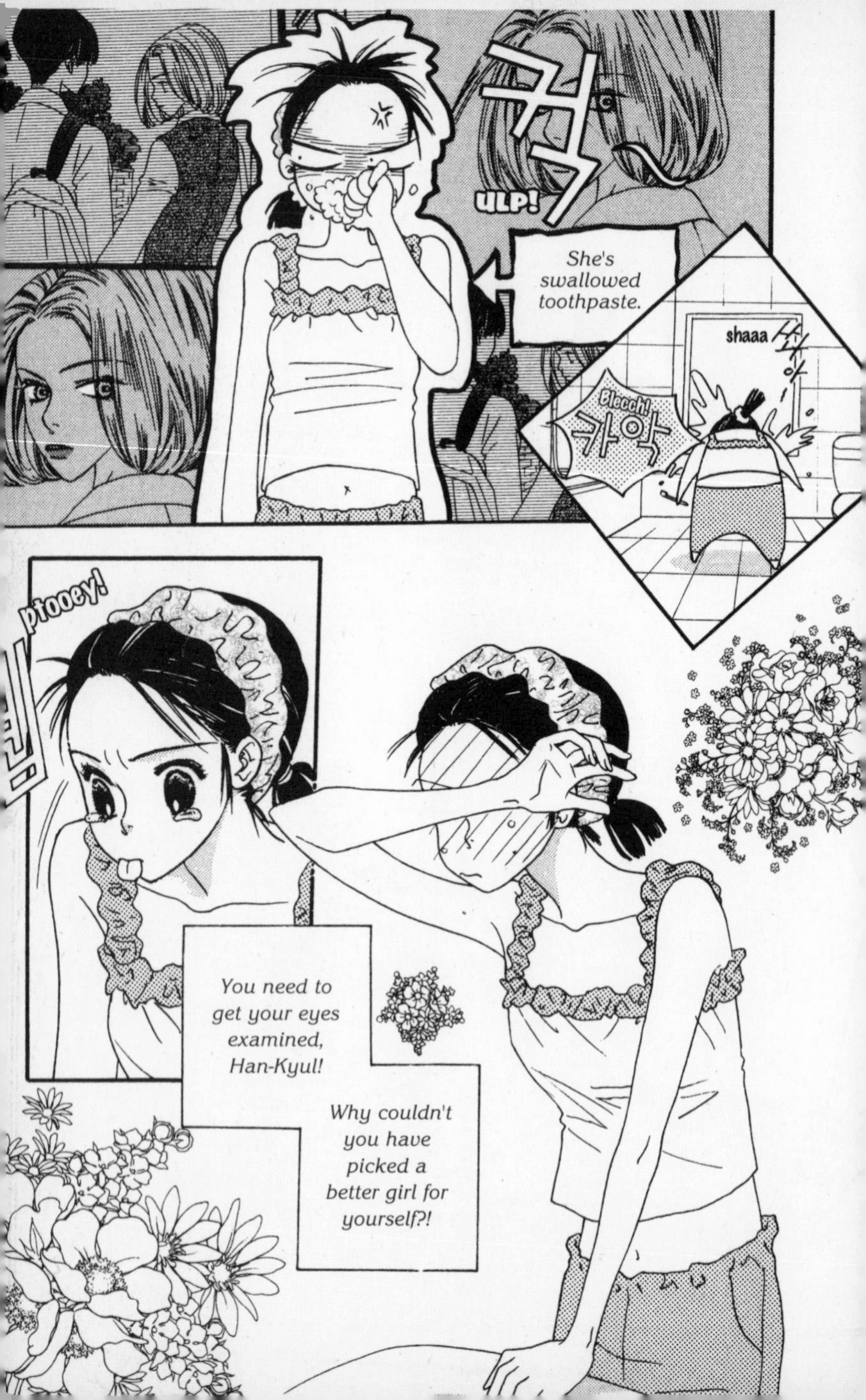
ULP!
She's swallowed toothpaste.
shaaa
Blecch!
ptooey!
You need to get your eyes examined, Han-Kyul!
Why couldn't you have picked a better girl for yourself?!

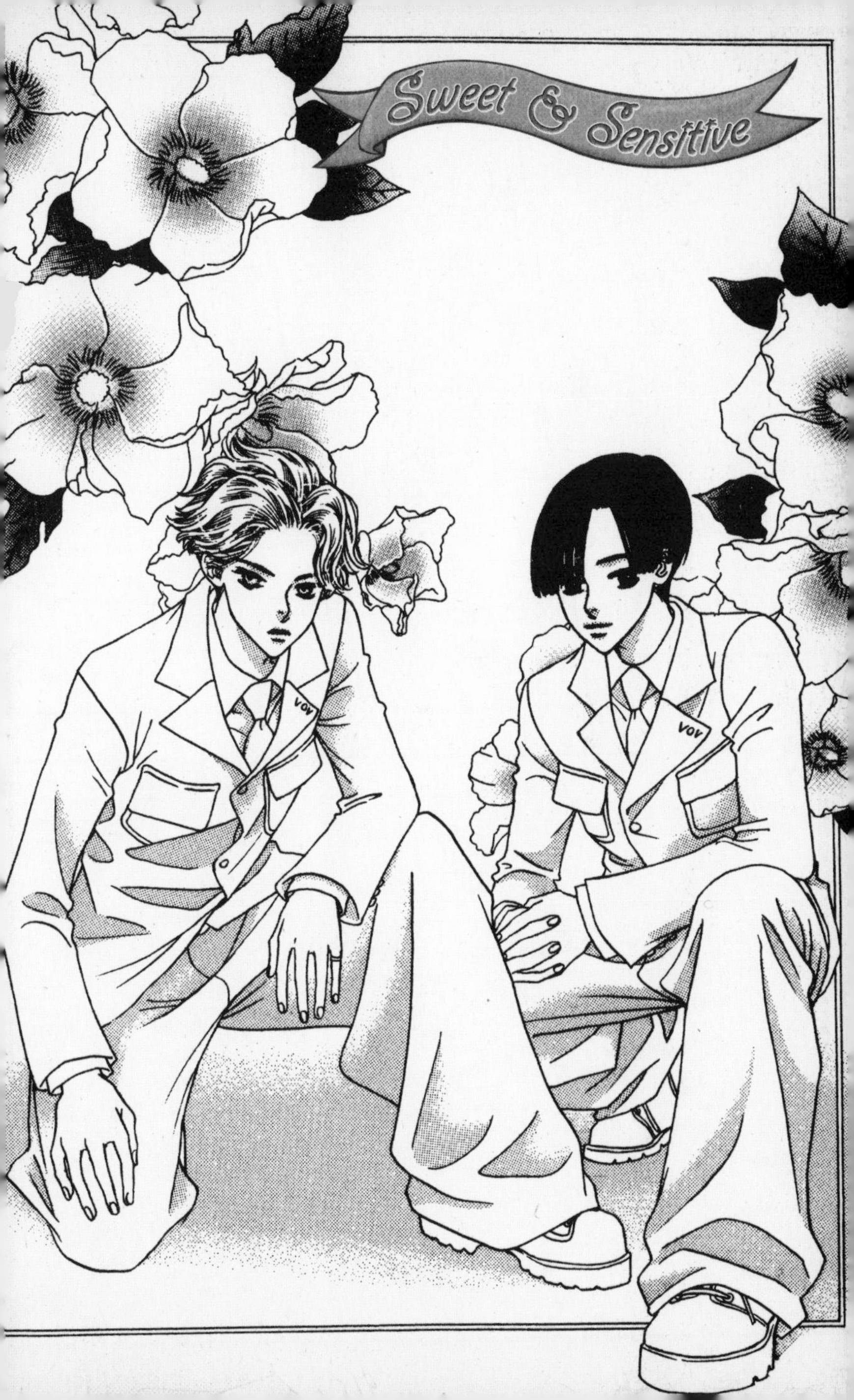
Sweet & Sensitive
VOV
VOV

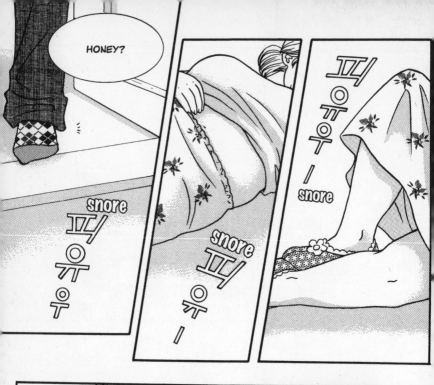

HONEY?

snore

snore

snore

snore

...

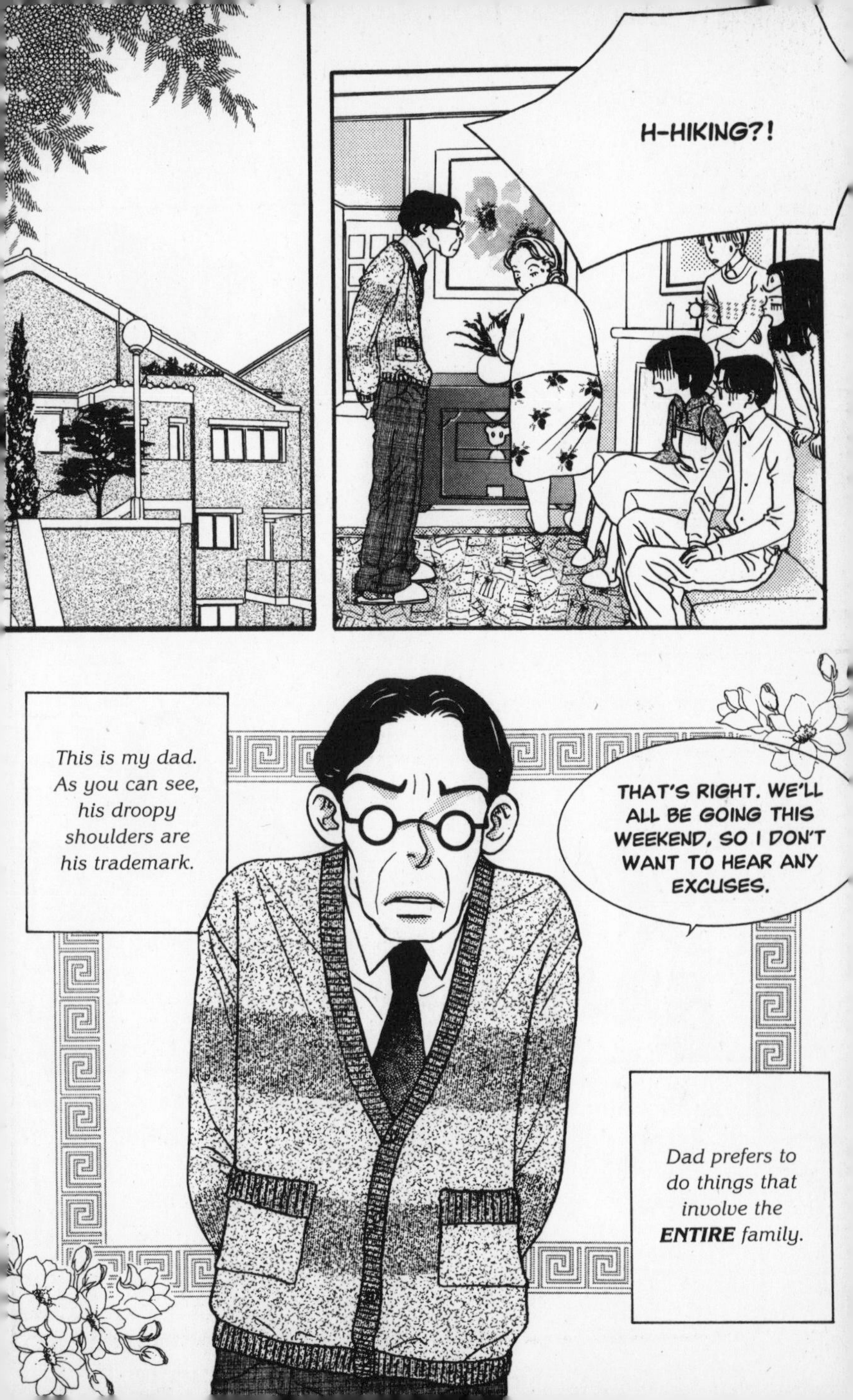
H-HIKING?!
This is my dad. As you can see, his droopy shoulders are his trademark.
THAT'S RIGHT. WE'LL ALL BE GOING THIS WEEKEND, SO I DON'T WANT TO HEAR ANY EXCUSES.
Dad prefers to do things that involve the ENTIRE family.

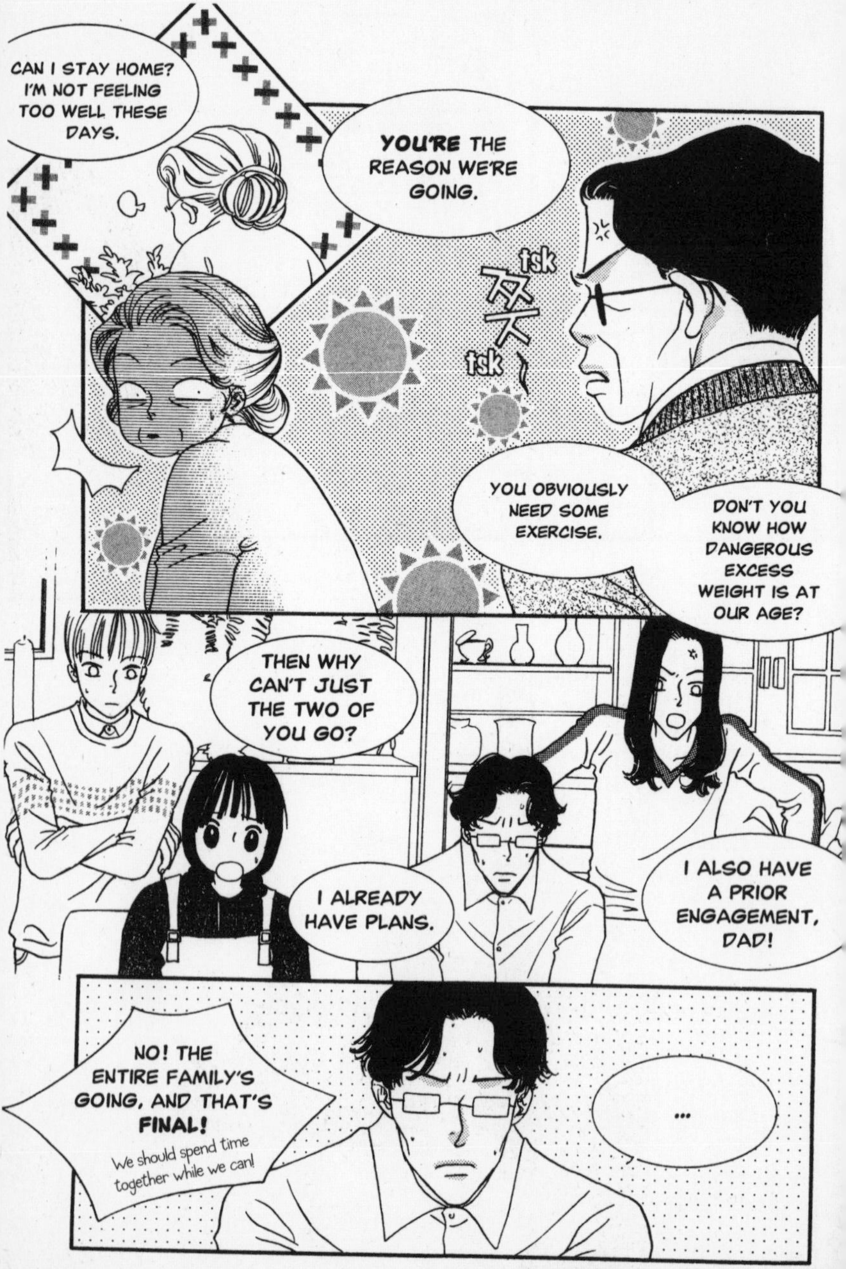
CAN I STAY HOME? I'M NOT FEELING TOO WELL THESE DAYS.
YOU'RE THE REASON WE'RE GOING.
tsk
tsk
YOU OBVIOUSLY NEED SOME EXERCISE.
DON'T YOU KNOW HOW DANGEROUS EXCESS WEIGHT IS AT OUR AGE?
THEN WHY CAN'T JUST THE TWO OF YOU GO?
I ALREADY HAVE PLANS.
I ALSO HAVE A PRIOR ENGAGEMENT, DAD!
NO! THE ENTIRE FAMILY'S GOING, AND THAT'S FINAL!
We should spend time together while we can!
...

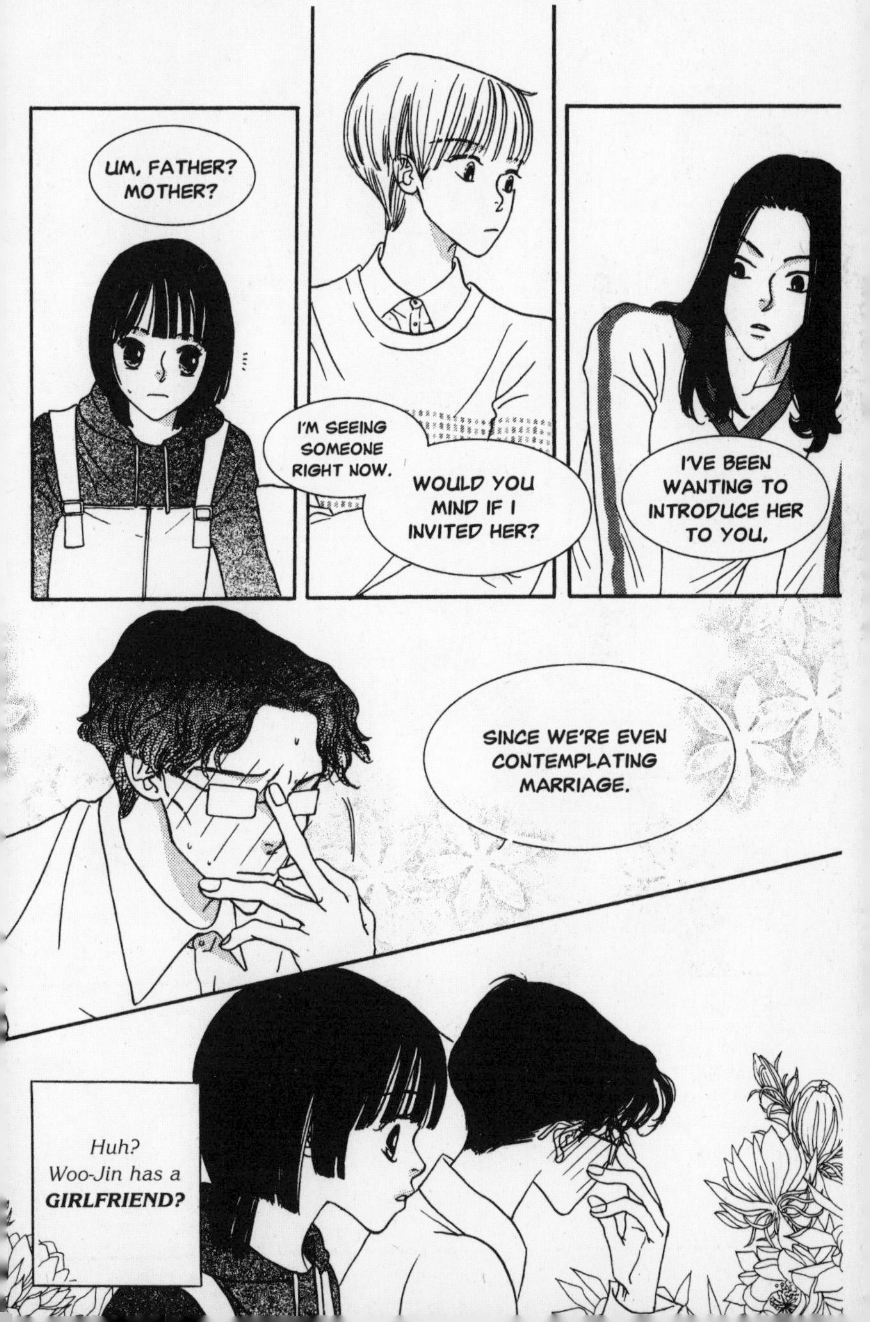
UM, FATHER? MOTHER?
I'M SEEING SOMEONE RIGHT NOW.
WOULD YOU MIND IF I INVITED HER?
I'VE BEEN WANTING TO INTRODUCE HER TO YOU,
SINCE WE'RE EVEN CONTEMPLATING MARRIAGE.
Huh? Woo-Jin has a **GIRLFRIEND?**

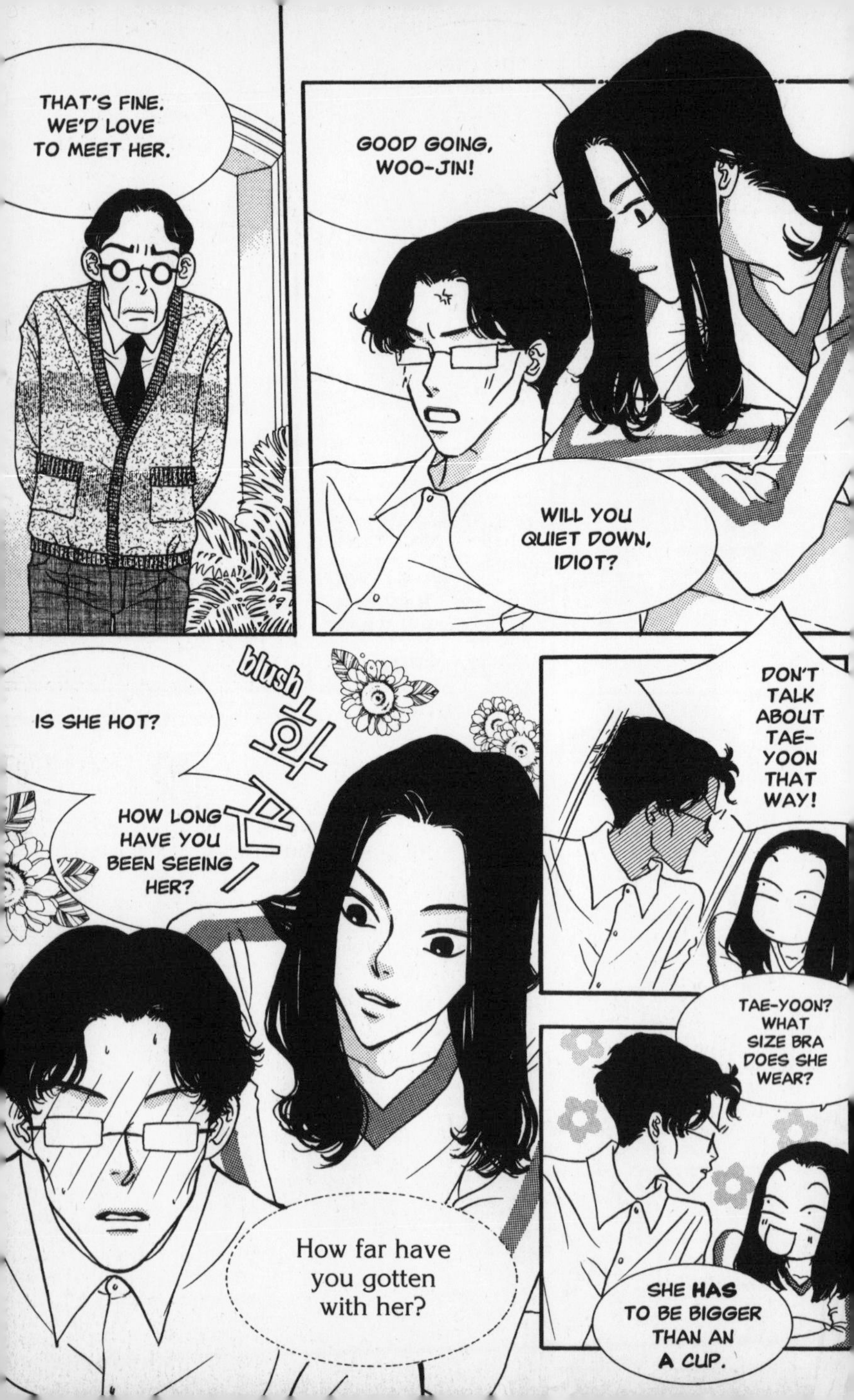
THAT'S FINE. WE'D LOVE TO MEET HER.
GOOD GOING, WOO-JIN!
WILL YOU QUIET DOWN, IDIOT?
IS SHE HOT?
blush
HOW LONG HAVE YOU BEEN SEEING HER?
How far have you gotten with her?
DON'T TALK ABOUT TAE-YOON THAT WAY!
TAE-YOON? WHAT SIZE BRA DOES SHE WEAR?
SHE **HAS** TO BE BIGGER THAN AN A CUP.

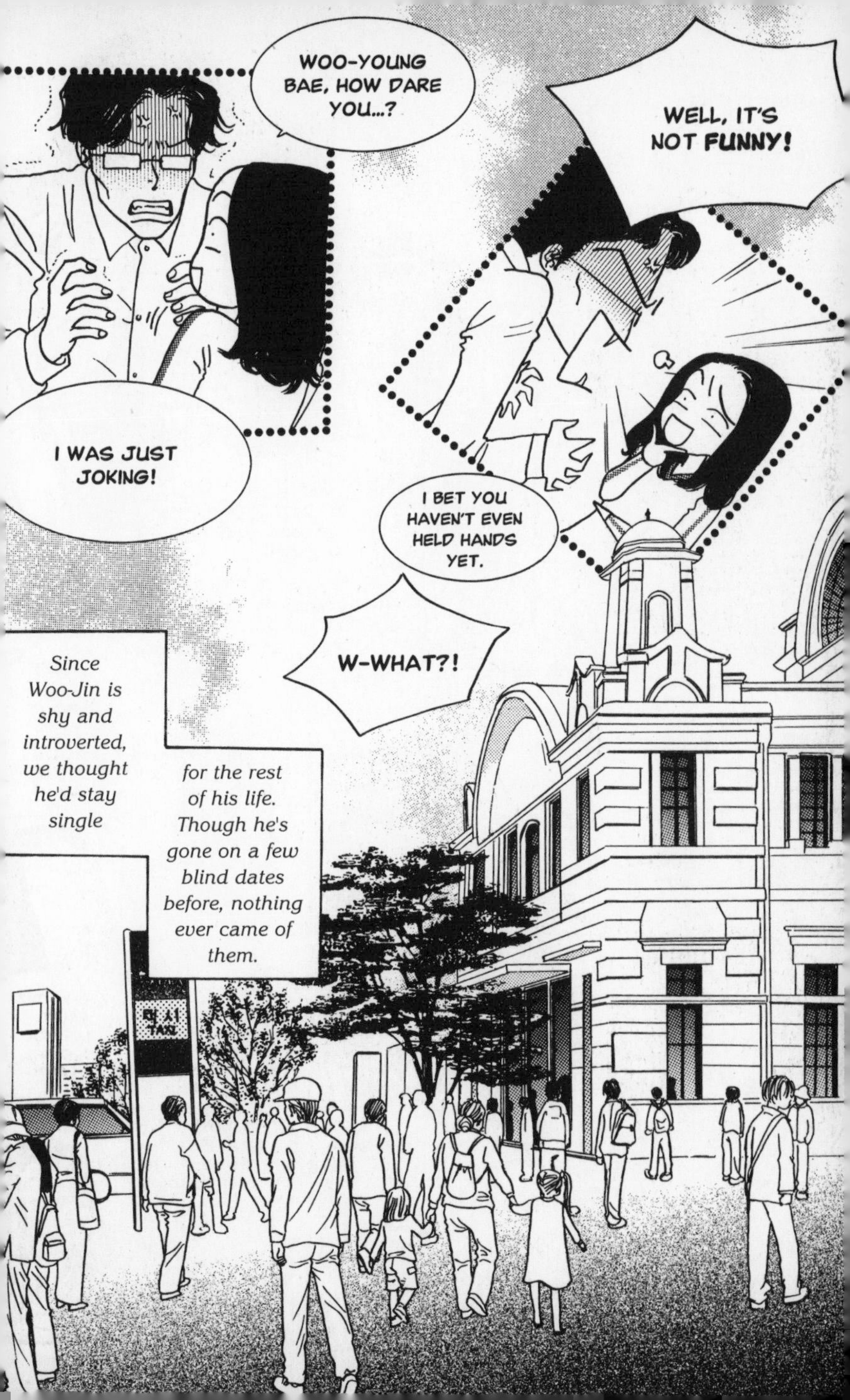

WOO-YOUNG BAE, HOW DARE YOU...?
I WAS JUST JOKING!
WELL, IT'S NOT FUNNY!
I BET YOU HAVEN'T EVEN HELD HANDS YET.
W-WHAT?!
Since Woo-Jin is shy and introverted, we thought he'd stay single
for the rest of his life. Though he's gone on a few blind dates before, nothing ever came of them.

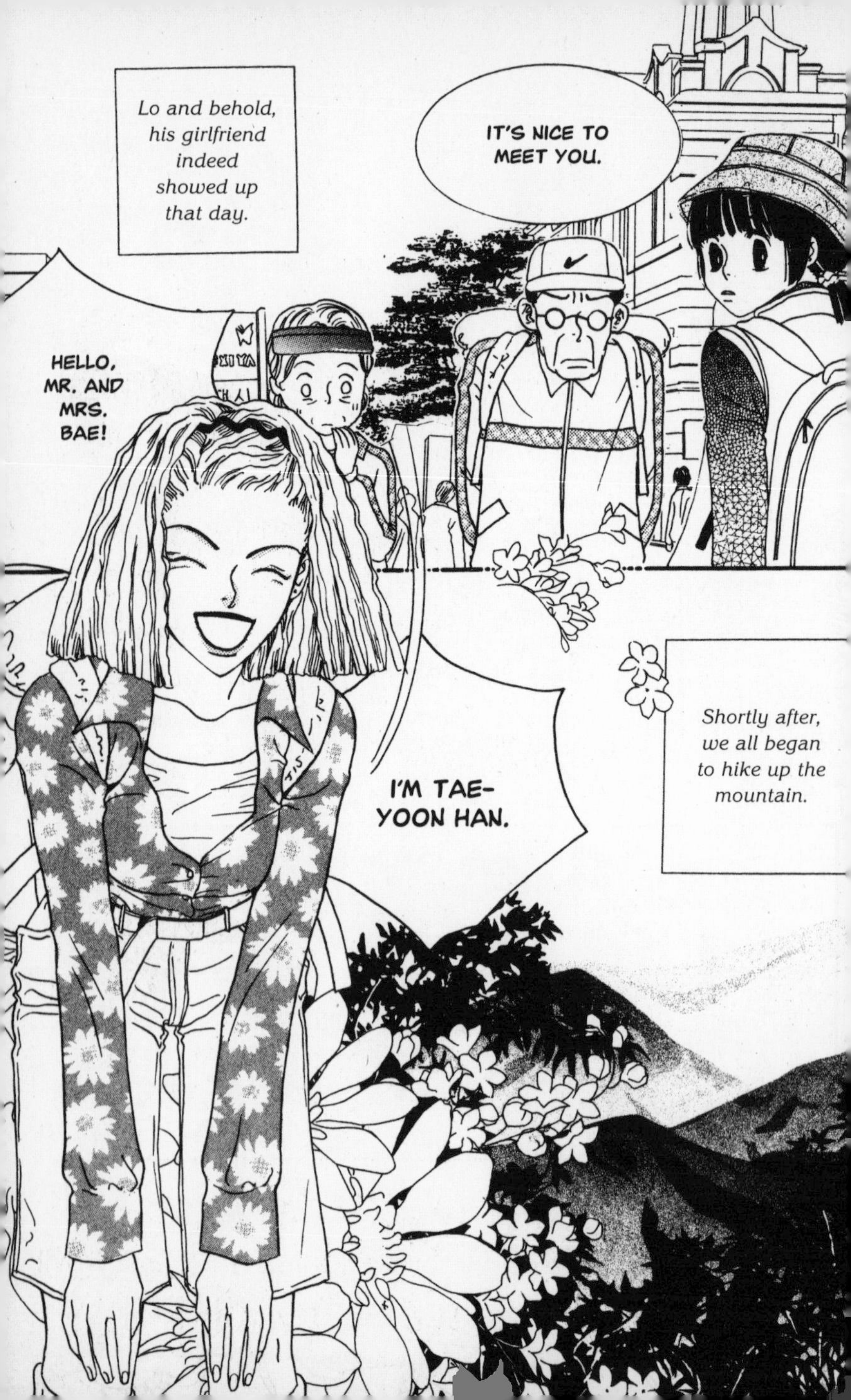
Lo and behold, his girlfriend indeed showed up that day.
IT'S NICE TO MEET YOU.
HELLO, MR. AND MRS. BAE!
I'M TAE-YOON HAN.
Shortly after, we all began to hike up the mountain.

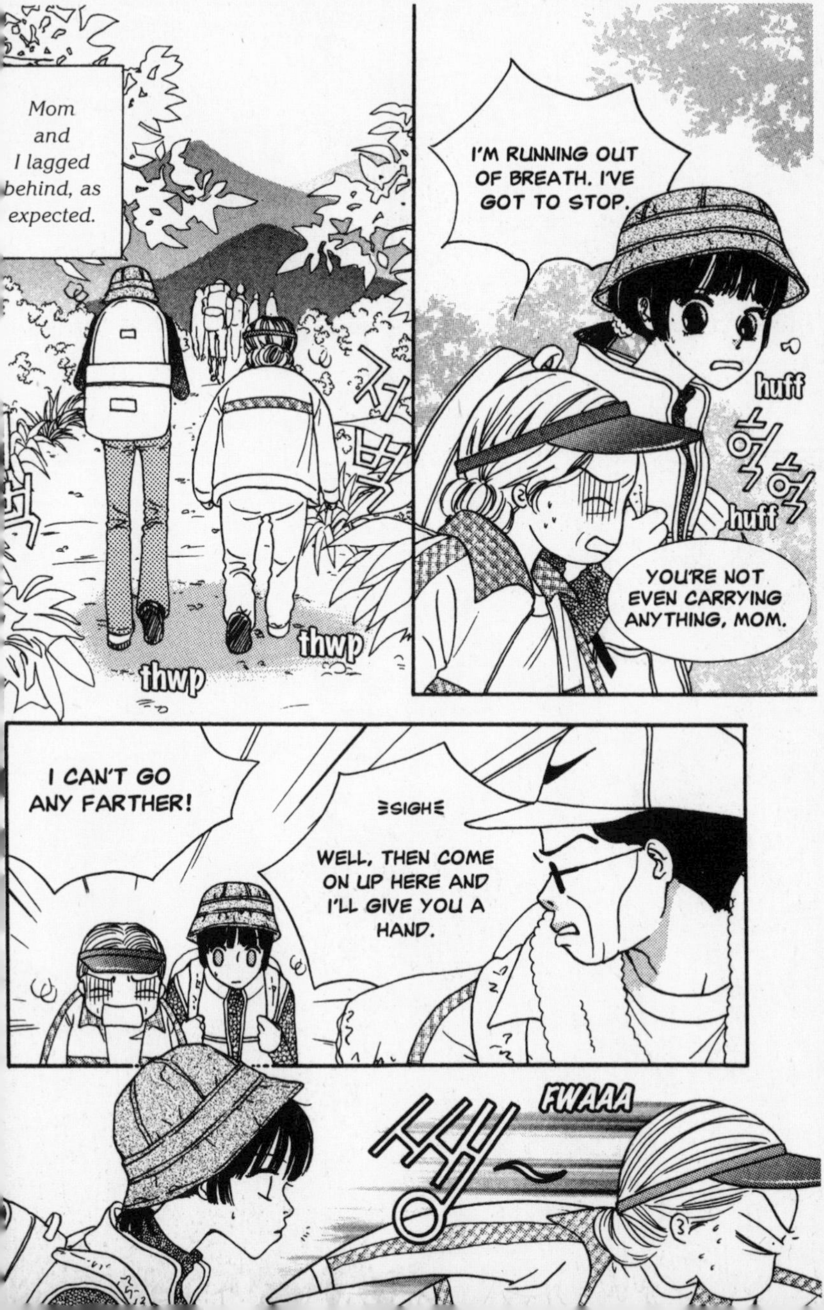
Mom and I lagged behind, as expected.
thwp
thwp
I'M RUNNING OUT OF BREATH. I'VE GOT TO STOP.
huff
헉헉
huff
YOU'RE NOT EVEN CARRYING ANYTHING, MOM.
I CAN'T GO ANY FARTHER!
SIGH
WELL, THEN COME ON UP HERE AND I'LL GIVE YOU A HAND.
FWAAA
쌩

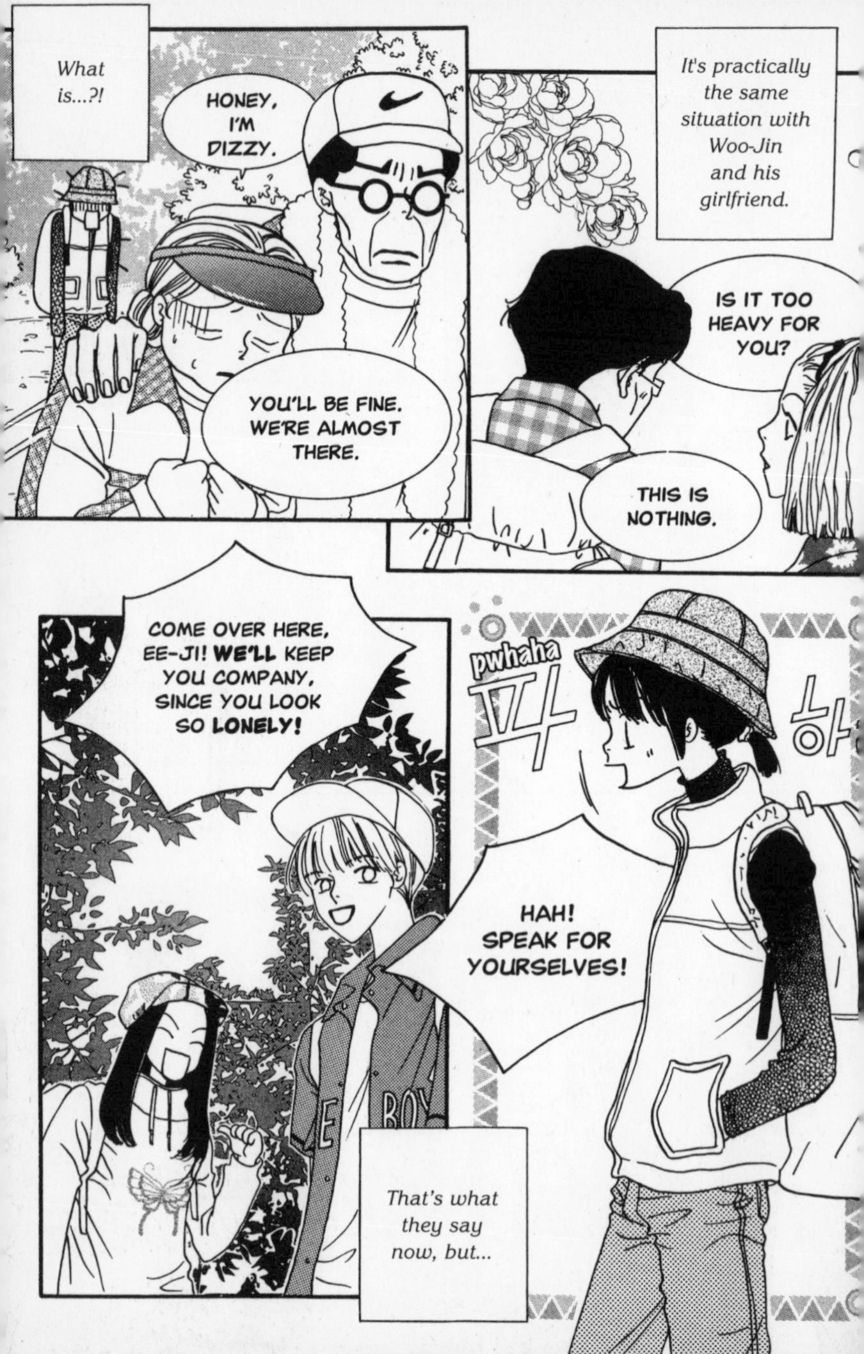

What is...?!
HONEY, I'M DIZZY.
YOU'LL BE FINE. WE'RE ALMOST THERE.
It's practically the same situation with Woo-Jin and his girlfriend.
IS IT TOO HEAVY FOR YOU?
THIS IS NOTHING.
COME OVER HERE, EE-JI! WE'LL KEEP YOU COMPANY, SINCE YOU LOOK SO LONELY!
pwhaha
파하
HAH! SPEAK FOR YOURSELVES!
That's what they say now, but...

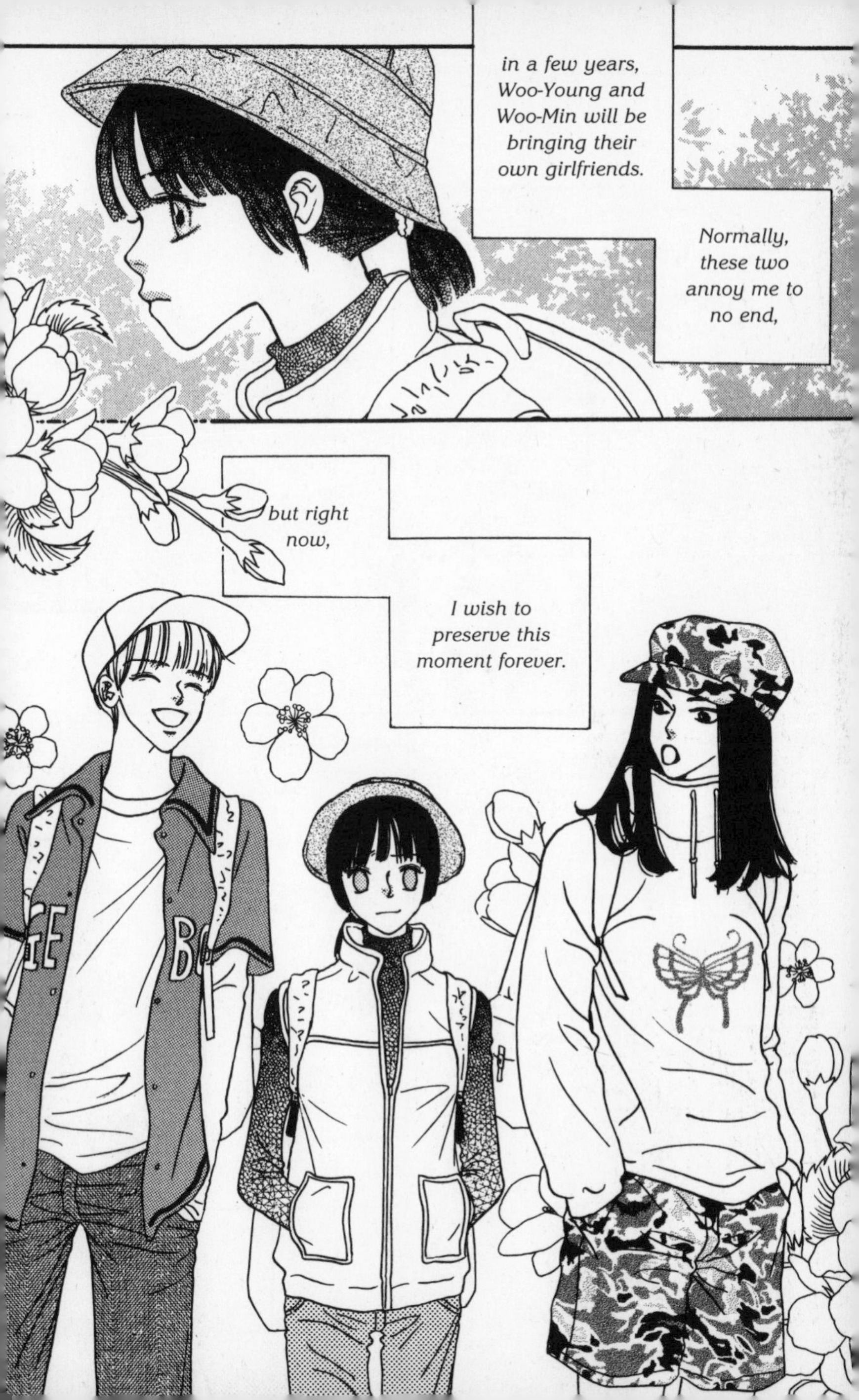
in a few years, Woo-Young and Woo-Min will be bringing their own girlfriends.
Normally, these two annoy me to no end,
but right now,
I wish to preserve this moment forever.

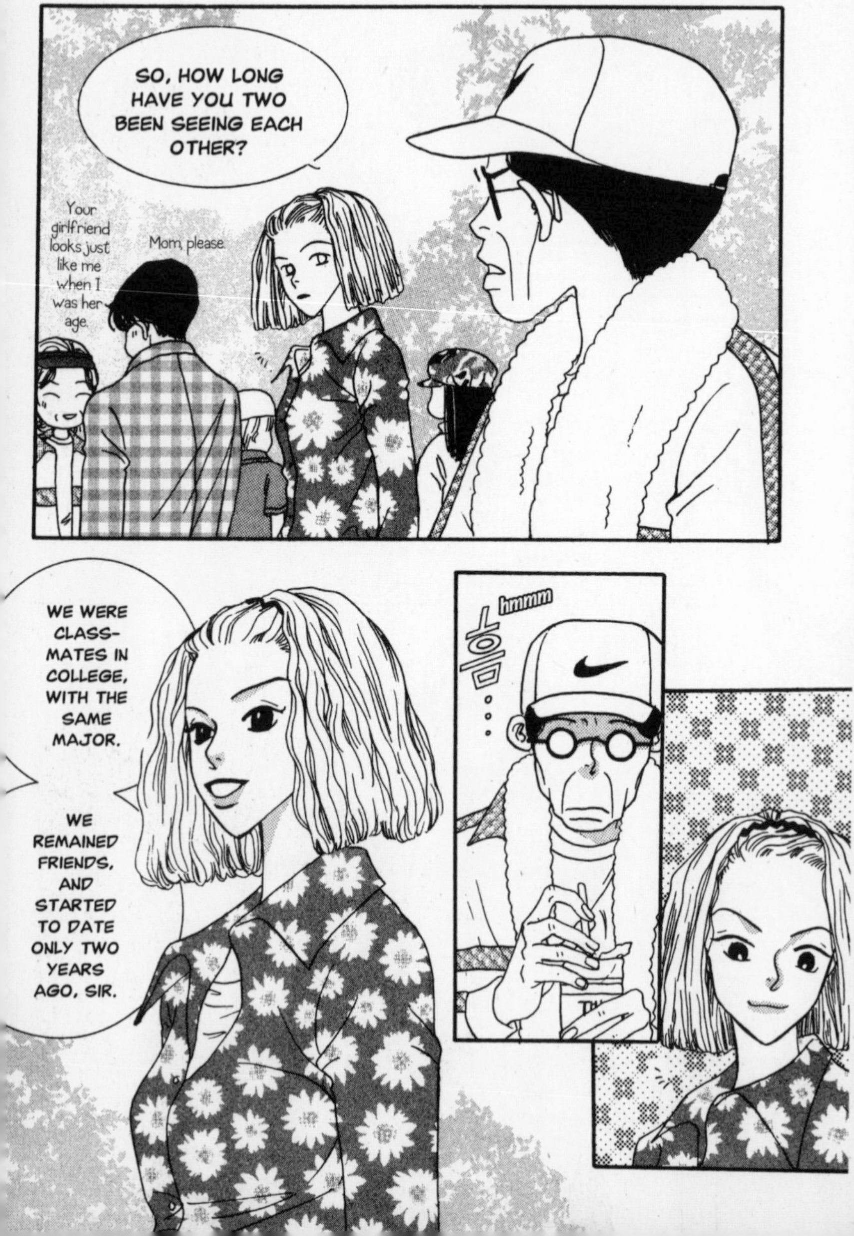
SO, HOW LONG HAVE YOU TWO BEEN SEEING EACH OTHER?
Your girlfriend looks just like me when I was her age.
Mom, please.
WE WERE CLASS-MATES IN COLLEGE, WITH THE SAME MAJOR.
WE REMAINED FRIENDS, AND STARTED TO DATE ONLY TWO YEARS AGO, SIR.
hmmm
흠...

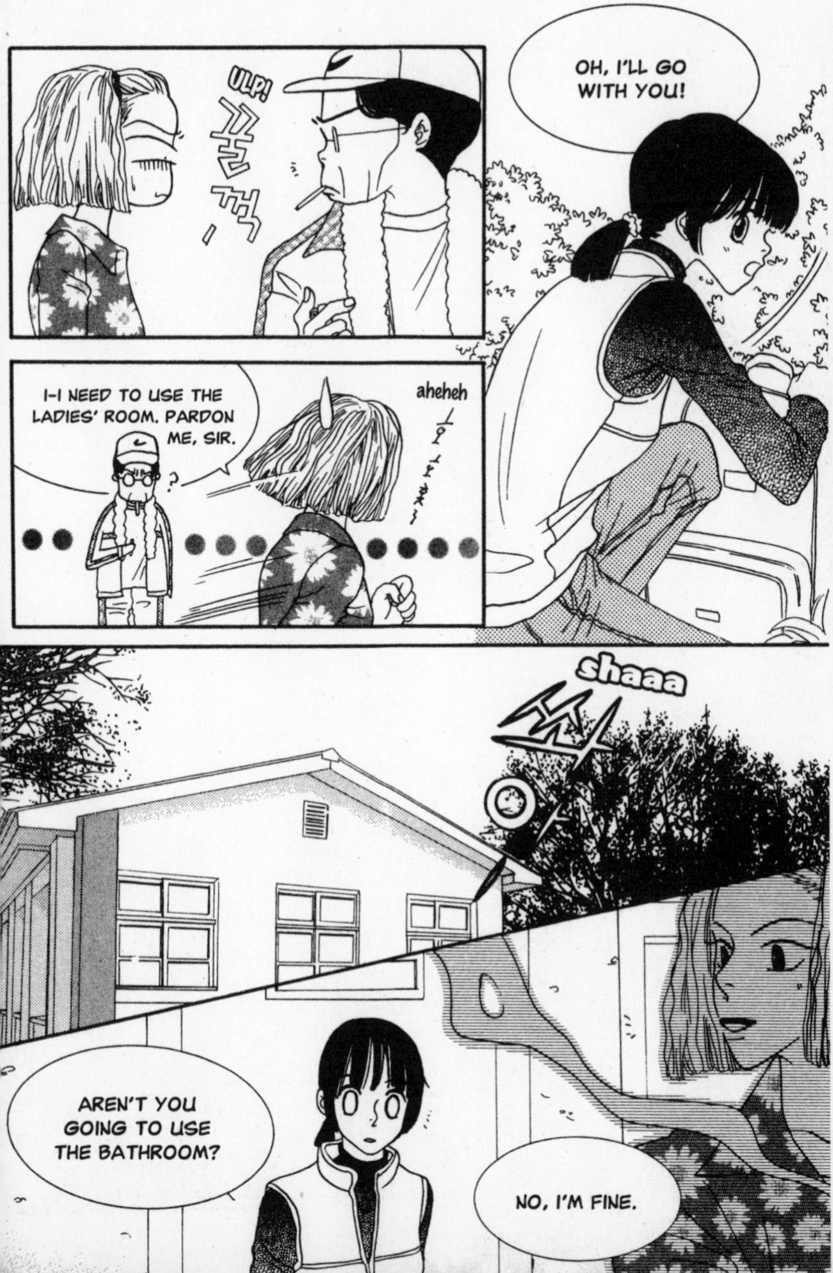
ULP!
꿀꺽
I-I NEED TO USE THE LADIES' ROOM. PARDON ME, SIR.
?
aheheh
OH, I'LL GO WITH YOU!
shaaa
AREN'T YOU GOING TO USE THE BATHROOM?
NO, I'M FINE.

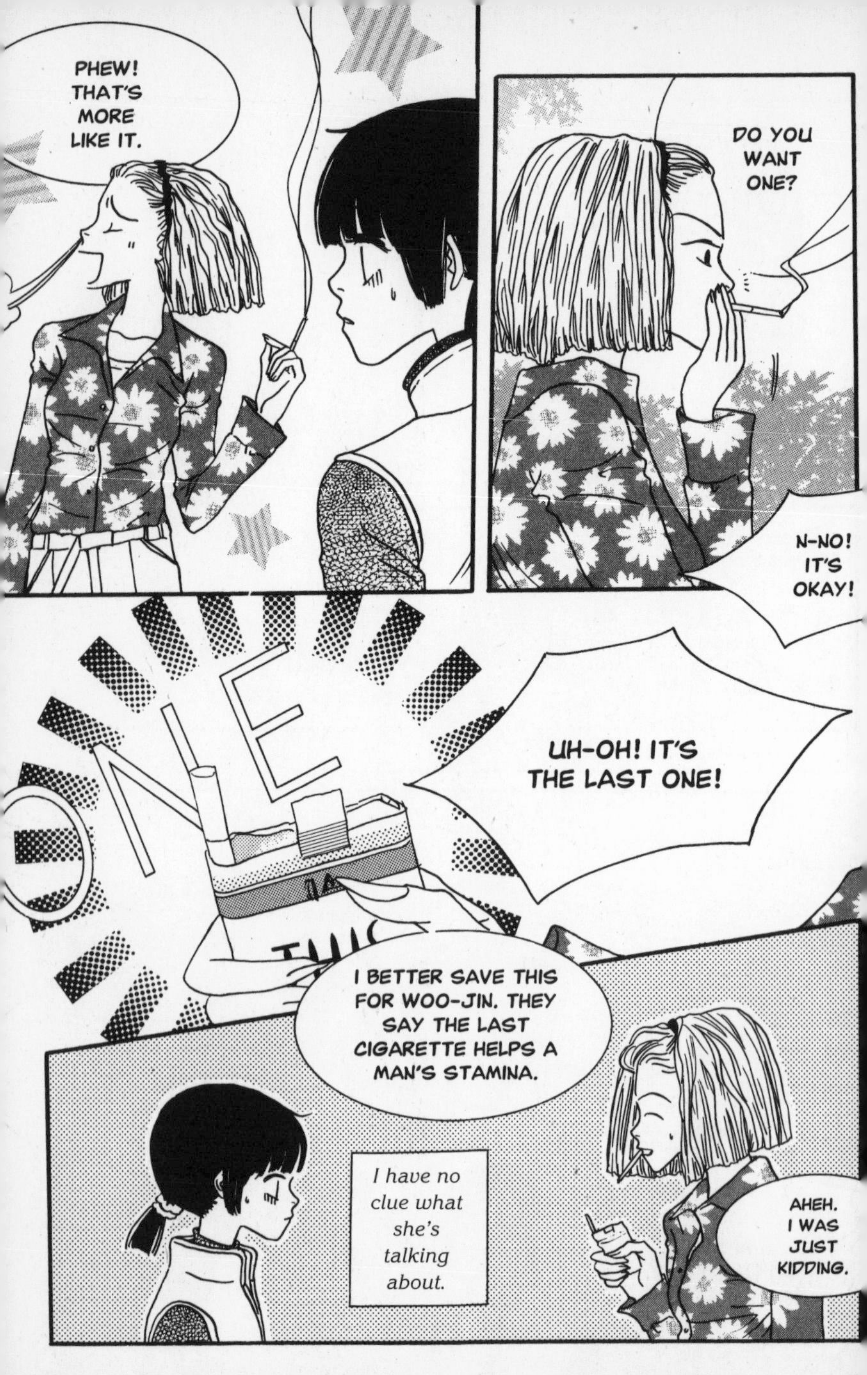
PHEW! THAT'S MORE LIKE IT.
DO YOU WANT ONE?
N-NO! IT'S OKAY!
UH-OH! IT'S THE LAST ONE!
I BETTER SAVE THIS FOR WOO-JIN. THEY SAY THE LAST CIGARETTE HELPS A MAN'S STAMINA.
I have no clue what she's talking about.
AHEH. I WAS JUST KIDDING.

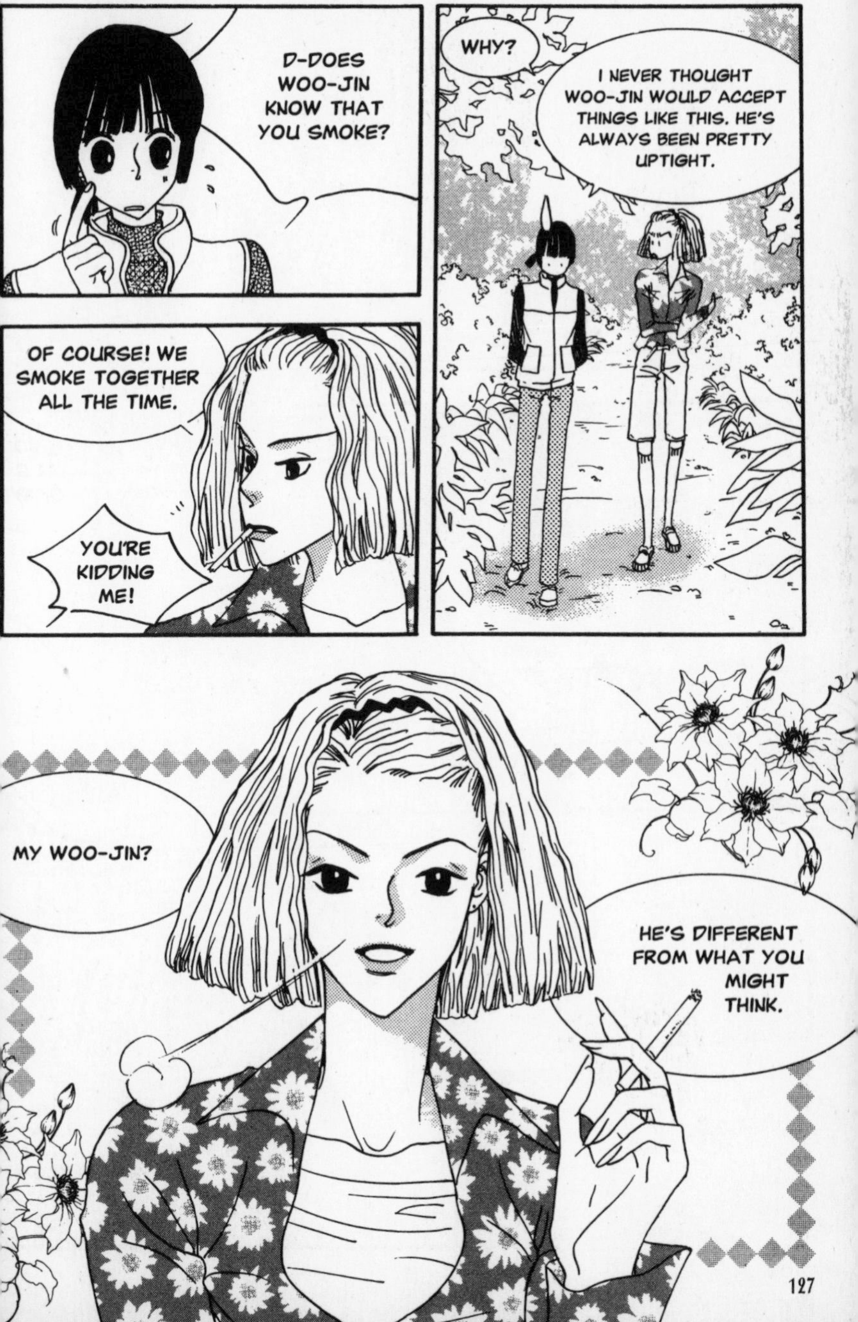
D-DOES WOO-JIN KNOW THAT YOU SMOKE?
WHY?
I NEVER THOUGHT WOO-JIN WOULD ACCEPT THINGS LIKE THIS. HE'S ALWAYS BEEN PRETTY UPTIGHT.
OF COURSE! WE SMOKE TOGETHER ALL THE TIME.
YOU'RE KIDDING ME!
MY WOO-JIN?
HE'S DIFFERENT FROM WHAT YOU MIGHT THINK.

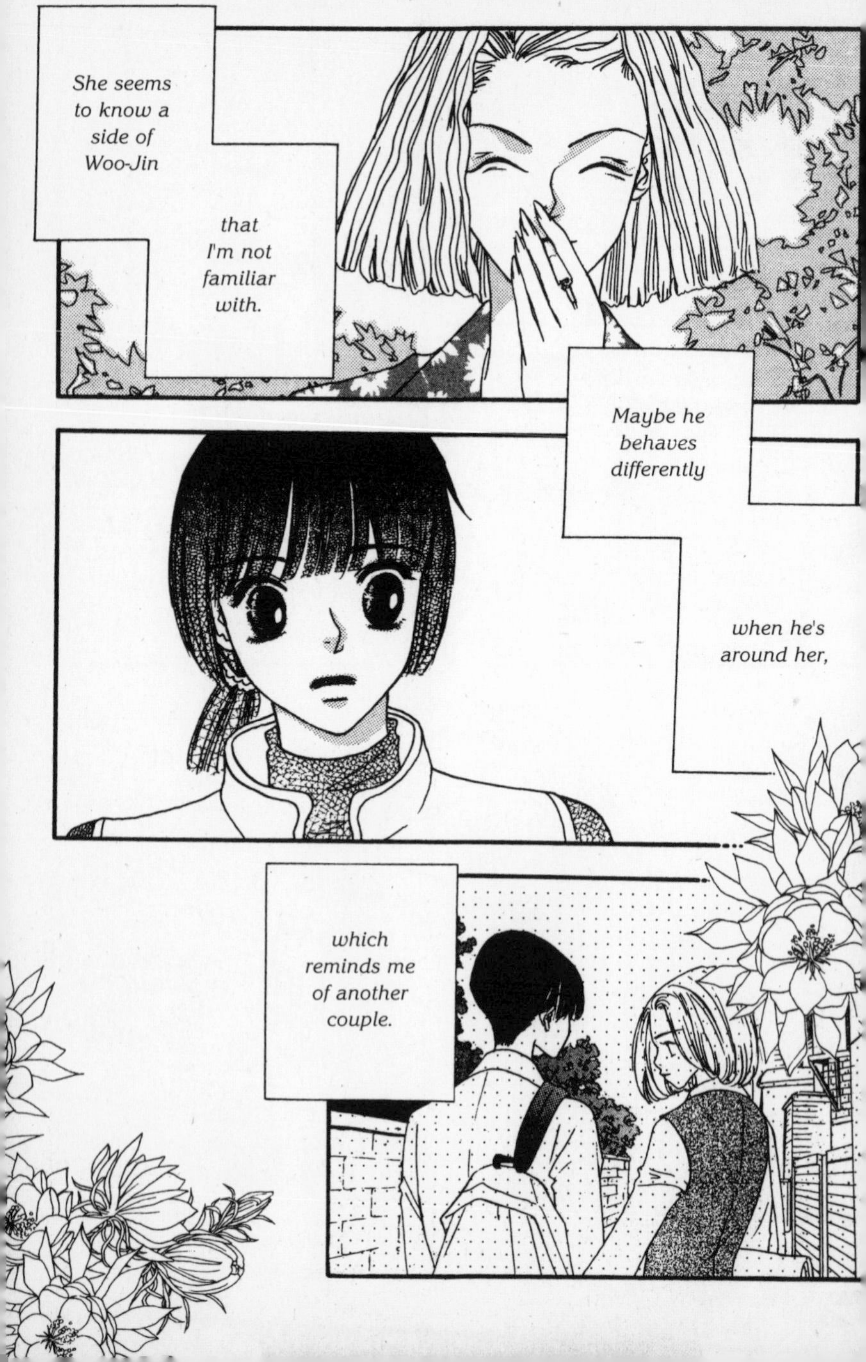
She seems to know a side of Woo-Jin
that I'm not familiar with.
Maybe he behaves differently
when he's around her,
which reminds me of another couple.

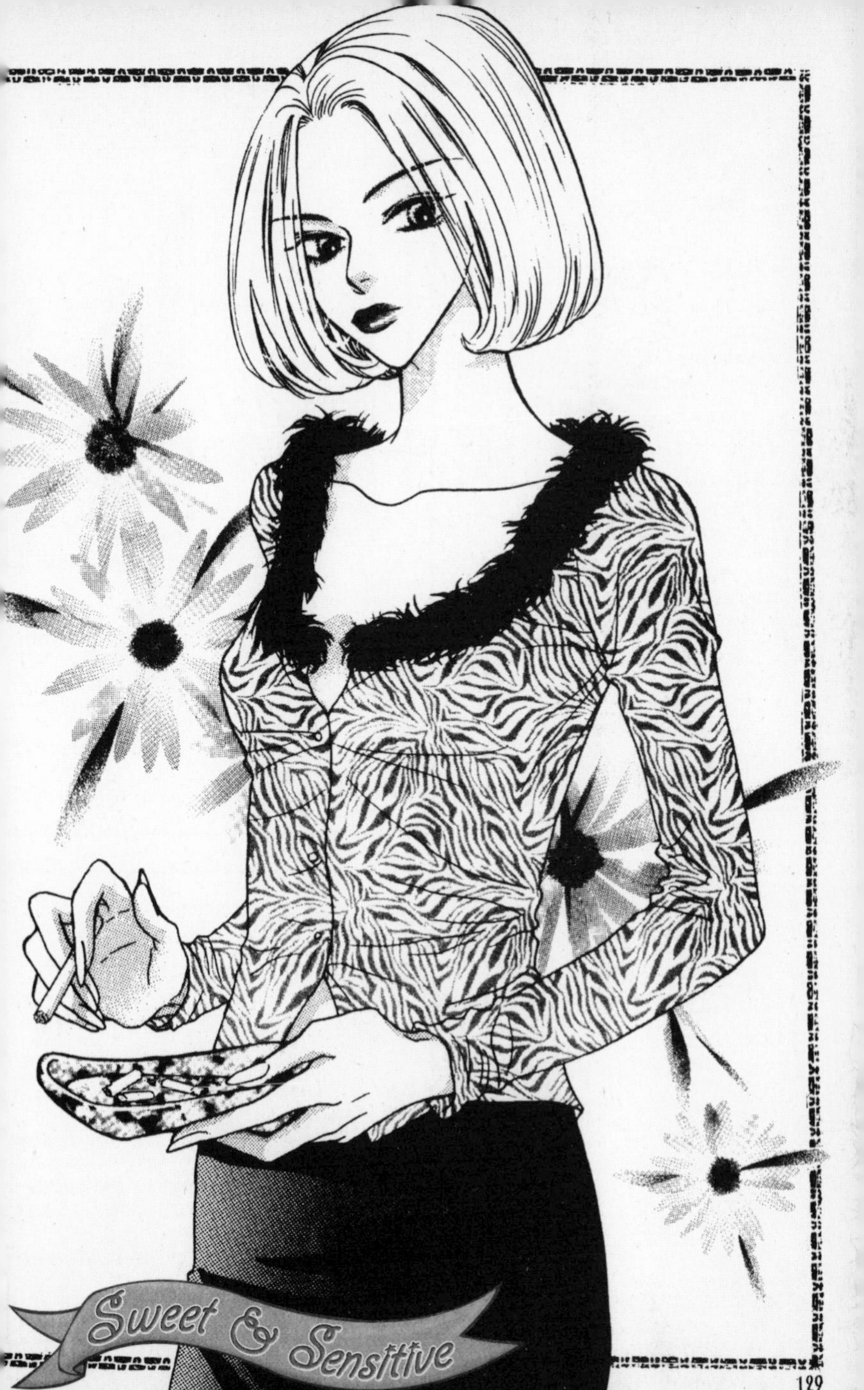
Sweet & Sensitive

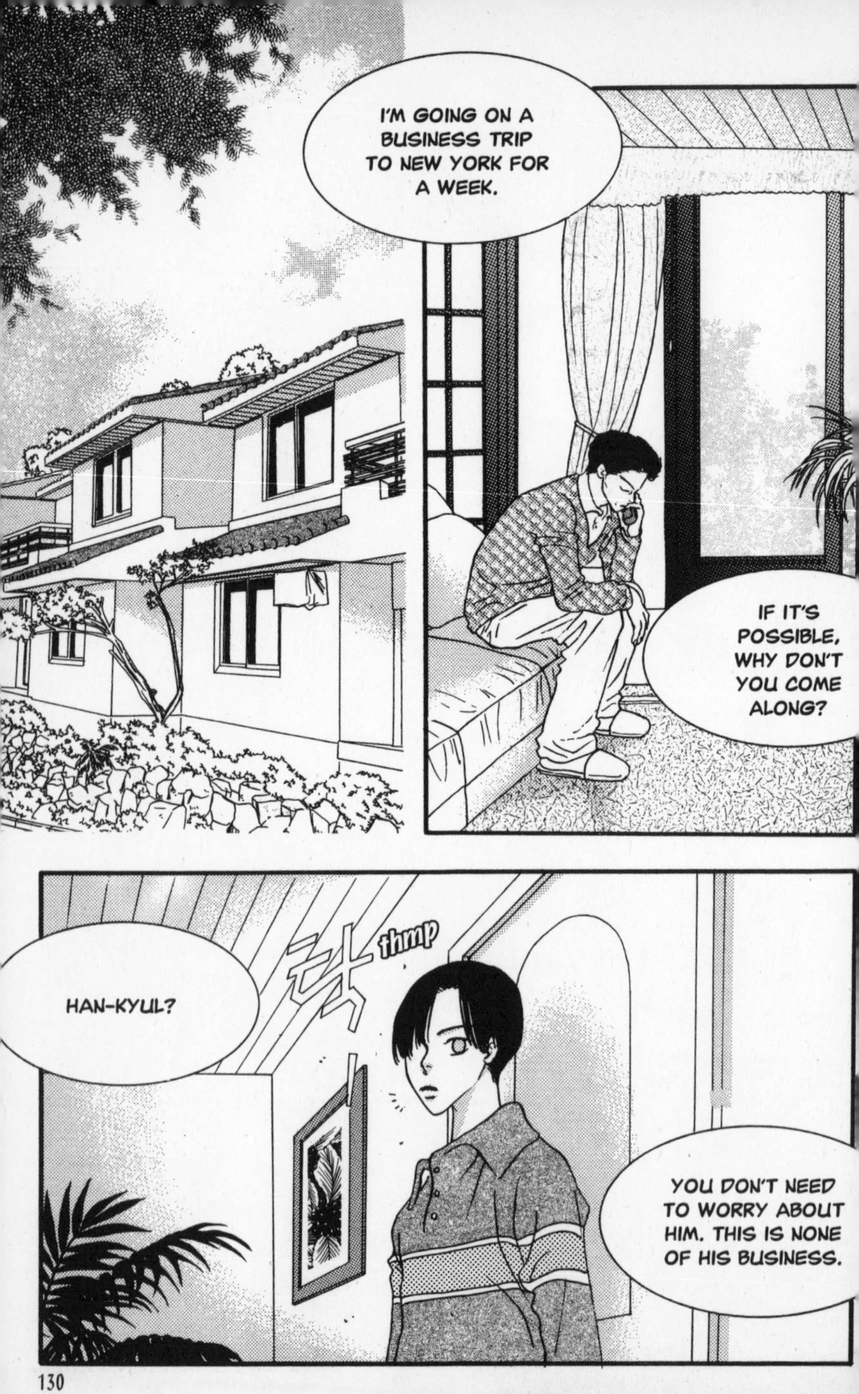
I'M GOING ON A BUSINESS TRIP TO NEW YORK FOR A WEEK.
IF IT'S POSSIBLE, WHY DON'T YOU COME ALONG?
thmp
HAN-KYUL?
YOU DON'T NEED TO WORRY ABOUT HIM. THIS IS NONE OF HIS BUSINESS.

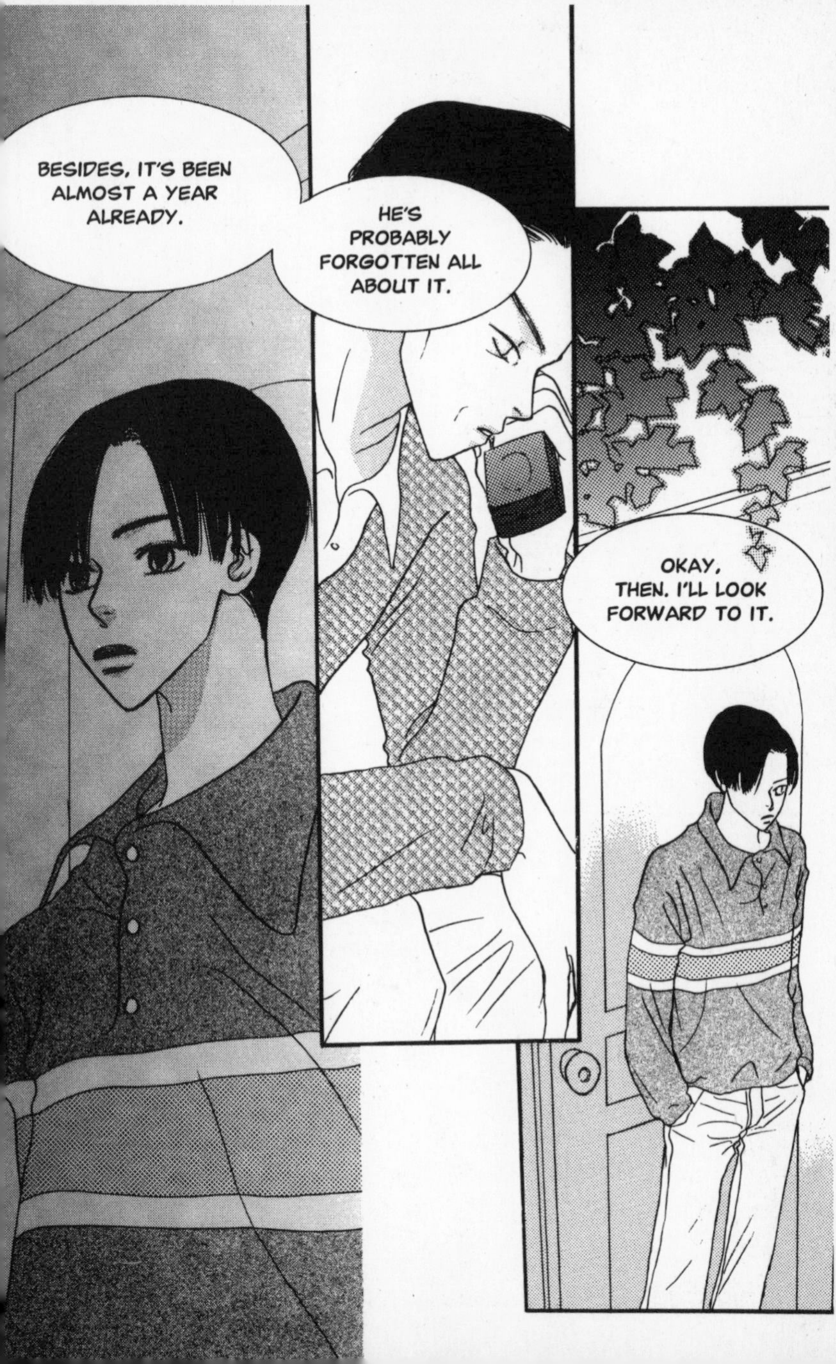
BESIDES, IT'S BEEN ALMOST A YEAR ALREADY.
HE'S PROBABLY FORGOTTEN ALL ABOUT IT.
OKAY, THEN. I'LL LOOK FORWARD TO IT.

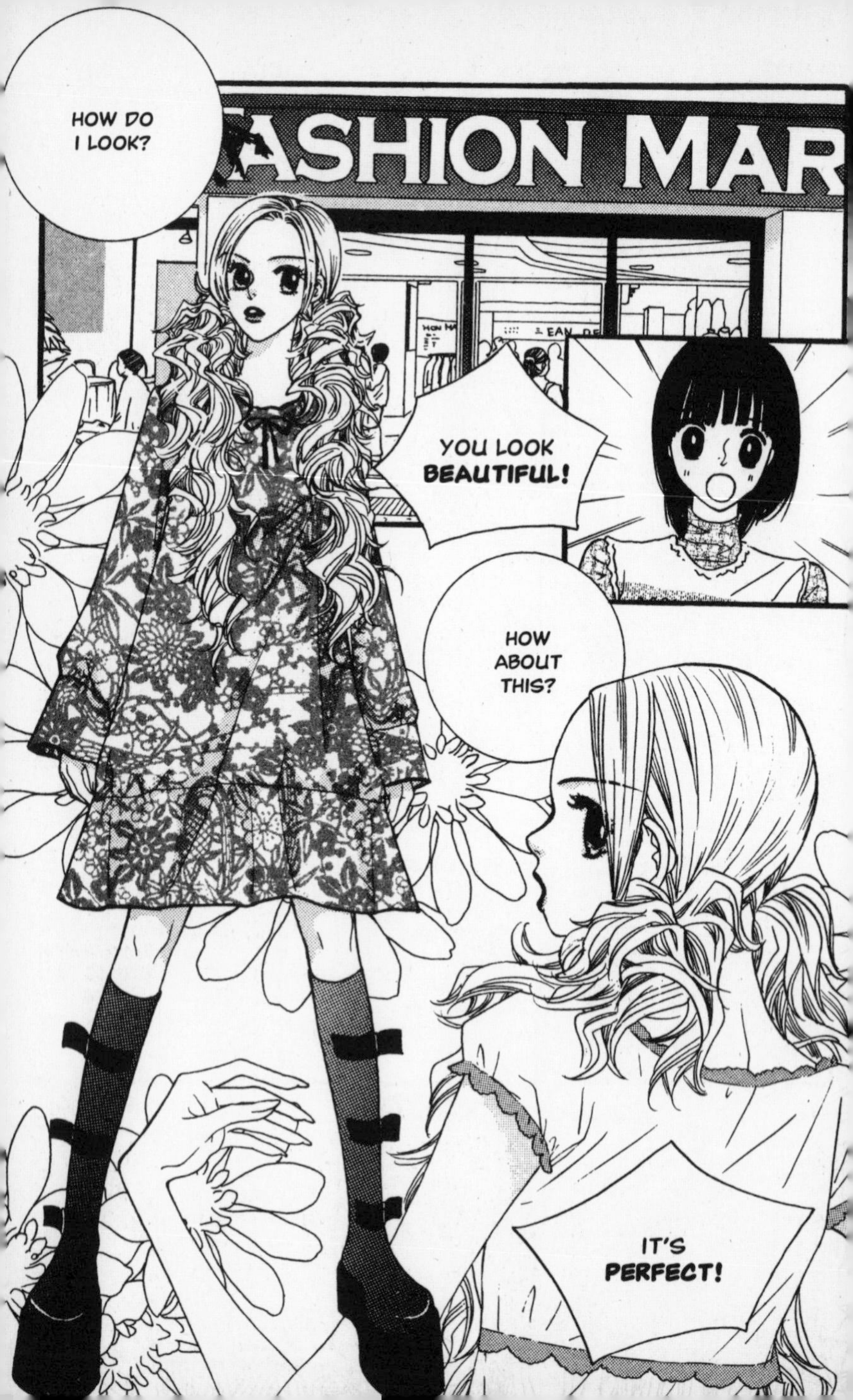
HOW DO I LOOK?
ASHION MAR
YOU LOOK BEAUTIFUL!
HOW ABOUT THIS?
IT'S PERFECT!

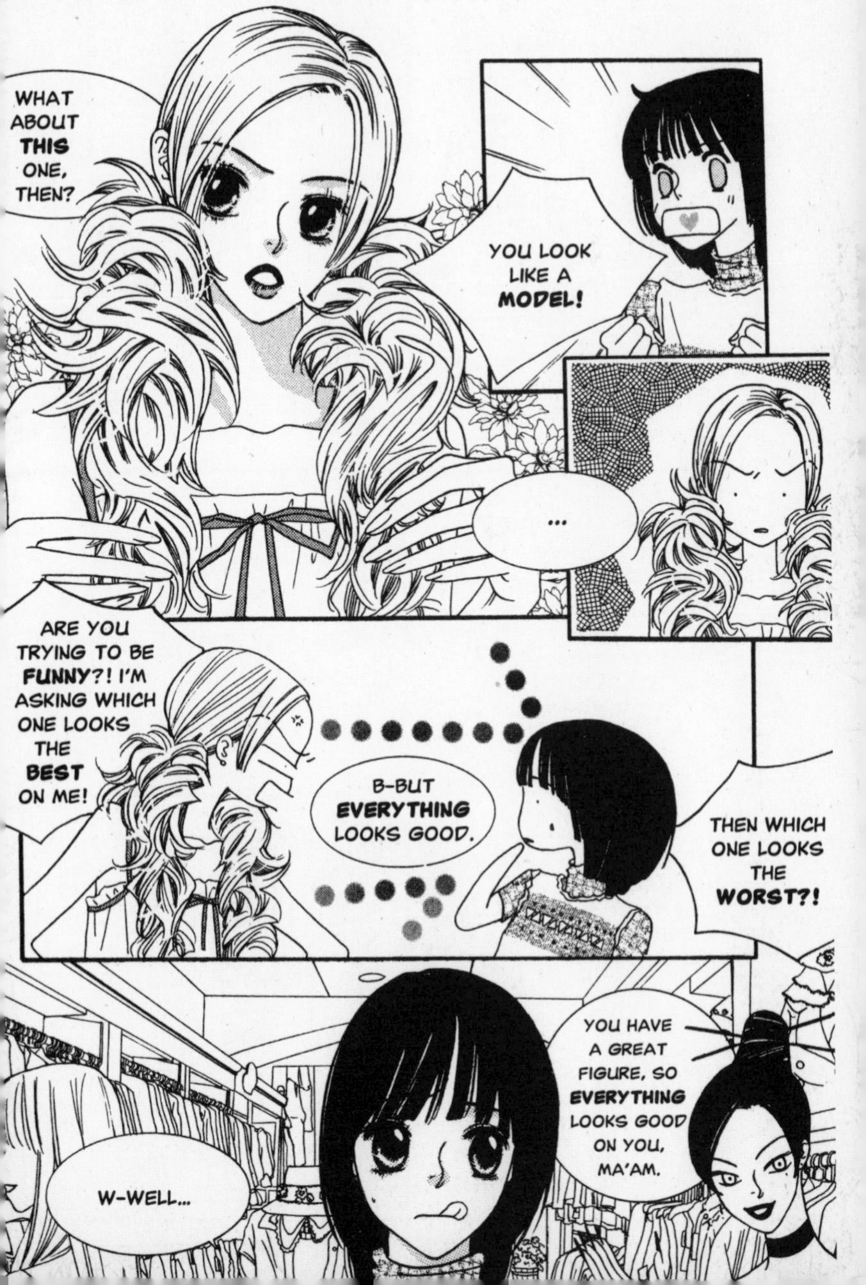
WHAT ABOUT THIS ONE, THEN?
YOU LOOK LIKE A MODEL!
...
ARE YOU TRYING TO BE FUNNY?! I'M ASKING WHICH ONE LOOKS THE BEST ON ME!
B-BUT EVERYTHING LOOKS GOOD.
THEN WHICH ONE LOOKS THE WORST?!
YOU HAVE A GREAT FIGURE, SO EVERYTHING LOOKS GOOD ON YOU, MA'AM.
W-WELL...

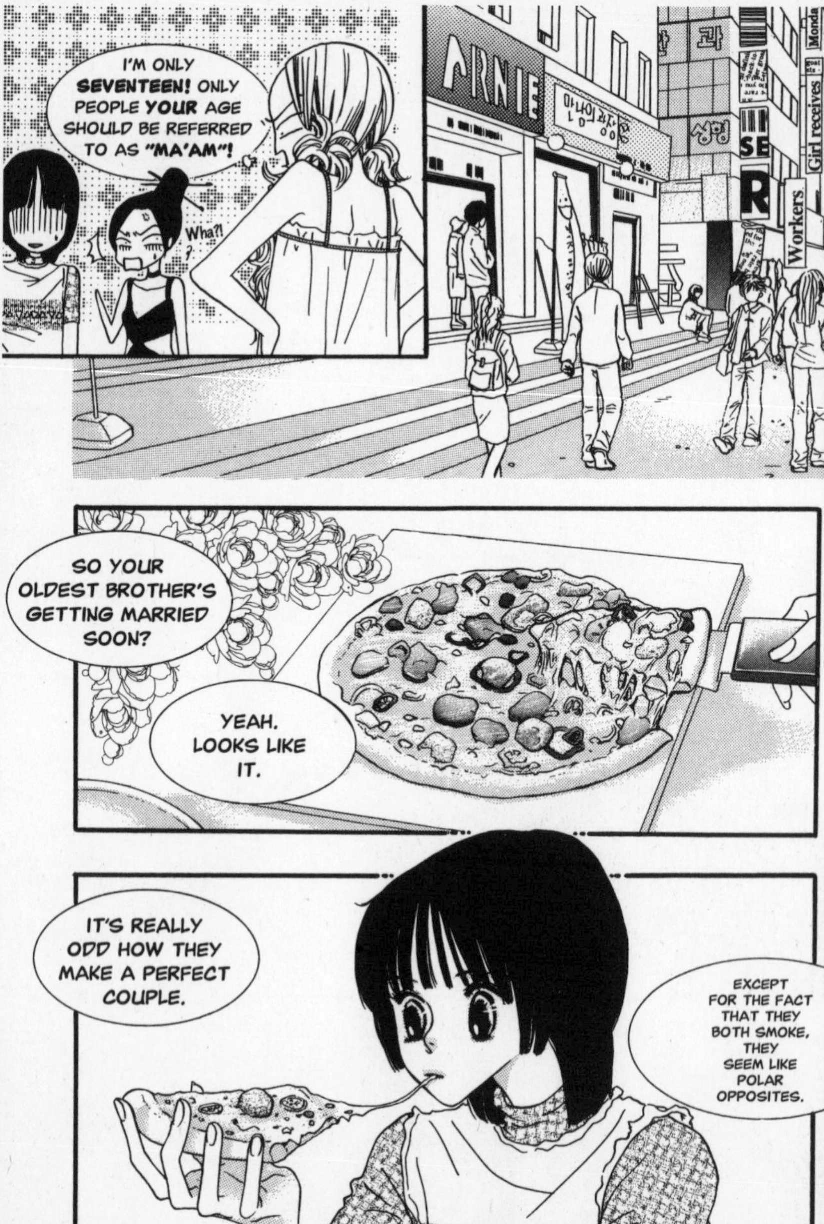
I'M ONLY SEVENTEEN! ONLY PEOPLE YOUR AGE SHOULD BE REFERRED TO AS "MA'AM"!
Wha?!
ARNIE
Workers
Girl receives
SO YOUR OLDEST BROTHER'S GETTING MARRIED SOON?
YEAH. LOOKS LIKE IT.
IT'S REALLY ODD HOW THEY MAKE A PERFECT COUPLE.
EXCEPT FOR THE FACT THAT THEY BOTH SMOKE, THEY SEEM LIKE POLAR OPPOSITES.

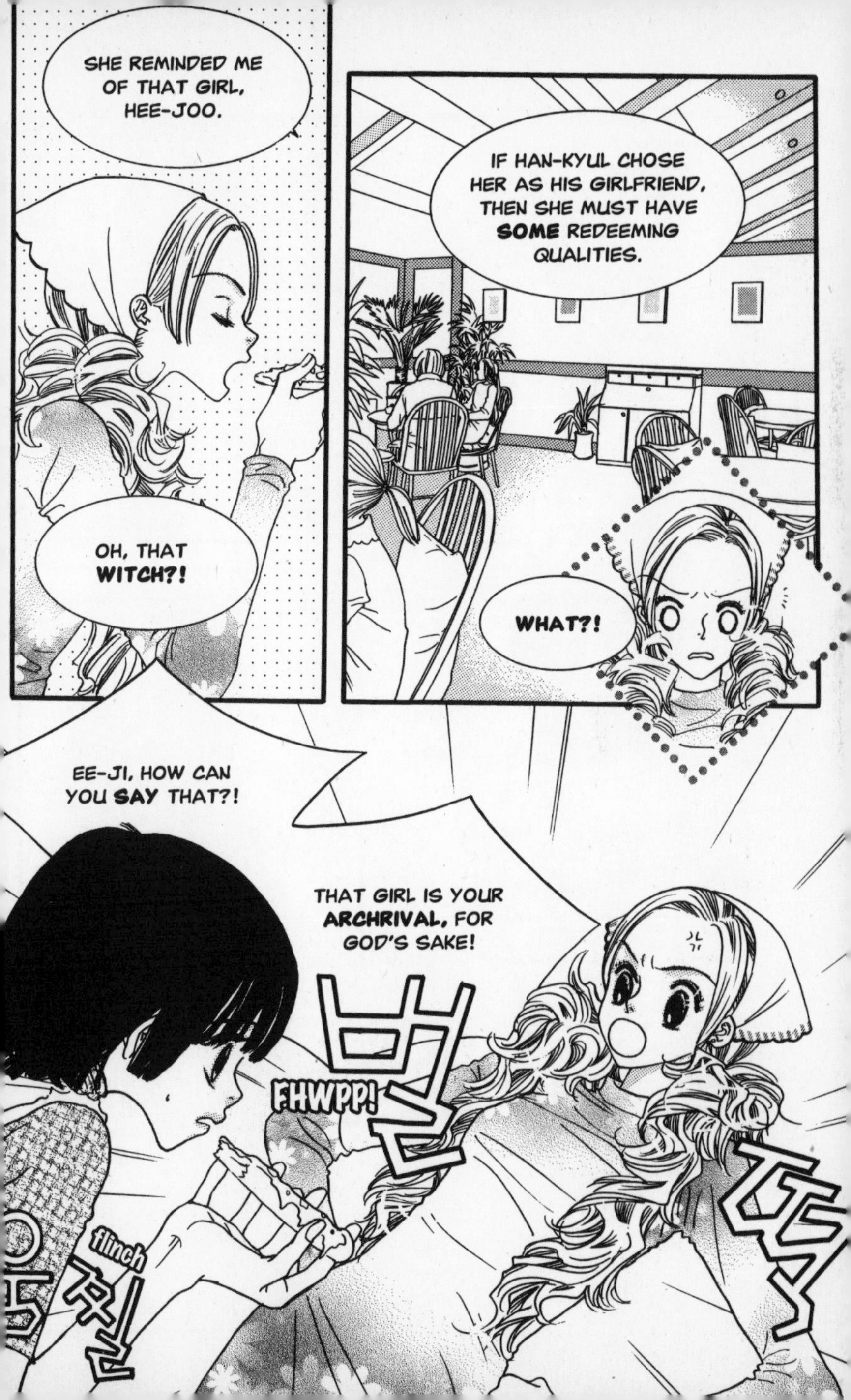

SHE REMINDED ME OF THAT GIRL, HEE-JOO.
IF HAN-KYUL CHOSE HER AS HIS GIRLFRIEND, THEN SHE MUST HAVE SOME REDEEMING QUALITIES.
OH, THAT WITCH?!
WHAT?!
EE-JI, HOW CAN YOU SAY THAT?!
THAT GIRL IS YOUR ARCHRIVAL, FOR GOD'S SAKE!
FHWPP!
flinch

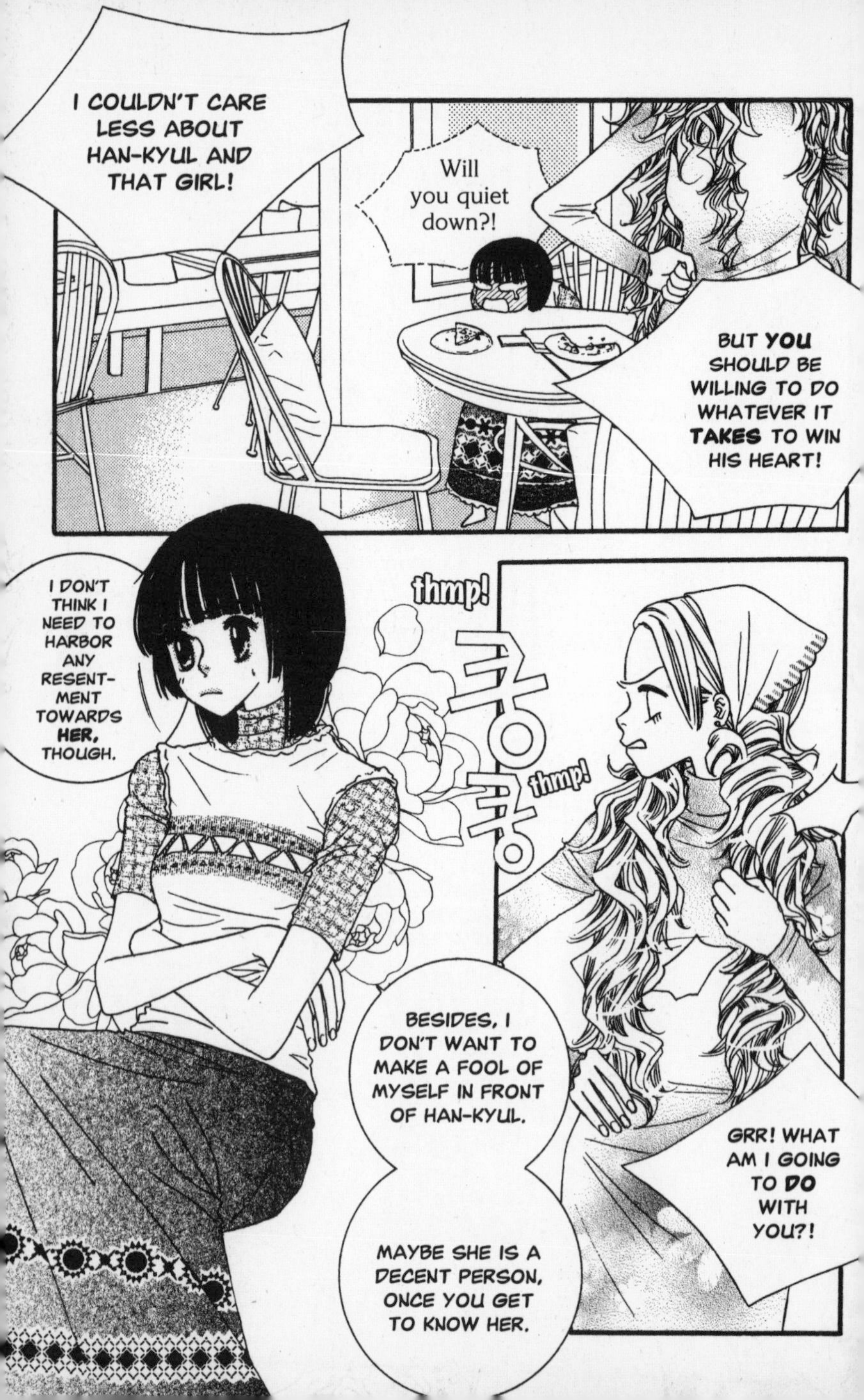

I COULDN'T CARE LESS ABOUT HAN-KYUL AND THAT GIRL!
Will you quiet down?!
BUT **YOU** SHOULD BE WILLING TO DO WHATEVER IT **TAKES** TO WIN HIS HEART!
I DON'T THINK I NEED TO HARBOR ANY RESENT-MENT TOWARDS **HER,** THOUGH.
thmp!
쿵
thmp!
쿵
BESIDES, I DON'T WANT TO MAKE A FOOL OF MYSELF IN FRONT OF HAN-KYUL.
MAYBE SHE IS A DECENT PERSON, ONCE YOU GET TO KNOW HER.
GRR! WHAT AM I GOING TO **DO** WITH YOU?!

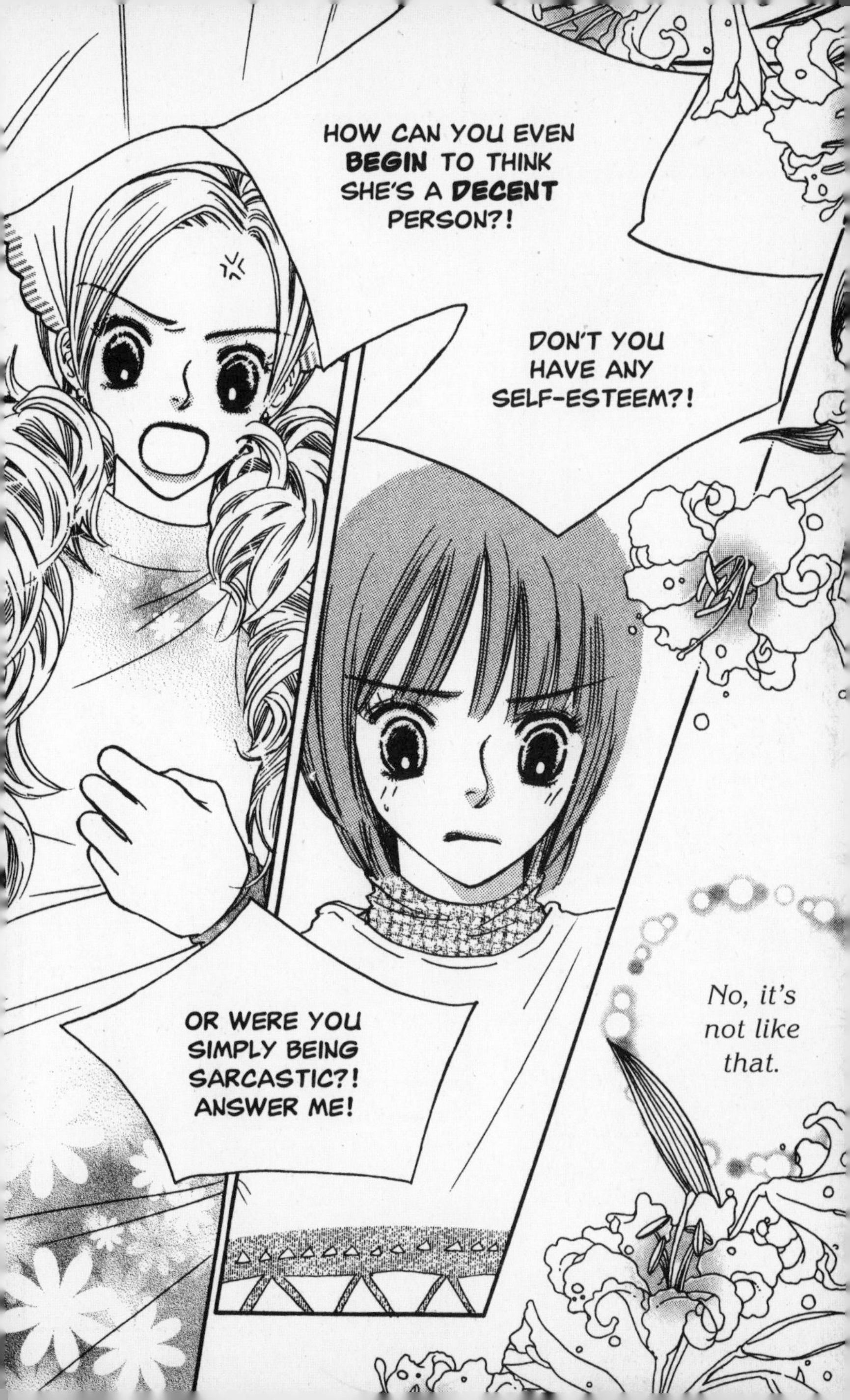
HOW CAN YOU EVEN **BEGIN** TO THINK SHE'S A **DECENT** PERSON?!
DON'T YOU HAVE ANY SELF-ESTEEM?!
No, it's not like that.
OR WERE YOU SIMPLY BEING SARCASTIC?! ANSWER ME!

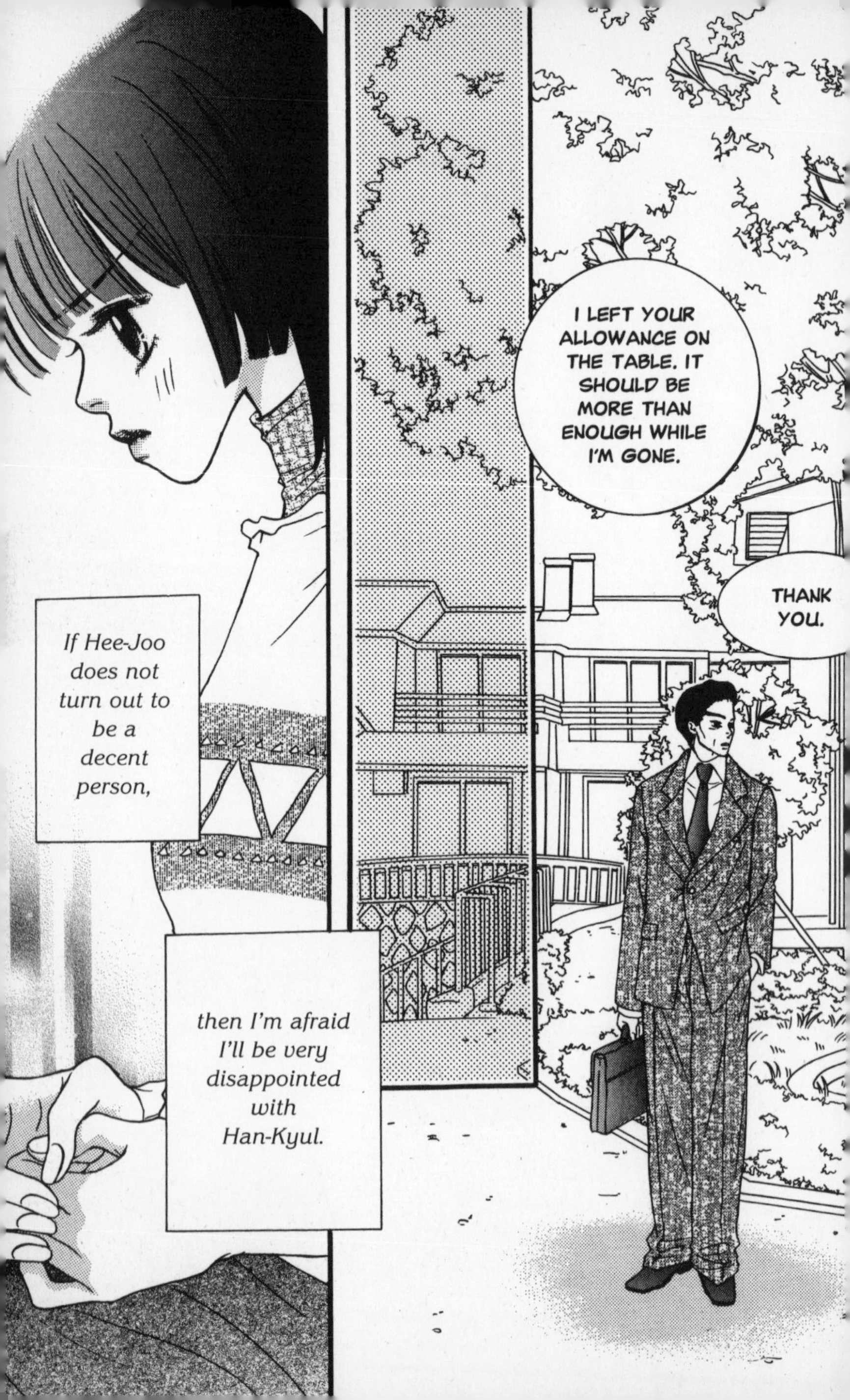
If Hee-Joo does not turn out to be a decent person,
then I'm afraid I'll be very disappointed with Han-Kyul.
I LEFT YOUR ALLOWANCE ON THE TABLE. IT SHOULD BE MORE THAN ENOUGH WHILE I'M GONE.
THANK YOU.

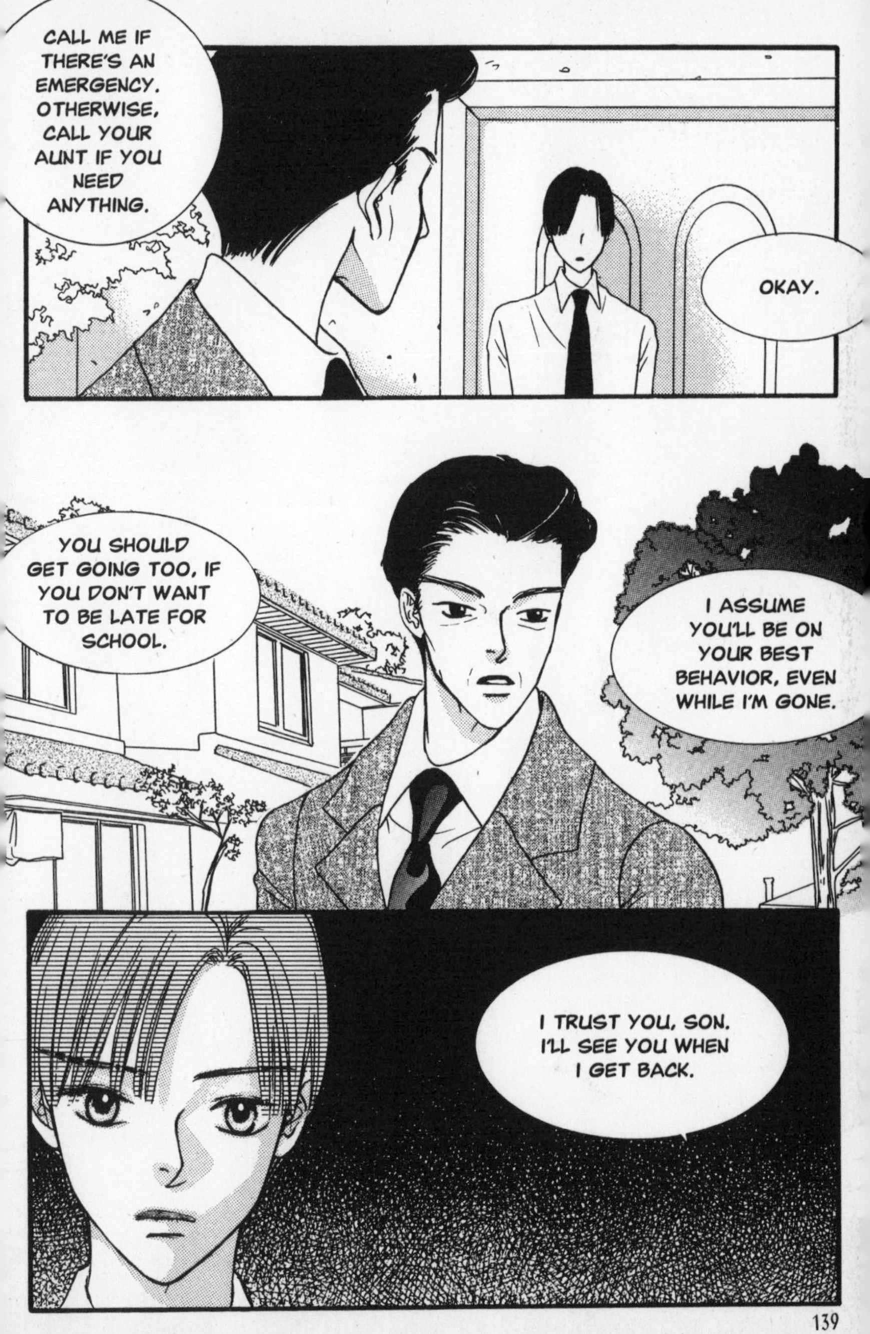
CALL ME IF THERE'S AN EMERGENCY. OTHERWISE, CALL YOUR AUNT IF YOU NEED ANYTHING.
OKAY.
YOU SHOULD GET GOING TOO, IF YOU DON'T WANT TO BE LATE FOR SCHOOL.
I ASSUME YOU'LL BE ON YOUR BEST BEHAVIOR, EVEN WHILE I'M GONE.
I TRUST YOU, SON. I'LL SEE YOU WHEN I GET BACK.

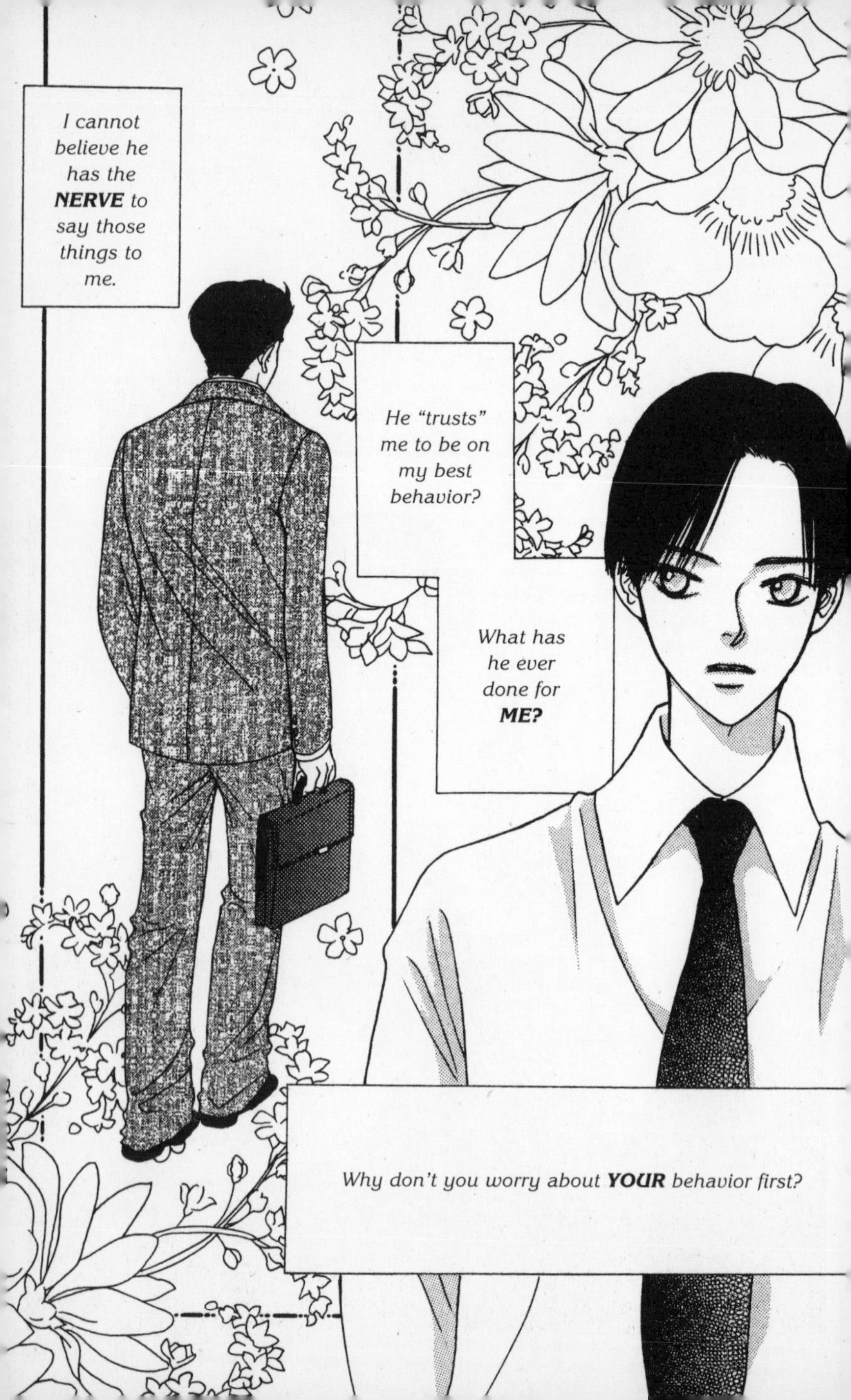
I cannot believe he has the NERVE to say those things to me.
He "trusts" me to be on my best behavior?
What has he ever done for ME?
Why don't you worry about YOUR behavior first?

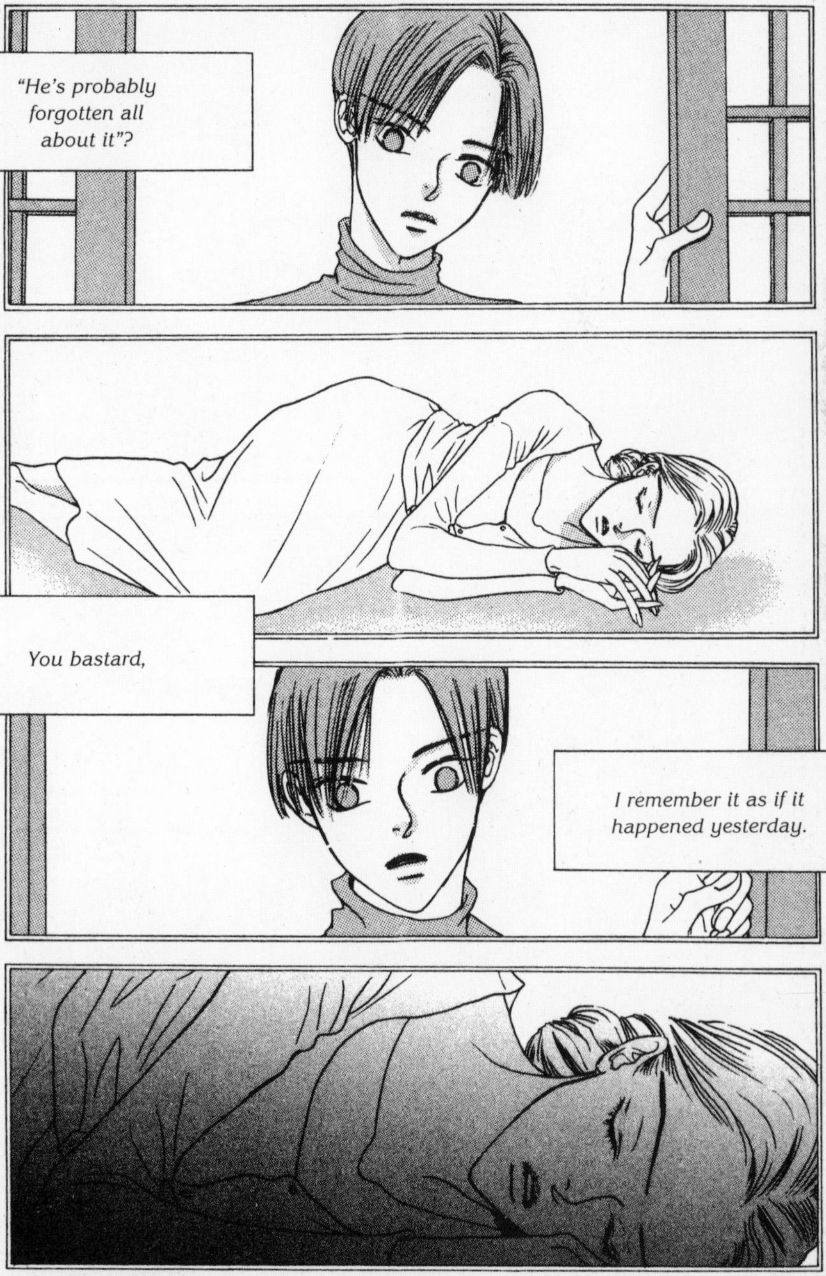
"He's probably forgotten all about it"?
You bastard,
I remember it as if it happened yesterday.

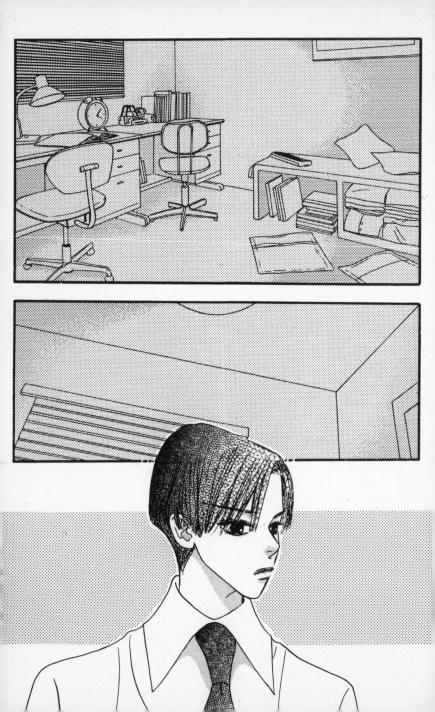

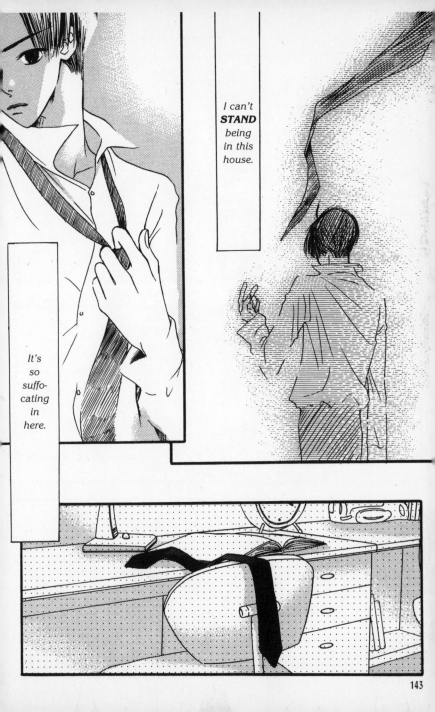

I can't **STAND** being in this house.

It's so suffocating in here.

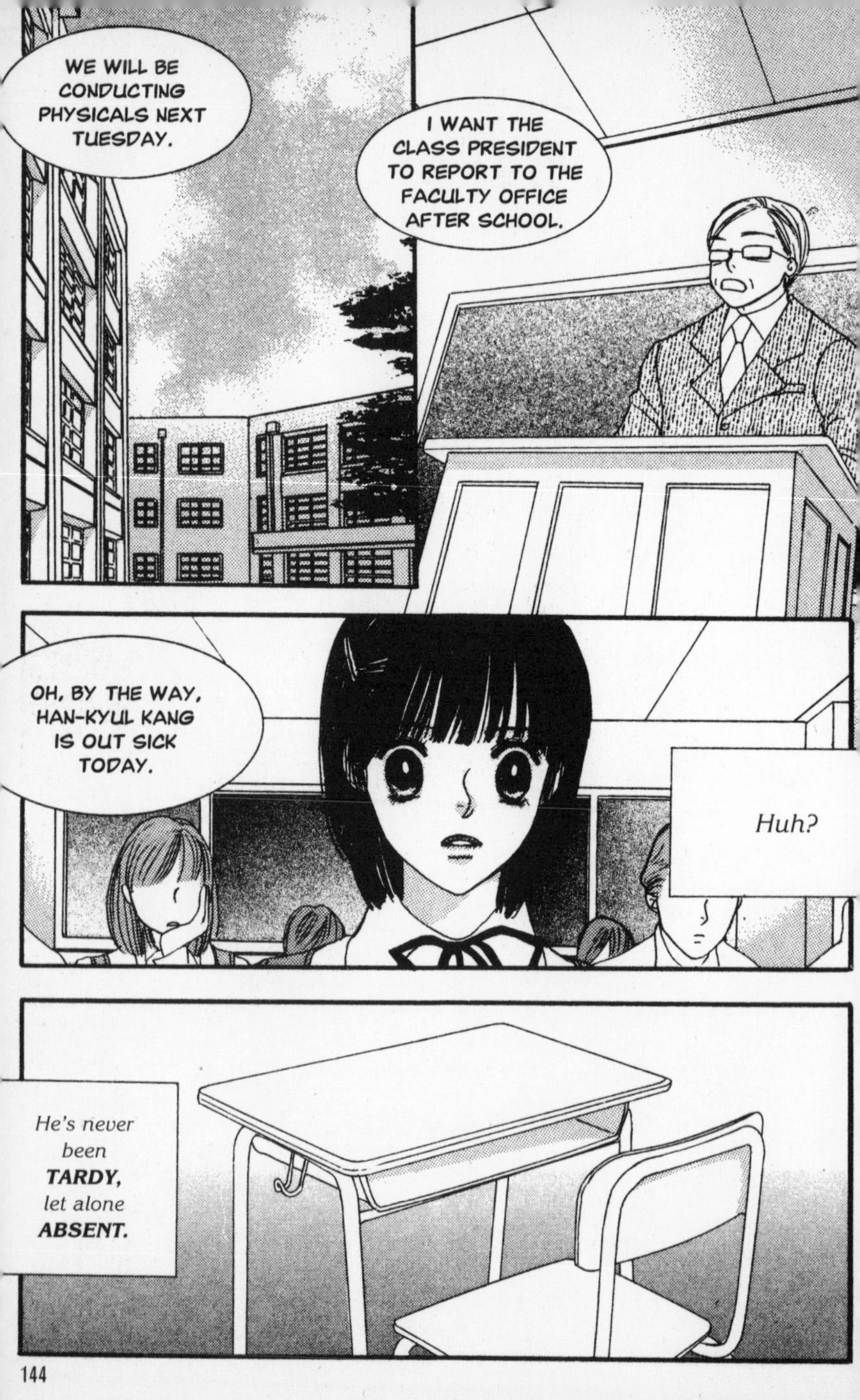
WE WILL BE CONDUCTING PHYSICALS NEXT TUESDAY.
I WANT THE CLASS PRESIDENT TO REPORT TO THE FACULTY OFFICE AFTER SCHOOL.
OH, BY THE WAY, HAN-KYUL KANG IS OUT SICK TODAY.
Huh?
He's never been TARDY, let alone ABSENT.

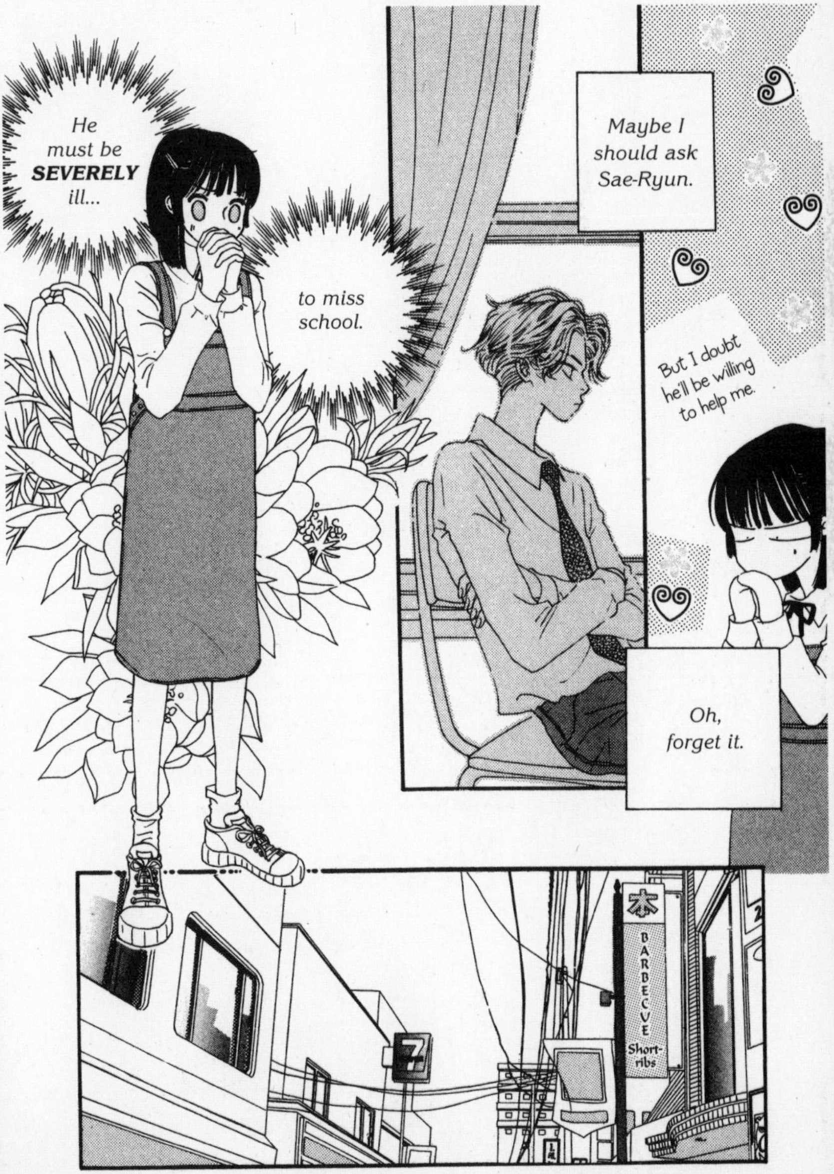
He must be **SEVERELY** ill...
to miss school.
Maybe I should ask Sae-Ryun.
But I doubt he'll be willing to help me.
Oh, forget it.
BARBECUE
Short-ribs

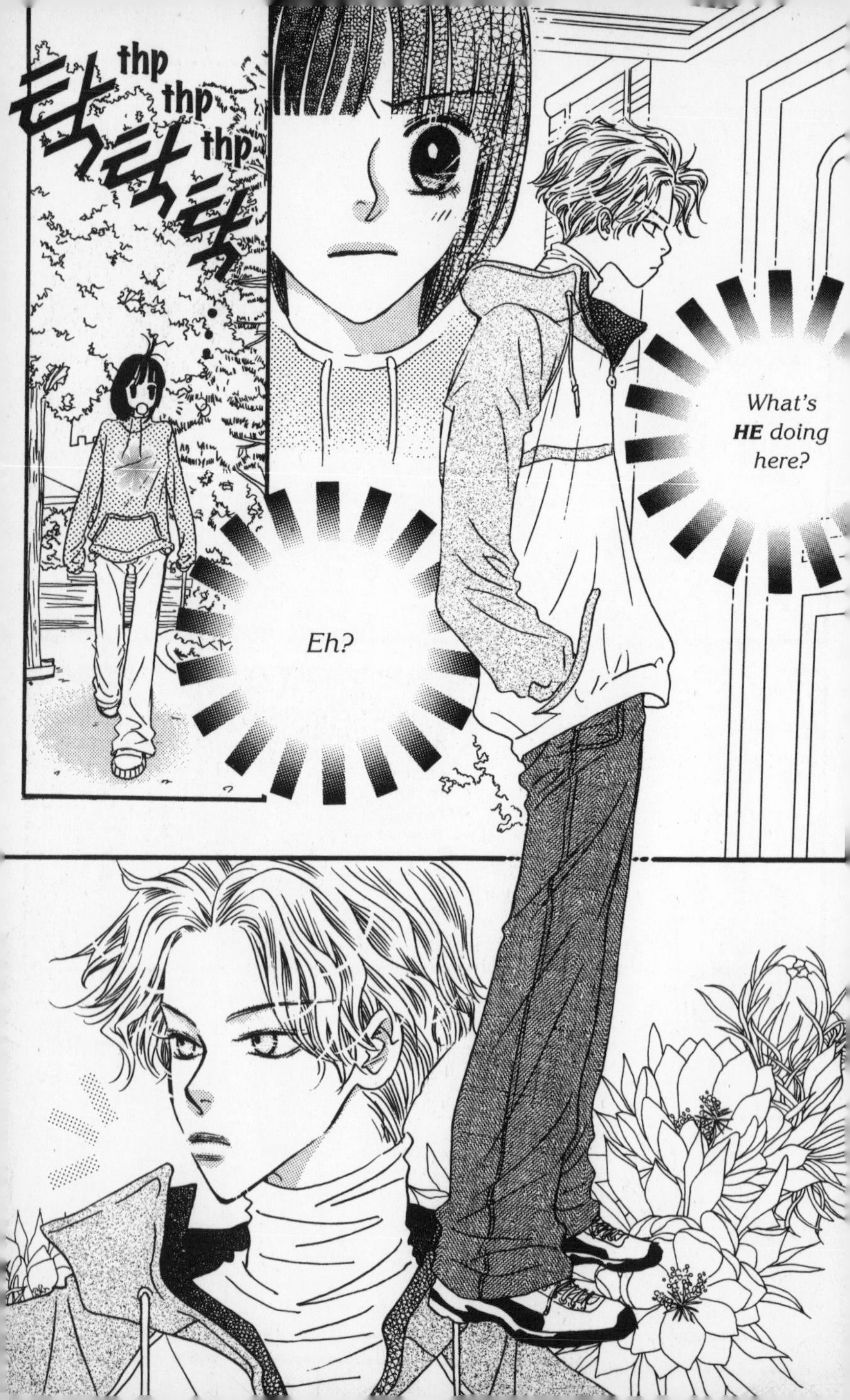
thp
thp
thp
What's **HE** doing here?
Eh?

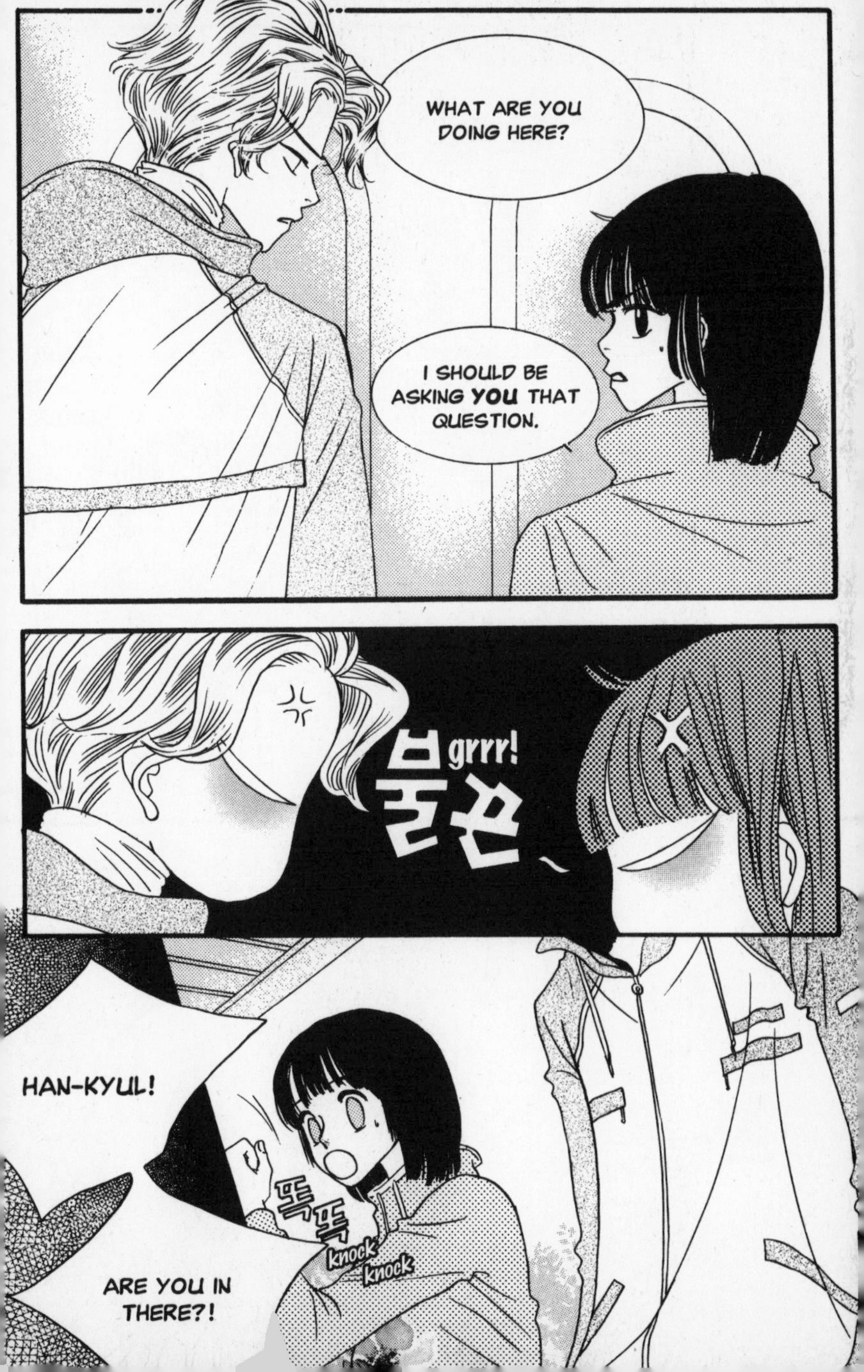
WHAT ARE YOU DOING HERE?
I SHOULD BE ASKING **YOU** THAT QUESTION.
불끈
grrr!
HAN-KYUL!
똑똑
knock knock
ARE YOU IN THERE?!

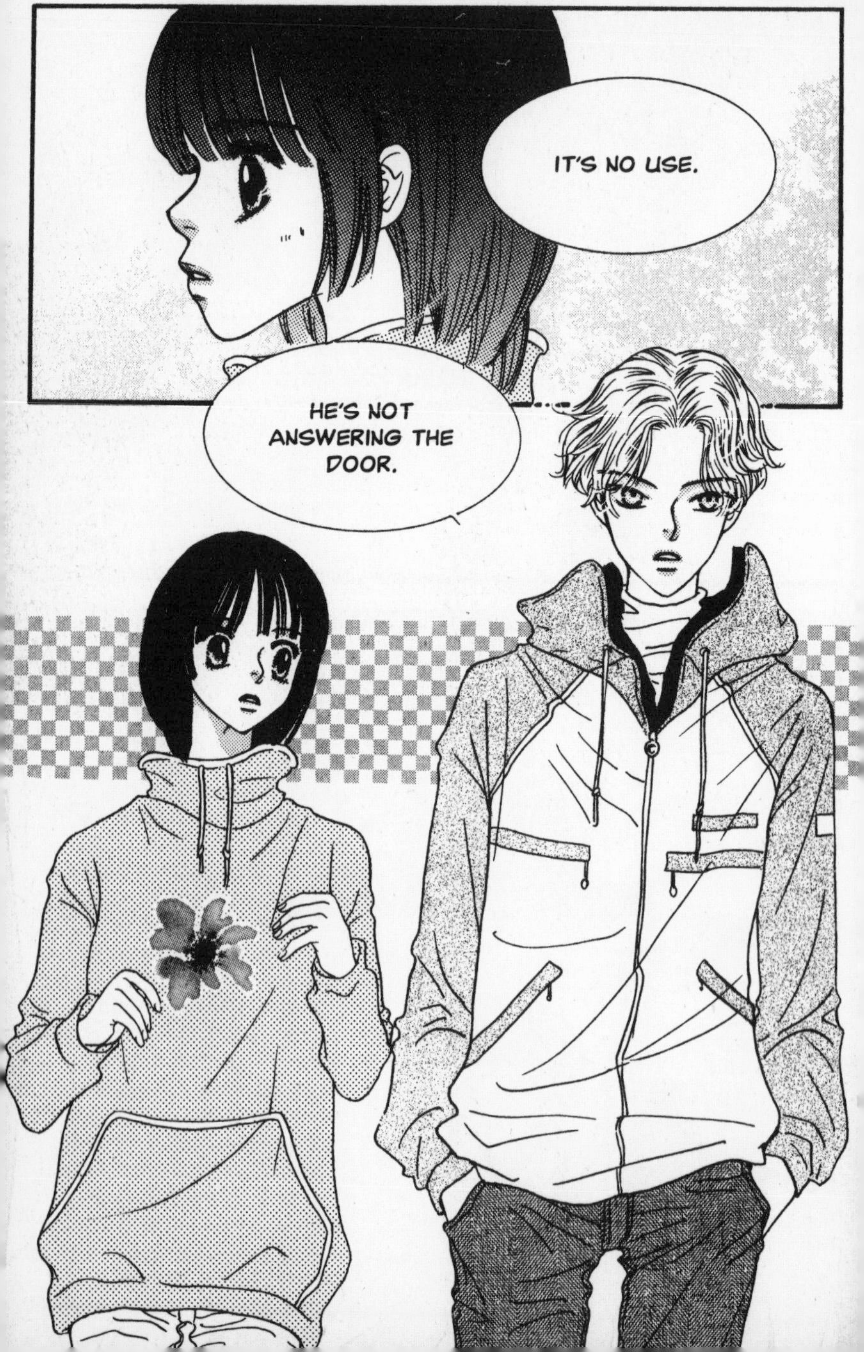
IT'S NO USE.
HE'S NOT ANSWERING THE DOOR.

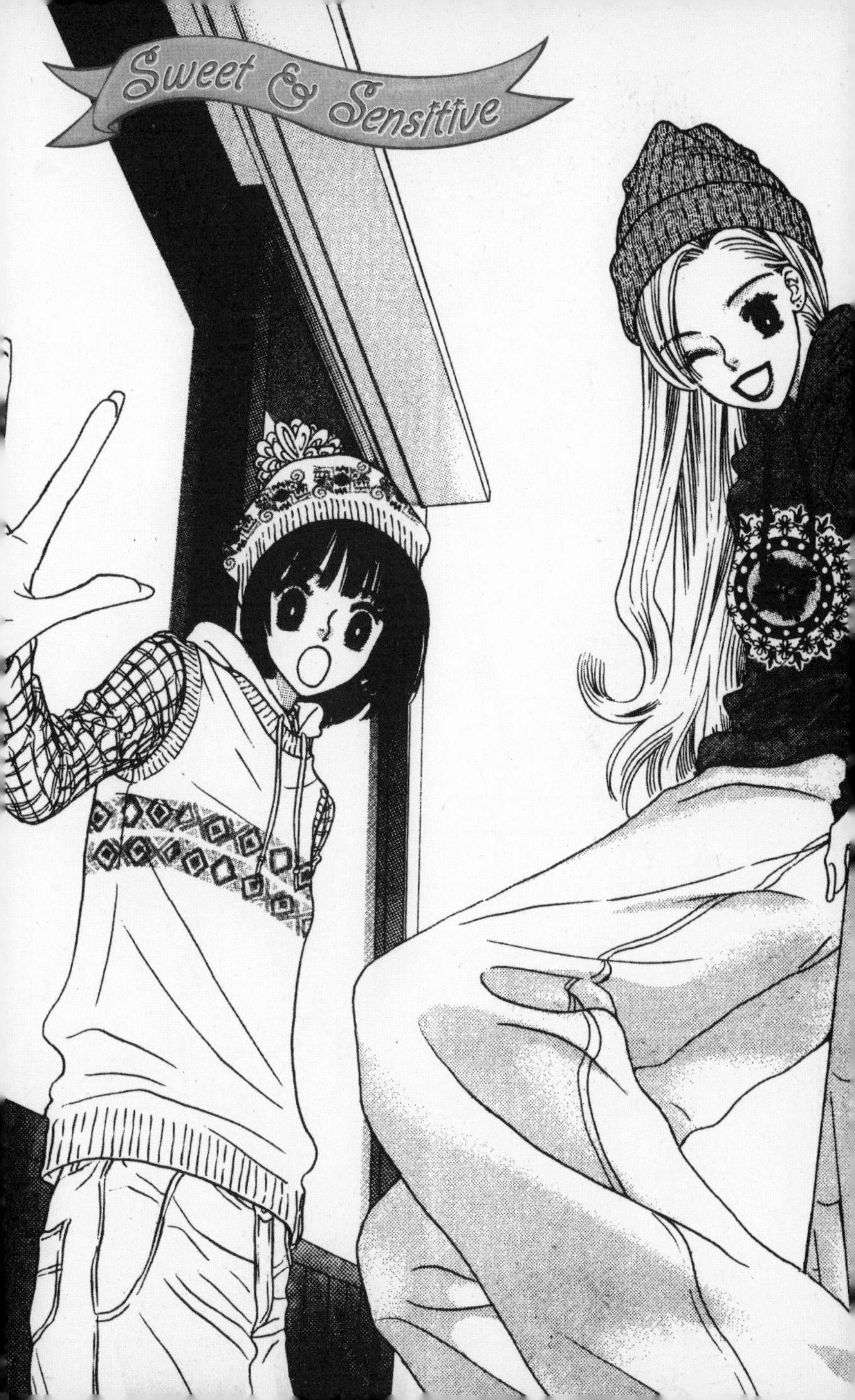
Sweet & Sensitive

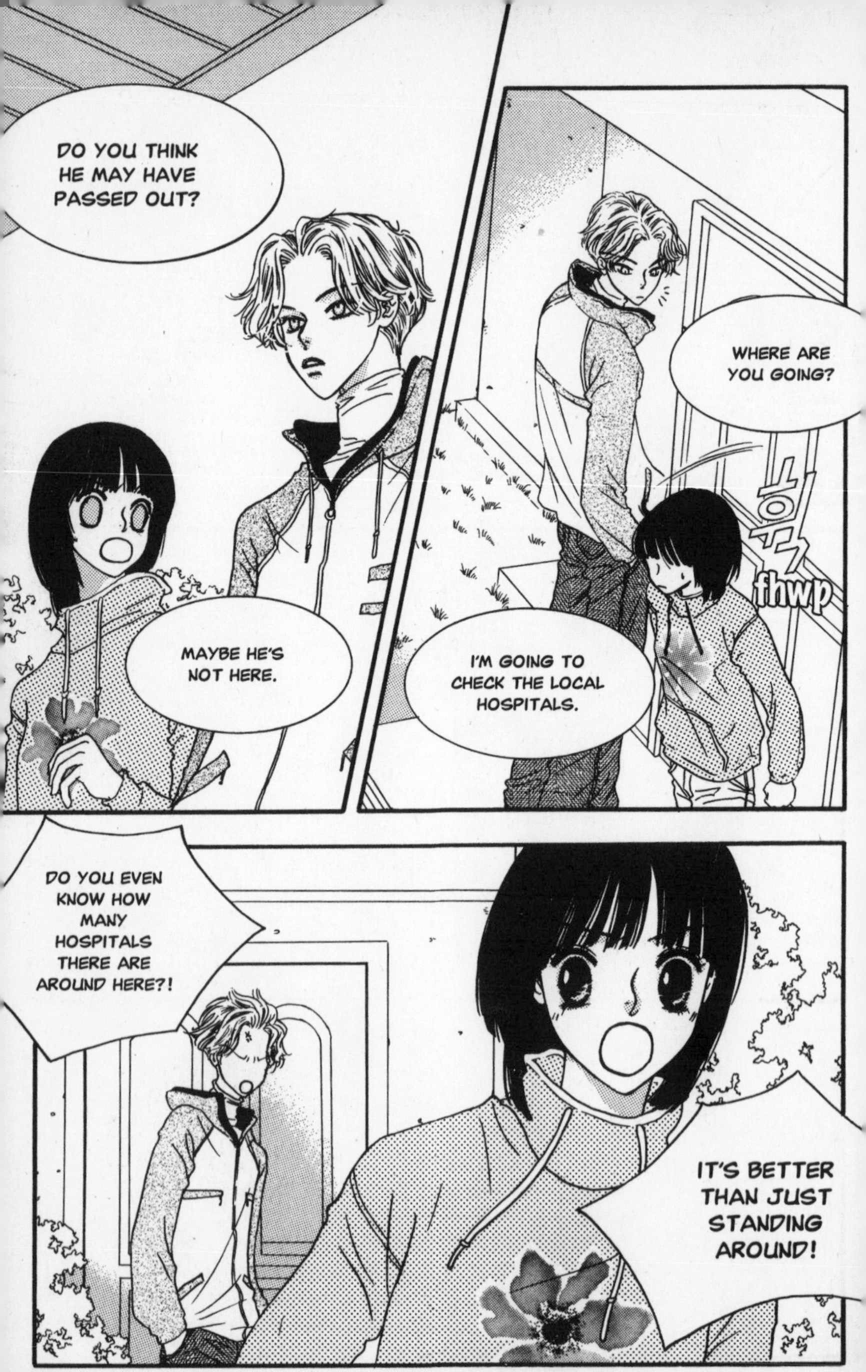
DO YOU THINK HE MAY HAVE PASSED OUT?
MAYBE HE'S NOT HERE.
WHERE ARE YOU GOING?
fhwp
I'M GOING TO CHECK THE LOCAL HOSPITALS.
DO YOU EVEN KNOW HOW MANY HOSPITALS THERE ARE AROUND HERE?!
IT'S BETTER THAN JUST STANDING AROUND!

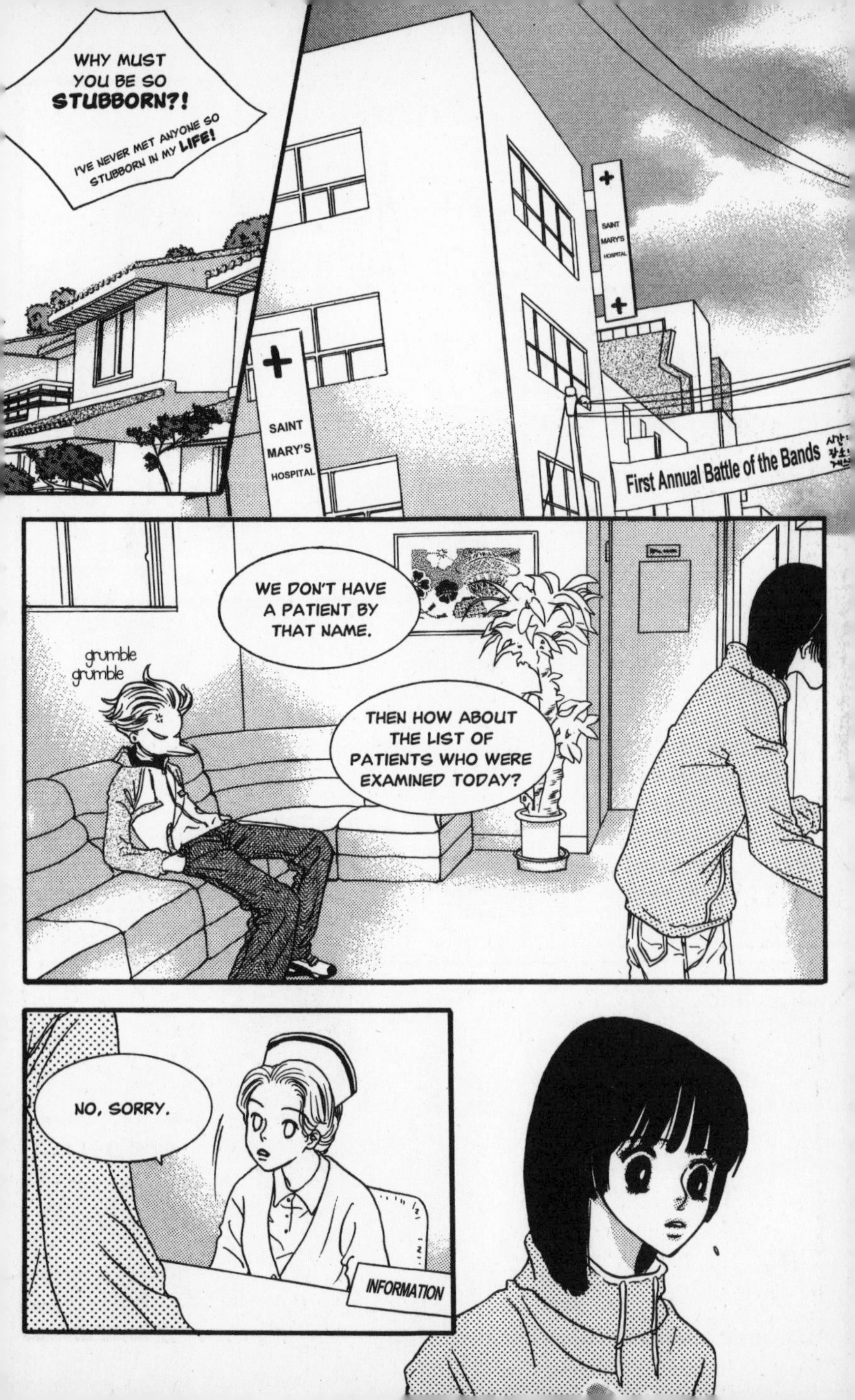
WHY MUST YOU BE SO STUBBORN?!
I'VE NEVER MET ANYONE SO STUBBORN IN MY LIFE!
SAINT MARY'S HOSPITAL
SAINT MARY'S HOSPITAL
First Annual Battle of the Bands
WE DON'T HAVE A PATIENT BY THAT NAME.
grumble grumble
THEN HOW ABOUT THE LIST OF PATIENTS WHO WERE EXAMINED TODAY?
NO, SORRY.
INFORMATION

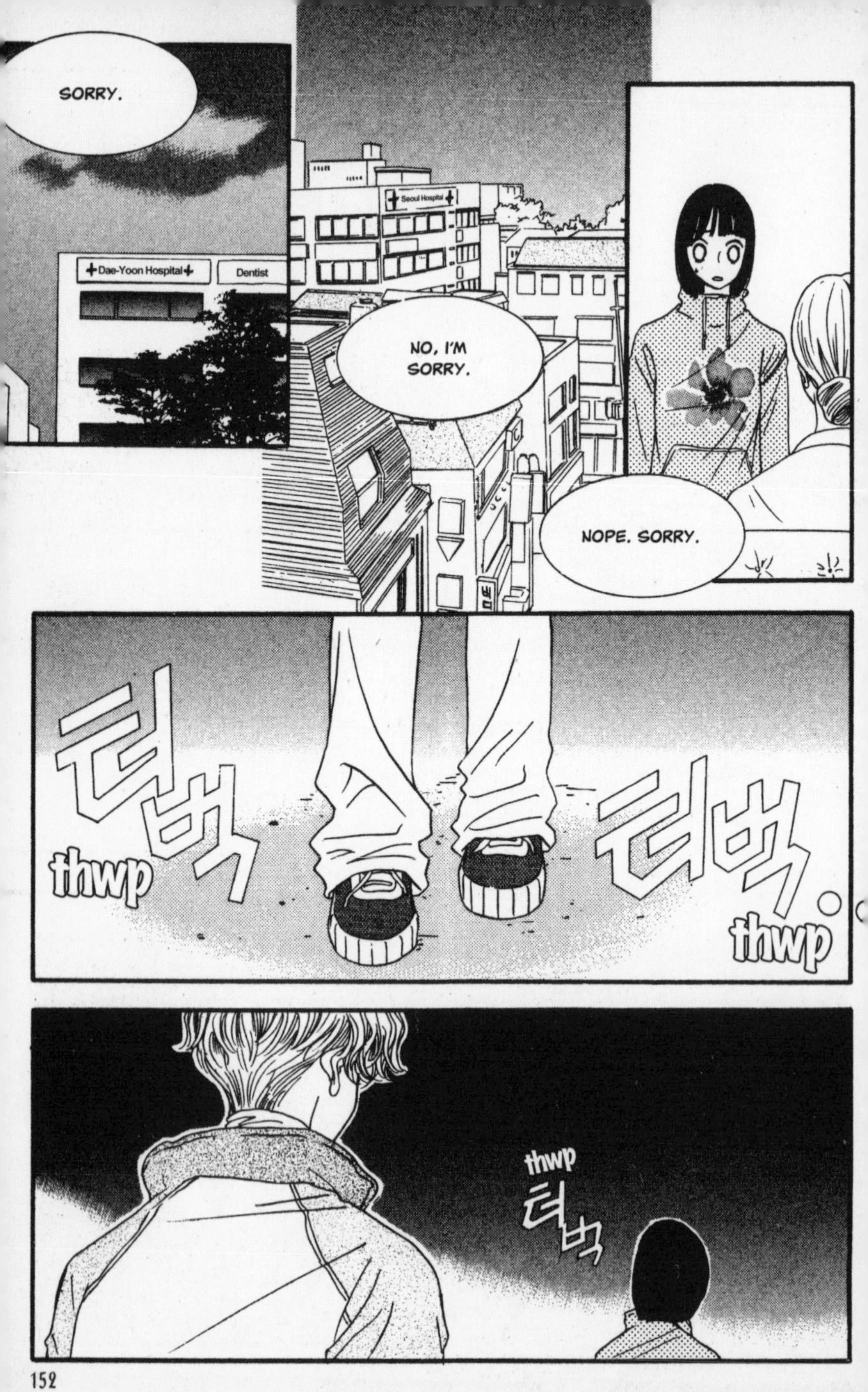
SORRY.
Dae-Yoon Hospital
Dentist
Seoul Hospital
NO, I'M SORRY.
NOPE. SORRY.
터벅
thwp
터벅
thwp
thwp
터벅

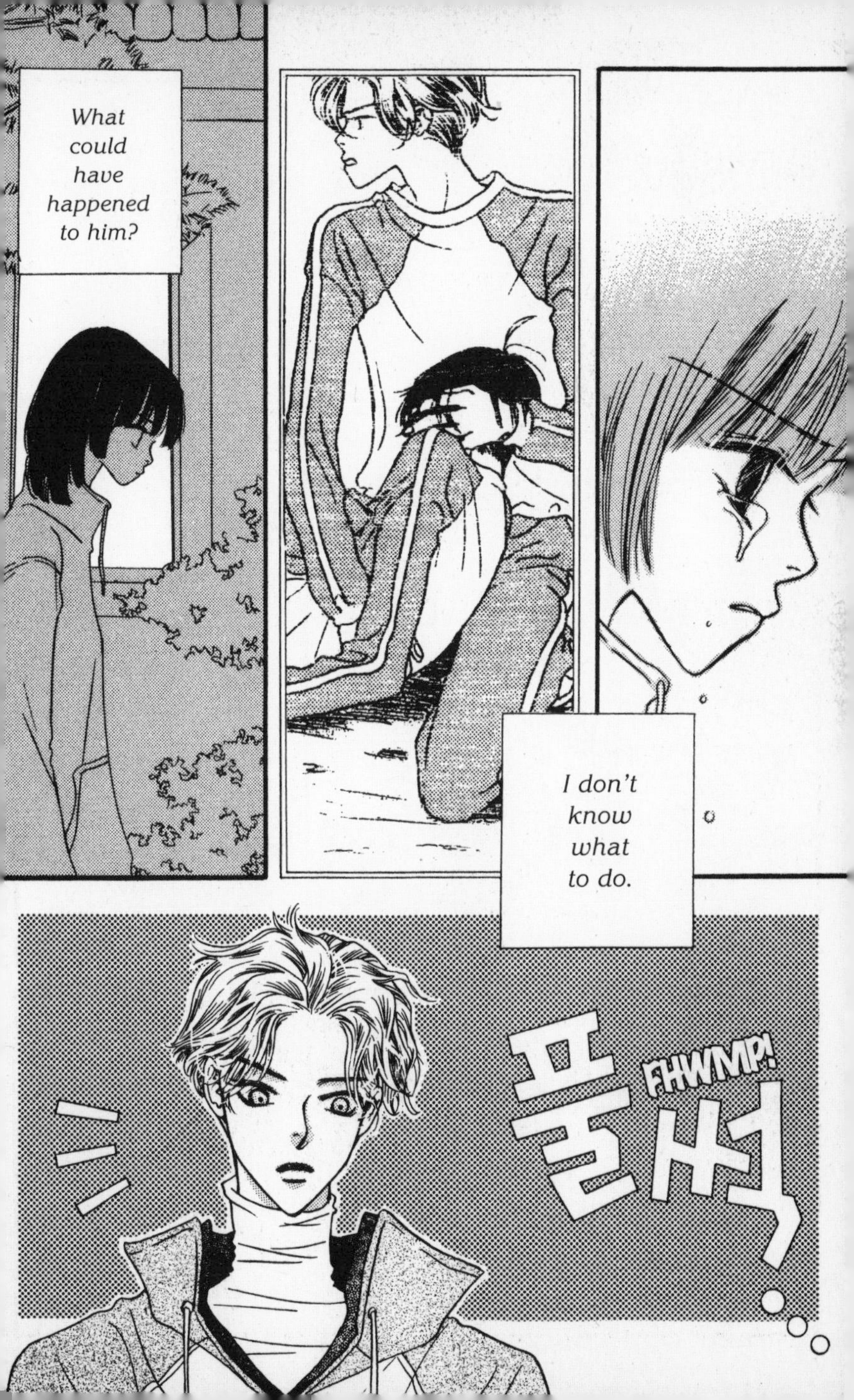
What could have happened to him?
I don't know what to do.
FHWMP!

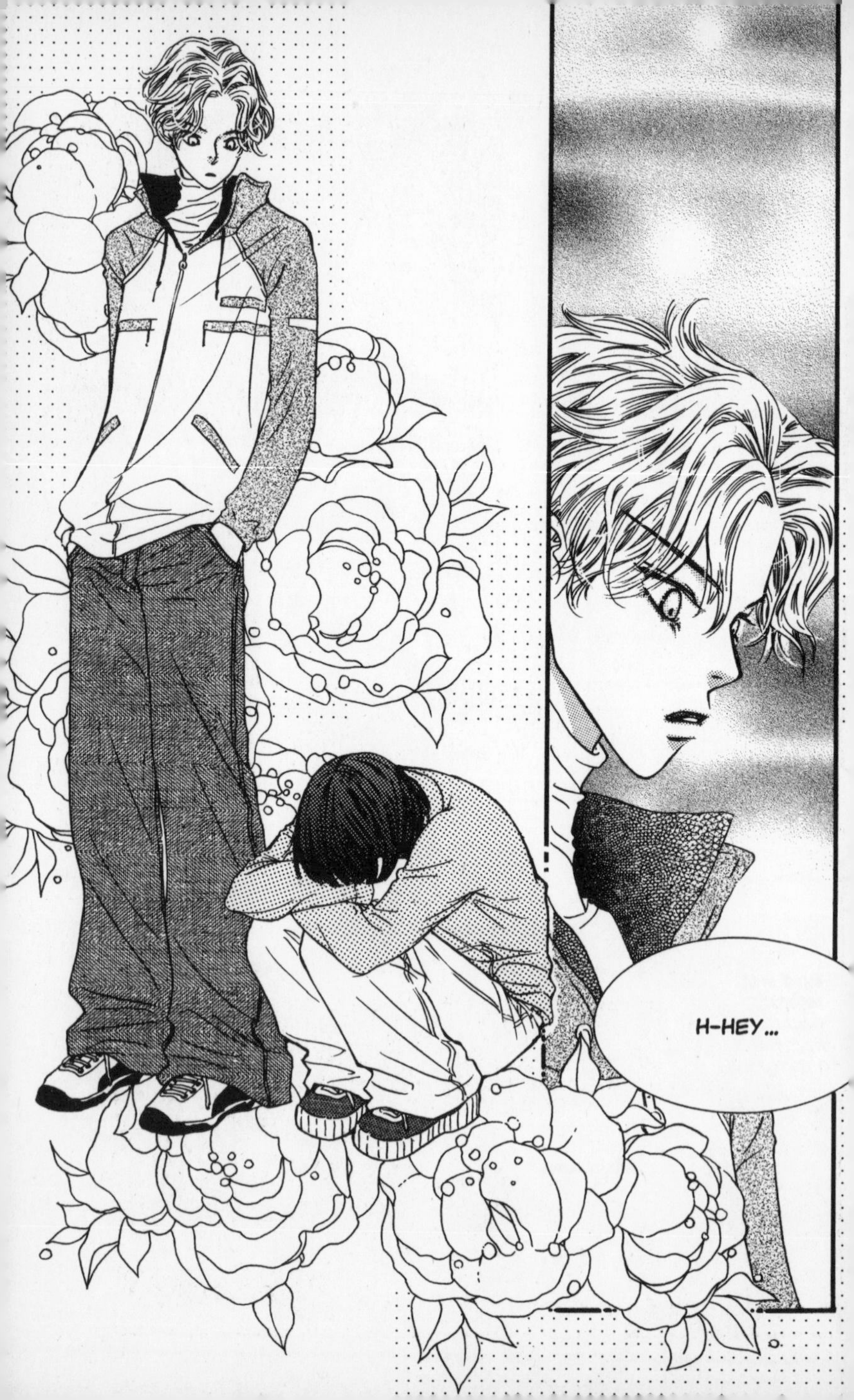
H-HEY...

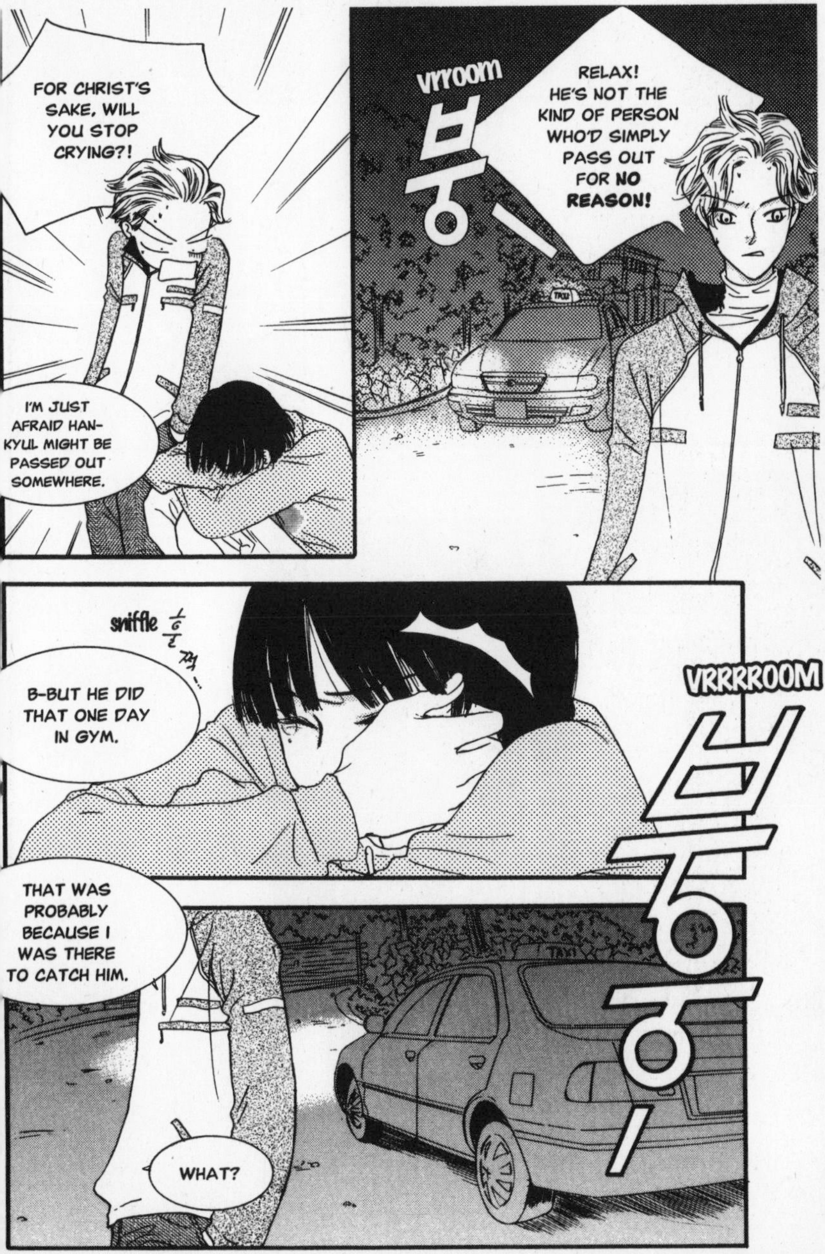

FOR CHRIST'S SAKE, WILL YOU STOP CRYING?!
I'M JUST AFRAID HAN-KYUL MIGHT BE PASSED OUT SOMEWHERE.
VRROOM
붕
RELAX! HE'S NOT THE KIND OF PERSON WHO'D SIMPLY PASS OUT FOR NO REASON!
sniffle
B-BUT HE DID THAT ONE DAY IN GYM.
VRRRROOM
THAT WAS PROBABLY BECAUSE I WAS THERE TO CATCH HIM.
WHAT?

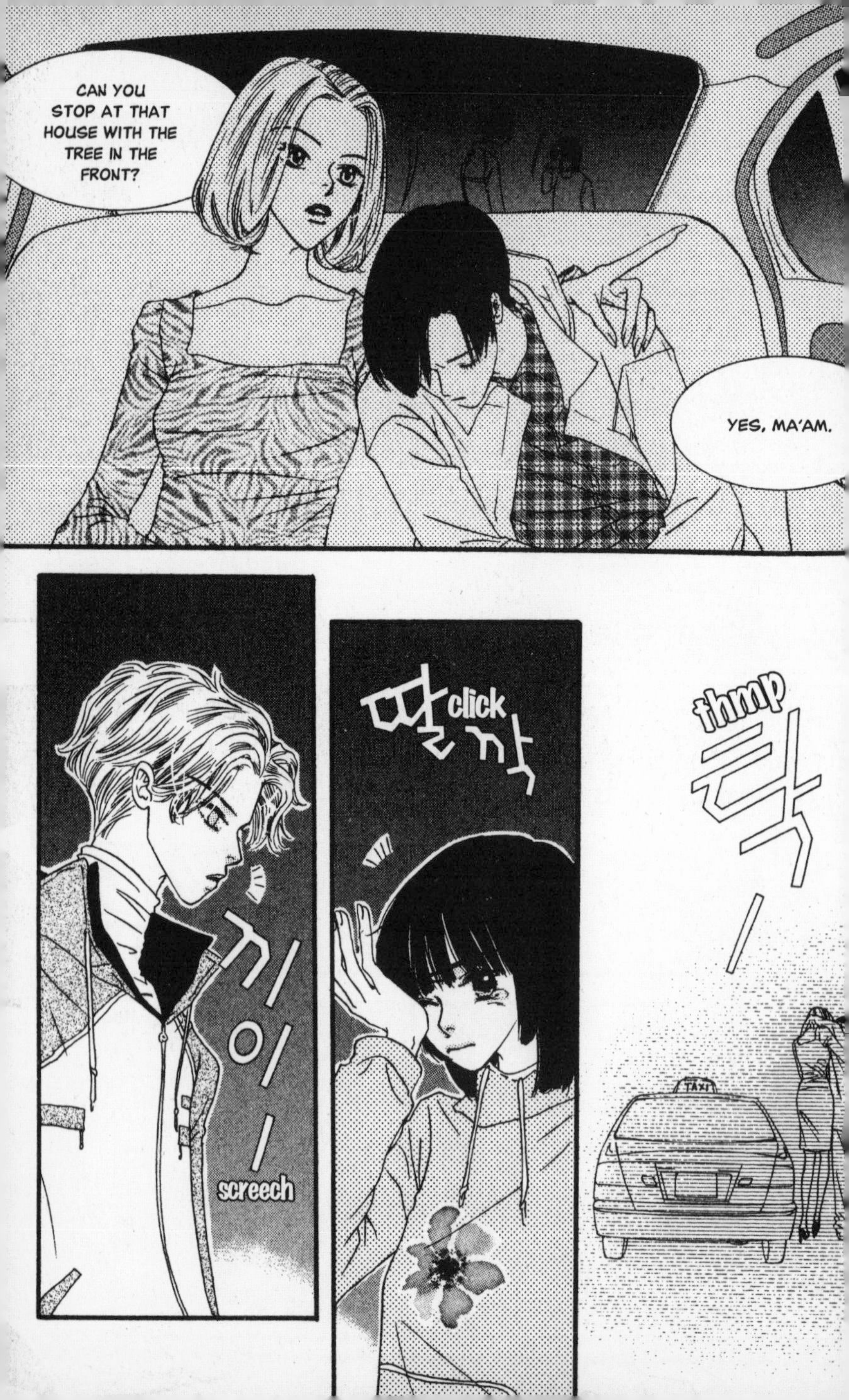
CAN YOU STOP AT THAT HOUSE WITH THE TREE IN THE FRONT?
YES, MA'AM.
thmp
click
screech

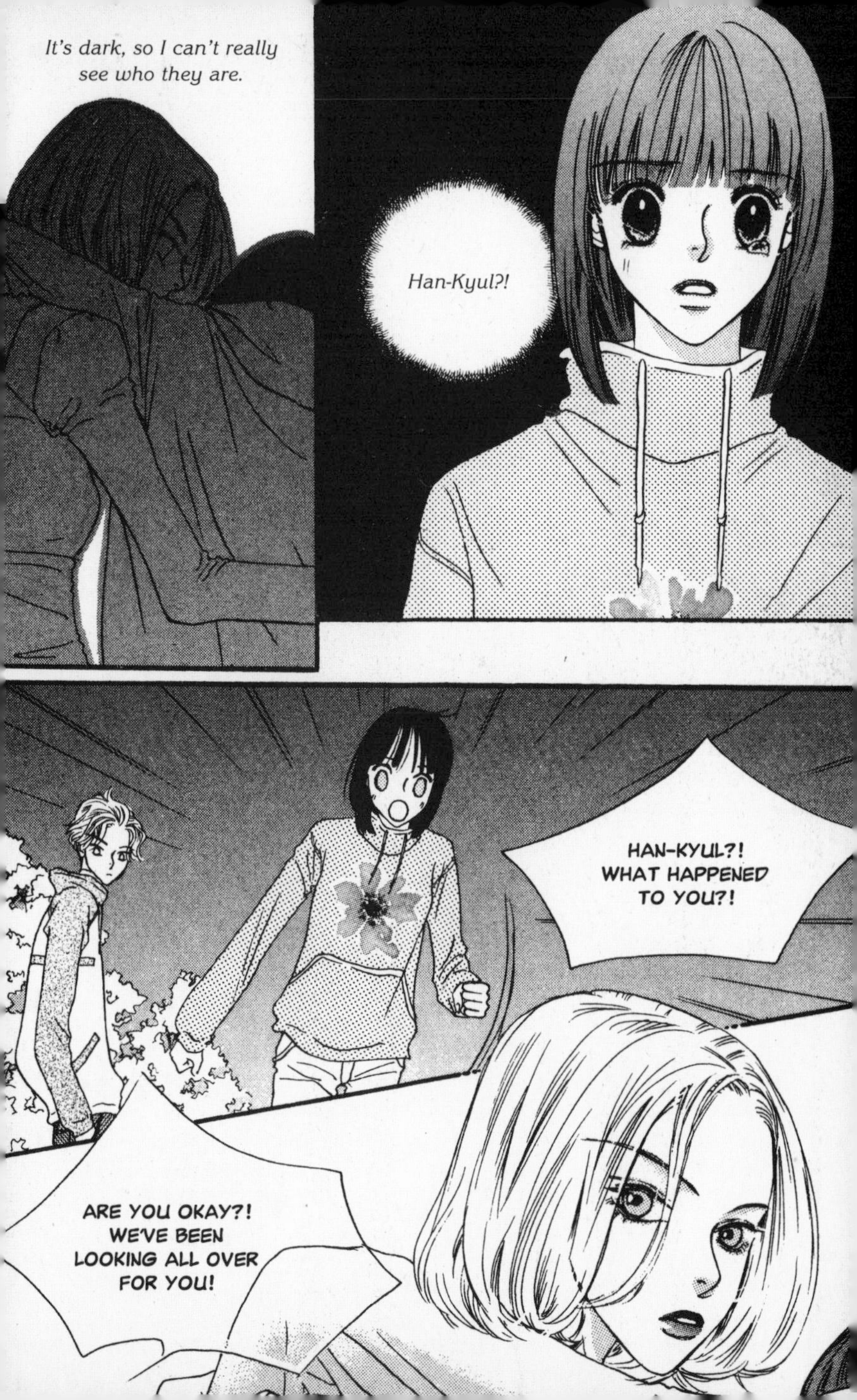
It's dark, so I can't really see who they are.
Han-Kyul?!
HAN-KYUL?! WHAT HAPPENED TO YOU?!
ARE YOU OKAY?! WE'VE BEEN LOOKING ALL OVER FOR YOU!

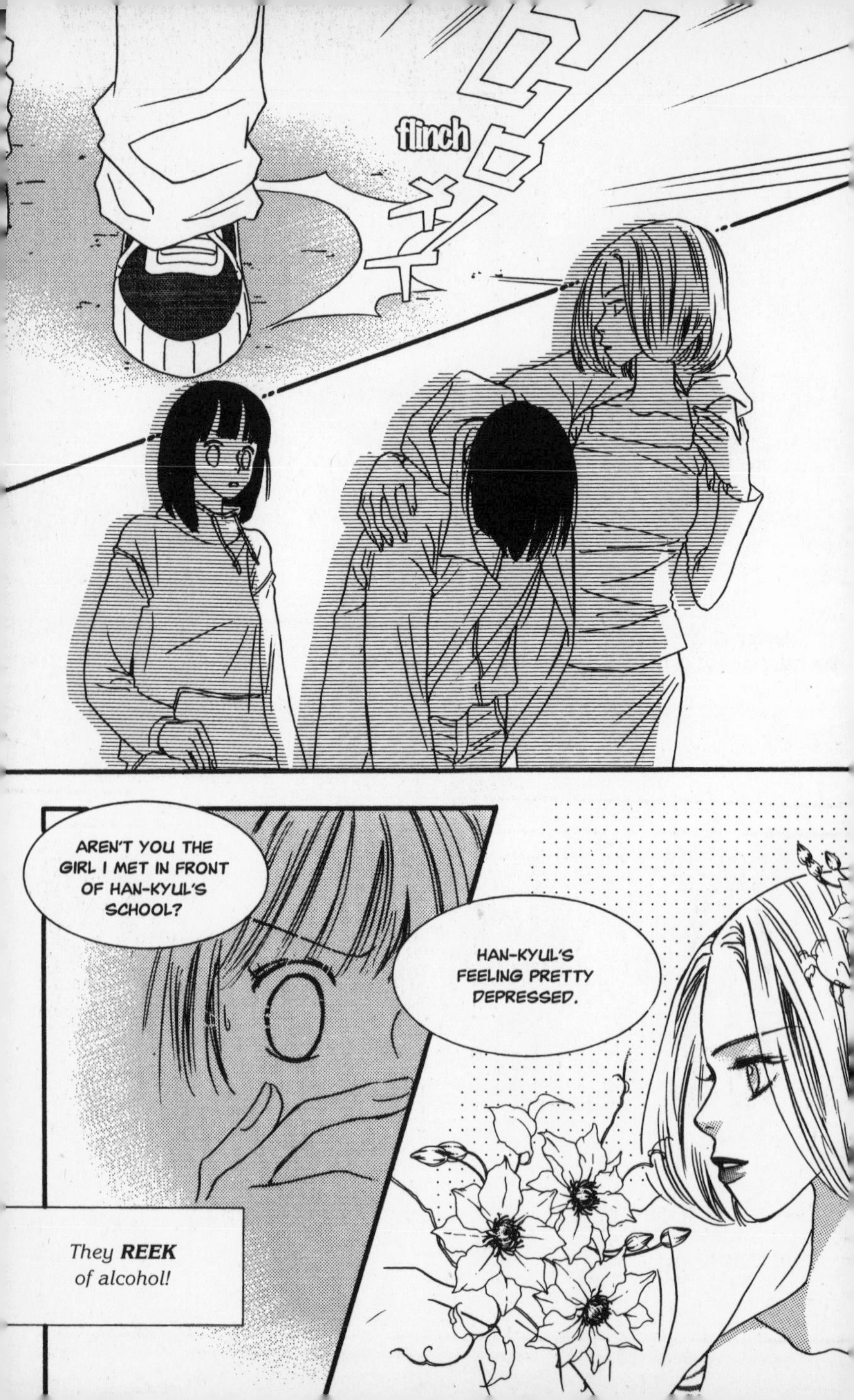
flinch
AREN'T YOU THE GIRL I MET IN FRONT OF HAN-KYUL'S SCHOOL?
HAN-KYUL'S FEELING PRETTY DEPRESSED.
They REEK of alcohol!

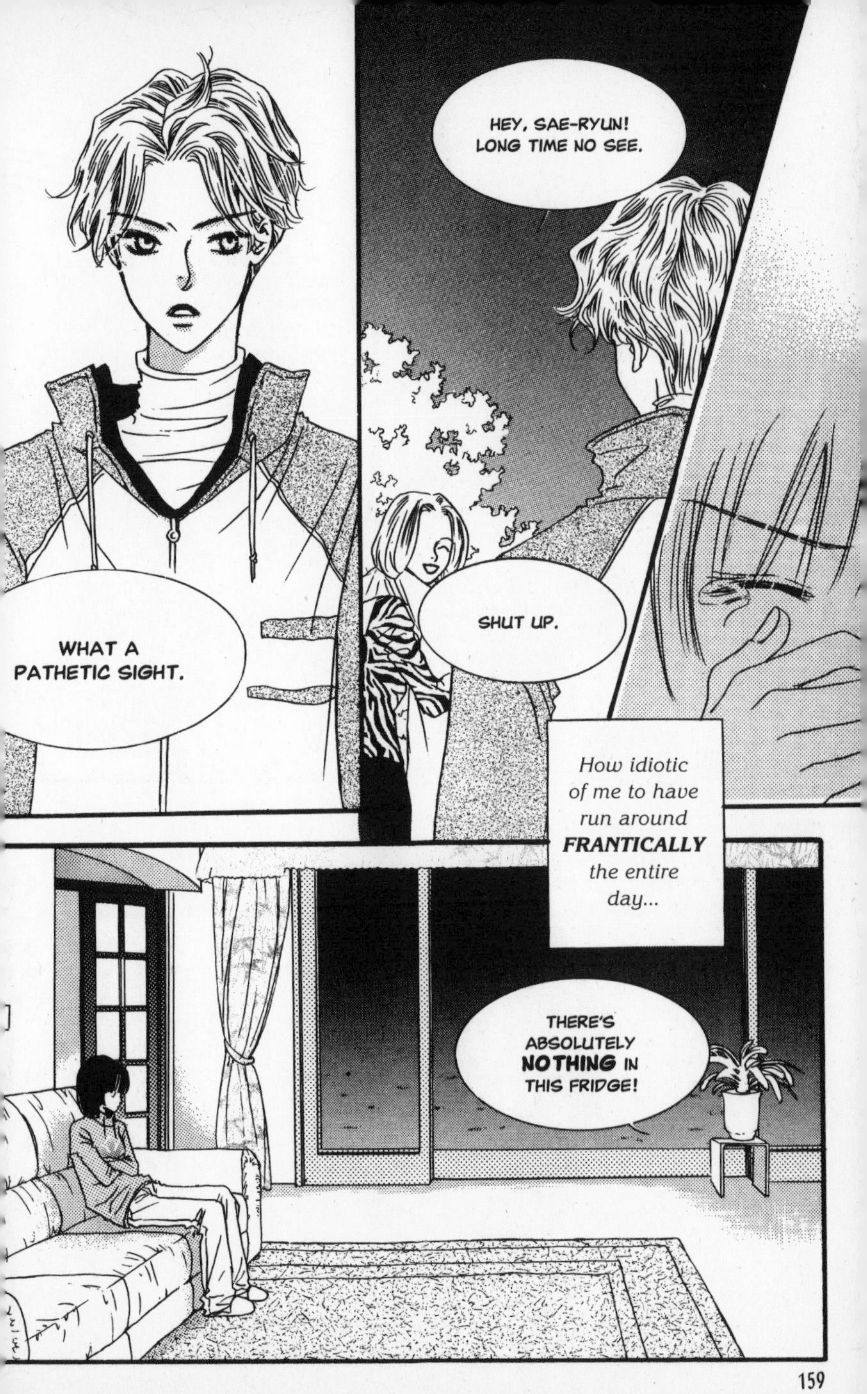
WHAT A PATHETIC SIGHT.
HEY, SAE-RYUN! LONG TIME NO SEE.
SHUT UP.
How idiotic of me to have run around **FRANTICALLY** the entire day...
THERE'S ABSOLUTELY **NOTHING** IN THIS FRIDGE!

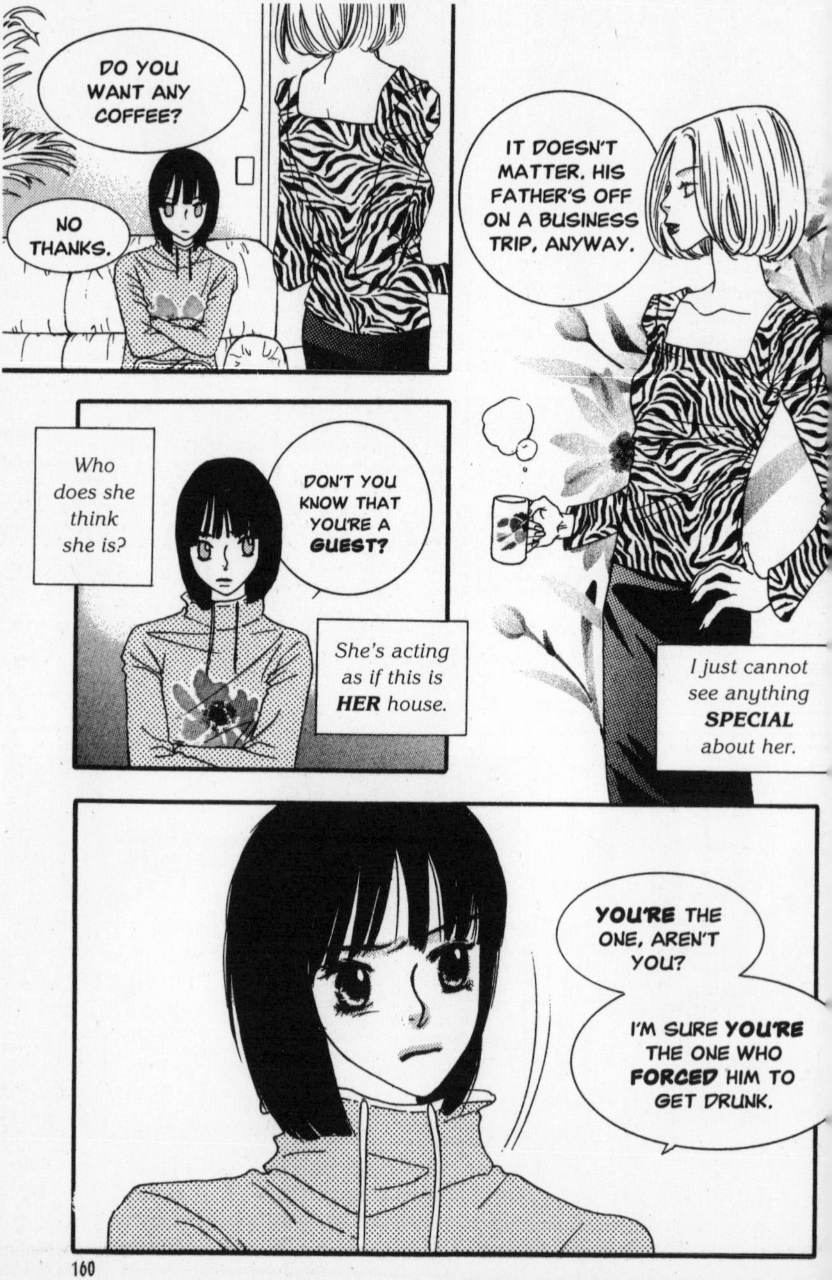
DO YOU WANT ANY COFFEE?
NO THANKS.
IT DOESN'T MATTER. HIS FATHER'S OFF ON A BUSINESS TRIP, ANYWAY.
Who does she think she is?
DON'T YOU KNOW THAT YOU'RE A GUEST?
She's acting as if this is HER house.
I just cannot see anything SPECIAL about her.
YOU'RE THE ONE, AREN'T YOU?
I'M SURE YOU'RE THE ONE WHO FORCED HIM TO GET DRUNK.

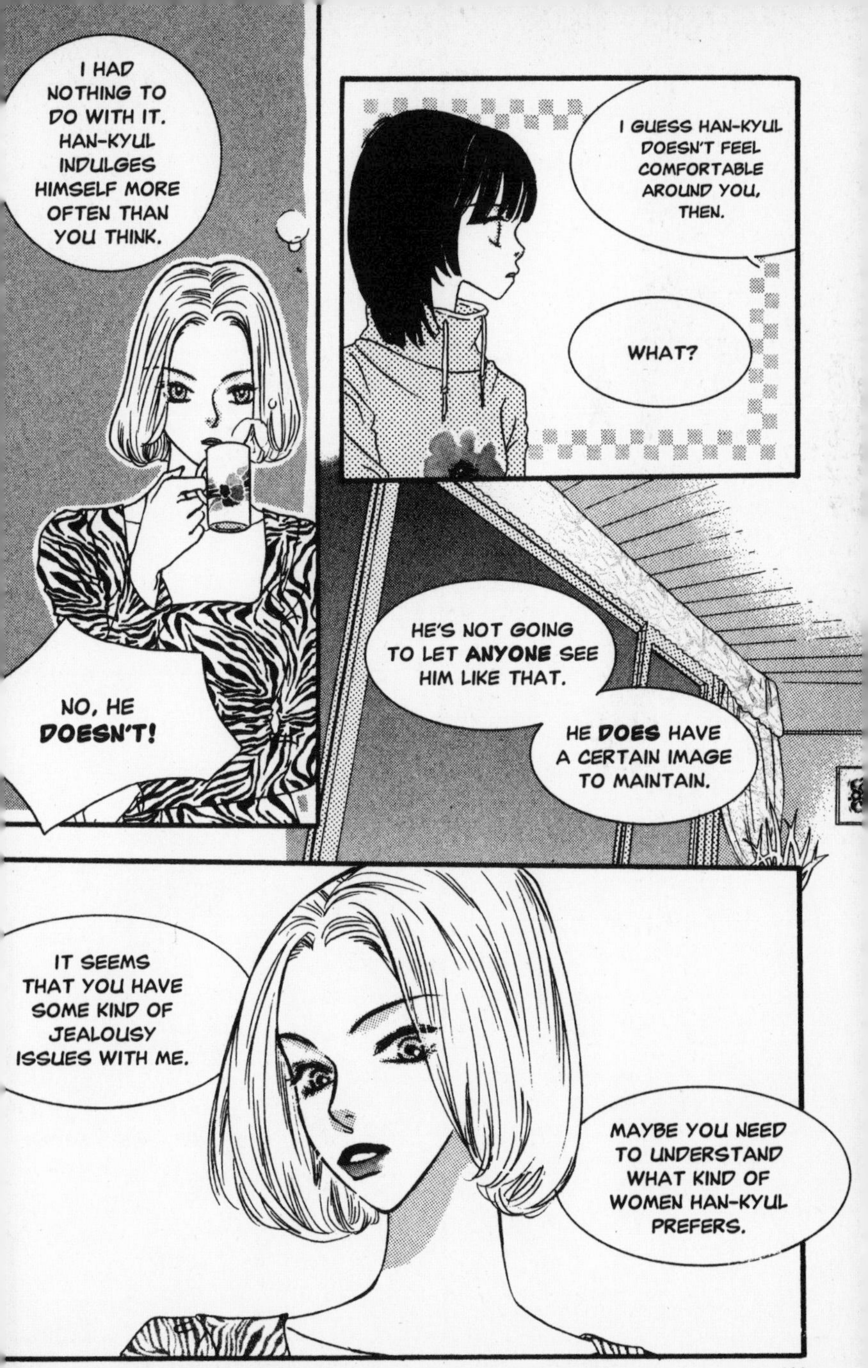
I HAD NOTHING TO DO WITH IT. HAN-KYUL INDULGES HIMSELF MORE OFTEN THAN YOU THINK.
I GUESS HAN-KYUL DOESN'T FEEL COMFORTABLE AROUND YOU, THEN.
WHAT?
NO, HE **DOESN'T!**
HE'S NOT GOING TO LET **ANYONE** SEE HIM LIKE THAT.
HE **DOES** HAVE A CERTAIN IMAGE TO MAINTAIN.
IT SEEMS THAT YOU HAVE SOME KIND OF JEALOUSY ISSUES WITH ME.
MAYBE YOU NEED TO UNDERSTAND WHAT KIND OF WOMEN HAN-KYUL PREFERS.

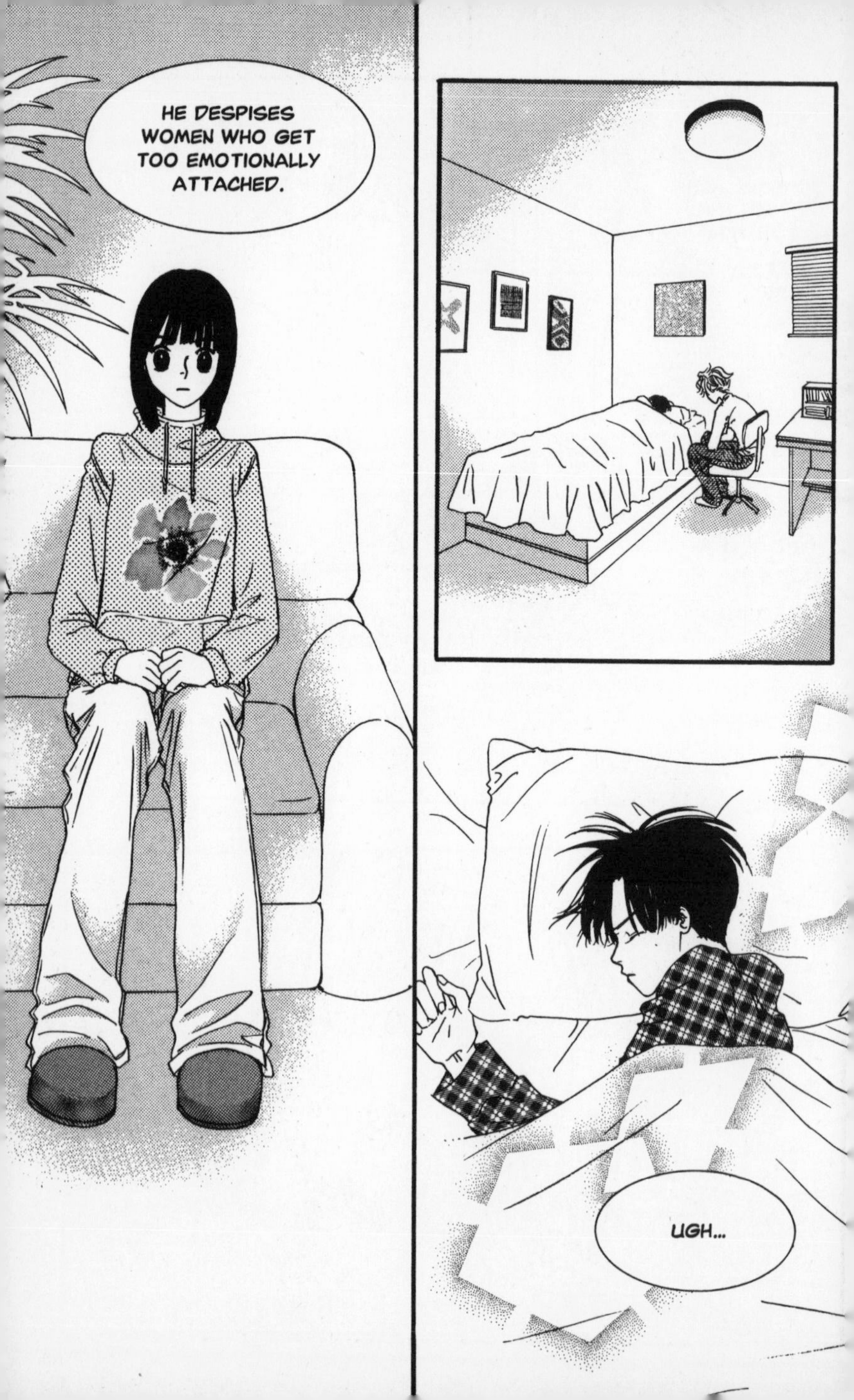
HE DESPISES WOMEN WHO GET TOO EMOTIONALLY ATTACHED.
UGH...

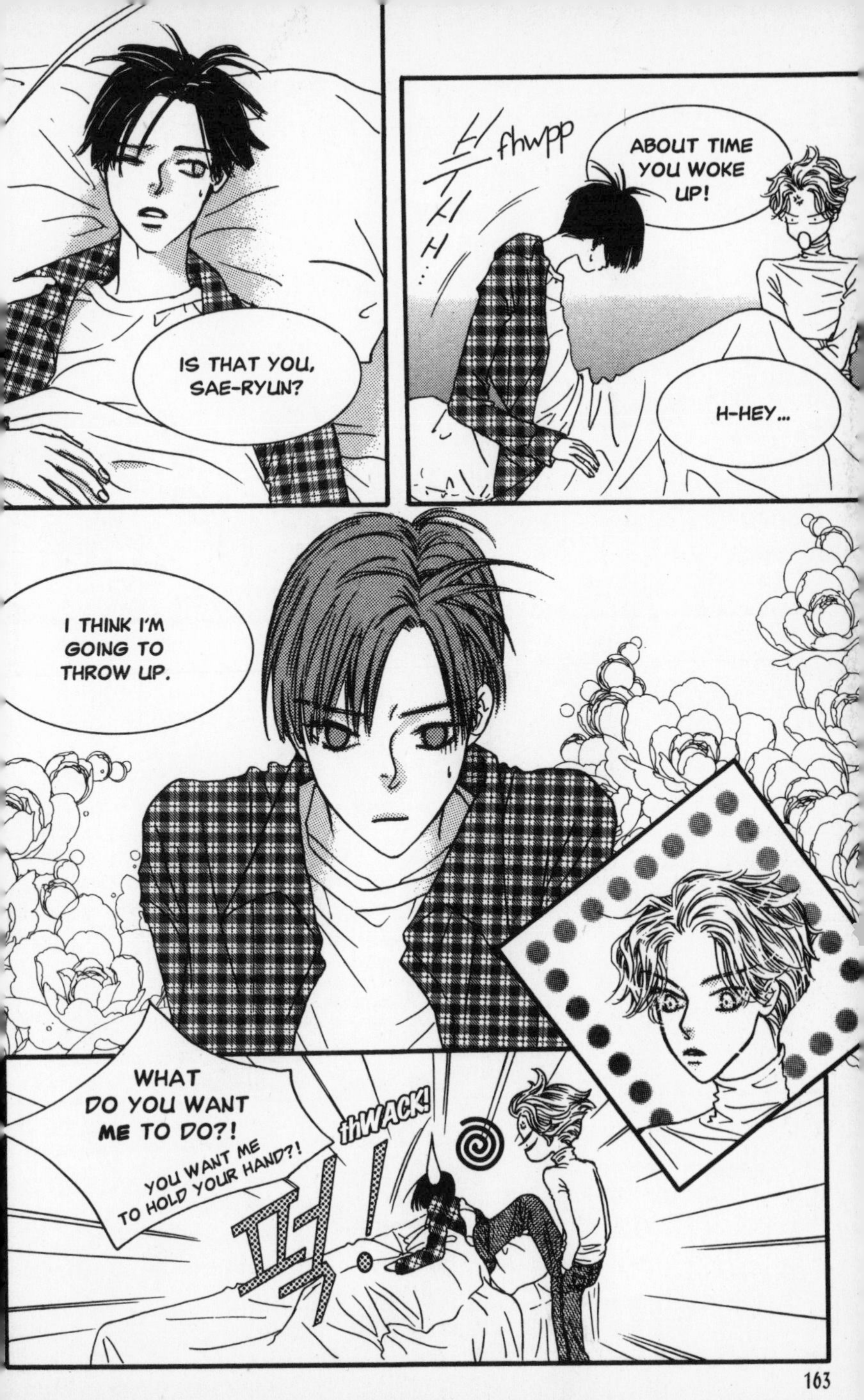
IS THAT YOU, SAE-RYUN?
fhwpp
ABOUT TIME YOU WOKE UP!
H-HEY...
I THINK I'M GOING TO THROW UP.
WHAT DO YOU WANT ME TO DO?!
YOU WANT ME TO HOLD YOUR HAND?!
thWACK!
퍽!

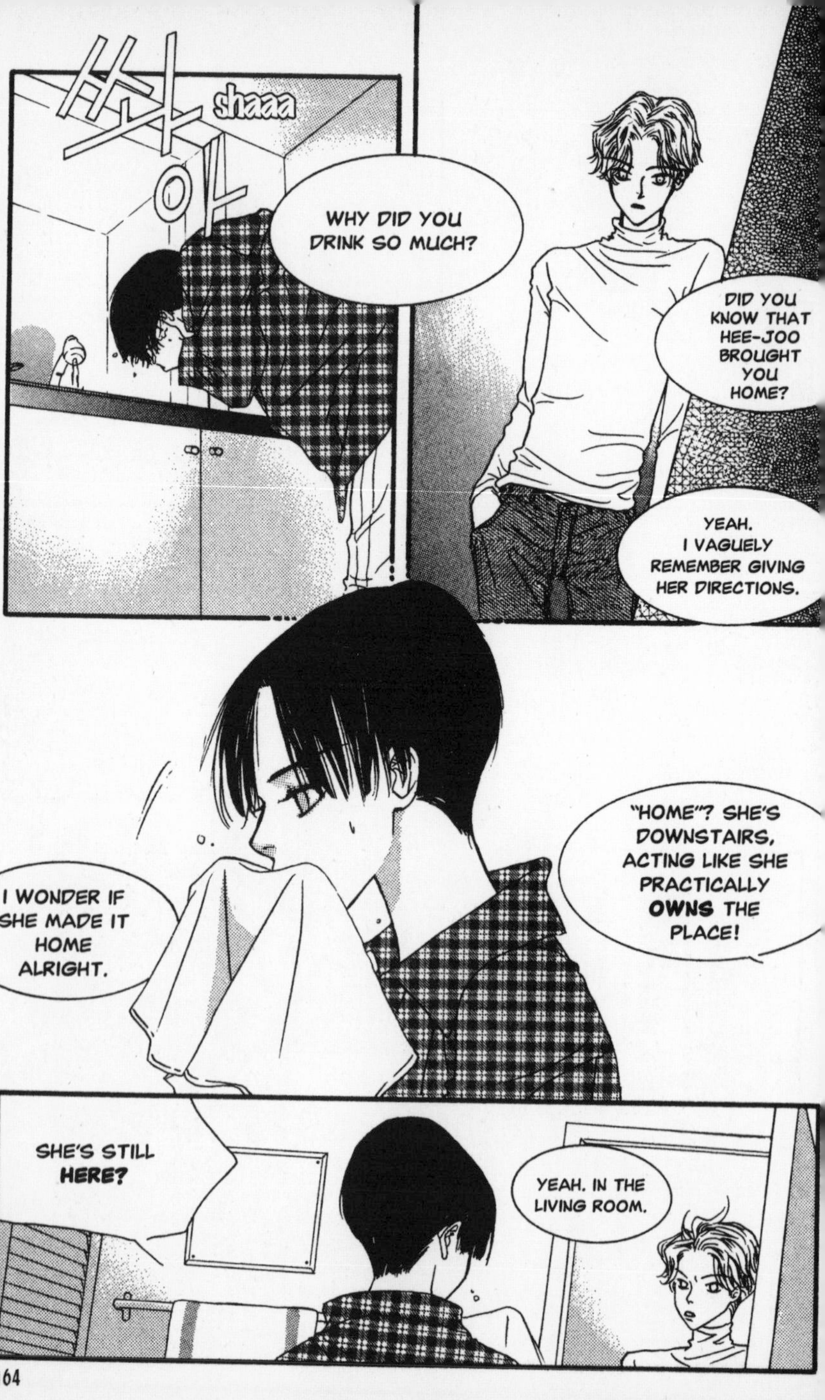
shaaa
WHY DID YOU DRINK SO MUCH?
DID YOU KNOW THAT HEE-JOO BROUGHT YOU HOME?
YEAH. I VAGUELY REMEMBER GIVING HER DIRECTIONS.
I WONDER IF SHE MADE IT HOME ALRIGHT.
"HOME"? SHE'S DOWNSTAIRS, ACTING LIKE SHE PRACTICALLY **OWNS** THE PLACE!
SHE'S STILL **HERE?**
YEAH. IN THE LIVING ROOM.

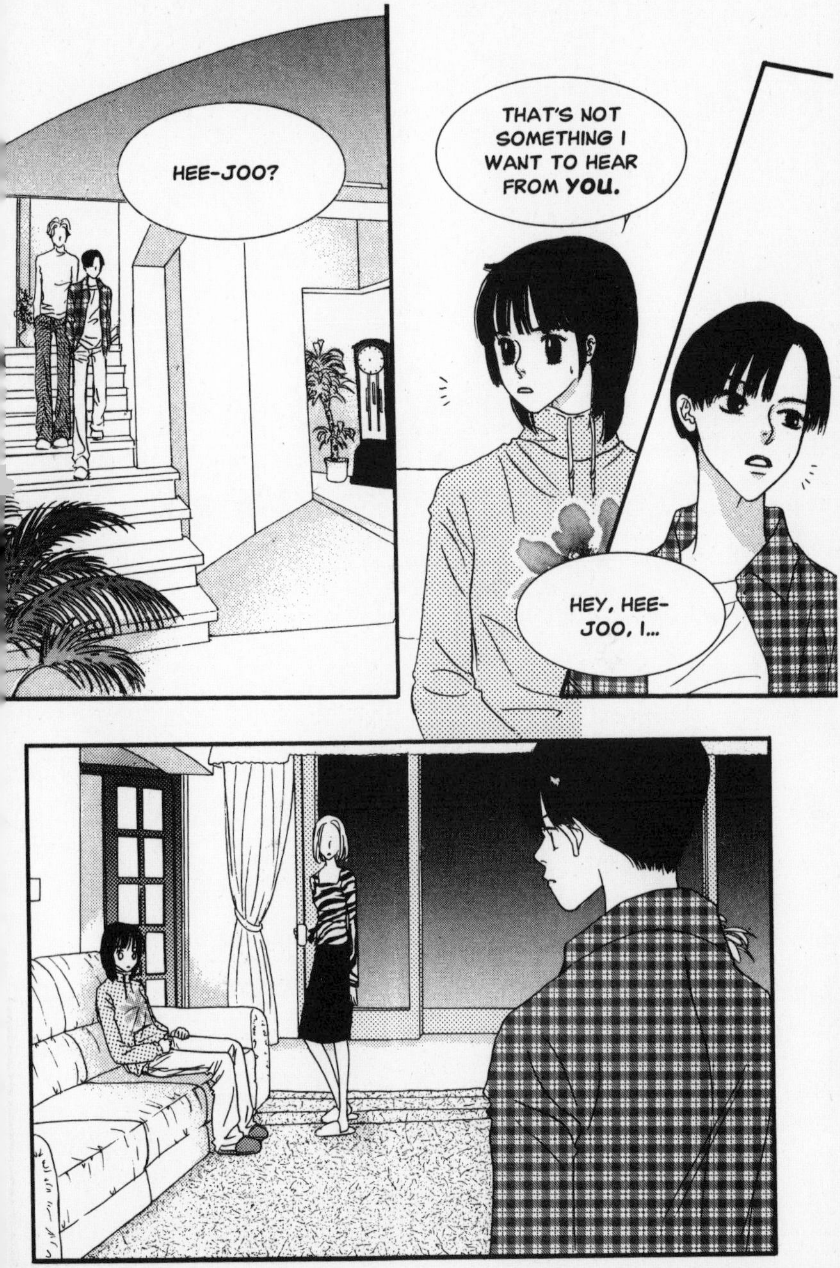
HEE-JOO?
THAT'S NOT SOMETHING I WANT TO HEAR FROM YOU.
HEY, HEE-JOO, I...

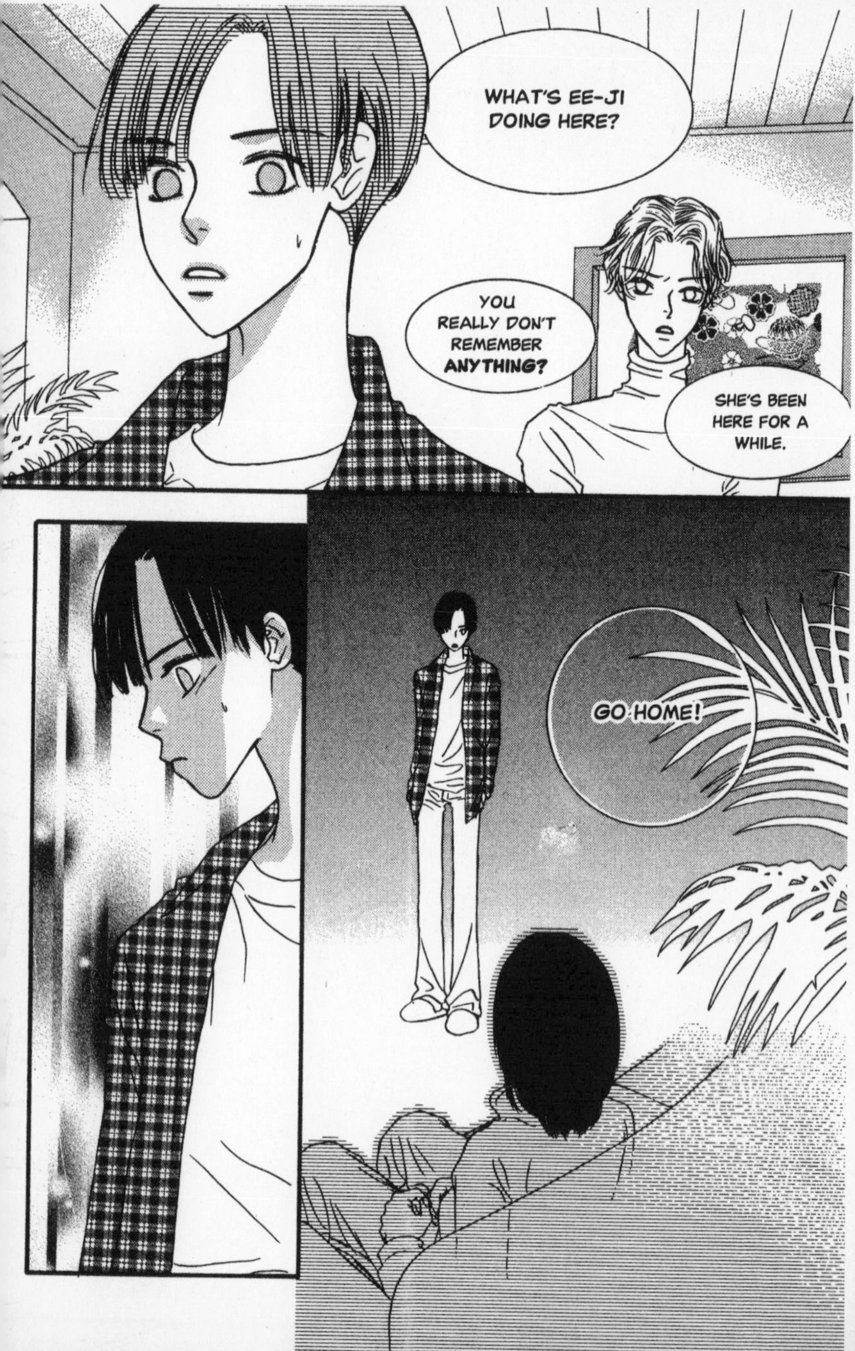
WHAT'S EE-JI DOING HERE?
YOU REALLY DON'T REMEMBER ANYTHING?
SHE'S BEEN HERE FOR A WHILE.
GO HOME!

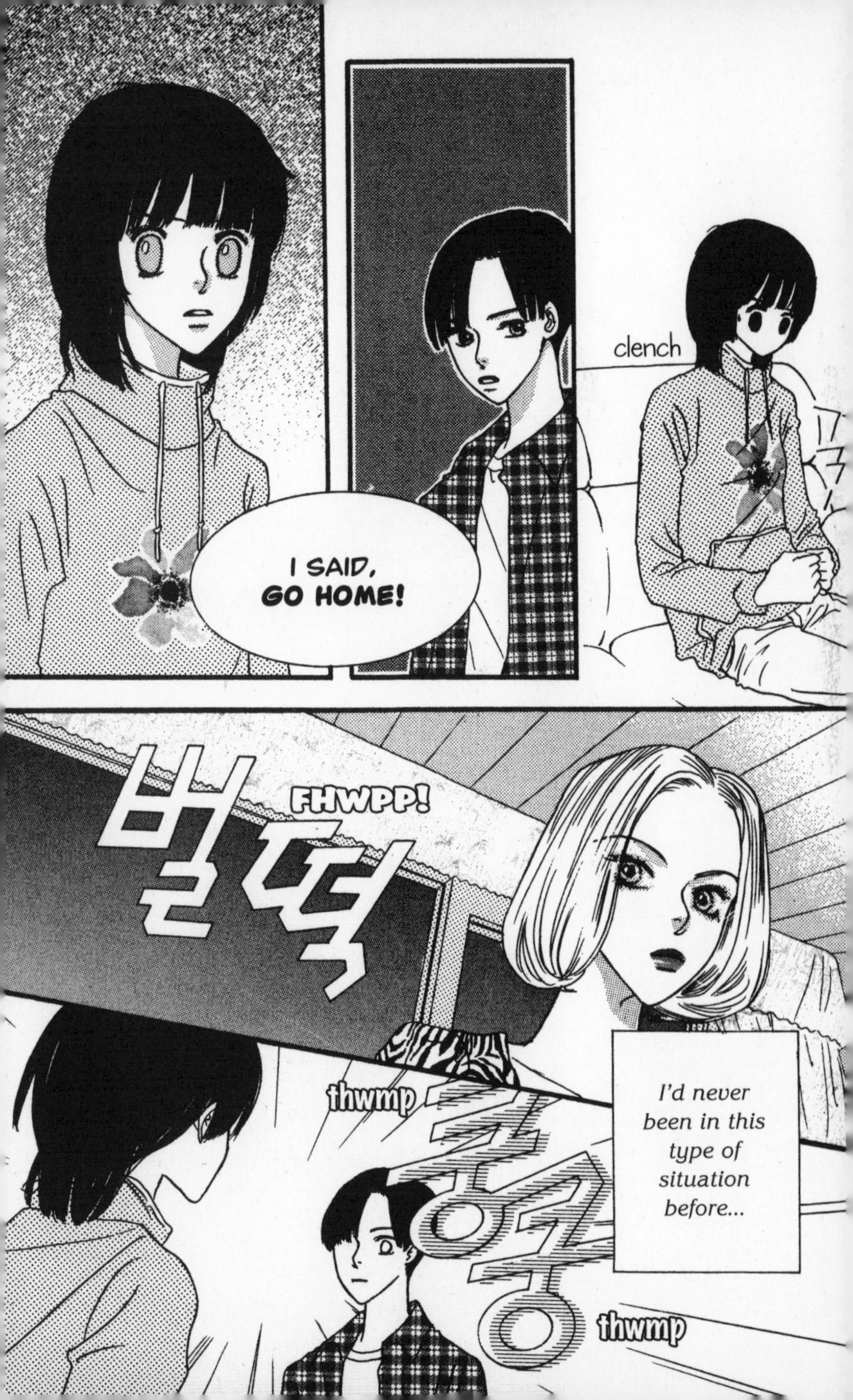

I SAID, GO HOME!
clench
벌떡
FHWPP!
I'd never been in this type of situation before...
thwmp
thwmp

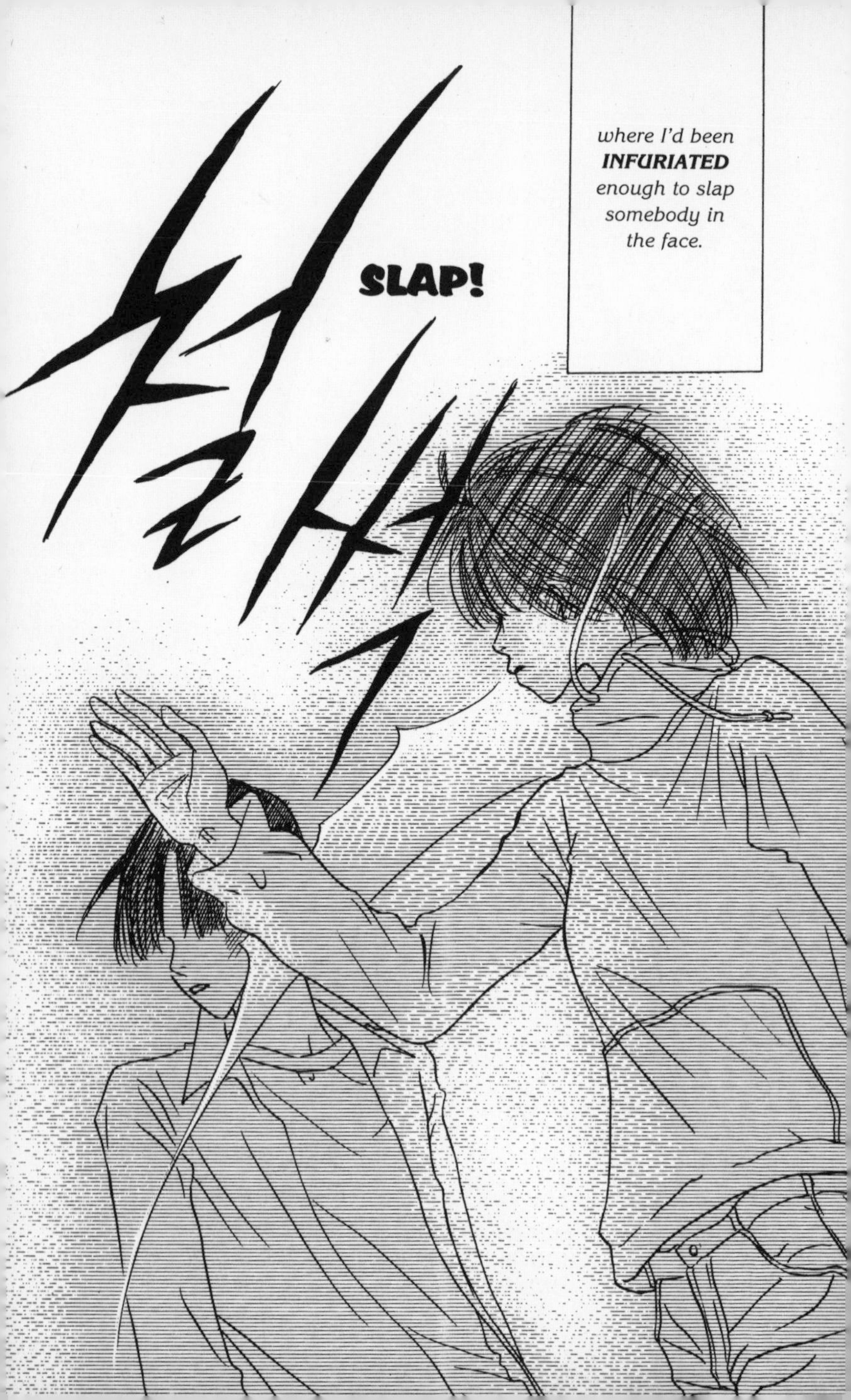
where I'd been INFURIATED enough to slap somebody in the face.
SLAP!

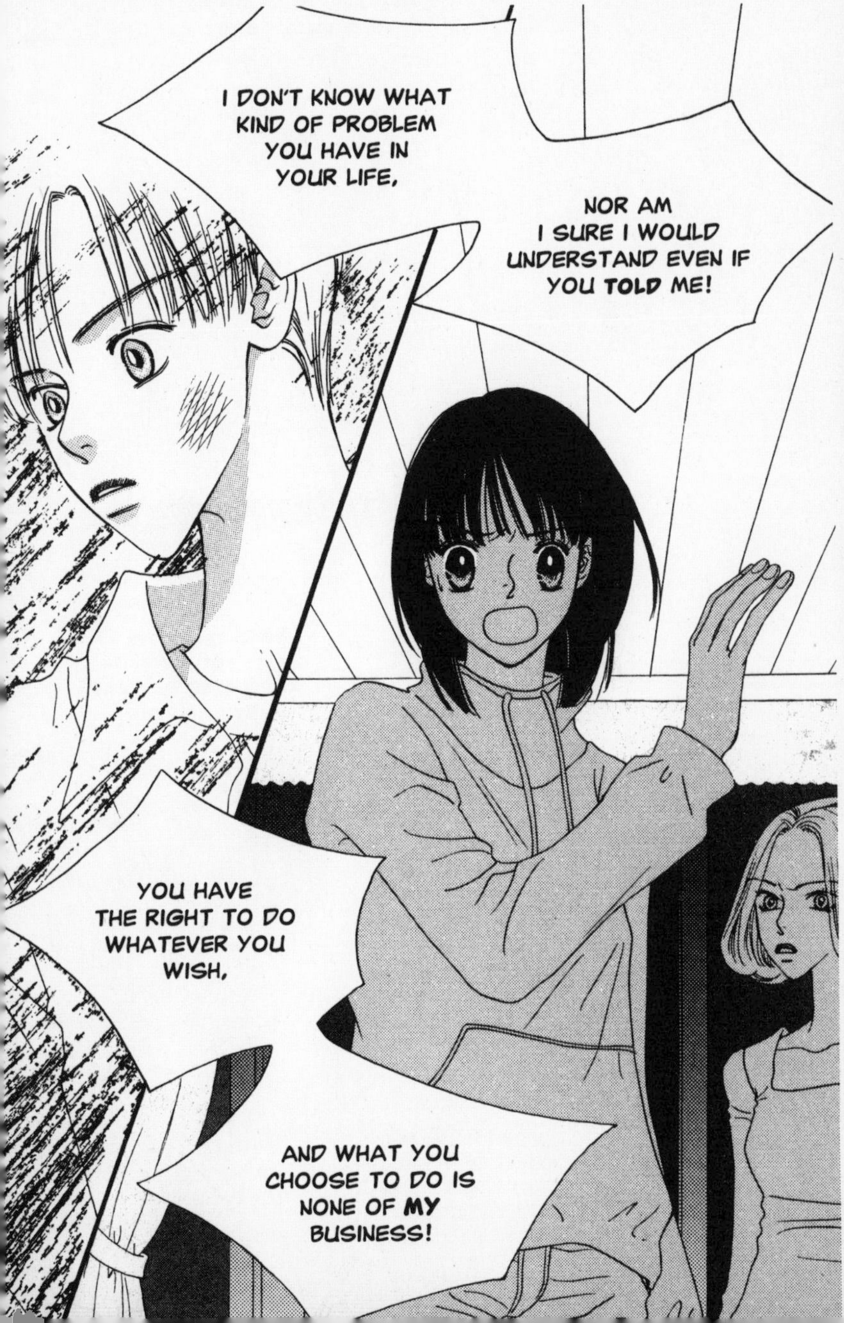
I DON'T KNOW WHAT KIND OF PROBLEM YOU HAVE IN YOUR LIFE,
NOR AM I SURE I WOULD UNDERSTAND EVEN IF YOU TOLD ME!
YOU HAVE THE RIGHT TO DO WHATEVER YOU WISH,
AND WHAT YOU CHOOSE TO DO IS NONE OF MY BUSINESS!

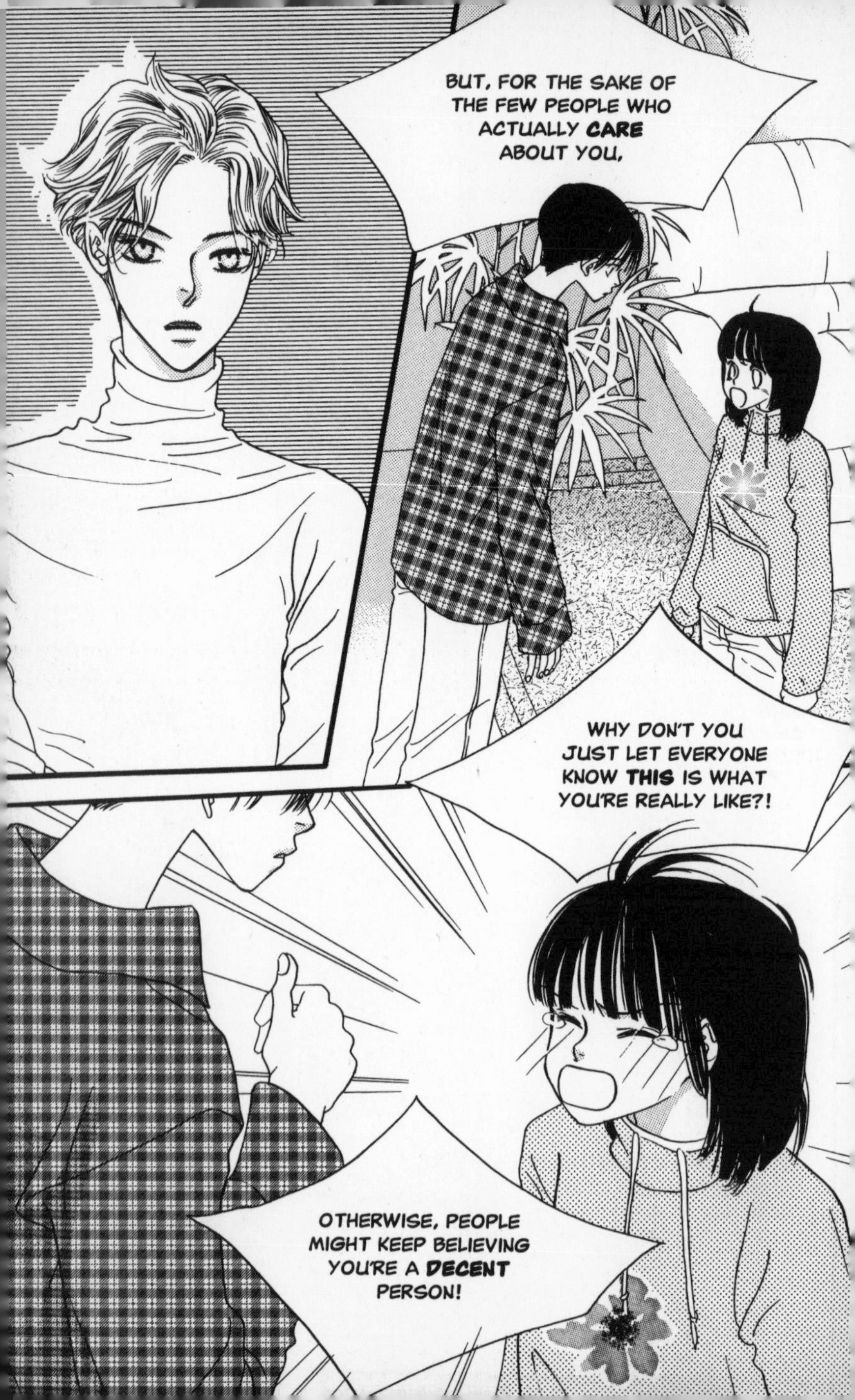
BUT, FOR THE SAKE OF THE FEW PEOPLE WHO ACTUALLY **CARE** ABOUT YOU,
WHY DON'T YOU JUST LET EVERYONE KNOW **THIS** IS WHAT YOU'RE REALLY LIKE?!
OTHERWISE, PEOPLE MIGHT KEEP BELIEVING YOU'RE A **DECENT** PERSON!

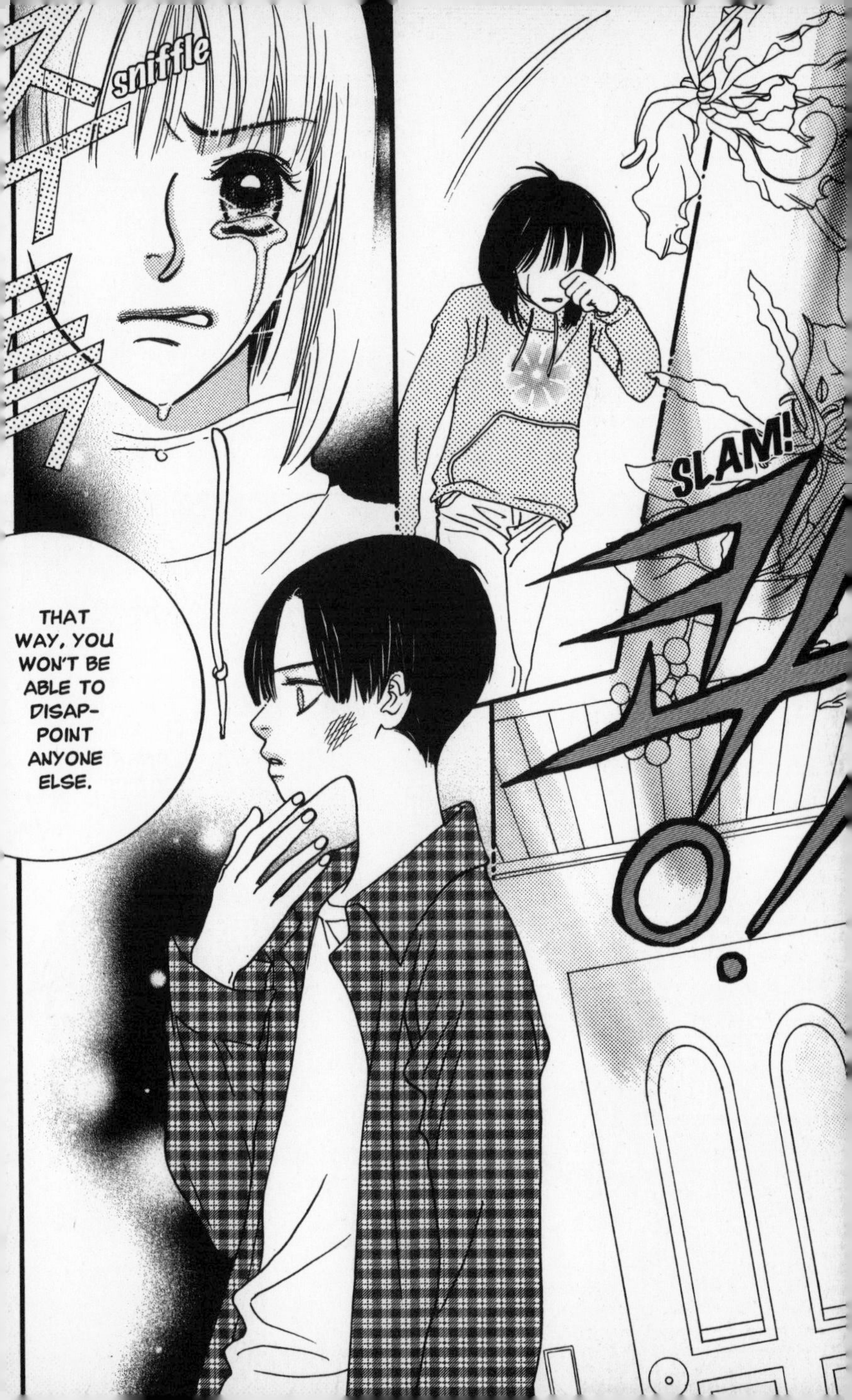
SLAM!
sniffle
THAT WAY, YOU WON'T BE ABLE TO DISAP-POINT ANYONE ELSE.

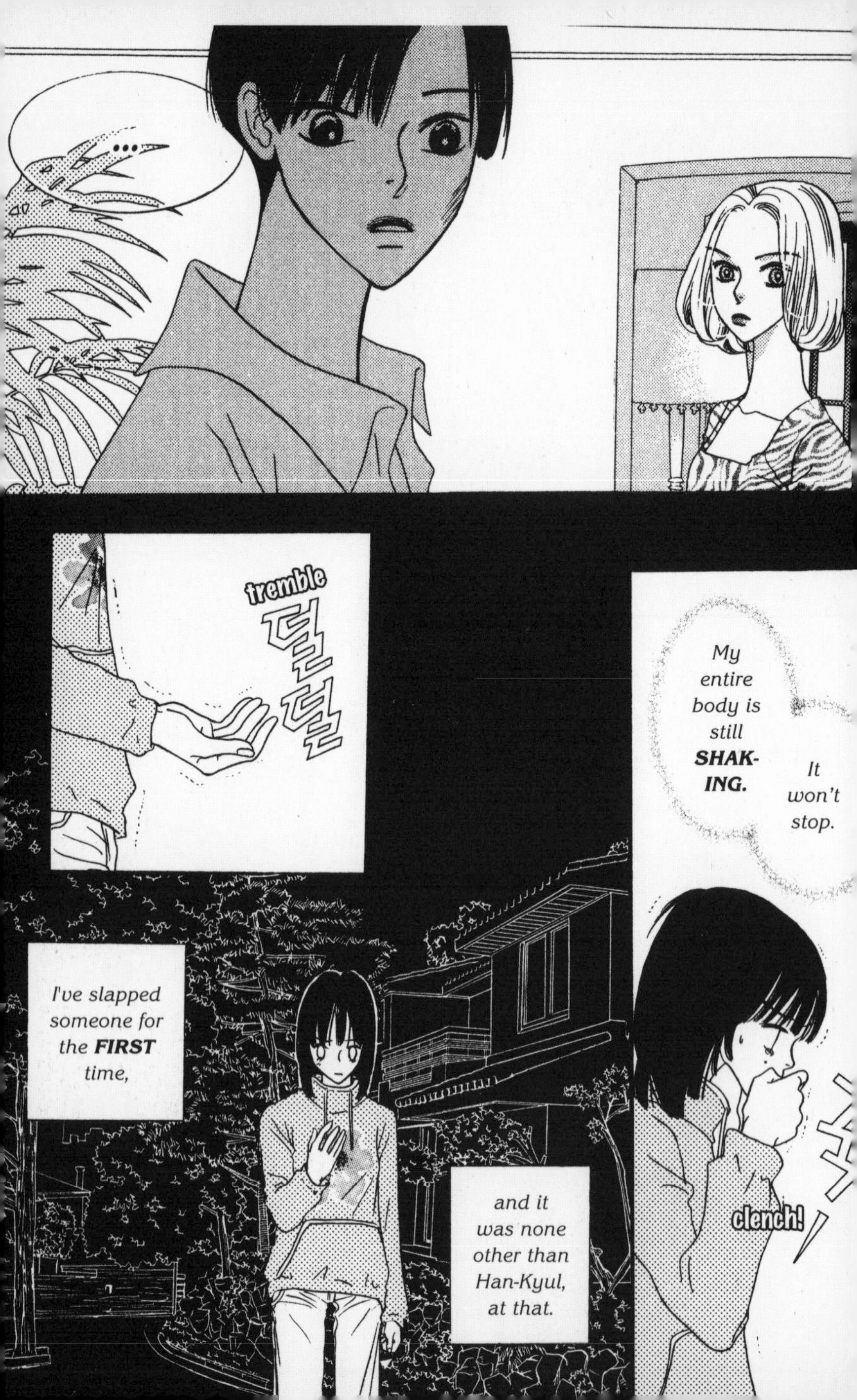
...
tremble
덜덜
My entire body is still SHAKING.
It won't stop.
I've slapped someone for the FIRST time,
and it was none other than Han-Kyul, at that.
clench!

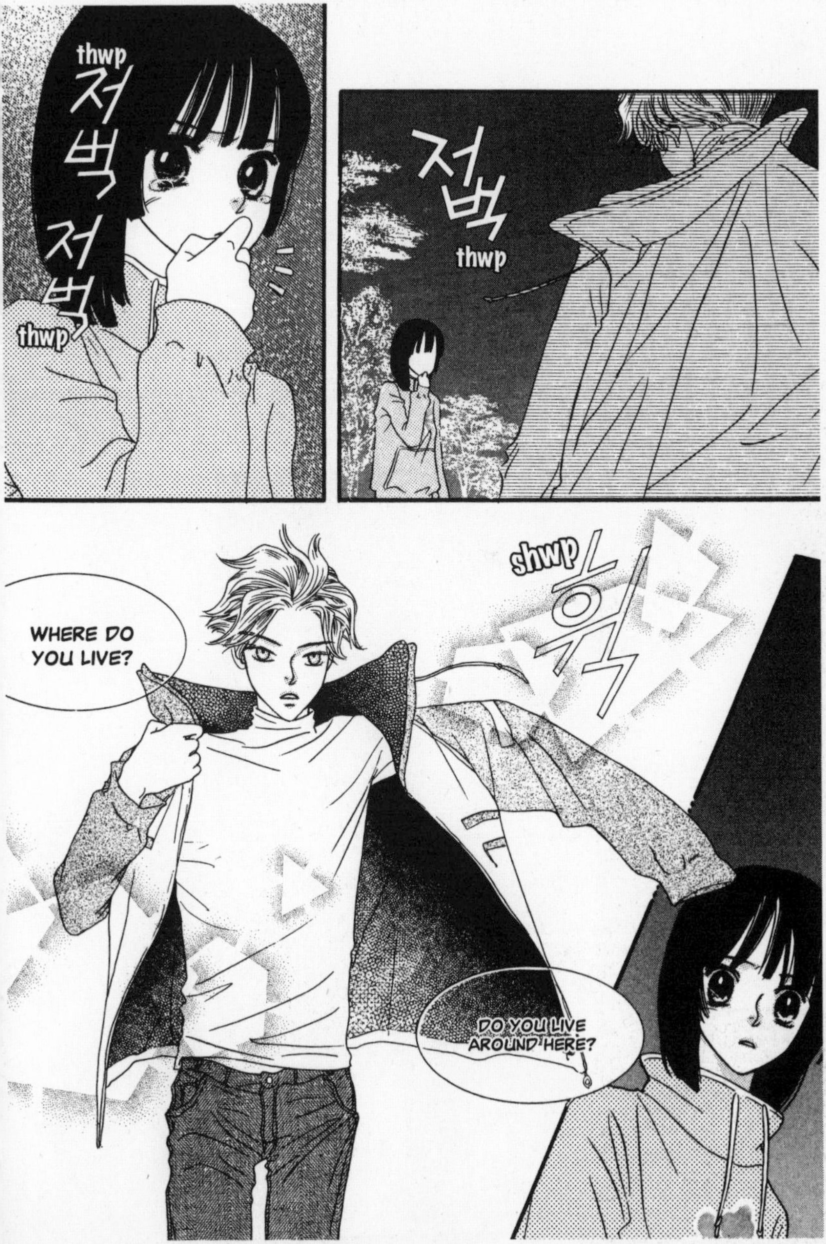
thwp
저벅 저벅
thwp
thwp
shwp
휙
WHERE DO YOU LIVE?
DO YOU LIVE AROUND HERE?

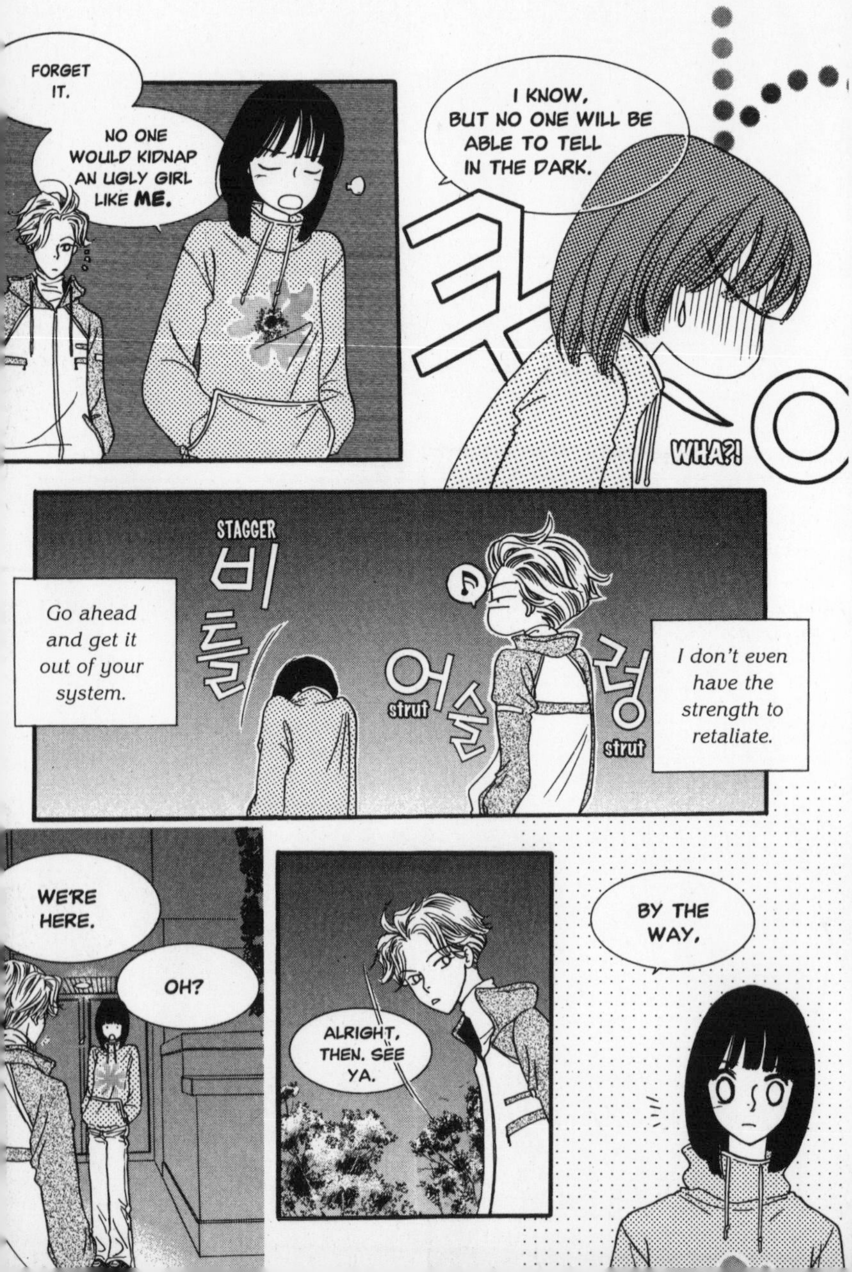
FORGET IT.
NO ONE WOULD KIDNAP AN UGLY GIRL LIKE ME.
I KNOW, BUT NO ONE WILL BE ABLE TO TELL IN THE DARK.
WHA?!
Go ahead and get it out of your system.
STAGGER
비틀
어슬렁
strut
strut
I don't even have the strength to retaliate.
WE'RE HERE.
OH?
ALRIGHT, THEN. SEE YA.
BY THE WAY,

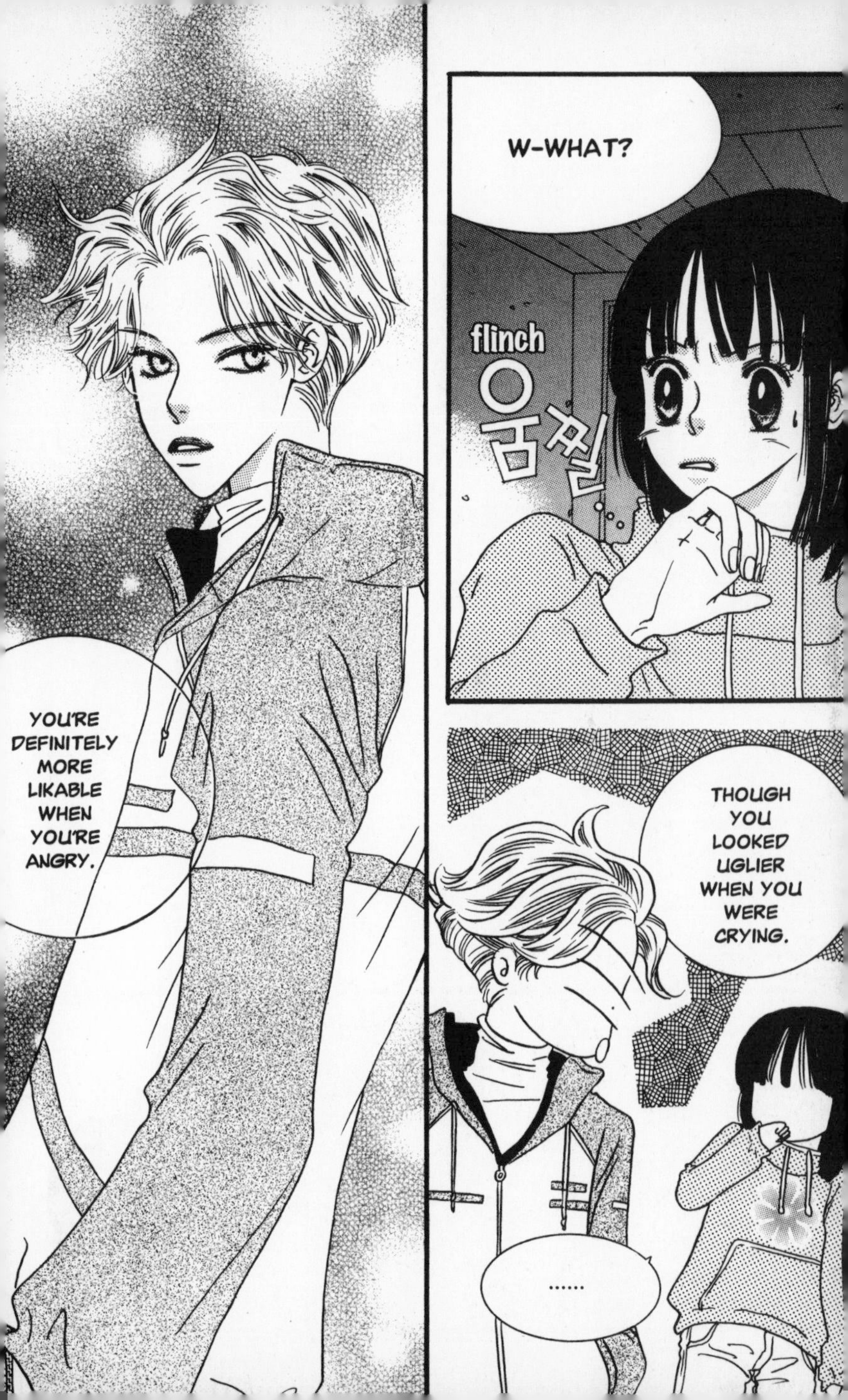
YOU'RE DEFINITELY MORE LIKABLE WHEN YOU'RE ANGRY.
W-WHAT?
flinch
움찔
THOUGH YOU LOOKED UGLIER WHEN YOU WERE CRYING.
......

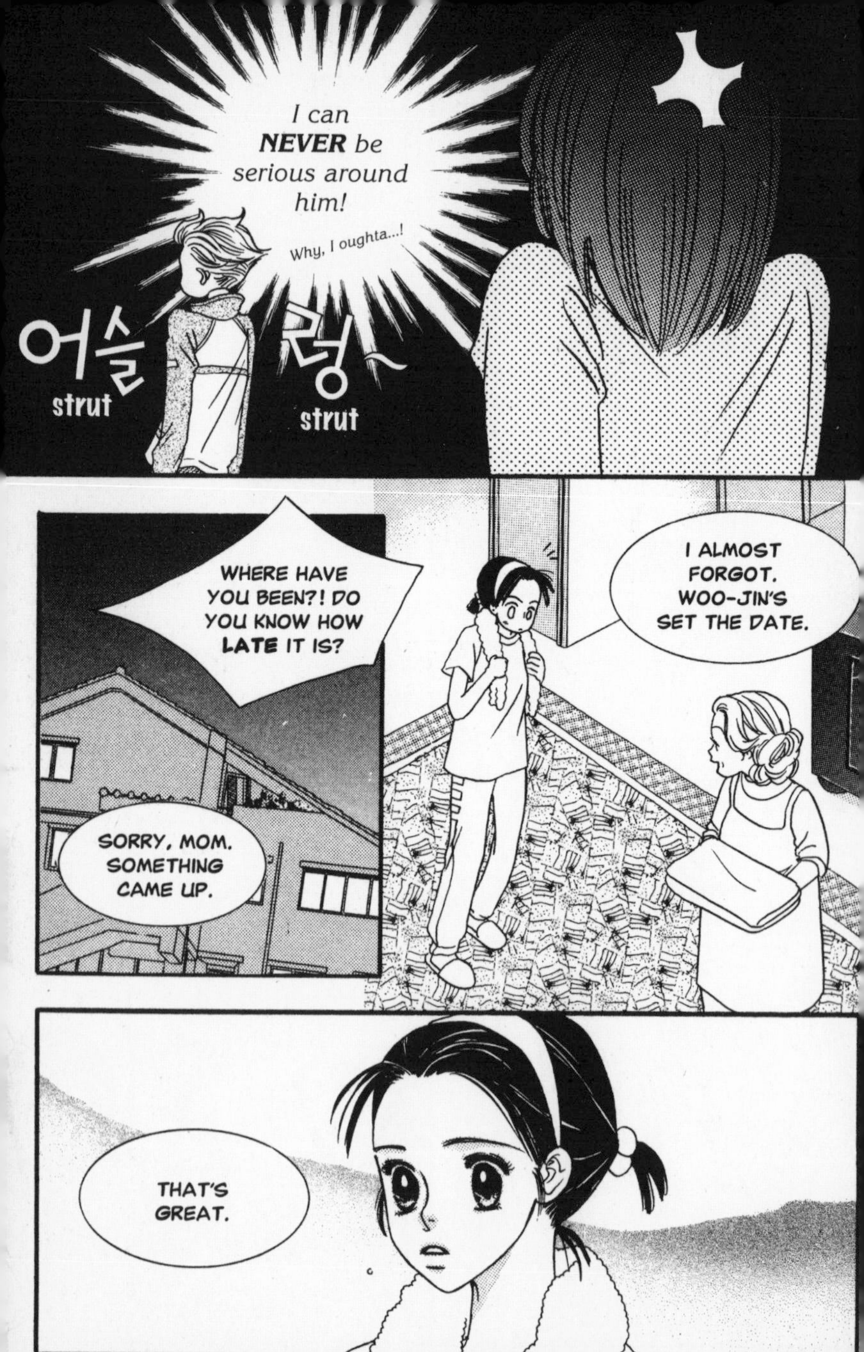
I can NEVER be serious around him!
Why, I oughta...!
어슬
strut
렁~
strut
WHERE HAVE YOU BEEN?! DO YOU KNOW HOW LATE IT IS?
SORRY, MOM. SOMETHING CAME UP.
I ALMOST FORGOT. WOO-JIN'S SET THE DATE.
THAT'S GREAT.

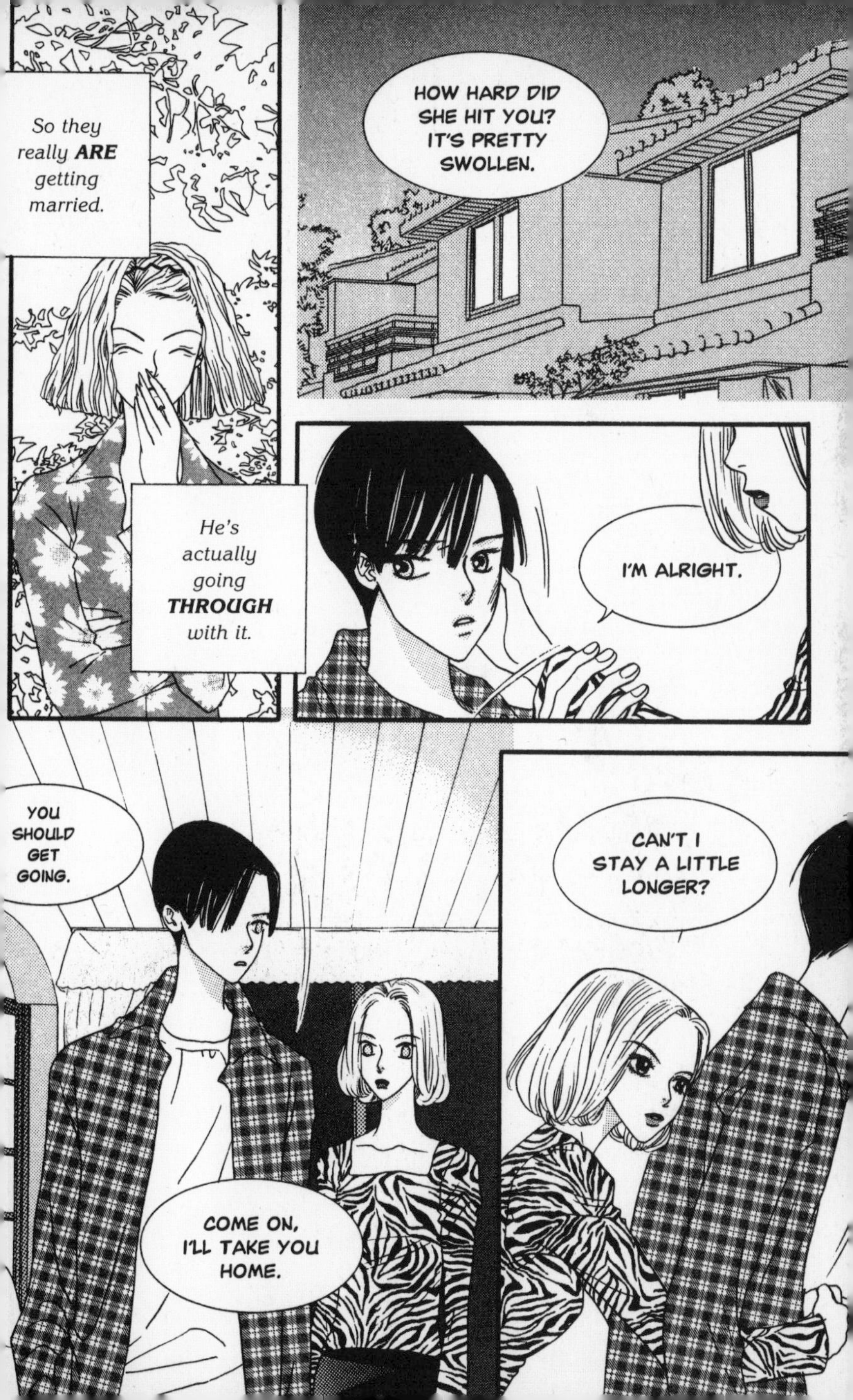
So they really **ARE** getting married.
HOW HARD DID SHE HIT YOU? IT'S PRETTY SWOLLEN.
He's actually going **THROUGH** with it.
I'M ALRIGHT.
YOU SHOULD GET GOING.
CAN'T I STAY A LITTLE LONGER?
COME ON, I'LL TAKE YOU HOME.

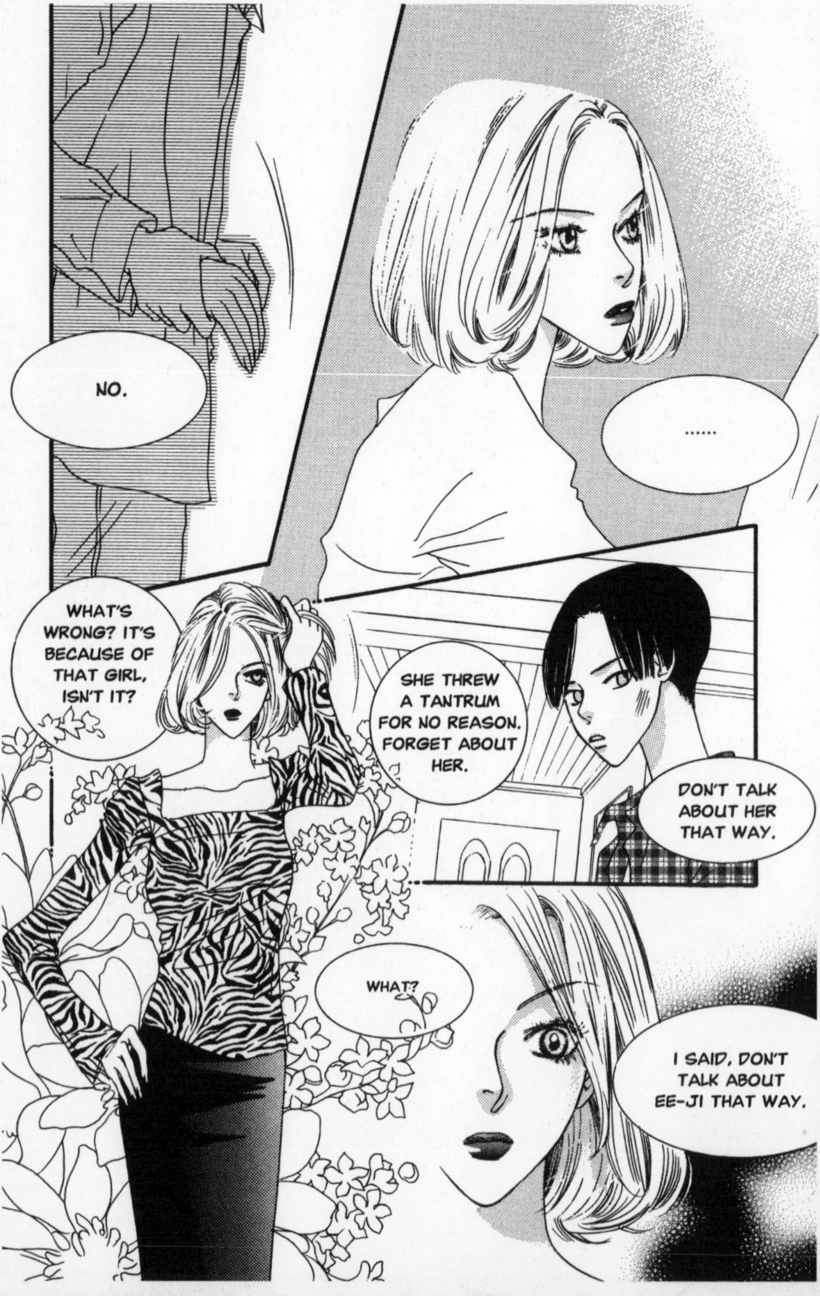
NO.
......
WHAT'S WRONG? IT'S BECAUSE OF THAT GIRL, ISN'T IT?
SHE THREW A TANTRUM FOR NO REASON. FORGET ABOUT HER.
DON'T TALK ABOUT HER THAT WAY.
WHAT?
I SAID, DON'T TALK ABOUT EE-JI THAT WAY.

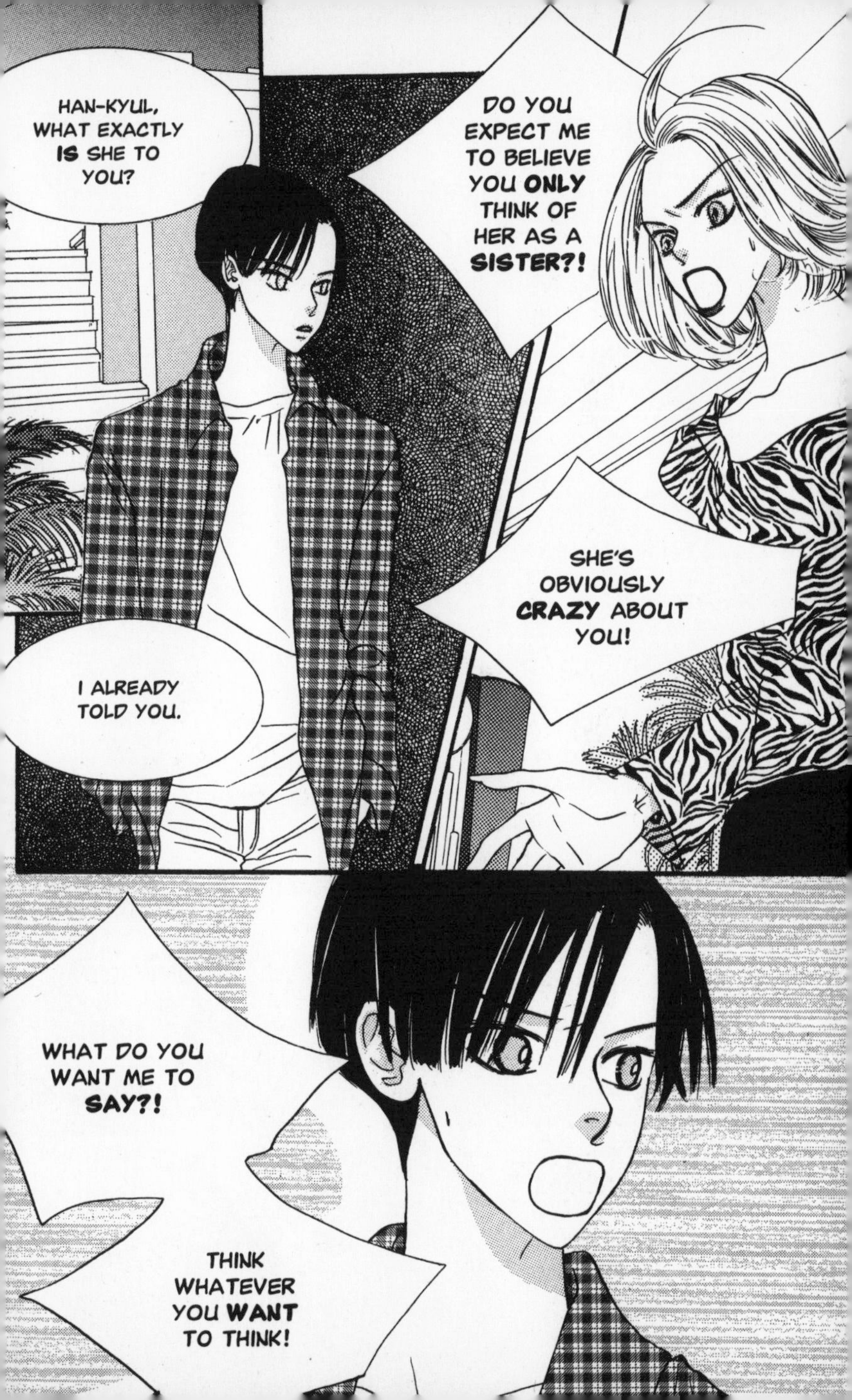
HAN-KYUL, WHAT EXACTLY IS SHE TO YOU?
I ALREADY TOLD YOU.
DO YOU EXPECT ME TO BELIEVE YOU ONLY THINK OF HER AS A SISTER?!
SHE'S OBVIOUSLY CRAZY ABOUT YOU!
WHAT DO YOU WANT ME TO SAY?!
THINK WHATEVER YOU WANT TO THINK!

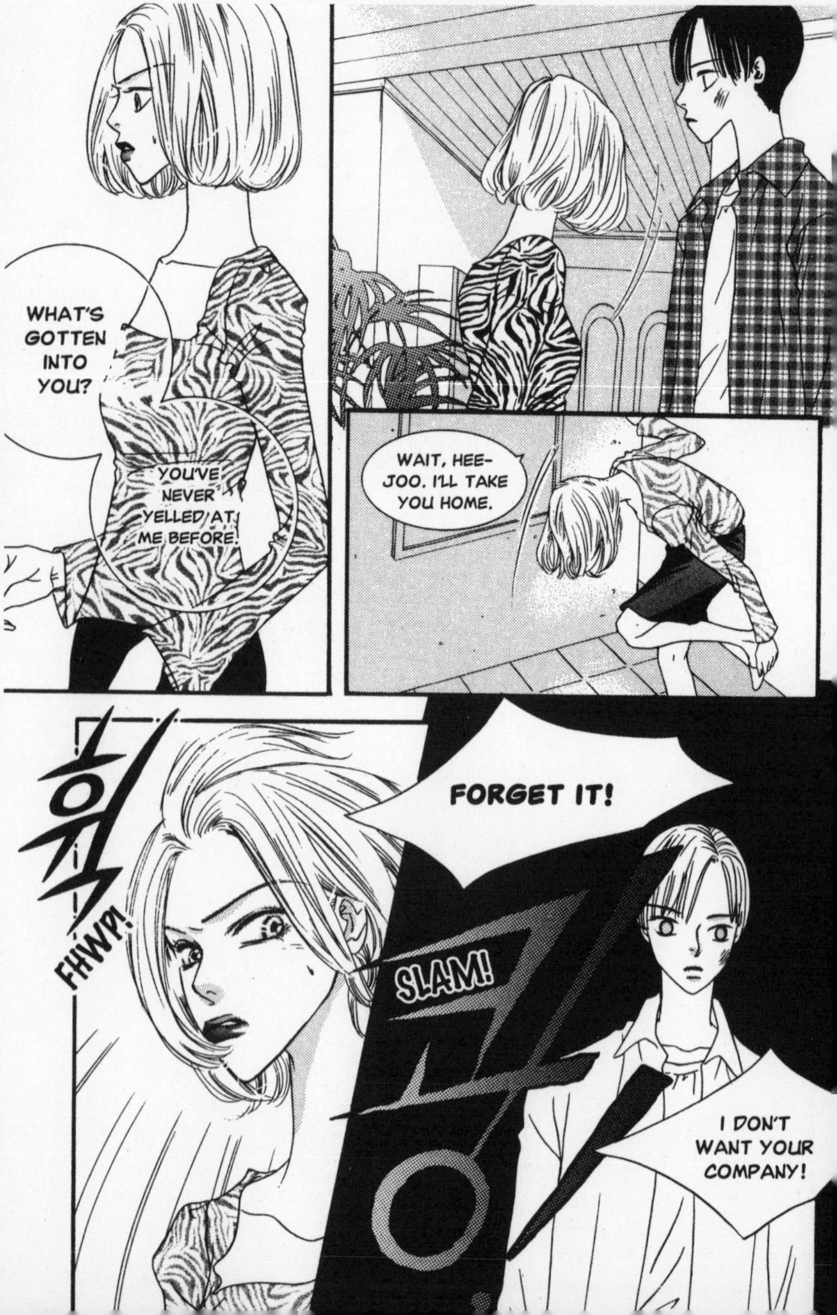
WHAT'S GOTTEN INTO YOU?
YOU'VE NEVER YELLED AT ME BEFORE.
WAIT, HEE-JOO. I'LL TAKE YOU HOME.
FHWP!
FORGET IT!
SLAM!
I DON'T WANT YOUR COMPANY!

What's gotten into me...?

Well, I always **DID** put up with her temper tantrums.

I met her when I was living with my grandparents.

I was drawn to her bold and straightforward personality,

which is **COMPLETELY** different from Ee-Ji's personality.

Thus, it surprised me to see Ee-Ji lash out like that.

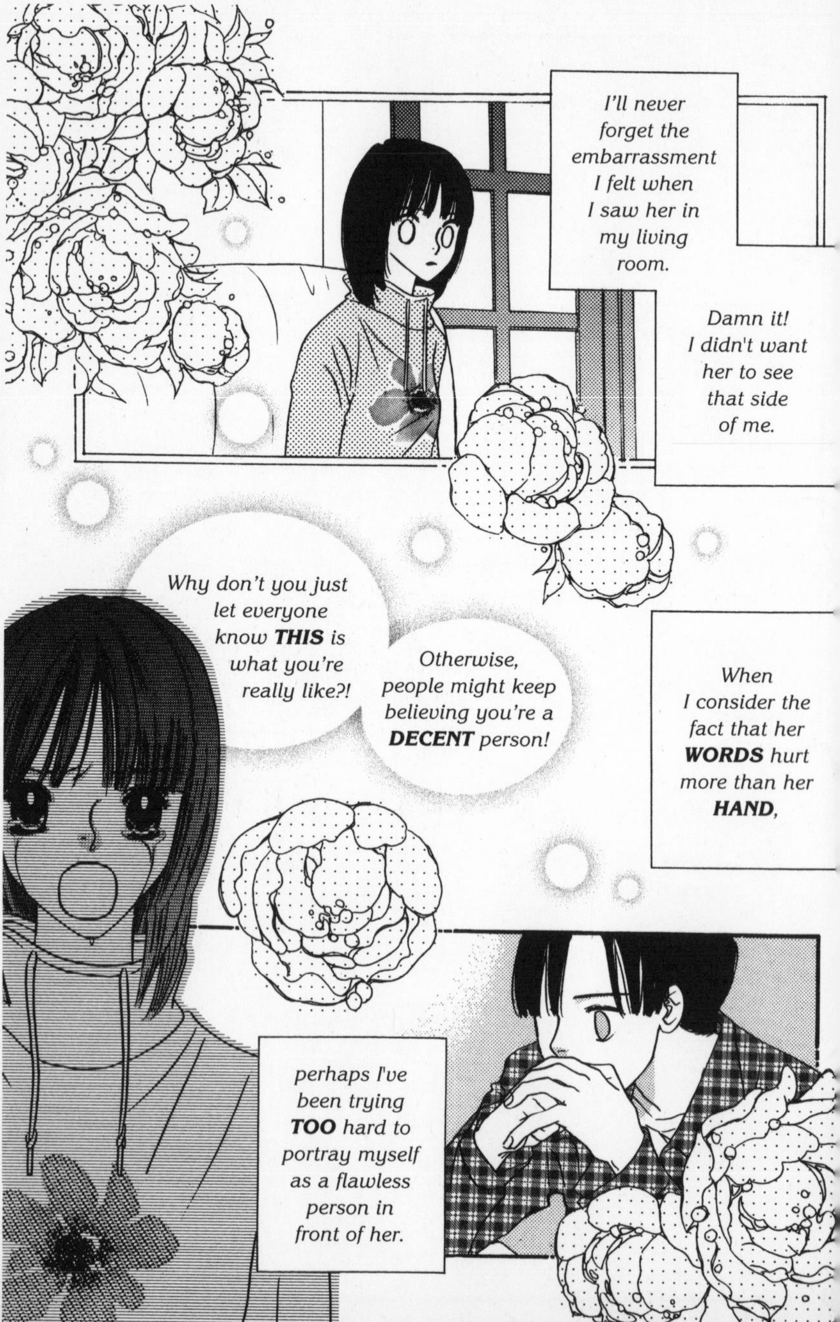
I'll never forget the embarrassment I felt when I saw her in my living room.
Damn it! I didn't want her to see that side of me.
Why don't you just let everyone know **THIS** is what you're really like?!
Otherwise, people might keep believing you're a **DECENT** person!
When I consider the fact that her **WORDS** hurt more than her **HAND**,
perhaps I've been trying **TOO** hard to portray myself as a flawless person in front of her.

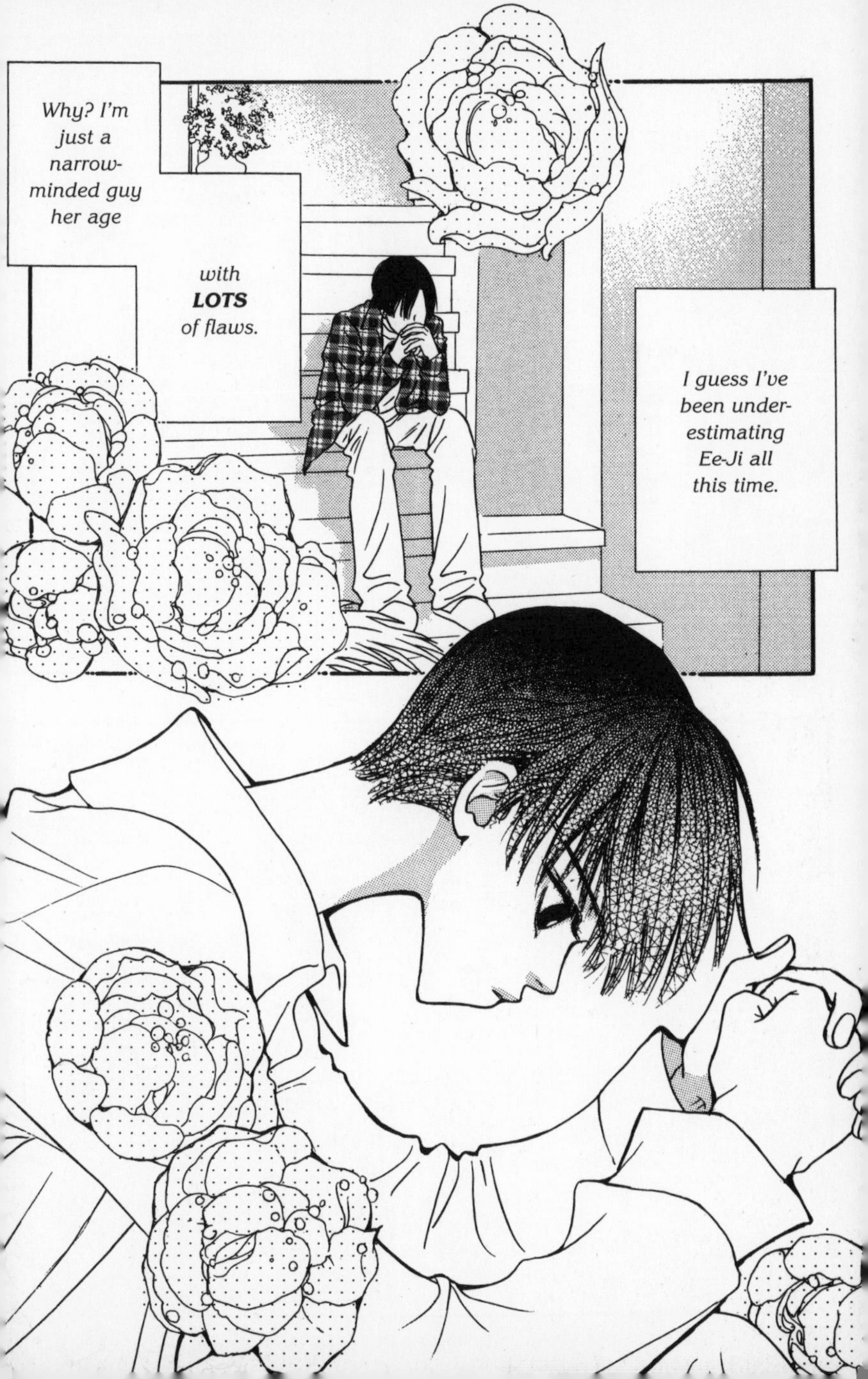

Why? I'm just a narrow-minded guy her age
with **LOTS** of flaws.
I guess I've been under-estimating Ee-Ji all this time.

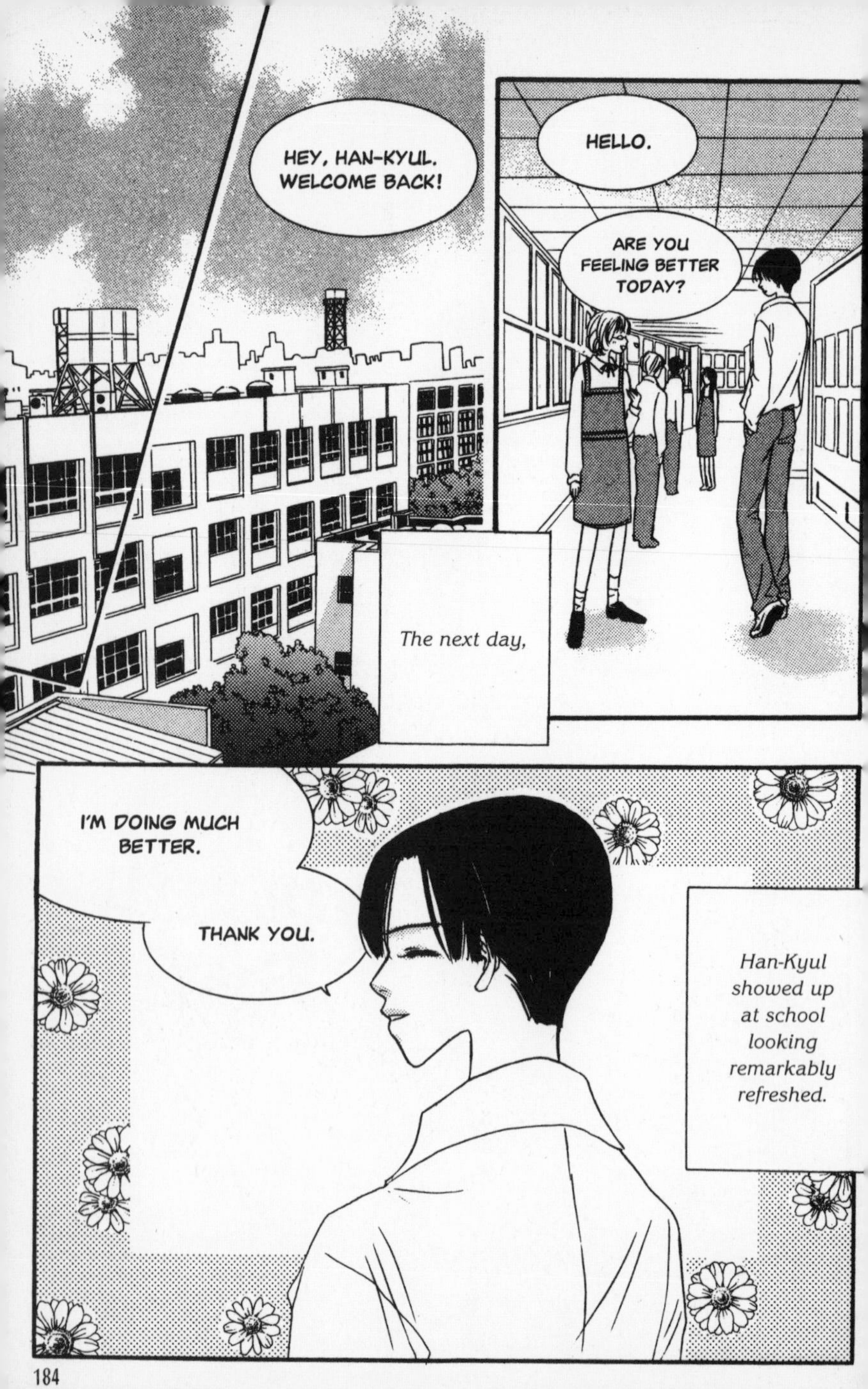
HEY, HAN-KYUL. WELCOME BACK!
HELLO.
ARE YOU FEELING BETTER TODAY?
The next day,
I'M DOING MUCH BETTER.
THANK YOU.
Han-Kyul showed up at school looking remarkably refreshed.

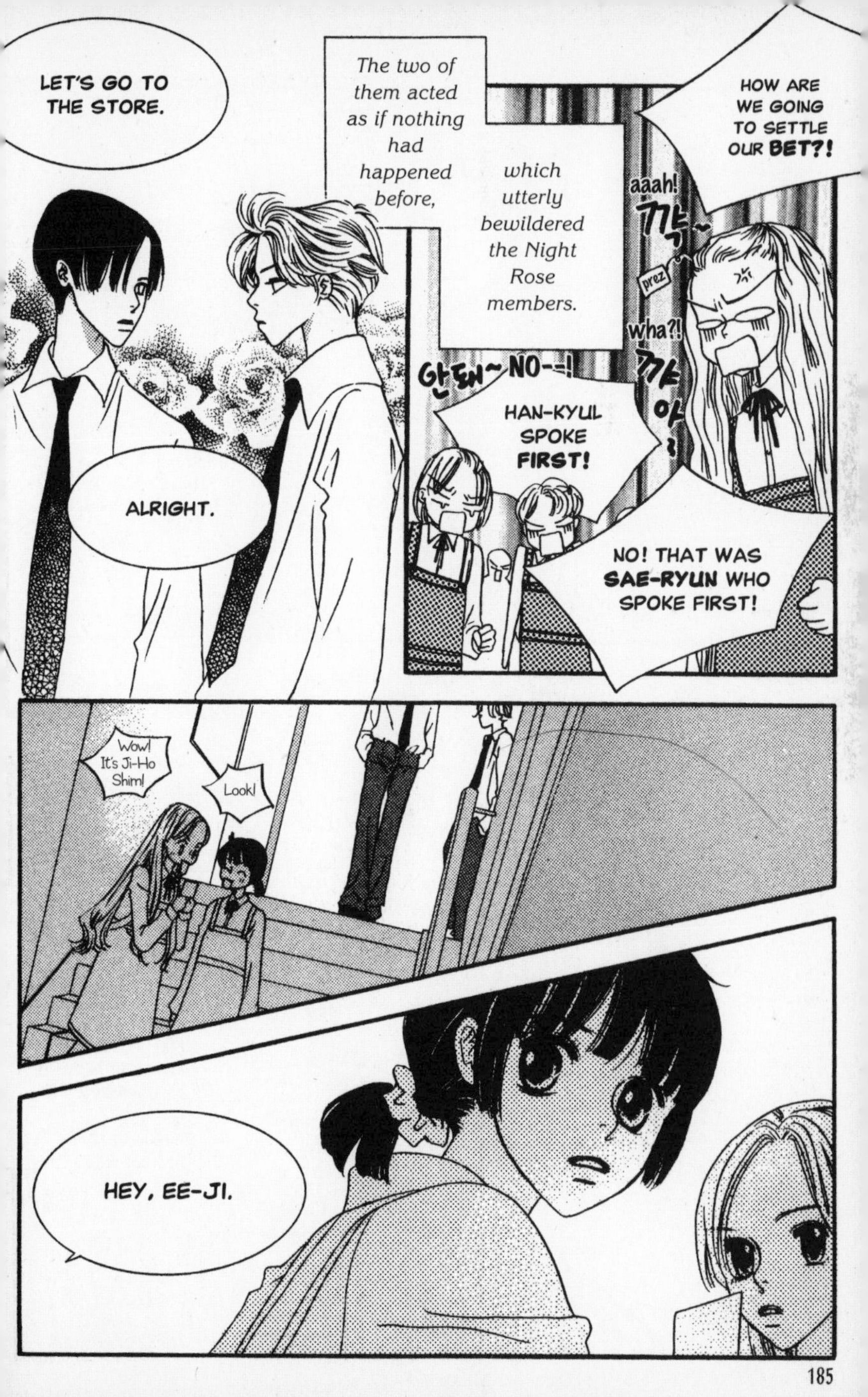

LET'S GO TO THE STORE.
The two of them acted as if nothing had happened before,
which utterly bewildered the Night Rose members.
HOW ARE WE GOING TO SETTLE OUR BET?!
aaah!
prez
wha?!
안돼~ NO--!
HAN-KYUL SPOKE FIRST!
NO! THAT WAS SAE-RYUN WHO SPOKE FIRST!
ALRIGHT.
Wow! It's Ji-Ho Shim!
Look!
HEY, EE-JI.

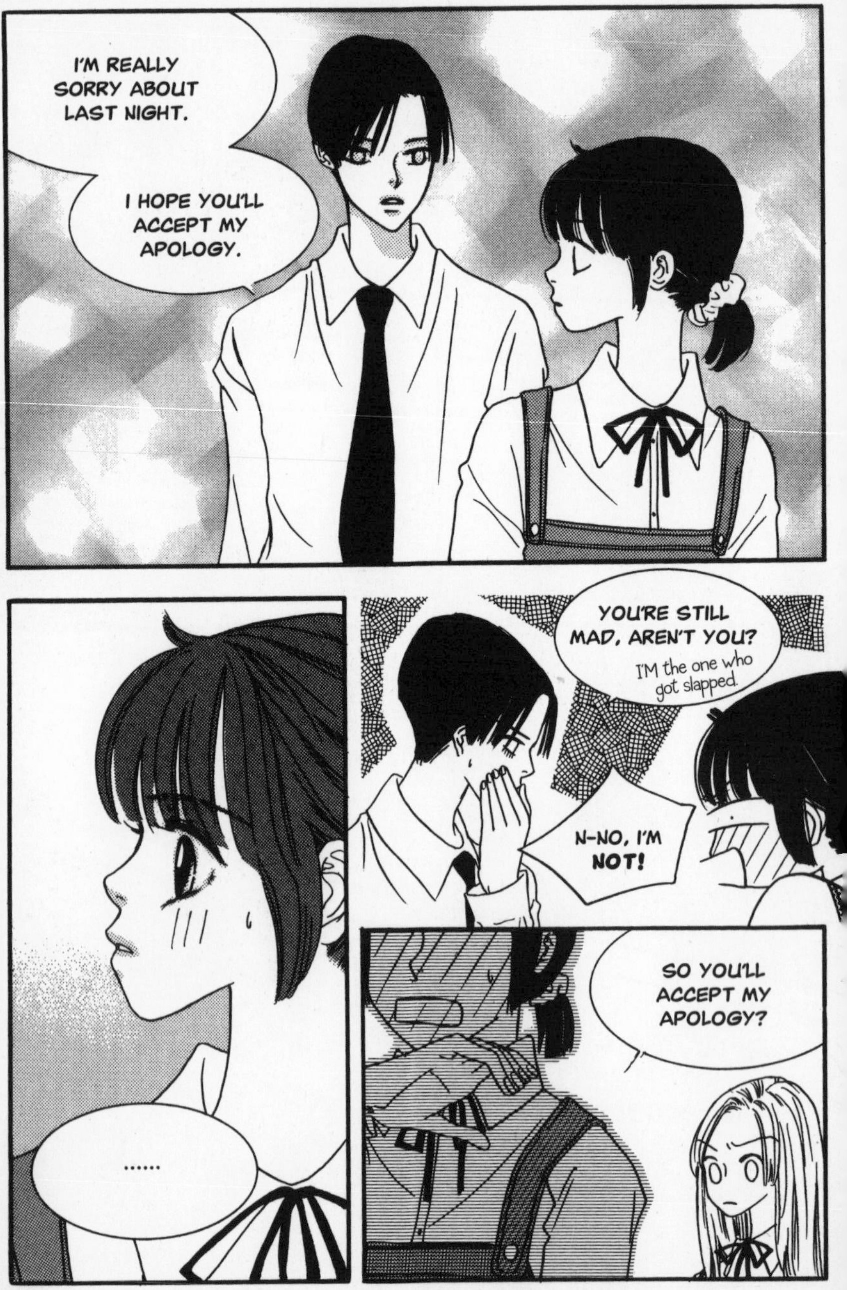
I'M REALLY SORRY ABOUT LAST NIGHT.
I HOPE YOU'LL ACCEPT MY APOLOGY.
......
YOU'RE STILL MAD, AREN'T YOU?
I'M the one who got slapped.
N-NO, I'M **NOT!**
SO YOU'LL ACCEPT MY APOLOGY?

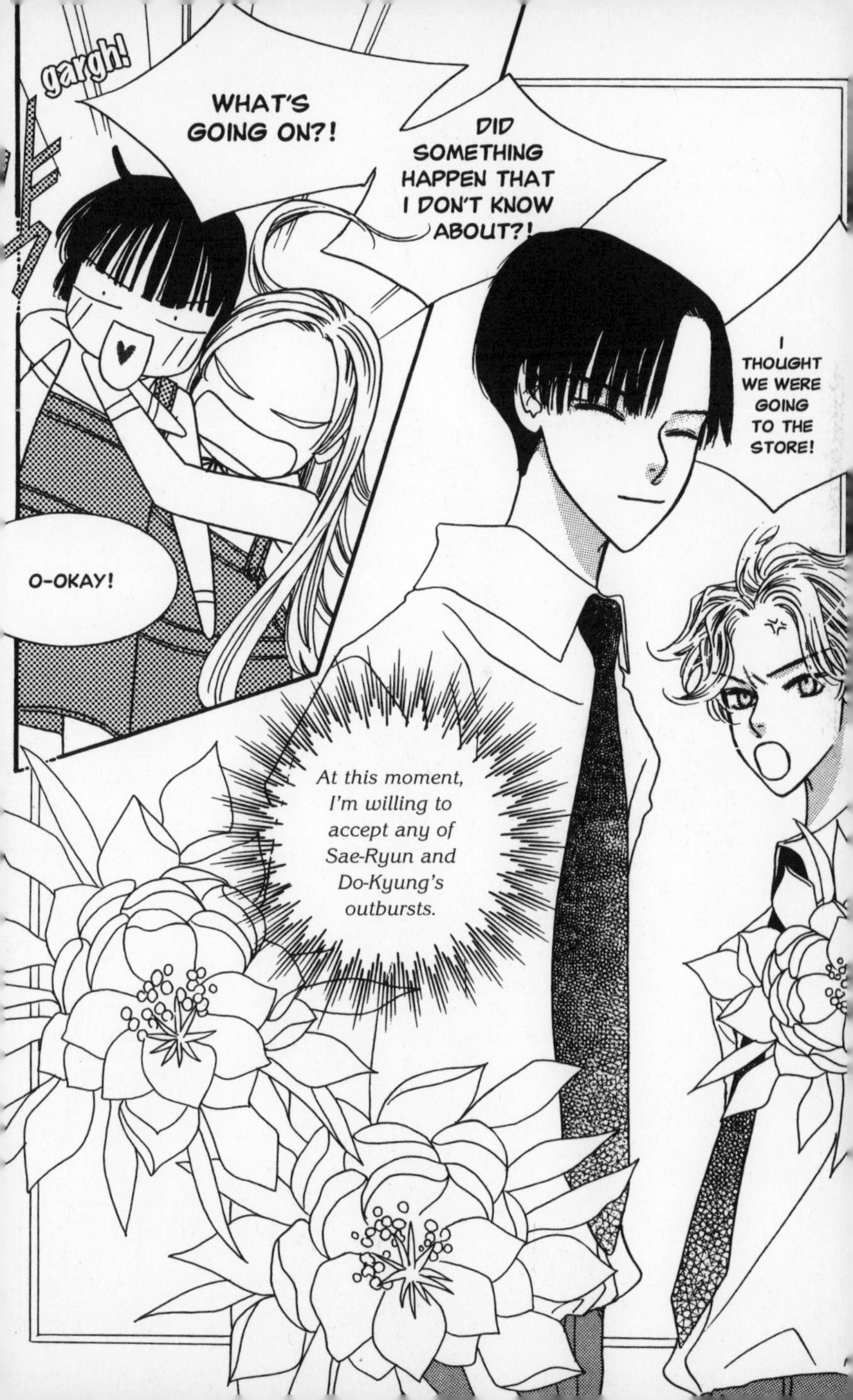
gargh!
WHAT'S GOING ON?!
DID SOMETHING HAPPEN THAT I DON'T KNOW ABOUT?!
I THOUGHT WE WERE GOING TO THE STORE!
O-OKAY!
At this moment, I'm willing to accept any of Sae-Ryun and Do-Kyung's outbursts.

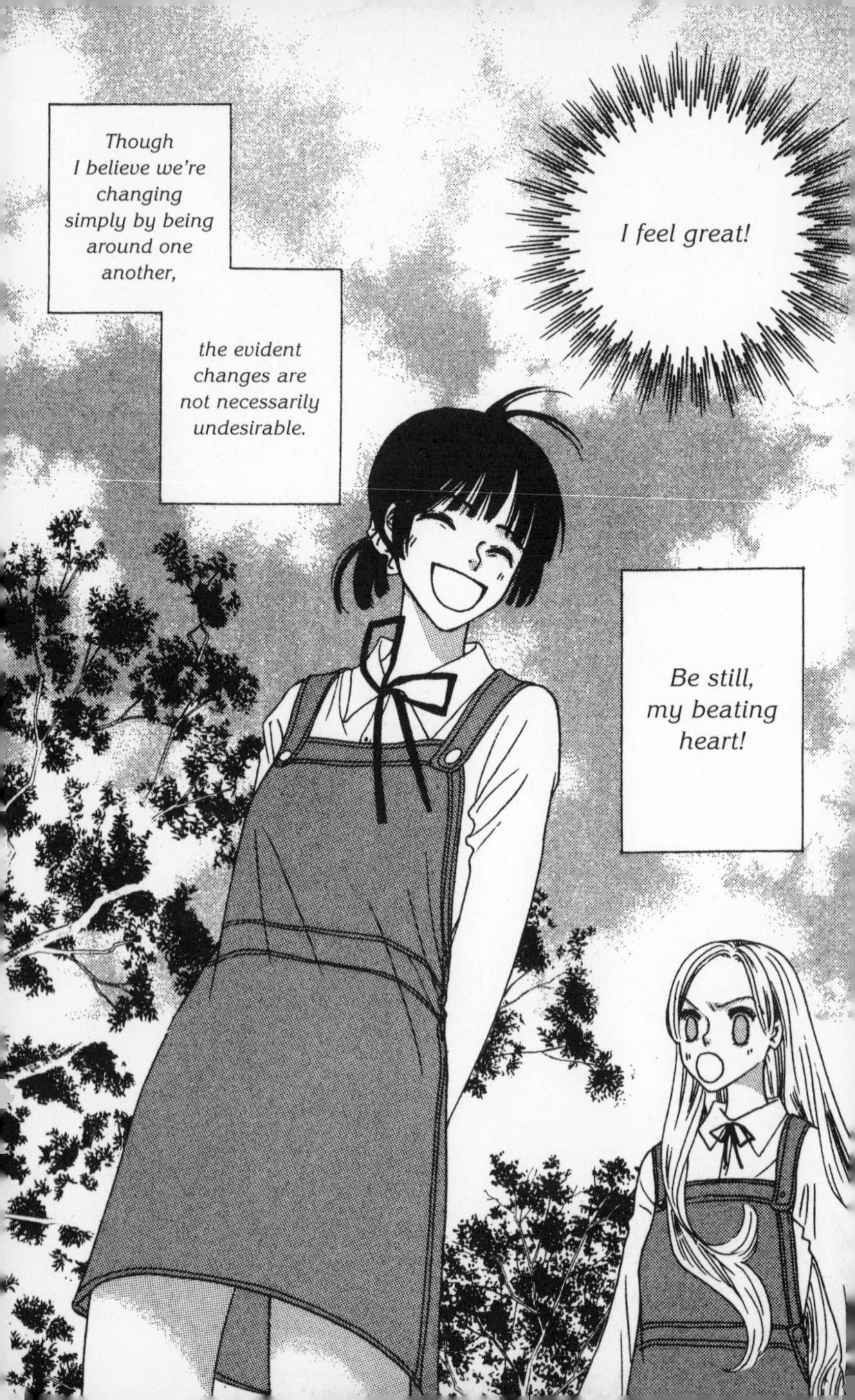
Though I believe we're changing simply by being around one another,
the evident changes are not necessarily undesirable.
I feel great!
Be still, my beating heart!

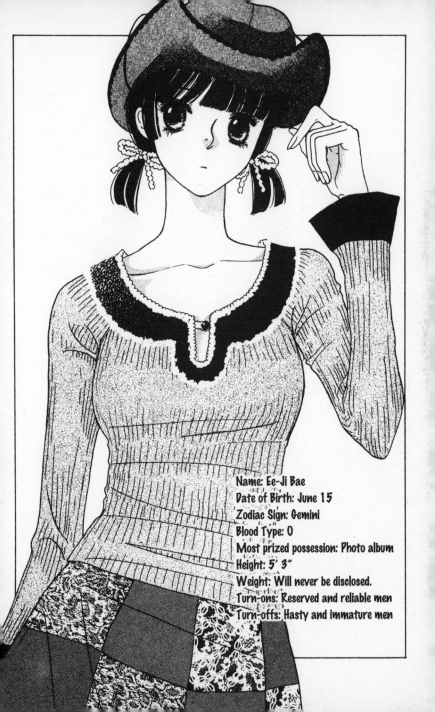

Name: Ee-Ji Bae
Date of Birth: June 15
Zodiac Sign: Gemini
Blood Type: O
Most prized possession: Photo album
Height: 5' 3"
Weight: Will never be disclosed.
Turn-ons: Reserved and reliable men
Turn-offs: Hasty and immature men

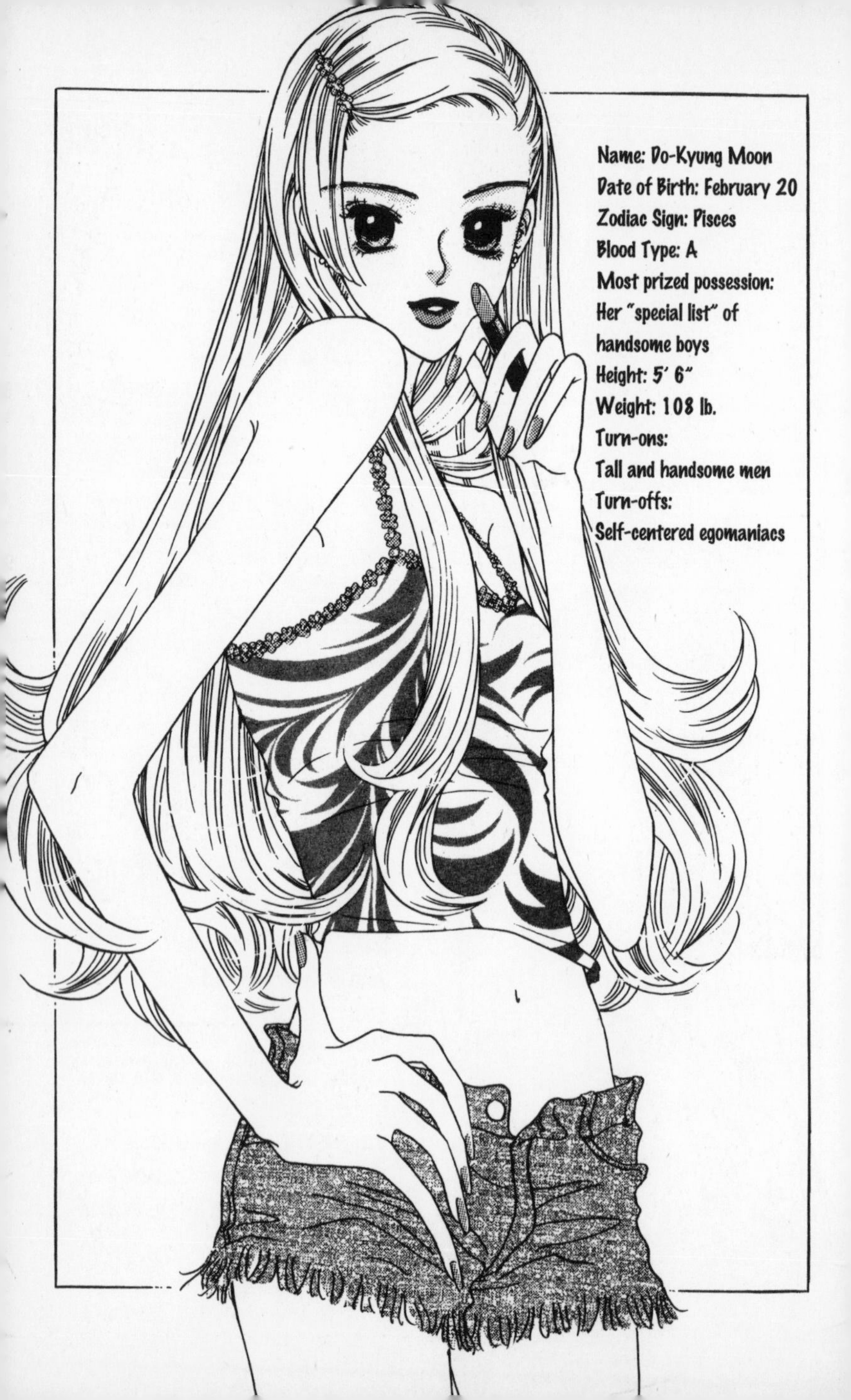
Name: Do-Kyung Moon
Date of Birth: February 20
Zodiac Sign: Pisces
Blood Type: A
Most prized possession:
Her "special list" of
handsome boys
Height: 5′ 6″
Weight: 108 lb.
Turn-ons:
Tall and handsome men
Turn-offs:
Self-centered egomaniacs

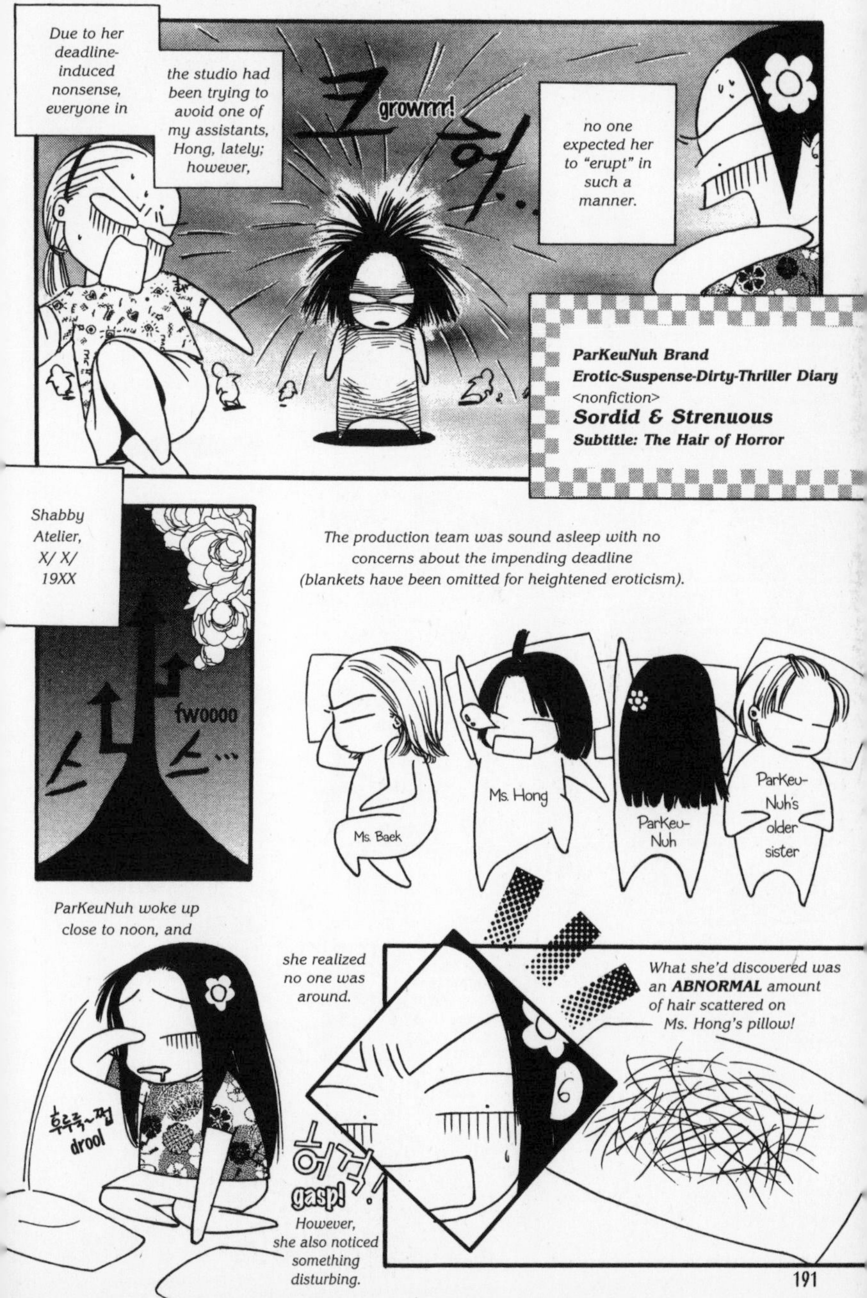
Due to her deadline-induced nonsense, everyone in
the studio had been trying to avoid one of my assistants, Hong, lately; however,
크허...
growrrr!
no one expected her to "erupt" in such a manner.
ParKeuNuh Brand
Erotic-Suspense-Dirty-Thriller Diary
<nonfiction>
Sordid & Strenuous
Subtitle: The Hair of Horror
Shabby Atelier, X/ X/ 19XX
스 스...
fwoooo
The production team was sound asleep with no concerns about the impending deadline (blankets have been omitted for heightened eroticism).
Ms. Baek
Ms. Hong
ParKeu-Nuh
ParKeu-Nuh's older sister
ParKeuNuh woke up close to noon, and
후루룩~쩝
drool
she realized no one was around.
What she'd discovered was an ABNORMAL amount of hair scattered on Ms. Hong's pillow!
헉!
gasp!
However, she also noticed something disturbing.

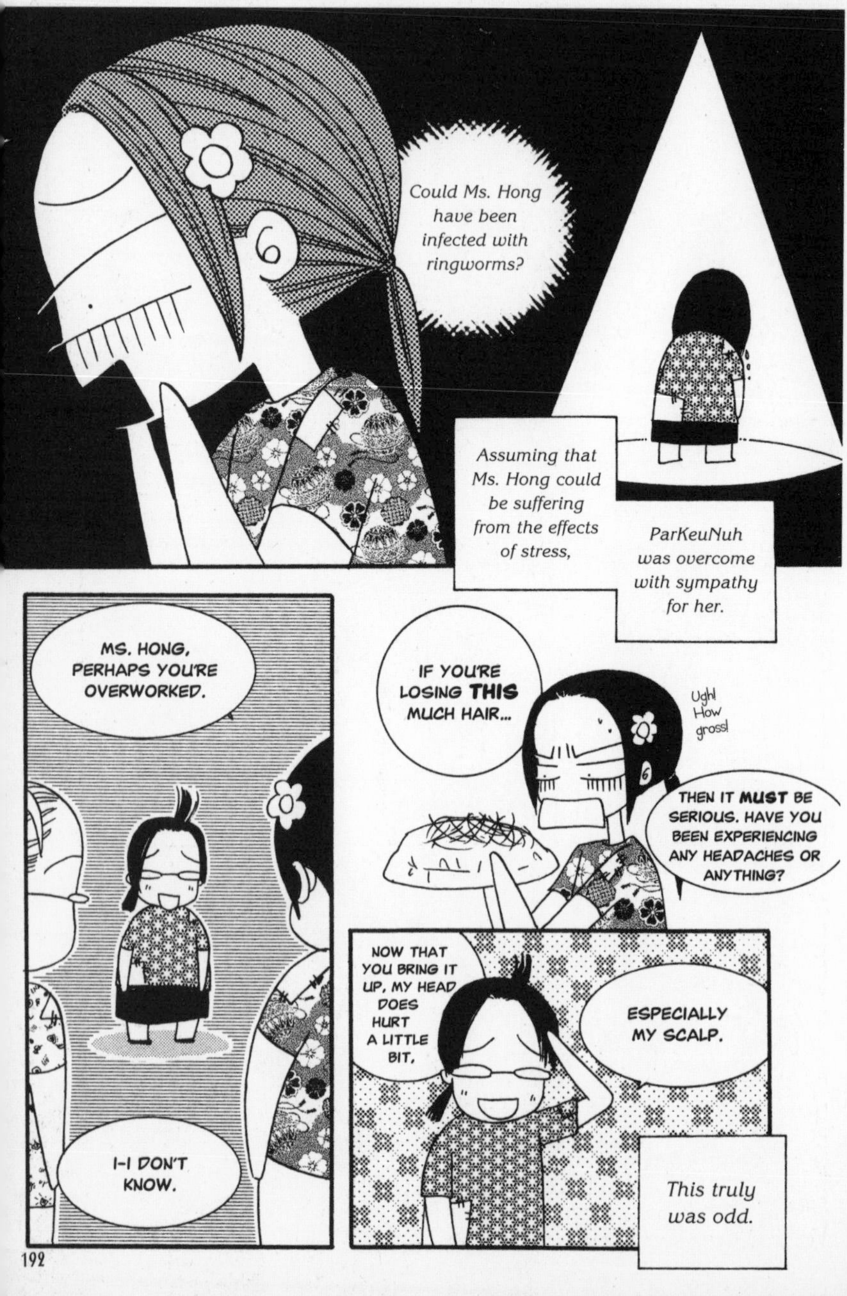
Could Ms. Hong have been infected with ringworms?
Assuming that Ms. Hong could be suffering from the effects of stress,
ParKeuNuh was overcome with sympathy for her.
MS. HONG, PERHAPS YOU'RE OVERWORKED.
I-I DON'T KNOW.
IF YOU'RE LOSING THIS MUCH HAIR...
Ugh! How gross!
THEN IT MUST BE SERIOUS. HAVE YOU BEEN EXPERIENCING ANY HEADACHES OR ANYTHING?
NOW THAT YOU BRING IT UP, MY HEAD DOES HURT A LITTLE BIT,
ESPECIALLY MY SCALP.
This truly was odd.

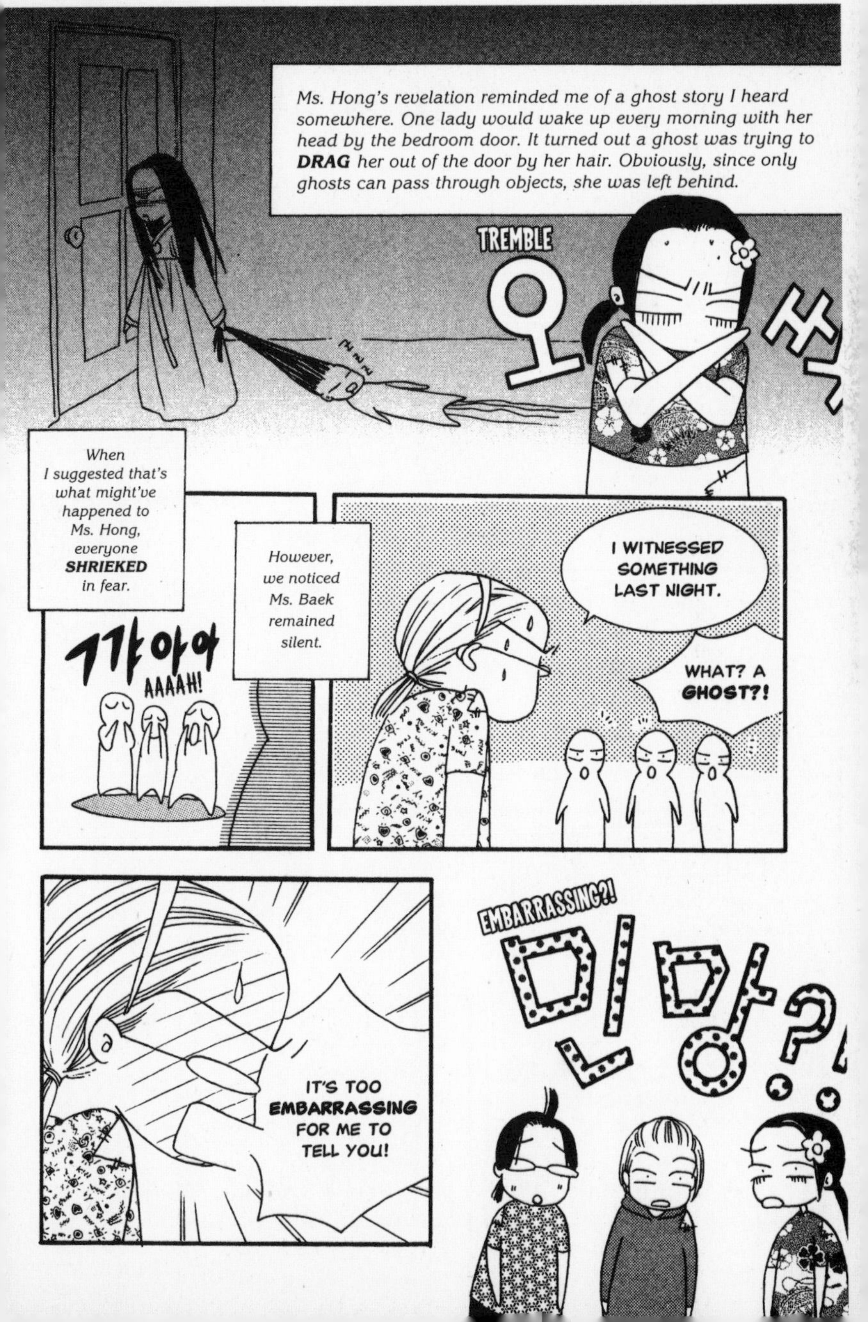

Ms. Hong's revelation reminded me of a ghost story I heard somewhere. One lady would wake up every morning with her head by the bedroom door. It turned out a ghost was trying to **DRAG** her out of the door by her hair. Obviously, since only ghosts can pass through objects, she was left behind.
TREMBLE
When I suggested that's what might've happened to Ms. Hong, everyone **SHRIEKED** in fear.
AAAAH!
However, we noticed Ms. Baek remained silent.
I WITNESSED SOMETHING LAST NIGHT.
WHAT? A GHOST?!
IT'S TOO EMBARRASSING FOR ME TO TELL YOU!
EMBARRASSING?!

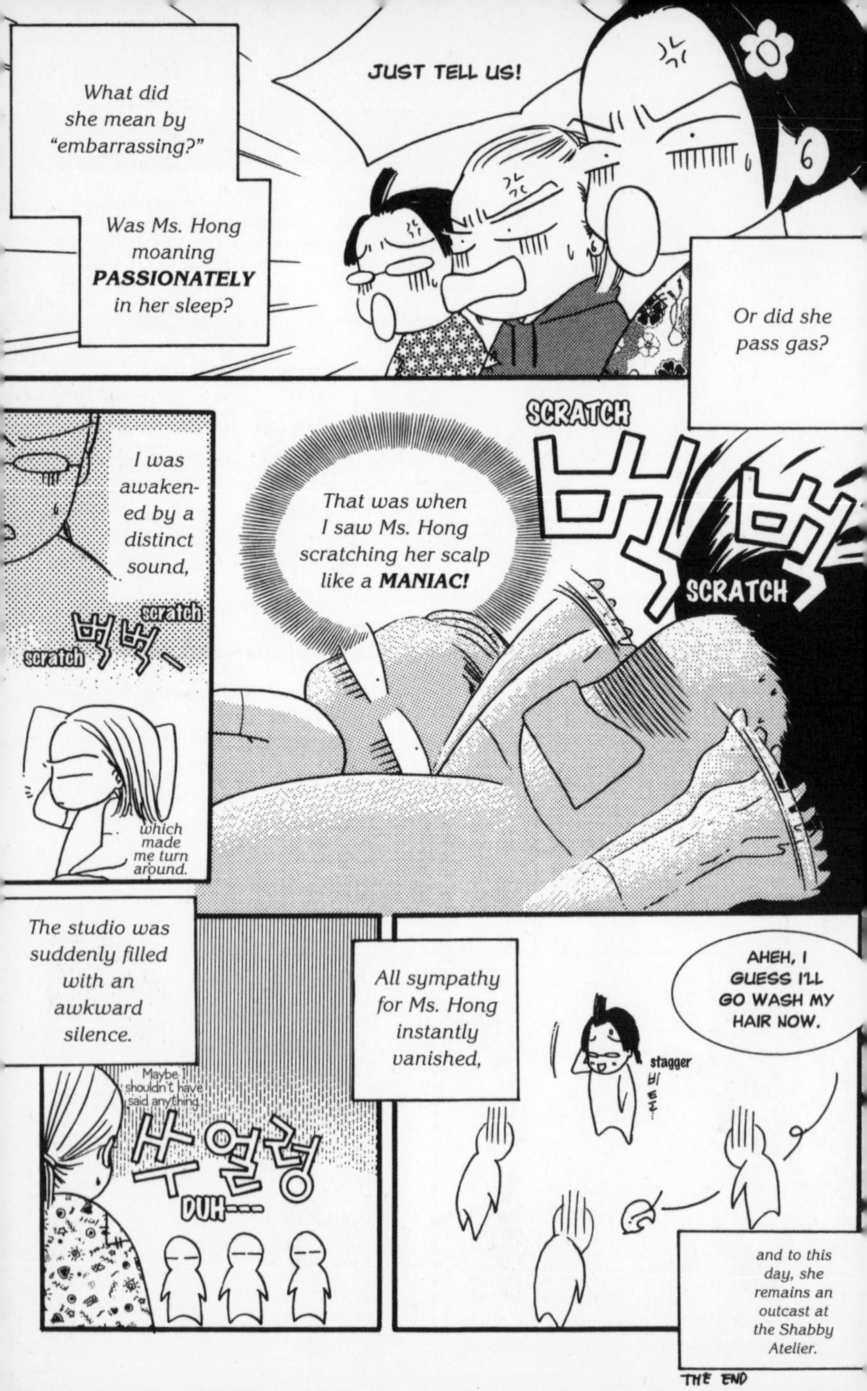

What did she mean by "embarrassing?"
Was Ms. Hong moaning **PASSIONATELY** in her sleep?
JUST TELL US!
Or did she pass gas?
I was awakened by a distinct sound,
scratch
scratch
which made me turn around.
That was when I saw Ms. Hong scratching her scalp like a **MANIAC!**
SCRATCH
SCRATCH
The studio was suddenly filled with an awkward silence.
Maybe I shouldn't have said anything.
DUH...
All sympathy for Ms. Hong instantly vanished,
AHEH, I GUESS I'LL GO WASH MY HAIR NOW.
stagger
and to this day, she remains an outcast at the Shabby Atelier.
THE END

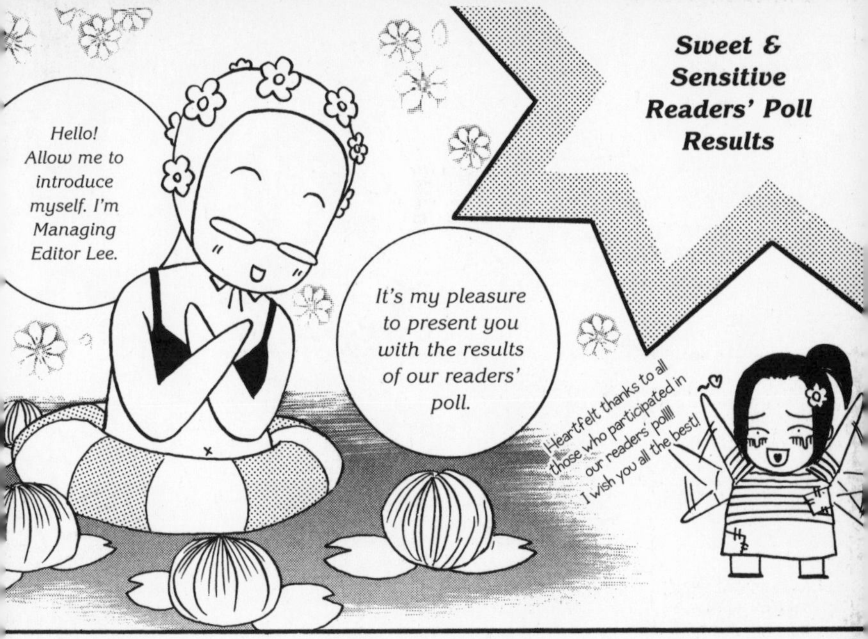

Sweet & Sensitive Readers' Poll Results
Hello! Allow me to introduce myself. I'm Managing Editor Lee.
It's my pleasure to present you with the results of our readers' poll.
Heartfelt thanks to all those who participated in our readers' poll!! I wish you all the best!

Poll 1: Character Drawing Contest · Poll 2-1: Favorite Character · Poll 2-5: Casting Suggestions

First Place:
Sae-Ryun Shin (49%)

Casting
- 1st Place: Ji-Ho Shim (25.2%)
- 2nd Place: Tae-Hyun Cha (10.7%)
- Co-3rd Place: Hyuk Jang, Seung-Hyun Kim
- Honorable Mention: Da-Mi Seo-Mun, Min-Shik Choi

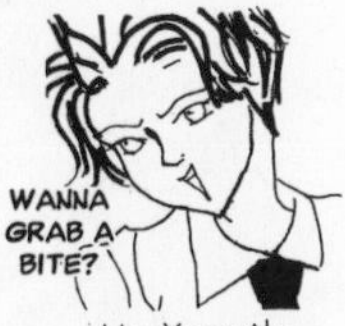

WANNA GRAB A BITE?

Hee-Young Ahn

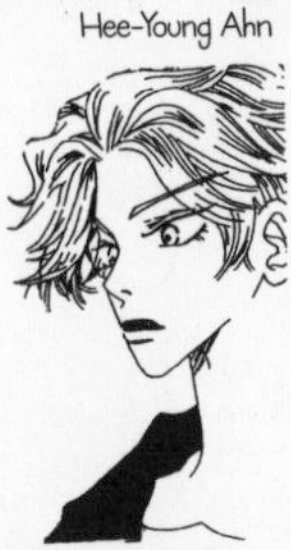

Hee-Jang Kim

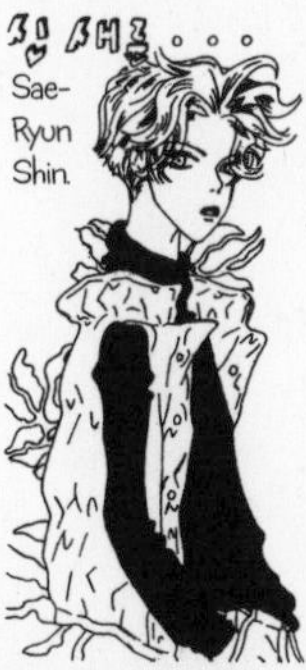

Sae-Ryun Shin.

Eun-Mi Kim

Second Place:
Ee-Ji Bae (18.3%)

Casting
- 1st Place: Rim Chae (22.7%)
- 2nd Place: Du-Na Bae, Na-Young Lee (7.6%)
- 4th Place: Eun-Kyung Im (5.3%)
- Honorable Mention: Sung-Eun Kim, ParKeuNuh, Qi Shu, Kyung-Rim Park

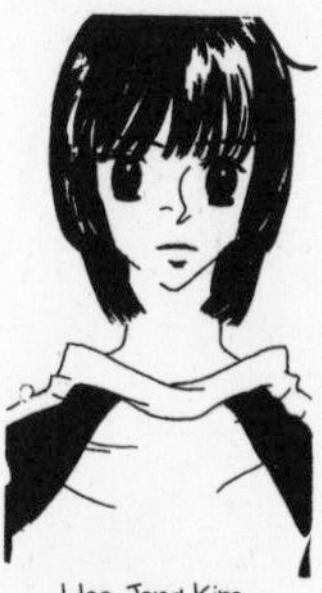

Hee-Jang Kim

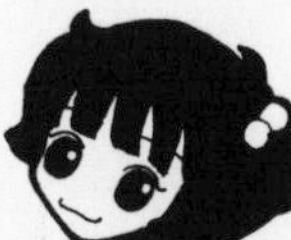

Eun-Jin Kim

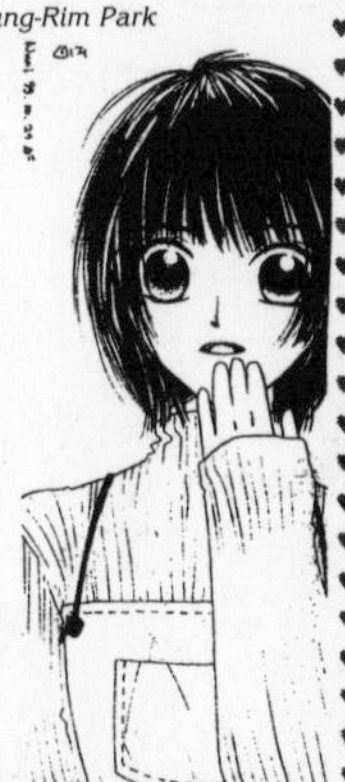

Eun-Won Lee

Third Place:
Do-Kyung Moon (13.3%)

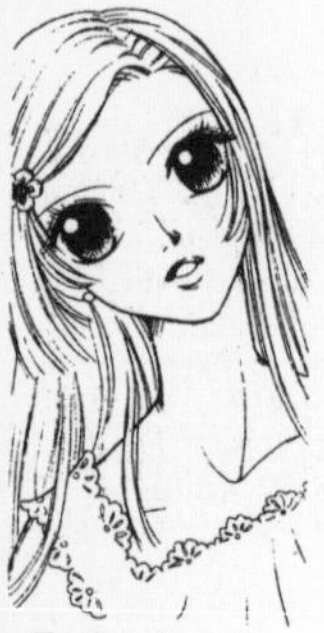

Eun-Won Lee

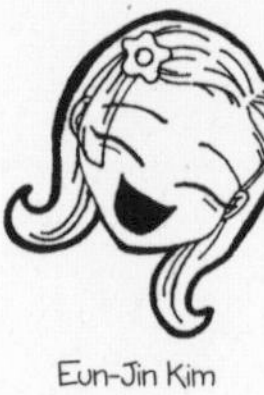

Eun-Jin Kim

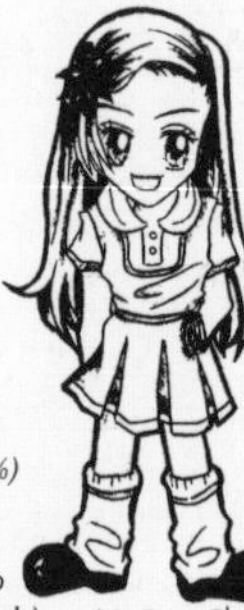

Mi-Jung Shim

Casting
- *1st Place: Hee-Sun Kim (21.2%)*
- *2nd Place: Min-Hee Kim (7.5%)*
- *3rd Place: Yoo-Jin Kim (5.5%)*
- *Honorable Mention: Kyung-Ah Choi (manhwa artist) Namie Amuro (if too expensive, then Ji-Yoon Park)*

Fourth Place:
Han-Kyul Kang (10%)

Casting
- *1st Place: Ji-Ho Shim (18.9%)*
- *2nd Place: Jae-Mo Ahn (7.4%)*
- *3rd Place: Kyu-Hwan Lee (6.8%)*
- *Honorable Mention: Ji-Eun Kim (cartoonist), Chan Jung, Suk-Kyu Han, Tai-Ji Seo, Oh-Joong Kwon, Shin-Yang Park*

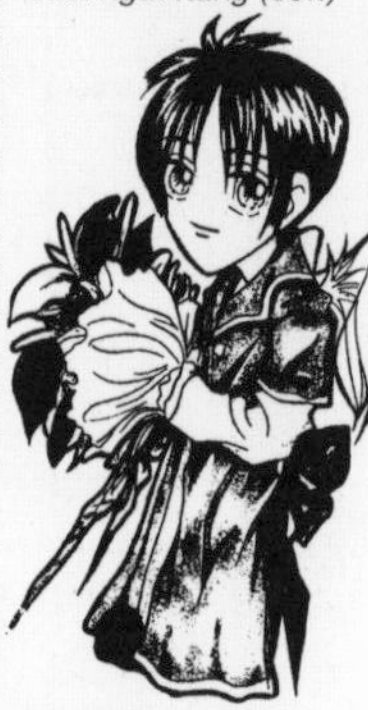

Mi-Jung Shim

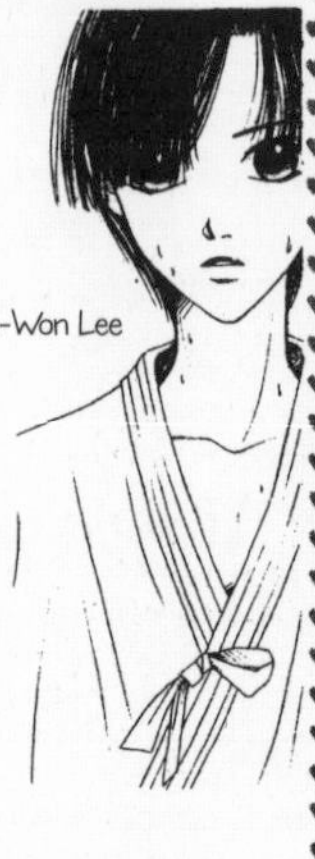

Eun-Won Lee

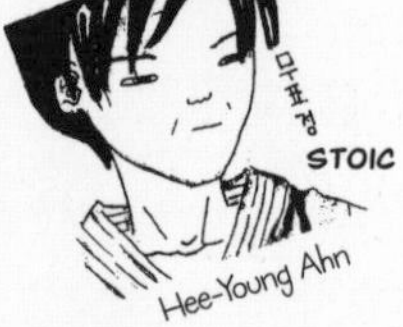
무표정
STOIC

Hee-Young Ahn

Poll 2-1: Best Scenes

First Place:
Ee-Ji's confession scene (18.4%)

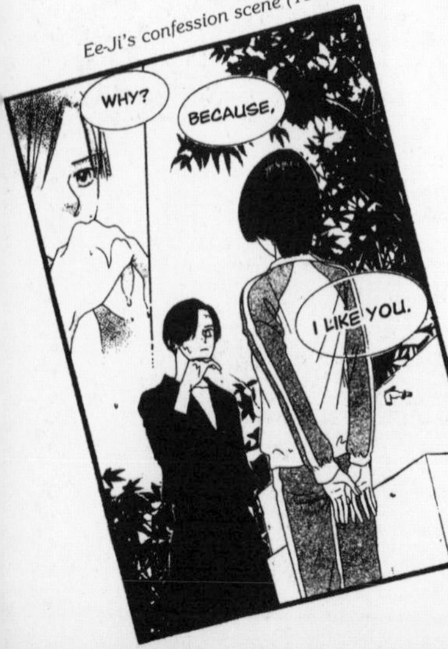
WHY?
BECAUSE,
I LIKE YOU.

Co-Second Place:
Do-Kyung witnessing naked Woo-Young (13.3%)

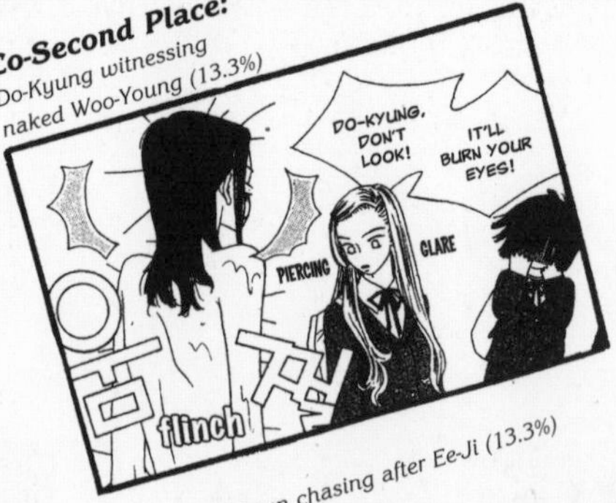
DO-KYUNG, DON'T LOOK!
IT'LL BURN YOUR EYES!
PIERCING
GLARE
flinch

Sae-Ryun chasing after Ee-Ji (13.3%)

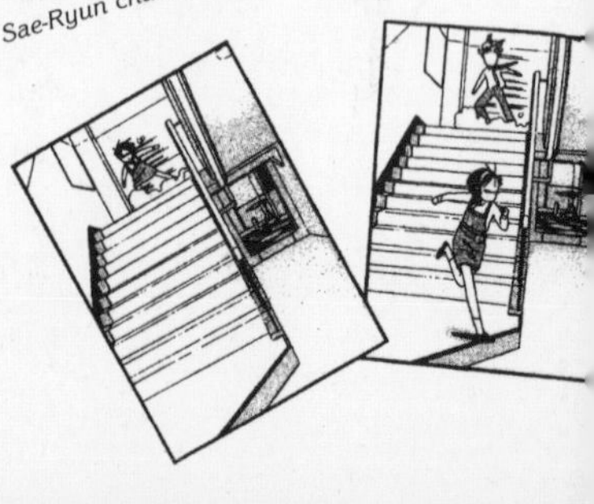

Poll 2-2: Best Line

First Place:
"You wanna grab a bite to eat?" (37.6%)

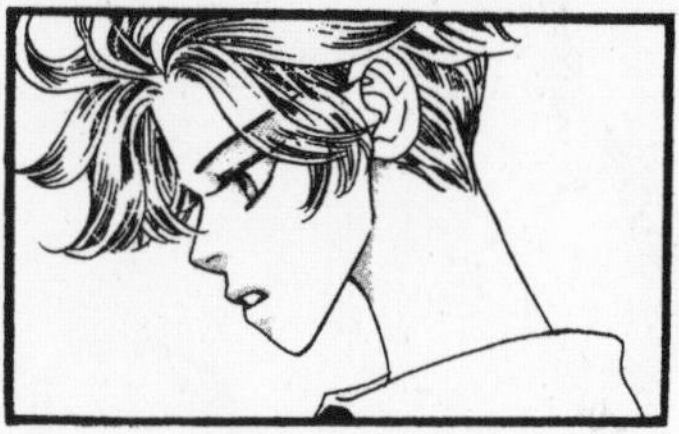

Second Place:
"Because I like you." (23.3%)

Third Place:
"Don't be rude to Ee-Ji." (15.9%)

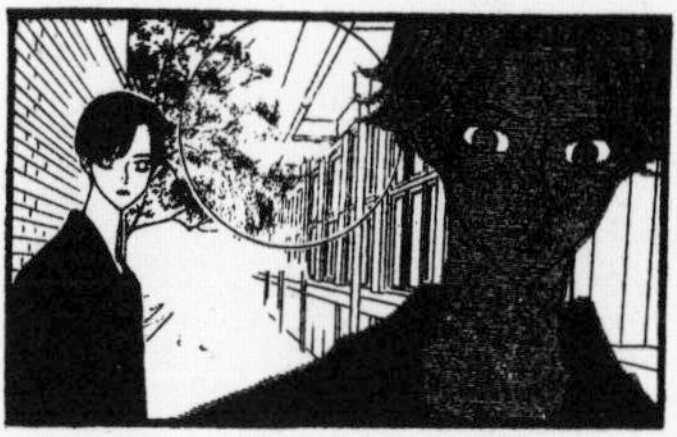

Poll 2-3: Best Couple

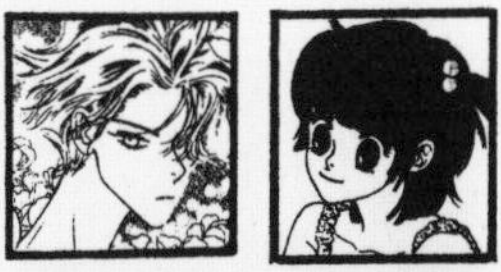

♡ **First Place:**
Sae-Ryun & Ee-Ji (38.4%)

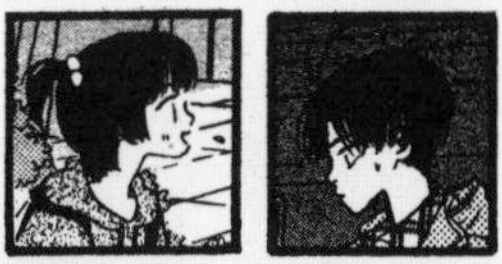

♡ **Second Place:**
Ee-Ji & Han-Kyul (36%)

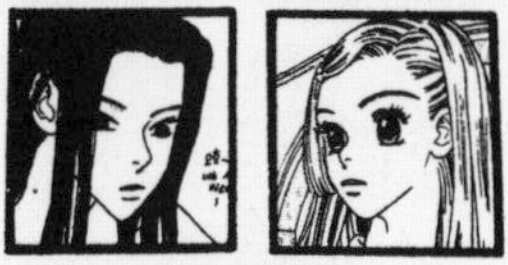

♡ **Third Place:**
Woo-Young & Do-Kyung (9.6%)

Honorable Mention:

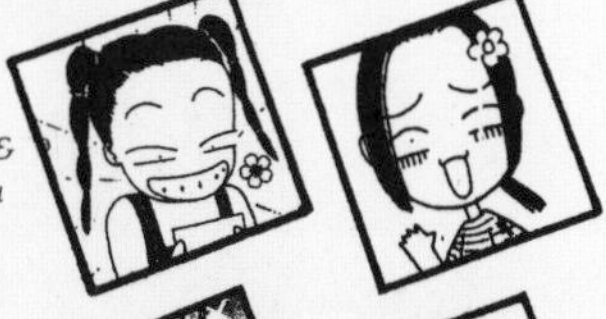

♡ Woo-Young & ParKeu Nuh (1.6%)

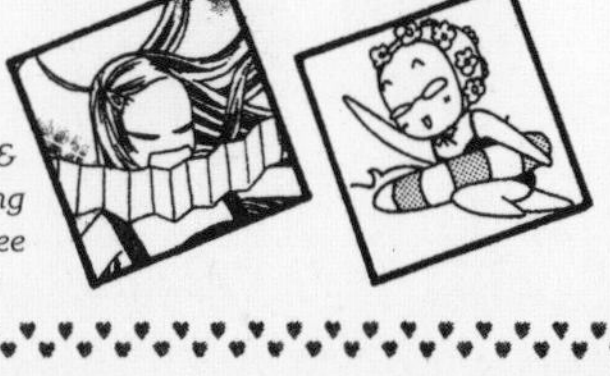

♡ Do-Kyung & Managing Editor Lee (0.8%)

Poll 2-4: Worst Couple

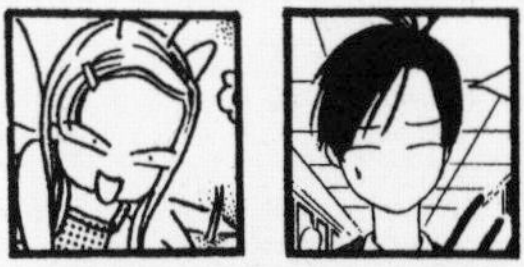

♡ **First Place:**
Do-Kyung & Han-Kyul (26.7%)

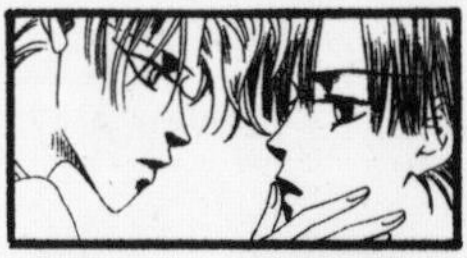

♡ **Second Place:**
Sae-Ryun & Han-Kyul (23.3%)
Illustrated by Yeh-Seul Ahn

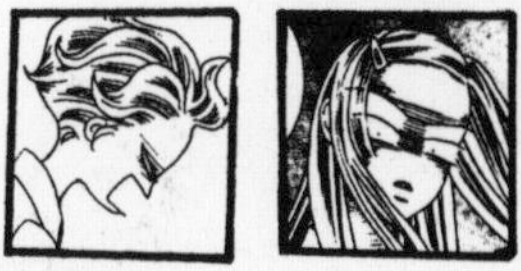

♡ **Third Place:**
Sae-Ryun & Do-Kyung (17.2%)

Honorable Mention:

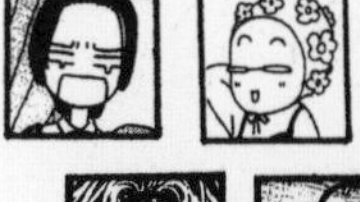

♡ Ee-Ji & Managing Editor Lee (0.9%)

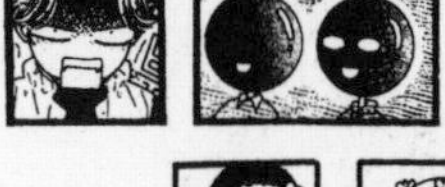

♡ Sae-Ryun & Ee-Ji's "unattractive" friends (1.7%)

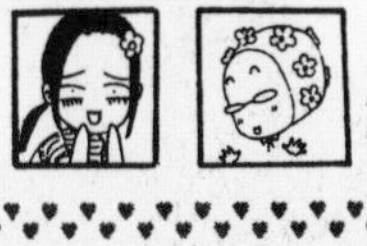

♡ ParKeu-Nuh & Managing Editor Lee (0.9%)

Cameo Suggestions,
Issue Editorial Department

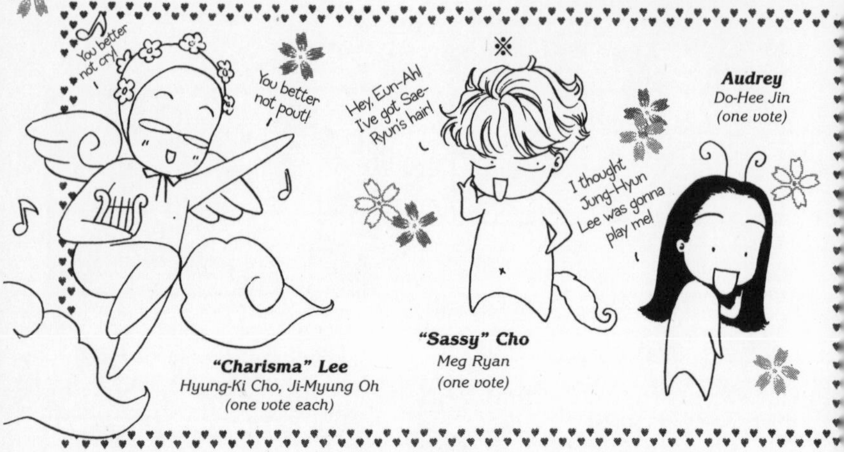
You better not cry!
You better not pout!
Hey, Eun-Ah! I've got Sae-Ryun's hair!
I thought Jung-Hyun Lee was gonna play me!

"Charisma" Lee
Hyung-Ki Cho, Ji-Myung Oh
(one vote each)

"Sassy" Cho
Meg Ryan
(one vote)

Audrey
Do-Hee Jin
(one vote)

Readers' Poll Postscript

Our sincerest apologies for not being able to include more of your drawings. Interestingly, most of you thought the casting questions were the hardest. In the "Worst Couple" category, many thought Do-Kyung might beat up on Han-Kyul pretty regularly if they got together, and that a match between Do-Kyung and Sae-Ryun would be like throwing gasoline into a raging fire. One of the readers nearly wrote a term paper regarding this category! Thank you all for participating. ♡

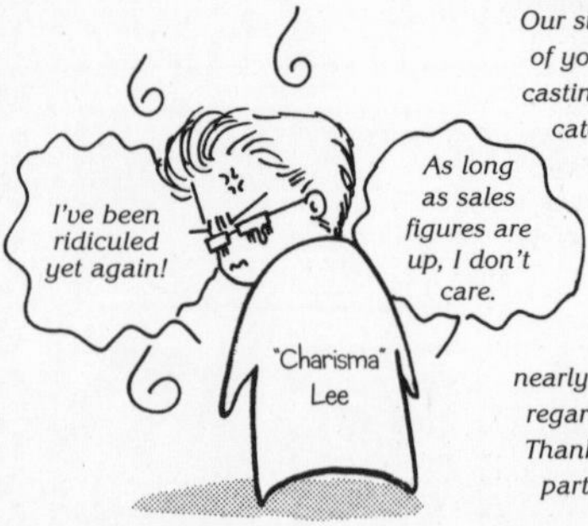
I've been ridiculed yet again!
As long as sales figures are up, I don't care.
"Charisma" Lee

**In reality, the sales figures have little to do with the extent of Lee's ridicule.*

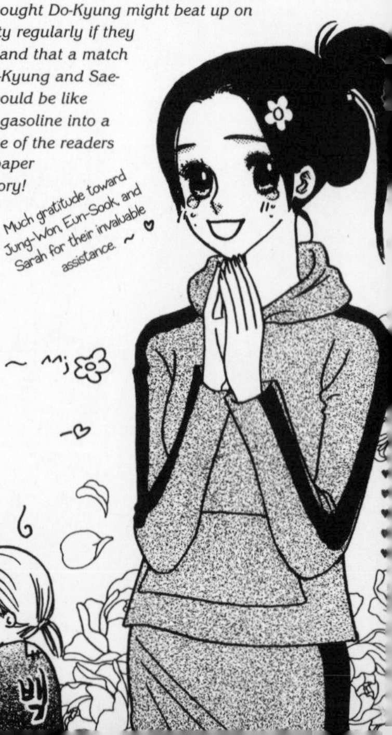
Much gratitude toward Jung-Won, Eun-Sook, and Sarah for their invaluable assistance. ~ ♡

Hello, this is ParKeuNuh. ~ ^^;

Thank you all for reading S & S.
Volume Three is on its way.
Much thanks to my staff. ~♡

February, 2000 ParKeuNuh

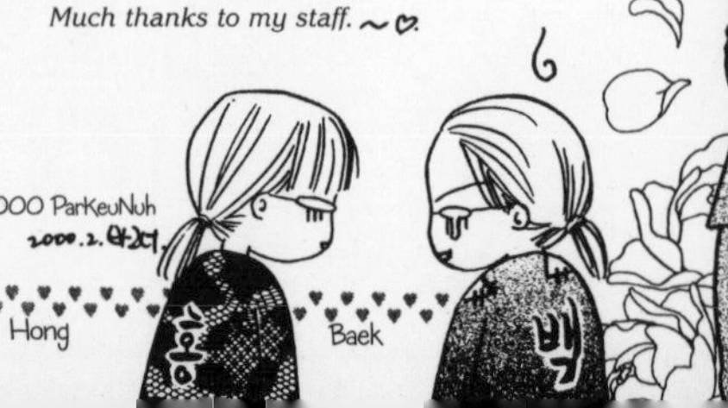
Hong
Baek

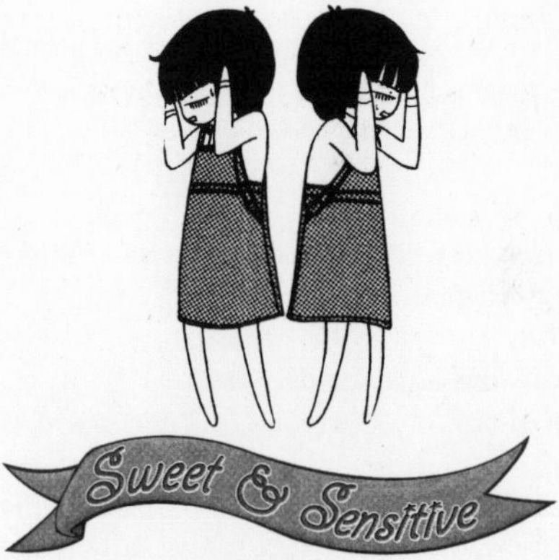
Sweet & Sensitive

Volume 3

Coming Soon...

Sweet & Sensitive Volume 02

PG. 69

I even saw her wearing make-up the other day.
In Korea, the public school education system discourages extravagant usage of cosmetics, such as lipstick or eyeliners.

PG. 99

Upperclassmen
In Korea, it's customary for underclassmen to bow and use formal language with their upperclassmen. Unfortunately, there are many incidents in Korean schools where the respect given to upperclassmen is abused.

PG. 103

Uniform
In most Korean schools (especially middle schools and high schools), students are required to wear uniforms.

PG. 110

Shocked expressions on bystanders faces
In Korea, public displays of affection are highly discouraged, especially among teenagers.

PG. 125

I-I need to use the ladies' room.
In Korea, smoking in front of your future parents-in-law is considered highly disrespectful, regardless of gender.

PG. 126

A man's stamina
Because of the prevalence of heavy smokers in Korea, there are several humorous sayings about cigarettes. In addition to the one featured in the dialogue, another claims that you will be cursed if you throw away a cigarette that has only been half-smoked.

LETTER FROM THE ADV MANGA TRANSLATION STAFF

Dear Reader,

On behalf of the ADV Manga translation team, thank you for purchasing an ADV book. We are enthusiastic and committed to our work, and strive to carry our enthusiasm over into the book you hold in your hands.

Our goal is to retain the true spirit of the original Korean book. While great care has been taken to render a true and accurate translation, some cultural or readability issues may require a line to be adapted for greater accessibility to our readers. At times, manhwa titles that include culturally-specific concepts will feature a "Translator's Notes" section, which explains noteworthy references to the original text.

We hope our commitment to a faithful translation is evident in every ADV book you purchase.

Sincerely,

Javier Lopez
Lead Translator

Jason An

Simon Jung

ADV Manga™

Sweet & Sensitive

3

The most dreaded of high school events rolls around and Ee-Ji is sweating—it's time for physicals and the school-wide weigh-ins. After scheming her way out of the public humiliation, Ee-Ji becomes something of a high school celebrity. She could use her newfound respect to impress Han-Kyul, but a conversation with her new sister-in-law leaves Ee-Ji completely disenchanted with ideas of true love and marriage. While indecision warps her mind, new confusion is added to the mix with a secret admirer! With love in the air and high school heroics under her belt, Ee-Ji's on top of the world, but she could stumble and fall if she doesn't play her cards right!

© 2000 Park Eun-Ah, DAIWON C.I., Inc.

www.adv-manga.com

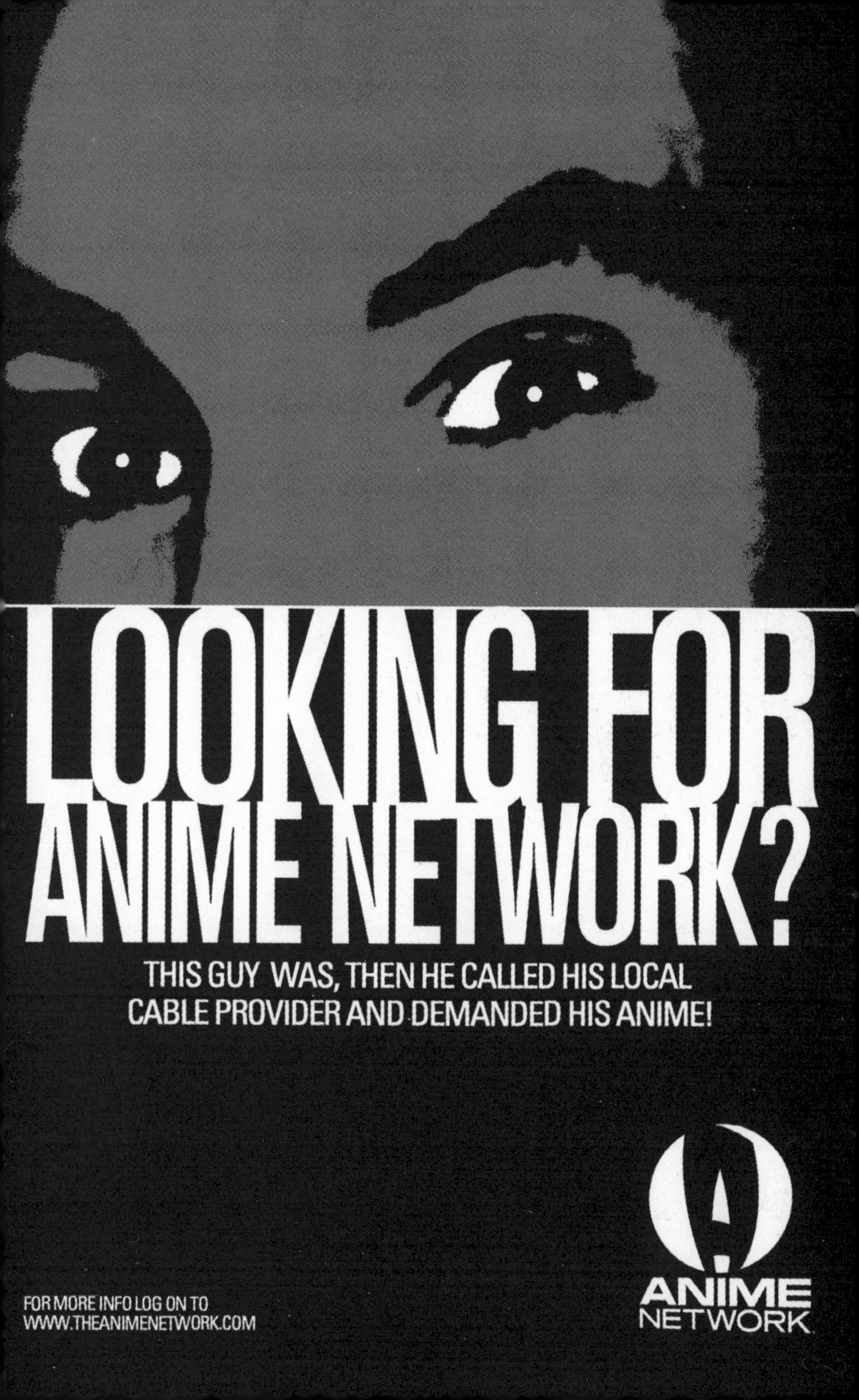
LOOKING FOR ANIME NETWORK?
THIS GUY WAS, THEN HE CALLED HIS LOCAL CABLE PROVIDER AND DEMANDED HIS ANIME!
FOR MORE INFO LOG ON TO WWW.THEANIMENETWORK.COM
ANIME NETWORK

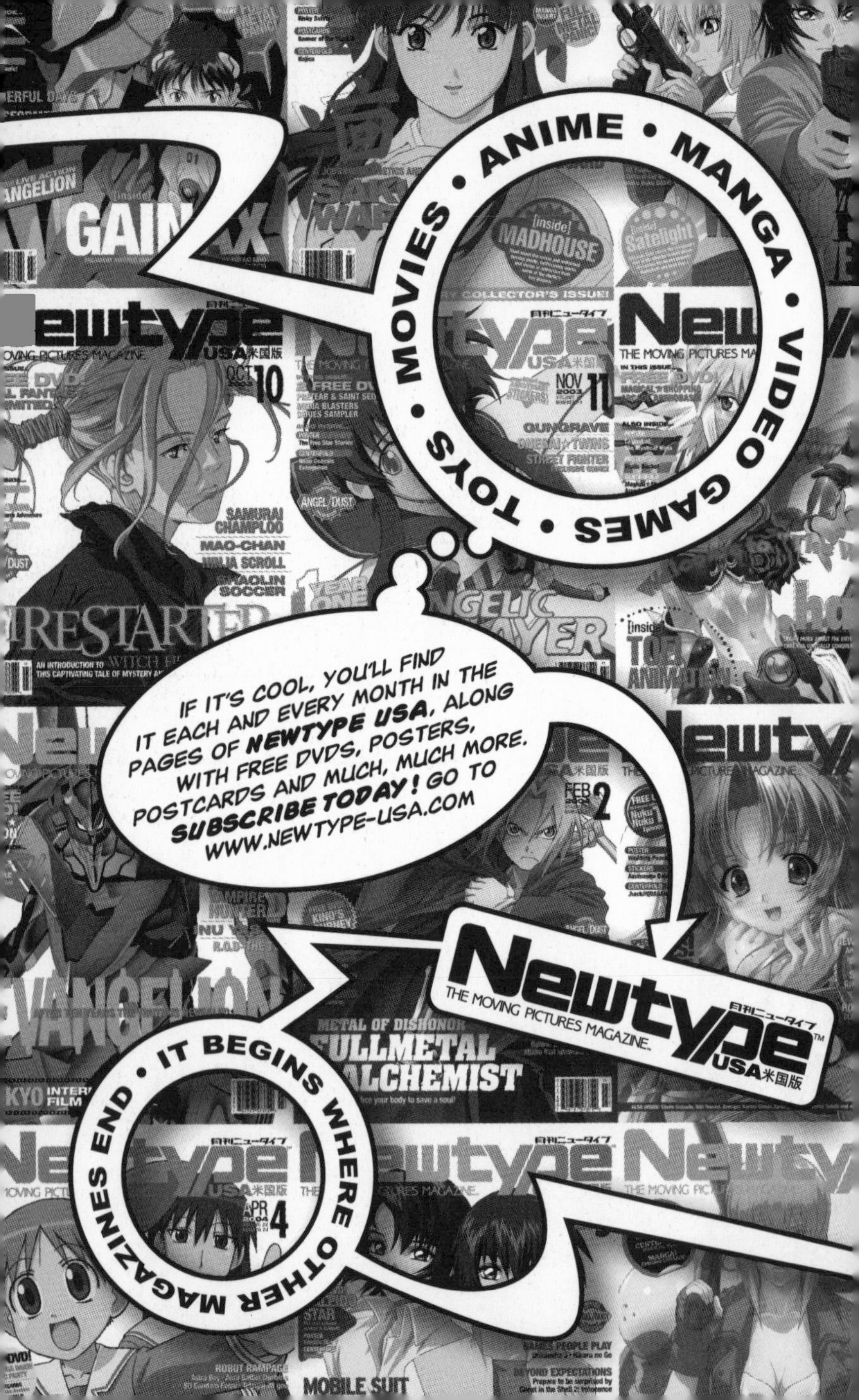
ANIME • MANGA • VIDEO GAMES • TOYS • MOVIES •
IF IT'S COOL, YOU'LL FIND IT EACH AND EVERY MONTH IN THE PAGES OF NEWTYPE USA, ALONG WITH FREE DVDS, POSTERS, POSTCARDS AND MUCH, MUCH MORE. SUBSCRIBE TODAY! GO TO WWW.NEWTYPE-USA.COM
Newtype USA
THE MOVING PICTURES MAGAZINE.
IT BEGINS WHERE OTHER MAGAZINES END •

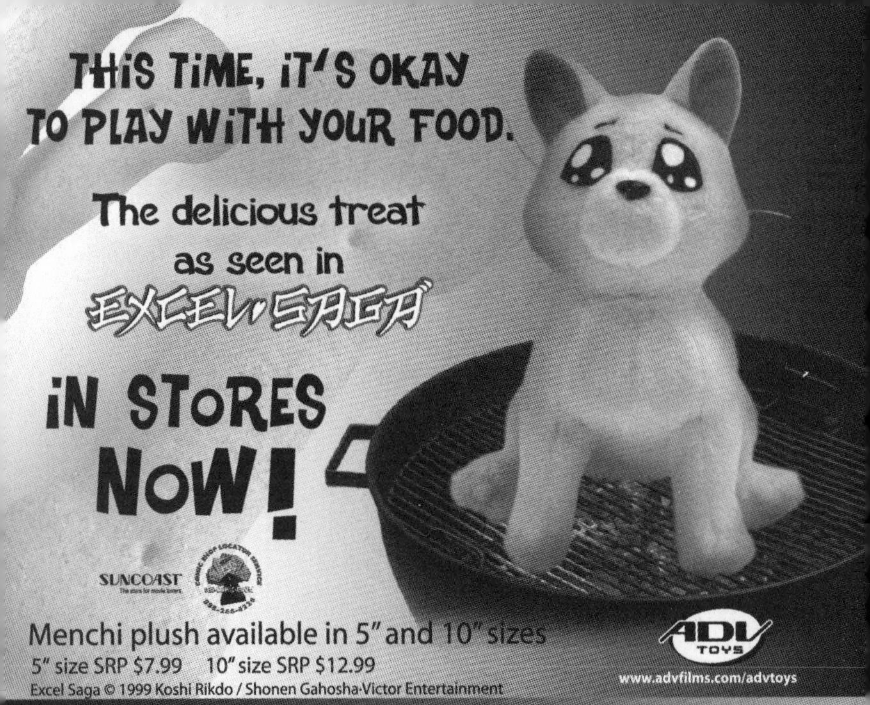
THIS TIME, IT'S OKAY TO PLAY WITH YOUR FOOD.
The delicious treat as seen in
EXCEL SAGA
IN STORES NOW!
SUNCOAST
Menchi plush available in 5″ and 10″ sizes
5″ size SRP $7.99 10″ size SRP $12.99
Excel Saga © 1999 Koshi Rikdo / Shonen Gahosha·Victor Entertainment
ADV TOYS
www.advfilms.com/advtoys

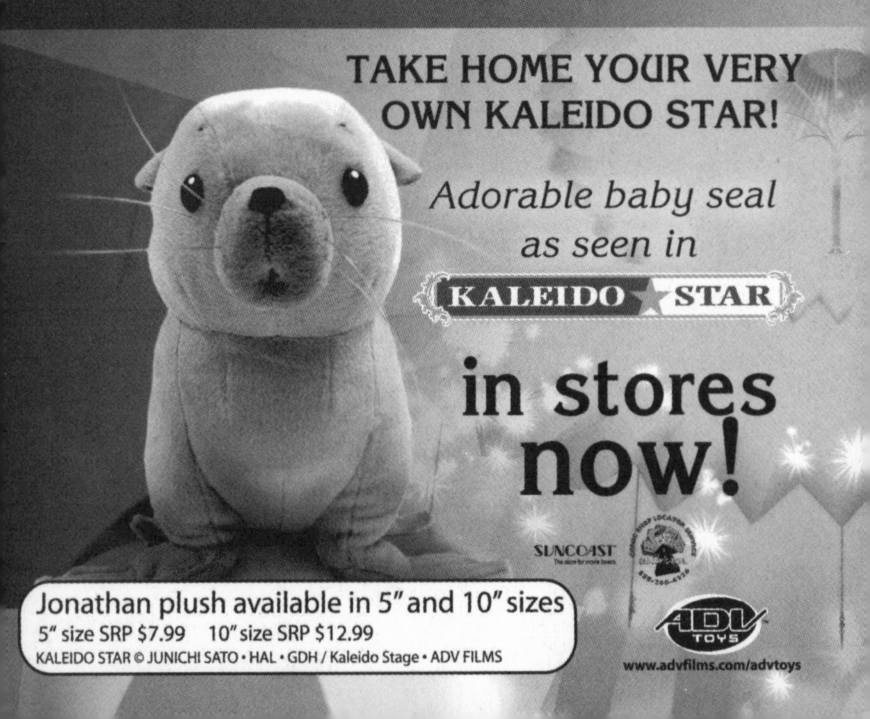
TAKE HOME YOUR VERY OWN KALEIDO STAR!
Adorable baby seal as seen in
KALEIDO STAR
in stores now!
SUNCOAST
Jonathan plush available in 5″ and 10″ sizes
5″ size SRP $7.99 10″ size SRP $12.99
KALEIDO STAR © JUNICHI SATO • HAL • GDH / Kaleido Stage • ADV FILMS
ADV TOYS
www.advfilms.com/advtoys

The New Legend of Snow White

Prétear

TO SAVE THE WORLD FROM THE PRINCESS OF DISASTER...

Himeno must find the power within to become the Prétear, the one who can bring the life-giving Leafe to a dying world. But she is troubled as she learns who the Princess of Disaster was before her heart turned into icy steel. Could Himeno share the same fate?

Read the book that inspired the hit anime!

PRÉTEAR VOL. 2
BY KAORI NARUSE AND JUNICHI SATOU
AUGUST 2004 · $9.99 · ALL AGES
ALSO AVAILABLE: PRÉTEAR VOL. 1

www.adv-manga.com